six
Defragment your hard disk once a month or so.

Use a utility like the Norton Utilities Speed Disk to rearrange all your documents and applications on your hard disk so the hard disk can work at optimum efficiency. Make sure you back up all your work before you defragment. See Chapter 17 for details.

seven
Keep only ONE copy of the system software in the Mac at a time.

You can have only one System Folder on your hard disk, with one System file in it, and you should not normally put any floppy disks into your Mac that have system software on them. See "Be Kind to Your Hard Disk" in Chapter 6 for details.

eight
Keep your System file small and keep your System Folder tidy.

Keep only the fonts and sound you really need in your System file, and keep only the utilities and accessories in your System Folder. See "Using Suitcase" in Chapter 17 for a way to reduce the number of fonts in your System file.

nine
If you have an external hard drive, make sure it is on whenever the Mac is on.

Start the external drive before you start your Mac, and turn off the external drive after you shut down and turn off the Mac. See Chapter 6 for details.

ten
If you have two or more external hard drives, make sure they have different ID numbers.

Set the SCSI ID numbers to be something other than 0 (zero) or 7, and make sure they are different from each other. See "Connect and Initialize the Hard Drive Properly" in Chapter 6 for details.

Books that Work
Just Like Your Mac

As a Macintosh user, you enjoy unique advantages. You enjoy a dynamic user environment. You enjoy the successful integration of graphics, sound, and text. Above all, you enjoy a computer that's fun and easy to use.

When your computer gives you all this, why accept less in your computer books?

At SYBEX, we don't believe you should. That's why we've committed ourselves to publishing the highest quality computer books for Macintosh users. Externally, our books emulate the Mac "look and feel," with powerful, appealing illustrations and easy-to-read pages. Internally, our books stress "why" over "how," so you'll learn concepts, not sequences of steps. Philosophically, our books are designed to help you get work done, not to teach you about computers.

In short, our books are fun and easy to use—just like the Mac. We hope you find them just as enjoyable.

For a complete catalog of our publications:

SYBEX, Inc.
2021 Challenger Drive, Alameda, CA 94501
Tel: (510) 523-8233/(800) 227-2346 Telex: 336311
Fax: (510) 523-2373

SYBEX is committed to using natural resources wisely to preserve and improve our environment. As a leader in the computer book publishing industry, we are aware that over 40% of America's solid waste is paper. This is why we have been printing the text of books like this one on recycled paper since 1982.

This year our use of recycled paper will result in the saving of more than 15,300 trees. We will lower air pollution effluents by 54,000 pounds, save 6,300,000 gallons of water, and reduce landfill by 2,700 cubic yards.

In choosing a SYBEX book you are not only making a choice for the best in skills and information, you are also choosing to enhance the quality of life for all of us.

Anybody's
MAC BOOK

Anybody's
MAC® BOOK

Tom Cuthbertson

SAN FRANCISCO ■ PARIS ■ DÜSSELDORF ■ SOEST

Acquisitions Editor: Dianne King
Developmental Editor: Kenyon Brown
Copy Editor: Brendan Fletcher
Technical Editors: Nick Dargahi, Celia T. Stevenson, Dan Tauber
Word Processors: Ann Dunn, Susan Trybull
Book Designer: Suzanne Albertson
Technical Art: Delia Brown
Screen Graphics: Cuong Le
Typesetter: Deborah Maizels
Proofreader/Production Assistant: Janet K. Boone
Indexer: Nancy Guenther
Cover Designer: Thomas Ingalls + Associates
Cover Illustrator: Harumi Kubo

SYBEX is a registered trademark of SYBEX Inc.

TRADEMARKS: SYBEX has attempted throughout this book to distinguish proprietary trademarks from descriptive terms by following the capitalization style used by the manufacturer.

SYBEX is not affiliated with any manufacturer.

Every effort has been made to supply complete and accurate information. However, SYBEX assumes no responsibility for its use, nor for any infringement of the intellectual property rights of third parties which would result from such use.

Copyright ©1992 SYBEX Inc., 2021 Challenger Drive, Alameda, CA 94501. World rights reserved. No part of this publication may be stored in a retrieval system, transmitted, or reproduced in any way, including but not limited to photocopy, photograph, magnetic or other record, without the prior agreement and written permission of the publisher.

Library of Congress Card Number: 91-68338
ISBN: 0-89588-866-1

Manufactured in the United States of America
10 9 8 7 6 5 4 3 2 1

For Colleen!

Acknowledgments

More than thanks to Colleen for supporting me through the maelstrom. Also, many thanks to these among the friends and computer cohorts who helped me, answered my endless questions, and gave me their support so I could put my heart and mind into this book:

My developmental editor, Ken Brown; my editor, Brendan Fletcher; and my technical editors, Dan Tauber and Celia Stevenson of Sybex.

The editorial and production team at SYBEX: Ann Dunn and Susan Trybull, word processors; Deborah Maizels, typesetter; Janet Boone, proofreader; Cuong Le, screen graphics; Delia Brown, technical illustrations; and Suzanne Albertson, book designer.

My hardworking procedure drafters: Isaiah Carew (FileMaker Pro and Excel), Tracey Smith (PageMaker and Illustrator), Nancy Dannenberg (Quicken), Nick Dargahi (Networking), and Dan Tauber (E-mail).

The Computerware Santa Cruz team of Isaiah Carew, Eric Kopf, Kevin Quigley, Max Fischer, Steve Nakagawa, Dave Watson, Vaino Kees, Cathy and Mike Boucher, and Timothy Marshall; and Rose Meagher of the Computerware Training Center.

Bill McDermott, the wonderful chief leprechaun of the MaCruzers user's group, and Scott Sandow, the chairman of that group.

Keri Walker and Kate Paisley at Apple Computer; and Erica Sandstedt, Lisa Dronzek, Kelly Anne Marshall, and Dianne Jackson of Apple Support.

J.H. Alexander at Preferred Publishers, Freda Cook of Aldus, Karen Umholt of Broderbund, Jan Jacobs of Fifth Generation, David Schargel of Aladdin Systems, Nancy Stevenson of Symantec, Dave Miller of Intuit, Beth Regardz of Cabrillo College, Kevin Verboort (and a lot of other helpful people whose names I didn't get) of Microsoft Word Support, Jeffrey Hing of SCO, Howard Schneider of Canyon Consultants, David Mays of Dave's Computer Services in Santa Cruz, and Jim Rolens and Debra Spencer.

Clair, Sam, Cory, Ian, Tosh, Dylan, and Chancy (Kid Pix Cunsultants), and Jim Jones.

Contents at a Glance

Introduction	xxvii

PART ONE
Introducing the Macintosh   1

1	Meet the Macintosh	3
2	Meet the Mouse and the Desktop	31
3	Printing	55

PART TWO
System 7 for Anybody   87

4	Working with Applications and Documents	89
5	Using Folders to Organize Your Files	111
6	Storage: Hard and Floppy Disks	123
7	Checking and Adjusting Memory	151
8	Customizing Your Mac	163

PART THREE
Applications for the Mac   183

9	Word Processors	185
10	Graphics Applications	213

11	Page Layout Applications	255
12	Spreadsheets	289
13	Databases	323
14	Managing Personal Finances	349
15	Integrating Your Work	371

PART FOUR

Utilities and Communications for the Mac 391

16	Time-Saving Utilities	393
17	Organizer Utilities	409
18	Data Protection and Recovery Utilities	439
19	HyperCard	463
20	Networking	475
21	Electronic Mail	507

APPENDICES

A	Graphics File Formats	527
B	Installing the System Software on a Customized Mac	531
	Index	535

Contents

Introduction

PART ONE
Introducing the Macintosh

1 MEET THE MACINTOSH — 3
What's Inside Your Mac? — 4
Which Mac for You? — 7
    Macintosh Classic, Classic II, and Macintosh Plus — 7
    Macintosh SE/30 — 9
    Macintosh LC — 9
    Macintosh IIsi, IIci, IIfx — 10
    Macintosh Quadra 700 and 900 — 12
    Portable and PowerBook Macs — 12
Setting Up Your Mac — 14
    Basic Setup Steps — 15
    Special Setup Steps for Mac Models — 15
    Extra Connections — 16
Getting the First Smile from Your Mac — 17
Shutting Down Your Mac — 18
Setting Up Your Hard Disk for Future Startups — 19
Troubleshooting Hardware and Installation Problems — 23

2 MEET THE MOUSE AND THE DESKTOP — 31
Introducing the Desktop — 33
Using the Mouse — 34

Selecting, Dragging, and Opening Icons	35
Choosing Commands from Menus	36
Using the Keyboard	37
Showing and Hiding Help Balloons	39
Doing Things to Windows	40
Dragging Things to the Trash	42
Using Dialog and Alert Boxes	43
Troubleshooting Problems with the Mouse and the Desktop	46

3 PRINTING 55

Which Printer for You?	56
Inkjet Printers	57
Laser Printers	57
Dot-Matrix Printers	58
Setting Up Printing in the Chooser	58
Setting Up a Direct Connection to a Printer	59
Setting Up a Network Connection to a Printer	60
Taking Care of Your Printer	62
Care and Feeding of a StyleWriter	62
Care and Feeding of a DeskWriter	63
Care and Feeding of a LaserWriter	64
Care and Feeding of an ImageWriter	67
Printing Documents	68
Using the PrintMonitor	69
Using Page Setup for Special Printing Needs	70
Printing a Window in the Finder	72
Printing a Snapshot of the Screen	72
Using the Right Fonts for Your Printer	73
Kinds of Fonts	73
Installing Fonts	76
Removing Fonts	77

Using Key Caps to Compare Fonts	78
Using Accented Characters	79
Troubleshooting Problems with Printing	80

PART TWO
System 7 for Anybody 87

4 WORKING WITH APPLICATIONS AND DOCUMENTS 89

Introducing Applications and Documents	90
Installing an Application	92
Opening an Installed Application	94
Opening a Document	94
Saving Your Work on a Document	97
Saving a Document for the First Time	97
Saving as You Edit	98
Special Saving Techniques	99
Managing Your Applications	100
Opening Applications from the Apple Menu	100
Switching between Applications	101
Managing Your Documents	103
Finding Misplaced Documents	103
Switching between Documents	104
Changing Your Desktop View of Documents and Folders	105
Using List Views	106
Troubleshooting Problems with Applications and Documents	108

5 USING FOLDERS TO ORGANIZE YOUR FILES 111

Creating Folders	113
Naming and Nesting Folders	114

Using List Views to Work with Folders	117
Troubleshooting Problems with Files and Folders	119

6 STORAGE: HARD AND FLOPPY DISKS 123

Introducing Hard Disks	124
Introducing Floppy Disks	125
Bytes, Kilobytes, Megabytes	126
Which Disk for You?	127
Care and Feeding of a Hard Disk	129
Connect and Initialize the Hard Drive Properly	129
Turn the External Drive On First, and Turn It Off Last	130
Be Kind to Your Hard Disk	131
Save and Back Up	132
Defragment the Hard Disk Before It Fills Up	133
Care and Feeding of Floppy Disks	135
Floppy Disk Precautions	135
Preparing a Floppy Disk for Use	136
Floppy Disks for Different Uses	136
The Startup Disk	137
System Disks and Application Disks	137
Data Disks	137
Backing Up System and Application Disks	138
Copying an Entire Floppy Disk	139
Locking and Unlocking a Floppy Disk	141
Erasing a Floppy Disk	142
Checking Disk Capacity	142
Troubleshooting Problems with Hard and Floppy Disks	143

7 CHECKING AND ADJUSTING MEMORY 151

Monitoring Your Memory Use	153
Adjusting Application Allocations	155

Adjusting the Disk Cache	157
Troubleshooting Problems with Memory	159

8 CUSTOMIZING YOUR MAC — 163

Looking Around Your System Folder	164
Specifying Startup Applications and Documents	166
Using Special Customizing Files	167
Using Control Panels	169
General Controls Settings	171
Brightness Control Settings	172
Color Control Settings	172
Keyboard Control Settings	175
Mouse Control Settings	176
Sound Control Settings	176
Views Control Settings	177
Memory Control Settings	179
Closing Control Panels	179
Customizing Icons	179
Troubleshooting Customization Problems	180

PART THREE
Applications for the Mac — 183

9 WORD PROCESSORS — 185

Which Word Processor for You?	187
Word Processors for Big Writing Jobs	187
A Word Processor for Everyday Jobs	188
Bargain Word Processors	188
Using Microsoft Word	189
Opening a Document	189
Entering Text	191
Editing Text	192

Moving and Replacing Text via the Clipboard	194
Using the Ruler to Format Text	195
Changing Text Style	199
Saving and Printing a Word Document	200
Using MacWrite II	**201**
Opening a Document	201
Entering Text	202
Editing Text	203
Using the Ruler to Format Text	204
Changing Text Style	207
Saving and Printing a MacWrite II Document	208
Troubleshooting Problems with Your Word Processor	209

10 GRAPHICS APPLICATIONS 213

Which Graphics Application for You?	214
A Great Beginner's Graffic Application	215
Workhorse Applications that Paint and Draw	215
High-Power Drawing Applications	216
Using Kid Pix	217
Opening a Document	217
Drawing Lines	219
Undoing and Erasing Mistakes	219
Placing Stamps	220
Painting with the Wacky Brush	221
Painting an Area with the Paint Can	221
Saving and Printing a Kid Pix Document	222
Using SuperPaint	222
Opening a Document	223
Creating a Shape	225
Drawing Freehand Outlines	227
Drawing and Refining a Detailed Shape	227
Filling Closed Areas with the Paint Can	229

Adding Text in the Draw Layer	230
Saving and Printing a SuperPaint Document	231
Using Adobe Illustrator	232
Opening a New Document	232
Starting Off with a Sketch	235
Creating a Closed Path	236
Splitting a Closed Path into Two Shapes	237
Matching Two Closed Paths	240
Filling a Closed Path with a Shade of Gray	244
Creating and Hiding a Blend	245
Adding a Freehand Drawing to a Graphic	247
Adding Text to a Graphic	249
Using Layers for Depth Effects	250
Saving and Printing an Illustrator Document	250
Troubleshooting Problems with Graphics Applications	252

11 PAGE LAYOUT APPLICATIONS — 255

Which Page Layout Application for You?	257
An Inexpensive Page Layout Tool for Small Jobs	257
Page Layout Applications for Big Jobs	258
Using PageMaker	259
Making a Rough Sketch and Collecting Files	260
Opening a Document	261
Making Preliminary Page Settings	262
The PageMaker Document Window	264
Creating Master Pages	265
Placing Text	268
Placing a Graphic	270
Changing Your View of the Page	270
Adjusting Text Blocks	272
Adjusting the Layout of a Document	273

Changing Font Size and Style for Headings	276
Wrapping Text around a Graphic	279
Saving and Printing a PageMaker Document	281
Troubleshooting Problems in PageMaker	282

12 SPREADSHEETS — 289

Which Spreadsheet for You?	290
High-Power Spreadsheet Applications	291
Budget Spreadsheet Applications	291
Using Excel	292
Starting a New Document	293
Entering Some Data	294
Changing Type Style and Format	296
Using Insert	297
Using the Font Dialog Box	298
Range Selection and Changing the Number Format	298
Using Formulas	299
Using the Fill Function	301
Absolute Cell Referencing	301
Completing the Spreadsheet	302
Using Charts	303
Saving and Printing an Excel Document	305
Using Resolve	306
Starting a New Document	307
Entering Some Data	308
Changing Type Style and Format	310
Inserting a Row	311
Selecting a Range and Changing Number Format	312
Using Formulas	312
Using the Fill Function	314
Absolute Cell Referencing	314

Completing the Spreadsheet	316
Using Charts	317
Troubleshooting Problems with Spreadsheet Applications	318

13 DATABASES — 323

Which Database Application for You?	325
Relational Databases	325
Flat-File Databases	328
Budget Databases	328
Using FileMaker Pro	329
Designing a Database	329
Opening a Document	330
Setting Up the Fields	331
Entering Records	332
Using the Toolbar	334
Sorting Records	335
Finding Records	337
Changing Your Layout	338
Adding to the Database	339
Creating a Mailing	341
Saving and Printing a FileMaker Pro Document	346
Troubleshooting Problems with FileMaker Pro	347

14 MANAGING PERSONAL FINANCES — 349

Which Money Managing Application for You?	350
Bargain Budgeting Tools	351
High-Cost Financial Management Applications	351
Using Quicken	352
Creating a File for Your Quicken Accounts	352

Opening a New Account	354
Using the Check Register	355
Recording a Check in the Register	356
Entering Deposits in the Register	358
Correcting Mistakes in the Register	358
Using Categories	359
Choosing a Category or Transfer Account	360
Setting Up a Category	360
Writing Checks	361
Memorizing Transactions	363
Printing	364
Printing Checks on a Page-Oriented Printer	365
Printing Checks on a Continuous-Feed Printer	366
Creating Reports	366
Troubleshooting Problems with Quicken	367

15 INTEGRATING YOUR WORK — 371

Cutting, Copying, and Pasting	373
Introducing the Clipboard	373
Cutting and Pasting to Move Parts of Documents	374
Copying and Pasting	375
Copying Parts of Documents between Applications	376
Using the Scrapbook	378
Undoing Clipboard Mistakes	381
Dynamic Updating with Links	381
Linking a Text Document to a Spreadsheet	381
Special Considerations for Linked Documents	382
Publishing and Subscribing to Parts of Documents	384
Troubleshooting Problems with Data Integration	386

PART FOUR
Utilities and Communications for the Mac — 391

16 TIME-SAVING UTILITIES — 393
  Which Time-Saving Utilities for You? — 395
    Utilities that Get at Things Quickly — 395
    Utilities that Do Your Repetitive Work for You — 396
  Using Norton Fast Find — 397
  Using HAM — 398
  Using Norton KeyFinder — 401
  Using HotKeys MacroMaker — 402
  Troubleshooting Problems with Time-Saving Utilities — 406

17 ORGANIZER UTILITIES — 409
  Which Organizer Utilities for You? — 411
    Utilities that Organize Your Resources — 411
    Utilities that Organize and Defragment Your Hard Drive — 412
    Other Organizer Utilities and Screen Savers — 412
  Using Suitcase — 413
    Creating a Fonts Folder — 415
    Building Font Family Suitcases — 419
    Organizing Suitcases into Sets — 422
    Making Font Sets Available — 426
  Using Adobe Type Manager — 426
  Using Norton Speed Disk — 428
  Troubleshooting Problems with Organizer Utilities — 432

18 DATA PROTECTION AND RECOVERY UTILITIES — 439
  Which Data Protection Utilities for You? — 441
    Antiviral Utilities — 441
    Backup Utilities — 442
    File Recovery Utilities — 443
  Using SAM — 444
  Using Disinfectant — 447
  Using Fastback Plus — 448
    Doing Your First Big Backup — 448
    Daily and Partial Backups — 451
    Restoring a File to Your Hard Disk — 451
  Using Redux — 455
  Using the Norton Disk Doctor — 458
  Using Norton UnErase — 459
  Troubleshooting Problems with Data Protection Utilities — 461

19 HYPERCARD — 463
  Using HyperCard Stacks — 465
    Starting HyperCard and Opening a Stack — 465
    Adding and Sorting Address Cards — 467
    Finding Cards in the Stack — 469
    Fixing Mistakes — 471
    Printing — 471
    Quitting HyperCard — 472
  Troubleshooting Problems with HyperCard — 473

20 NETWORKING — 475
  AppleTalk and Ethernet Networks — 477
  Setting Up an AppleTalk Network — 479

Setting Up an EtherTalk Network	481
Installing EtherTalk Drivers	482
Selecting Your Network Connection	483
Connecting to a Shared Printer on the Network	484
Using a Print Server	485
Using an ImageWriter on the Network	486
Sharing Files on a Network	486
Distributed and Dedicated File Servers	487
Preparing to Share Files	488
Setting Up Your Macintosh as a File Server	490
Sharing a Folder with Everybody	490
Limiting Access Privileges	492
Shutting Off File Sharing on Your Computer	498
Getting Access to Other Users' Files	498
Logging In to a File Server and Getting a File	499
Login Shortcut: Creating Aliases	502
Disconnecting from Someone Else's Computer	502
Linking Programs	502
Troubleshooting Problems with Networks	503

21 ELECTRONIC MAIL   507

Which E-Mail System for You?	508
Using Microsoft Mail	510
Selecting a Mail Server	510
Starting E-Mail	513
Sending a Message	513
Replying to a Message	518
Using E-Mail inside Other Applications	519
Quitting Mail and Signing Off	520
Mail Etiquette	520

Using Information Services   521
        CompuServe   522
        MCI Mail   522
        Public Access Systems   523
    Troubleshooting E-Mail Problems   523

APPENDICES

A GRAPHICS FILE FORMATS   **527**

B INSTALLING THE SYSTEM SOFTWARE ON A CUSTOMIZED MAC   **531**

Index   535

Introduction

I would like to introduce you to a computer with a heart.

Meet the Macintosh, the computer that was made for your enjoyment. The whole intent of the Macintosh is to encourage you to do your best work, and to make working on a computer so easy that anybody can enjoy it.

Why is the Macintosh so nice to use? Because it was designed by people who cared. Of course, most computers are designed by folks who care about their product. But the Mac designers went beyond that; they didn't just care about the bits, bytes, bells and whistles. They cared about the people who would *use* the thing. As Mac software whiz Andy Hertzfeld said, "It's the product I want my best friends to have."

This attitude has continued to guide the development of the Mac to this day. With each improvement in the Mac's design—whether the change was to the hardware or to the system software that runs the Mac—Apple engineers have made ease of use their top priority. Now, with the introduction of System 7, the Mac is more powerful and friendlier than ever.

The History of the Mac

The Macintosh design didn't come out of nowhere, of course. By the late 1970s, engineers and dreamers at places like the Stanford Research Institute (SRI) and the Xerox Palo Alto Research Center (PARC) had come up with ideas like the mouse and the desktop. (The mouse is what you use to tell a computer what to do, and the desktop is the graphic display of all the things you work with on the computer.). But they didn't put the ideas into a box that anybody could afford. It took Steve Jobs, Steve Wozniak, Bill Atkinson, Andy Herzfeld, and a bunch of other wild-eyed, idealistic young computer fanatics at Apple to put the ideas together with hardware that actually worked and was actually affordable.

There's a great story about the day when the Apple team visited PARC and saw the working model of the Xerox desktop for the first time. The scholarly fellows at PARC began a quiet, orderly presentation of the first desktop, and all of a sudden, the Apple guys came unglued. Steve Jobs was bouncing around the room like a ping-pong ball, shouting about how revolutionary, how insanely great this interface was. Bill Atkinson walked right up the the screen of the PARC machine as the engineer was talking, and pushed his nose against the tube like a zombie. He was trying to watch individual pixels move so he could figure out how this wonderful thing worked.

The PARC research team was taken aback. They thought their computer was nice, but they didn't think it was *that* exciting. In point of fact, when they produced the Star computer, it was so big, slow, expensive, and ugly, it *wasn't* very exciting. It didn't sell well at all.

But the guys at Apple had seen the light. They developed the Lisa first; it had a nice desktop interface that worked pretty well, but it was pretty big, expensive, and slow too, so it didn't sell well, either. Then Burrell Smith, a self-taught hardware genius, created an elegant, small circuit board that did most of what the Lisa's many boards did, and it did it twice as fast. All of a sudden there was a desktop interface that did what you told it to do, instantly, and the circuitry for it could fit in a box about a third the size of the PARC Star.

The Macintosh team at Apple knew they really had something. They worked like crazy to get all the details ironed out, and put together a small, nonthreatening computer that was made and priced for the masses.

The first Macs were humble indeed, especially if you compare them with what we use today. The hardware had a long way to go; the first Mac didn't have a hard drive at all. But the heart of the thing, its clear, graphic interface and simple organization, has stayed almost exactly the same as the power of the computer has increased. A new user can still do most basic Mac functions on the desktop with the mouse, and without any fancy memorized commands. The Mac is still simple enough that anybody can learn to get along with it in a matter of minutes.

How This Book Can Help You

This book is a guide to using the Mac. It is designed to help you make the most of the desktop interface and all the things you can do with it. You can do *so much* with a Mac! Anybody can! No matter who you are or what you do, you can use a Mac to be more productive, more creative, and more self-sufficient. You don't have to be a nerd. You don't have to be an electronic wizard or a brilliant memorizer of obscure commands and jargon. You just point that mouse and click what you want! And almost anything you want is available on the Mac, from a kid's sketching pad to full-color magazine layout tools, from a button calculator to financial planning tools that can handle a corporation's budget. Of course, I couldn't have written a book big enough to cover every single application for every single task you can accomplish with a Mac, but I have tried to cover the basic tools that people commonly use for everyday work.

A Mac Book for Anybody

My goal in this book is to help you do more with your Mac. I want to help you get over that queasy feeling of being intimidated by new things on the computer.

Now, you don't have to be using your Mac to solve the whole world's woes to get that intimidated feeling. I remember my first day with the Mac; I was intimidated every time I pulled down a menu. I was scared I'd blow the thing up or something if I released the mouse button when the wrong command was highlighted. With that in mind, I wrote this book to help *all* of you get over the feeling of intimidation.

If you are new to the Mac and computers in general, the first chapters and the simple exercises for each application can help you get past being intimidated by the Mac itself. You are encouraged to feel your way into the use of the mouse, the keyboard, and the desktop, and then you are given easy things to do that give you confidence and a sense of how much fun it is to do work on the Mac. After writing a little memo or two and painting a few simple pictures, you'll forget you were ever afraid of menus.

If you have used your Mac some, but you are not getting much out of it because you feel intimidated by applications that you think might be hard to learn, or if the techniques of using the desktop seem too complex, this book will give you a quick, easy way to get into the powerful features of the Mac and its applications. You can use this book as a springboard, from just plugging along to really making the most of your Mac.

If you are an experienced Mac user, but you sometimes get stymied by some particularly intimidating problem with software or hardware, this book can help you solve your problems and forge ahead. There are not only problem-solving sections at the ends of all the chapters, there are also tips and tricks on every page. No matter how much you have used an application, there is always another trick you can learn to make it work better, and I have included all the best ones I know.

Help with System 7

No matter what level of experience you have, you may need some help adapting to System 7 and the ways that new applications take advantage of its features. All of the programs covered in this book are compatible with System 7, and all of the procedures were written with the System 7 user in mind. What's more, Part Two, "System 7 for Anybody," guides you through all of the important features of System 7, so you can make the most of all it offers.

If you are using a different version of the system software, this book can still help you. If you want to upgrade to System 7, there are plenty of details on how to make a smooth transition. If you want to stick with your version of the system software, you can still follow most of the procedures in the book and apply them to your situation.

How to Use This Book

This book is like a tree. The roots are in the first part. If you are new to the Macintosh and computing in general, read the first part carefully, working through the examples on your Mac as you go. Get your roots set firmly, and you can grow into a confident user of the Macintosh.

- Chapter 1 gives you a thorough introduction to the Mac, helps you decide which Mac is best for your needs, and tells you how to set up your Mac.
- Chapter 2 shows you how to use the mouse, the keyboard, and the desktop. It takes you through the basic techniques one step at a time and helps you master the fundamentals so that all your other work on the Mac will come more easily.

- Chapter 3 tells you how to print things you create on your Mac. It also helps you choose, set up, and maintain the printer that's right for you.

The second part of the book is like a tree's trunk. It describes the System 7 software, the structure that holds up the Mac interface and helps you do your work and store it. No matter what you do on the Mac, your efforts will depend on the structure described Part Two. You may not want to learn every detail in this part of the book right at first, but if you keep referring back to the section, your power as a user will increase dramatically.

- Chapter 4 covers the basic techniques of using applications and documents. Applications are the tools for your Mac work and documents are the products of your work on the Mac. You learn how to install and start applications, how to find and open documents, and how to switch between application and document windows as you work.
- Chapter 5 tells you how to organize your work on the Mac desktop. You learn to put all your documents in well-organized folders, so you can find things easily and move quickly from one item to another.
- Chapter 6 explains how to use hard and floppy disks to save your work. You also learn how to take care of your disks so that you'll never lose any important files.
- Chapter 7 shows you how to take care of your Mac's memory. Each Mac has only so much, and you learn how to make the most of what you have.
- Chapter 8 is about customizing your Mac so it looks, sounds, and works just the way you want it to.

The third and fourth parts of the book are like limbs, twigs, and leaves: once you have the basics down, you can branch out to work in whatever applications suit you, and you can take advantage of the utilities that will help you most. Just read the chapters that apply to your needs, and move ahead.

- Chapters 9 through 15 cover all of the basic types of applications you can use on the Mac. Each chapter tells you how to pick the application that will work best for you and how to start doing your work with it. There are chapters on word processing, page layout applications, painting and drawing applications, spreadsheets, databases, and money management applications. There is also a chapter that explains how to combine different kinds of work from different applications in a single, integrated document.
- Chapters 16 through 21 introduce helpful utilities and communications packages that can improve your life on the Mac. There are chapters on time-saving utilities, organizer utilities, data protection and recovery utilities, networking, and electronic mail.

Along the way, as you learn about the basics and then develop your own special field of Mac expertise, you may have some problems. The Mac is wonderful, but it is not perfect. Both the Mac and the software that runs on it were made by humans like you and me, and we all make mistakes. To take care of the problems you may encounter, there are troubleshooting sections at the ends of all the chapters. Whenever you have a problem, look at the end of the chapter that deals with what you are doing and see if your problem is covered. If it isn't covered in that chapter, look in the index; it might be covered under a different heading. With a little patience and effort, you can usually get the Mac running smoothly again in a matter of minutes.

One detail you should understand about the illustrations in this book—many were made by taking pictures of what was on my Mac's screen. They may look a bit different from what you see on your Mac.

My Mac shows shades of gray, so lots of things look three-dimensional on it; if your Mac shows only black and white, you won't see all those little shadows and shapes to the objects on the screen. Don't let the different scenery throw you; it all works the same.

In fact, the key to using this book and your Mac is to keep trying things, even if they seem a little new and different. The Mac will reward your efforts. That's why I say it is a computer with a heart: it encourages you to do your best. And my greatest hope is that this book can give you the same sort of encouragement.

PART one

Introduction to the Macintosh

The first part of this book is an introduction to the Macintosh for new users. You'll start by learning a bit about the Macintosh hardware (the pieces of machinery you set down on your desk) and software (the programs that go in the machinery and make it do what you want). You'll also learn how to set up your Mac and get it running.

Then you'll explore the basic techniques for using the Mac: how to use the mouse and the keyboard, how to maneuver around on the desktop that appears on the screen, and how to tell the Mac to do things. Finally, you'll learn how to print documents you produce on the Mac.

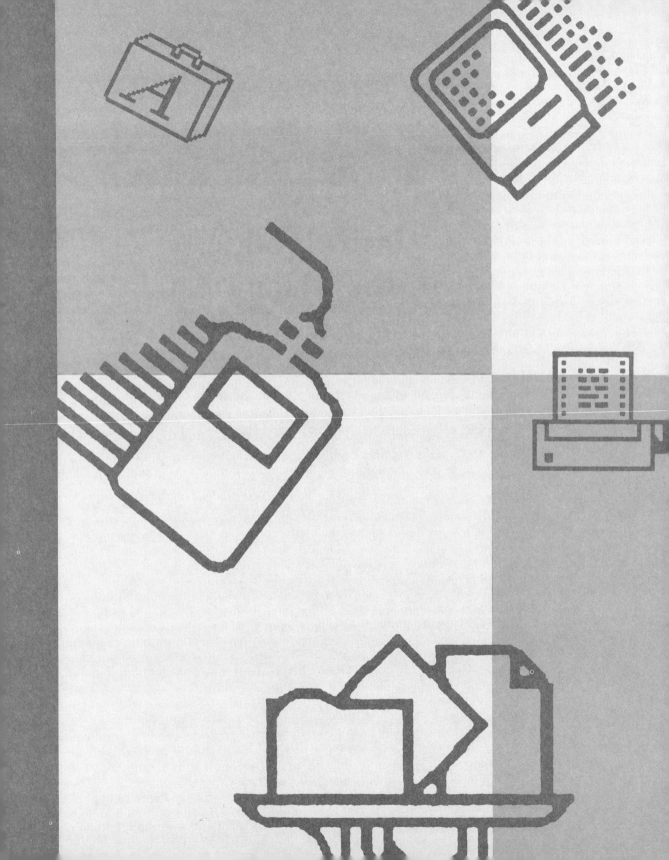

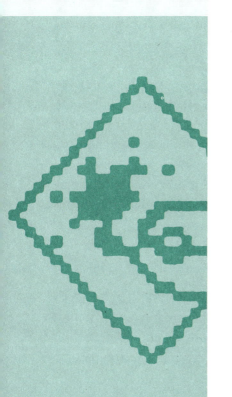

CHAPTER 1

Meet the Macintosh

The Macintosh is a simple machine. It was designed and built so you can use it without worrying about a lot of confusing details. But just because you'll find the Mac easy and pleasant to use, you shouldn't think that it's a frivolous toy with no power to do real computing work. You can find a Macintosh that will handle any kind of work you would want a computer to do, from word processing to desktop publishing, from keeping inventory to planning the national budget, from cartoon sketching to three-dimensional full-color computer-aided design.

This chapter will help you find and set up the Mac that's right for you. It introduces the different models of Macintosh and describes the features that make each model good for a particular use. If you have bought a Mac and it is set up already, you can skip the hints for choosing a Mac and setting up in this chapter. But if you are new to computers, read the "What's Inside Your Mac?" section that follows, so you'll understand some basics about the machine, and so you'll know what things are when I refer to them later on.

 ## What's Inside Your Mac?

A Macintosh computer isn't all that complicated, really. It sounds complicated if you describe every little part in great technical detail, but you don't *need* to understand all those details. So here are the parts of your Macintosh, described in nontechnical terms.

First, let's look at the outer, more obvious units. There are the parts of the computer that you interact with: the keyboard (with letter keys, numbers, symbols, and some special control keys), and the mouse, which you move around to make a little pointer or cursor scurry around on the screen. Anything you want to tell the computer to do, you can tell it by using these simple tools.

The messages you send to the computer from the keyboard and mouse are called the *input*. The results of your keyboard and mouse input are shown on the screen, or display, and are known as *output*. The output can be anything from text or numbers to three-dimensional views of space stations. All types of input and output are referred to as *data*.

The internal parts of the computer process and store the data. There is a part of the computer that is kind of like your brain, but it doesn't quite think, it processes data. Computer people call it the *CPU* (Central Processing Unit). The faster this little chip of silicon can process your data, the more it costs, and the more your Mac costs. Exception: Newer Macs tend to have quicker CPUs, even the cheaper models. People use all kinds of complex jargon and empirical details to describe how fast the CPU works, but the concept is simple: Cheap old Macs are slow, new Macs are quick, and pricey new Macs go like blazes.

The *memory* is the part of the computer that remembers things. There are several types of memory: ROM (Read Only Memory), and RAM (Random Access Memory), and a few others, but for your purposes, the RAM is the key. Your Mac's CPU needs memory it can use any time it wants, and that's what RAM is.

The more RAM your Mac has inside it, the more it can remember as it works on things. If your Mac doesn't have enough RAM, it works slowly, just as you write slowly if you keep forgetting the meanings of words you want to use. There is a vital difference between your memory and your Mac's, though. You can go to sleep and wake up in the morning and still remember *most* of what you had in your memory the day before.

Chapter 1

When you shut down your Mac for the night, everything in the RAM disappears.

Since your Mac forgets everything in the RAM when it's off, there has to be a place where your Mac can store things permanently. This is called disk storage. If you want to keep something from disappearing when you turn your Mac off, you save it on a disk.

There are two basic types of disks. *Floppy disks* go in a floppy disk drive slot at the front of your Mac, or in an external floppy disk drive that plugs into the back. A floppy disk drive is sort of a cross between a record player and a cassette player/recorder; it can write things onto the floppy disk and read things off it. It works *much* faster than a record player, though. A floppy disk can hold a fair amount of stuff, like a book's worth of text.

There are also *hard disks* (sometimes called hard drives; the disk and the drive are usually all in one unit). Hard drives can be inside the Mac or external, like floppy drives. A hard disk can hold much more than a floppy disk, like a personal library's worth of text, or more. Hard drives read and write data faster than floppy disk drives, too. Needless to say, the bigger a hard disk you have, the less you'll have to shuttle those slow little floppy disks in and out of your floppy drive. If your Mac doesn't have a hard disk inside it, you should get an external hard disk drive.

The parts of the Mac that I've described so far are all *hardware*. The last and most important part of the Mac is the *system software*, the coded instructions that make the whole system work. The combination of hardware and software that you interact with is called the *interface*. It is my humble opinion that the Macintosh interface is far and away the best one in the computer world.

For more information on the interface, see Chapter 2. For more information on memory and storage, see Chapters 6 and 7. For more information on the Mac's CPU and how the system software relates it to the other parts, see *Inside Macintosh*, a many-volume set published by Addison-Wesley for programmers, nerds, and the technically inclined.

Which Mac for You?

If you have not bought a Macintosh yet, first make sure you understand the basic concepts of what makes a Mac run, as described in the previous section. Then look at the descriptions of the different models, and decide which one will work best for your needs. No matter which model you buy, remember that you want the fastest CPU, the most memory (RAM), and the greatest amount of storage you can afford. The last two items are measured in *megabytes*, or Mbs. For example, the Classic II can come with 2Mb of RAM and a 40Mb hard drive. This configuration is sometimes shortened to 2/40.

Keep in mind the fact that you might need to expand your computer's features as you expand your work. For instance, if you are a graphic designer or artist, sooner or later you will want to take on work in color or grayscale formats. Some Macs can handle color and grayscale, others can be upgraded to handle them, and some cannot handle either color or grayscale, no matter what you do to them. If you're planning to work in color or grayscale but you can't afford a Mac that can handle these formats, you should at least buy one that can be expanded to do so, so you can move on up when you're ready.

Macintosh Classic, Classic II, and Macintosh Plus

These models are the basic, no-frills Macs. The Classic is similar to the older Plus, but its CPU is faster. A Classic II, such as the one in Figure 1.1, has a relatively speedy CPU, in a class with many computers that cost twice as much. Any Classic can (and for most uses should) have a 40Mb or 80Mb hard disk inside it. Alas, the Classic has a fan in it, which the Plus did not. This made the old Plus run warm (hence the nickname "toaster"), but it was wonderfully quiet.

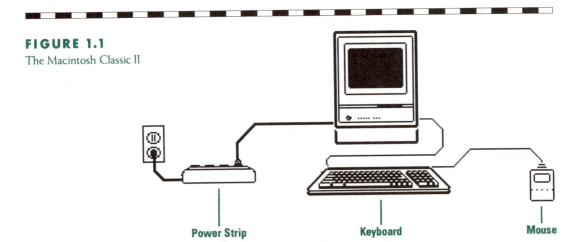

FIGURE 1.1
The Macintosh Classic II

Neither the Mac Plus nor either of the Classics can carry a tremendous amount of memory. You can get a Classic II with 4Mb of RAM, and that's enough to run System 7 with one or two applications. You can upgrade a Plus to 4Mb, and you can upgrade a Classic II to as much as 8Mb.

The Plus and the Classic have very good, clear screens, but they are small, and they cannot show true grayscale or color, so they are better for working with numbers and text than for doing professional graphics. They do not have any slot for expansion cards, so it is hard to adapt them for use with other monitors or things like Ethernet networks.

If you have a Plus or a Classic, you're in good company; there are lots of them around. They are often called "compact" Macs because the computer and the monitor or display screen are all built into one box. All you have do to prepare the Mac is plug in the power cord, mouse, and keyboard.

The simplicity of the Mac Plus and the Classics make them good for basic work such as word processing or database and spreadsheet applications, as long as you don't have to see large portions of a document at one time. Although they weigh too much to be considered truly portable, you can get them around quite easily as long as you don't have to carry them far. They are not a good choice for color or grayscale graphics work, nor are they designed for heavy-duty number crunching.

Macintosh SE/30

The SE/30 is a compact Mac, similar to the Plus and the Classic, but it costs more. That's because it has a quicker CPU, and a design that makes the best use of that CPU. It may also have a larger hard disk in it, and more memory. The SE has a slot for an expansion card, which means you can hook it up to a second monitor with color, or to an Ethernet network.

The SE is no longer in production, because it is going to be replaced by the less powerful Classic II. But until the design and the expansibility of the Classic are brought up to the SE's level, there are some things that the SE can do better, such as number crunching and working with complex black-and-white graphics.

Macintosh LC

This is the lowest-cost Macintosh that can support color. It comes without a display screen. As you can see in Figure 1.2, it is a modular model, meaning that it is made up of several components, or modules, as opposed to the all-in-one-box compact models. You can use either a color or a monochrome monitor with the LC. It has a slot for an expansion card, which can be used to extend its power or to allow the

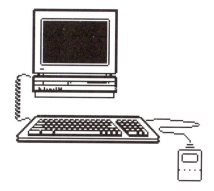

FIGURE 1.2
The Macintosh LC

use of Apple IIe software. The expansion slot can also be used to attach another monitor to the LC, or to attach it to an Ethernet network.

The LC does not have a particularly fast CPU. It is slower than the Classic II, and much slower than an SE or any of the current Mac II models (si, ci, fx). It comes with 2Mb or 4Mb of RAM, and either a 40Mb or 80Mb hard drive. Although you can expand the memory and the storage capacity of an LC, and you can connect things to it with the expansion slot, you cannot get past the limited speed of its CPU.

The LC is best suited for text and graphics work that do not require lots of number crunching. It is not a good choice if you need to move the computer often, or if you plan to expand your work into areas that require heavy CPU use, such as long spreadsheet calculations, page layout with lots of graphic formats, or complex color graphic design.

Macintosh IIsi, IIci, IIfx

These are all modular computers; each is a box that you have to put a display screen or monitor on top of, as shown in Figure 1.3, or next to, as shown in Figure 1.4. The main differences between the models are the speed of the CPU, the degree of expansibility, and the power of the color video support.

FIGURE 1.3
The Macintosh IIci with full-page monitor

FIGURE 1.4

The Macintosh IIfx with large color monitor

The si has a relatively slow CPU, although it is still faster than an LC or Classic II. It has built-in color video support, and you can add a video card to its single expansion slot for faster and better color display. The ci has a very fast CPU, and built-in color as well as slots for adding video and other expansion cards. The fx has the fastest CPU of the Mac II models. Although it has no video support built in, it can accept the fastest video cards and lots of other power cards in its six expansion slots.

These Macs are perfect for professionals who expect to expand their work to include number-crunching tasks or complex graphic work that requires the integration of a variety of formats. For example, a ci with a full-page monitor is perfect for page layout. An fx with a fast color video card and lots of RAM can be used as a workstation by an engineer designing three-dimensional objects. Scientists can use an fx for number crunching, or it can be set up a as a server for an AppleTalk or Ethernet network. The si is not powerful and fast enough for the highest-level design or network service, but it is good for lower-level color or grayscale graphic work.

Macintosh Quadra 700 and 900

These are the most powerful Macs. They are powerful enough to use as network servers on big Ethernet/AppleTalk networks, or they can be used as workstations for scientists, engineers, and high-tech designers who use three-dimensional applications or multicolored formats. The CPU of a Quadra like the one in Figure 1.5 is roughly twice as fast as the CPU of a Mac IIci, and about 20 percent faster than a Mac IIfx.

The options for these machines are staggering. For example, the 900 can have as much as 256Mb of RAM and a 400Mb hard disk inside; SCSI ports allow for almost unlimited external storage. The Quadras will support all kinds of different monitors, including many made by companies other than Apple. Input and output bottlenecks have been improved, so the Quadra's computing power doesn't have to wait for slow communication with other devices.

Portable and PowerBook Macs

The portable and PowerBook Macs are at a different extreme from the Quadras. They are masterpieces of miniaturization. They pack a surprising amount of power for their size, but they definitely have limits.

FIGURE 1.5
The Quadra 900

The portable Macintosh is smaller and somewhat lighter than a compact Mac, and it *all* fits in one unit. It can also run off a battery for a few hours. This is nice on trips, but most folks find it more convenient to plug the Mac in, rather than using the batteries and then having to plug *them* in for hours to recharge. This means the portable is better for using here and there, rather than on the way. At about 16 pounds, you don't want to lug it around too much, anyway.

The PowerBook Macs, like the one in Figure 1.6, are similar to the portable, but smaller and lighter yet. The 100 does not have any floppy disk drive, but you can connect an external floppy drive to it. It is one of the lightest of all "notebook-size" computers at only 5.2 pounds, ready-to-use. It is a light-duty computer, though; it has a slowish CPU, a small hard drive (20Mb) and a smaller, less readable screen than some other portables.

The 140 PowerBook is faster than the 100, and has a larger hard drive option (40Mb). There is an internal floppy drive, and the display is larger and clearer.

The 170 PowerBook is the fastest of the three PowerBooks, has the clearest display, and comes with a 40Mb hard drive, a floppy drive, and a built-in modem. But it costs a lot more, too.

All of the PowerBooks share some limitations. They cannot be expanded easily, nor can you add RAM easily. They cannot display color or grayscale graphics. Also, they have a slightly undersized keyboard, which takes a while to get used to if you are a touch-typist, and

FIGURE 1.6
The PowerBook Mac

the touch is unusual—somewhat squishy compared to the crisp feel of most Mac keyboards.

Instead of the mouse, the portable and PowerBooks have a built-in *trackball*. It is a ball in a socket in front of the keyboard. You use it to move the pointer, and you use the buttons next to it to click. The trackball is used as a way to keep the whole unit simple, and to save the space it takes to use a mouse. I don't like the trackball, but others may find it easy to adapt to.

Overall, the portable and PowerBook Macs are OK, but I think they are best used to fill very special needs, like recording changes in financial data or writing text while you are on an extensive trip with many stops and starts. Unless you have such needs, it makes more sense to get a compact. I have to tote my Classic II around at least once a month, and I don't mind it at all. Still, if I had to lug it through an airport four or six times a week, I might learn to love the trackball on a PowerBook real fast.

Setting Up Your Mac

The first thing you'll notice as you unpack any Mac is that it *looks* simple; there aren't hundreds of indescribable little parts and connectors that you have to put together. And there are very simple instructions for hooking things up, in the form of packets, numbered 1, 2, and 3. All you have to do is open packet 1, follow the instructions in the *Setting Up* booklet, and within about ten or fifteen minutes you'll have your Mac all connected and ready to go. If anything is unclear in the booklet, or if you have lost it, or bought your Mac secondhand, just read the basic setup steps that follow, and any special steps that apply to your model of Mac.

Basic Setup Steps

To hook up any Mac (except the Plus), you need to plug the power cord into a grounded outlet first, then plug in the mouse and the keyboard (the Plus has separate cables for the mouse and keyboard). All of the mouse and keyboard sockets have the little Apple Desktop Bus (ADB) icon, which looks like some kind of odd plumbing contraption.

The ADB plugs go in flat side up. You can plug the mouse into either the right or left end of the keyboard, depending on which hand you want to use on the mouse; just plug the keyboard cord into the other end. That's all there is to setting up, for the basic Mac. There are special steps for some models of the Mac, however; see the following paragraphs and read the notes that apply to your model.

One note of warning: Before turning the power switch on, make sure the Mac is placed where you want to use it. Don't move the Mac after it's on, expecially if there is a hard disk in it. You can ruin a hard disk by joggling it while it is spinning.

And another note for newcomers: If you have never used a Macintosh, insert the Macintosh Basics disk before you turn your Mac on. Push the disk into the disk drive slot on the front of your computer, with the label up and the metal end of the disk going in first. If you are familiar with the basics, just turn the Mac on and wait for the Happy Mac to appear.

Special Setup Steps for Mac Models

If you have a modular Macintosh, from an LC to any of the IIs to a Quadra, it requires a display or monitor. Set the computer on a flat, secure surface like the top of a table or desk. Put the monitor on top of the computer or near it. Plug in the power cords for both units. Then plug one end of the video cable into the monitor (if it isn't already attached), and plug the other end into the video port (socket) on the computer. This port has an icon under it that looks like a TV screen. If the connector at either end of the video cable has thumbscrews, screw them in tight.

If you have a Mac model that has expansion slots and you have an expansion card, unplug the power cord for the computer, then press the expansion card into place, as explained in the instructions included with the card. If those instructions are unclear, just have the people who sold you the card and the Mac put the card in for you; they should do this without charge.

If you have a model of Mac that accepts sound input and you want to add sounds to it, or if you use sound in your work on it, connect the microphone to the socket with the microphone above it, or connect your audio output plugs to the phono-plug adapter, as shown in the Apple *Setting Up* booklet.

If you have a portable or PowerBook Mac, you may wonder how to turn the thing on. In most cases, you can just press any key to power up. If that doesn't work, see the owner's guide.

No matter which model of Mac you have, if you have any other extra things to connect to it, such as an external disk drive, a printer, or a network cable, see the "Extra Connections" section below.

Extra Connections

By itself, a Mac is a sort of truncated creature. But you can hook all kinds of things up to it. Many are self-explanatory, such as trackballs and stylus pointers that plug into the ADB socket and replace the mouse, or modems that plug into the modem port (the socket with an icon that looks like a telephone), or printers that plug directly into the printer port. Just do your plugging in *before* you turn the Mac on, follow the instructions for the item you are connecting, and make sure you have the software to make use of the hardware you are connecting up.

There are some extra connections that take a little extra know-how, however. If you are connecting your Mac to a network, see Chapter 21 for cabling and software details. If you are hooking up an external hard drive, turn to "Connect and Initialize the Hard Disk Properly" in Chapter 6 for more information.

 ## Getting the First Smile from Your Mac

OK, so you have your Mac all set up where you want it and all the cables and cords are connected. Now it's time to turn the thing on and watch it smile at you. To get your Mac's first smile, just switch the power on. It beeps or strikes a nice musical chord, and then it whirrs quietly, and the screen gets bright, and you'll see the Happy Mac icon shown in Figure 1.7. In some cases, you may see the question mark icon shown in Figure 1.7 instead of a smile—just insert a startup disk if this happens, and you'll see the smile. (If you have a hard disk and saw the question mark icon, be sure to read "Setting Up Your Hard Disk for Future Start-ups" below. If you need help inserting the startup disk, see "The Happy Mac does not appear" later in this chapter.)

After the smiling Mac goes away, you see a little sign on the screen that says "Welcome to Macintosh." Now, I know that smiley faces and welcome mats can get trite. You can get sick of hearing "Have a nice day" from every clerk you deal with all day, especially if you're having an awful day. But the Mac doesn't force its smile on you repeatedly. In fact, once you've turned on the Mac a few times, you'll probably ignore the Happy Mac icon and the welcome screen. That's OK. But I think

FIGURE 1.7
Icons you may see when you start your Mac

Shutting Down Your Mac

they are a good sign. They remind me that at the very beginning, at the heart, if you will, the Mac is a positive machine, made to encourage us, the people who use it. Some other computers are not so nice.

When you have finished working on the Mac, you need to shut down the system software before you turn the computer off. If you are looking at the desktop, pull down the Special menu as shown in Figure 1.8, and choose Shut Down.

If you need more information about the desktop and how to use menus, see Chapter 2, "Meet the Mouse and the Desktop." After you choose Shut Down, the screen goes black. Mac II and Quadra models turn themselves off automatically. Mac Pluses, Classics, and LCs show you an alert box, telling you that it is now safe to switch off your Macintosh. Press the on/off switch on the back of the computer to turn the power off. If you have an external hard disk drive, you can turn it off after turning off the Mac. If you have a portable Mac, all you have to do is choose Shut Down from the Special menu, and the computer turns

FIGURE 1.8
Shutting down your Mac

itself off. If you want to put your portable in the half-off state that you get when you use Shut Down on other Macs, choose Sleep from the Special menu.

If you ever want to restart your Mac without turning it all the way off, you can either choose Restart from the Special menu, or you can click the Restart button in the alert box that appears after you choose Shut Down.

Warning: NEVER turn off the Mac without saving the work you are doing and ejecting any floppy disks in floppy disk drives! For information on ejecting disks, see the "Introducing Floppy Disks" section in Chapter 6. For information on saving, see Chapter 4.

 ## Setting Up Your Hard Disk for Future Startups

If you have an internal or external hard disk drive for your Mac, and you saw a blinking question mark icon instead of a Happy Mac when you switched the power on, you need to put the system software on your hard disk. (If you saw the Happy Mac, you can skip this section.) If you don't have a hard drive, you have to insert the System Startup disk in your floppy drive every time you start your Mac. That is a pain; if you can possibly afford it, buy an internal or external hard drive for your Mac, and put the system software on the hard disk.

The system software you need to put on the hard disk is on a series of floppy disks, beginning with Before You Install System 7, then Install 1, and so on. These disks are contained in the Number 2 Kit you received with your Mac. You may need to run an install floppy disk for your hard disk if it is a non-Apple hard disk. Do this before you install the system software. The following procedure explains how to copy the system software onto your hard disk, assuming that this is a first-time install.

The procedure takes some time, but don't try to take a shortcut and just drag a bunch of stuff off the install disks into your System Folder on your hard disk. It is *absolutely critical* that you get everything installed in the right place inside your System Folder; that means installing a whole set of system software that works together, and chucking out anything that won't work with the stuff you install. So do it once, and do it right, as described below. It'll save you an enormous amount of grief, believe me.

If you have a lot of special customizing files (INITs, CDEVs, DAs, extensions, control panels) and you have done a lot of customizing to the Finder itself, you should not do this first-time installing procedure. See Appendix B, "Installing the System Software on a Customized Mac."

If you are new to the Mac and to computing in general, work through Chapter 2, "Meet the Mouse and the Desktop," or at least take the Macintosh Basics tour before you do the following installation procedure. You need to be familiar with the mouse and how to use things on the desktop to complete this procedure.

1. Make sure you have HyperCard version 1.2.2 or later on your hard disk. If you don't have it installed, find the HyperCard disk that you received with your computer and copy HyperCard and the Home stack onto your hard disk. What's that? You're new to the Mac, and you don't know what the heck a Home stack is, much less how to copy it? That's OK. Just insert the HyperCard disk in your floppy drive, double-click the disk icon, then drag the HyperCard and Home stack icons shown in Figure 1.9 to your hard disk icon or hard disk window. For more information on HyperCard stacks and all that, see Chapter 19.

2. Insert the disk called Before You Install System 7 in your floppy disk drive.

3. Double-click the disk icon, then double-click the HyperCard stack, shown in Figure 1.10, named Before You Install System 7.

FIGURE 1.9
HyperCard icons

FIGURE 1.10
The Before You Install System 7 icon

4. On the Contents card that appears, click Compatibility Checker. This will find out if the software you have will work with the system software. If a dialog box appears with a Copy button, click Copy. A welcome screen for the Checker appears.

5. If there is a Set Up button in the welcome screen, click it. Then choose which disks you want to check. You probably just need to check your internal hard disk to make sure everything on it will work with the system software.

6. Click the Start Checking button. Messages tell you how the checking process is going.

7. Move any incompatible items out of your System Folder by clicking the Move Items button (if it appears).

8. When the final results of the check appear on the screen, click Print Report to print out the results. Then click Quit, close the Compatibility Checker disk window, and drag the disk to the Trash to eject it.

9. Back up any files you have created on your hard disk. Copy your documents and applications to floppy disks by inserting the disks and dragging the document and application icons to the floppy disk icons. Then shut down your Mac, as described earlier in this chapter.

10. Insert the Install 1 disk into the floppy drive in your Mac and turn it on. Click the OK button in the welcome screen to get the installer started.

11. Check the target hard disk named on the Easy Install screen, then click the Install button. If you want to install the system software on a hard disk other than the one named, click the Switch Disk button.

12. Insert the disks that the screen messages tell you to. When you see a message that installation was successful, click the Quit button. If you see a message that says installation was not successful, start the procedure over. If it fails again, get help from your dealer. When installation is successful and complete, a dialog box appears; click the Restart button in this dialog box. Your Mac restarts, running the system software you installed on your hard disk.

Congratulations. You now have the system software on your hard disk, and you can start up the Mac and use it without ever having to worry about what's running the show behind the scenes. One word of caution, though; make sure there is only *one* System Folder on your whole system, even if you have two or more hard disk drives. The only time you should ever have two sets of system software available to your Mac is when the system software in your hard drive is broken, and you have to use a floppy startup disk (such as Install 1) just to get the Mac going again and reinstall the system software on your hard drive.

Troubleshooting Hardware and Installation Problems

The following sections discuss the problems you can have in installing and starting up your Mac.

Mac doesn't start up.

The screen stays dark and you don't hear any startup beep or whirring of the hard drive. Like, you turn the switch on, and NUTHIN' happens. The Mac is not getting power. Check that the power cord is plugged in firmly. You'd be amazed how many people call Apple Support every day in a cold sweat, ranting about how their Mac has died, only to discover that it isn't plugged in right. Test the outlet by plugging a lamp or something into it, to make sure you are getting power there. Try turning the computer's power switch off and then on again.

If none of these things help, you either have a bad connection or a broken power supply in your Mac. If you can get another power cord for the Mac and swap it with yours, try that. No luck? Then it's time to take the Mac to a repair shop.

If you have an early Mac Plus, you may have lots of power supply failures unless you make sure the voltage is set to *exactly* 5 volts. Tell the shop to adjust the potentiometer to precisely 5 volts after they have replaced the power supply and warmed up the Mac for the first time to test it. You can also put a fan in your old Mac Plus to keep the power supply unit cool, but that means it will no longer be silent.

Screen stays dark.

The Mac beeps after you turn it on, and you hear the disk drive whirring, but nothing shows up on the screen. Something is wrong with your display. If you have a modular Mac with a separate monitor, check that the monitor is plugged in and turned on. Most monitors have a little light that goes on when you have turned them on.

If the monitor is on, or if you have a compact Mac with the screen in the same box with the computer, check the brightness control. On many Macs and monitors, there is a dial somewhere around the screen (usually on the side or under the front of the screen). On some compacts, such as the Classic, you have to adjust the brightness with menus and dialog boxes. This is a bit tough when you can hardly see the screen. Pull down the Apple menu at the far left end of your menu bar and choose Control Panels. When the window opens, double-click the brightness panel icon (the one with the sun in it). The control bar shown in Figure 1.11 appears. Drag the slide bar to the right to turn up the brightness until you can see the desktop bright and clear. (If you need help with these problems, see Chapter 2, "Meet the Mouse and the Desktop.")

If your Mac has been on a while and the screen goes dark, you may have a screen saver installed that is turning the screen black to preserve it. Just move or click the mouse or hit any key on the keyboard, and the screen saver will turn the screen on again.

If you try all the above fixes for a black screen and none of them work, it's time to take the monitor or the whole Mac to a good Mac shop for repairs.

FIGURE 1.11
Brightness control slide bar

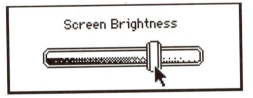

Glare on screen.

The Mac starts up OK, but when the desktop appears, you see a lot of glare from lights or things that are reflecting light in the room behind you. This can be hard on your eyes. The only fool-proof solution is to put the Mac in a place where there aren't any bright lights or reflections that will cause glare. Don't put it in front of a bright light or a window, though, because the contrast of the dark screen frame and the glare behind it is hard on your eyes too. Does this mean you have to sit in a cave to work on your Mac? No. I work in a room with a nice big window, but it is to the *side* of me and the Mac. I can look out at the sunlight filtering through the trees, but the sun can't shine directly on the screen or in my eyes.

Gray waves fluttering across screen.

You looked at your Mac from across the room and saw strange gray shadows fluttering in waves up and down the screen. Not to worry. You are not seeing ghosts. You are just seeing harmonic patterns of light and dark as they play tricks on your eye's nerve endings. If you ever see these fluttering forms when you are sitting right in front of the Mac, you should either see your qualified Mac technician and get the display fixed, or see your eye doctor.

The Happy Mac does not appear.

Your Mac is having trouble getting going on the system software that is available to it. You can tell more or less what the problem is by what icon you see instead of the Happy Mac.

If you see a disk icon with an X on it (like the one in Figure 1.12) and the floppy disk you put into the disk drive spits out, it just means that the floppy disk didn't have a System Folder with the system software on it. If you wait a moment, you should see the question mark disk icon. Then, if there is a System Folder with the system software on your hard disk, you'll soon see the Happy Mac.

If the disk icon with a flashing question mark on it (see Figure 1.12) stays on-screen, your Mac has looked around for the system software, and it is saying "Huh? I can't figure out what to do!" A few things could be wrong. The Mac didn't recognize your startup hard disk, or there are two hard disks with the same ID number and it can't figure out which one to go to for system software. Or maybe there isn't any system software available, because either you haven't got it on your hard disk, or you don't *have* a hard disk and you haven't inserted a floppy disk with the system software on it.

The simple answer to the question mark is to insert a startup floppy disk, such as Disk Tools, from your system software kit. Your Mac looks first in its floppy drive for the system software; when it finds it there, it displays the Happy Mac and starts up.

If you use a floppy as a startup disk and your hard disk icon doesn't show up on the desktop, see "Hard disk icon doesn't appear," later in this chapter. If you have a hard disk and its icon appears, you should set it up for future startups, as described earlier in this chapter. If you have two or more hard disks, including an internal one, you should make the internal one your startup disk, and change the numbers of the external drive or drives to numbers other than 0 (zero) or 7. Also, make sure only *one* System Folder, with *one* set of the system software, is available on your whole system.

FIGURE 1.12
The X and ? disk icons

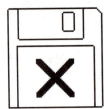

If you have only one hard drive, and the system software is on it, and you *still* get the question mark disk flashing at startup, or if the X disk and the question mark disk alternate back and forth, there is something wrong with the system software you installed. Reinstall it, making sure you follow all the steps in the "Setting Up Your Hard Disk for Future Startups" section earlier in this chapter. If you have two versions of the system software and you are using a utility such as Blesser or System Switcher to switch between versions, just switch to another version of the software and reinstall the faulty system software.

If you see the Sad Mac Icon (it looks more like a peevish drunk Mac to me; see Figure 1.13) you've got serious problems. Either the system software is damaged, or there is something wrong with the Macintosh hardware.

If you inserted a floppy disk, turn off the computer, then hold down the mouse button while you turn the Mac on again. This ejects the disk; try starting up again with a different startup disk. If the Sad Mac appears again, you may have a problem with the part of the Mac's memory (PRAM) that is supposed to recognize startup disks. To solve this problem, you have to zap the PRAM. If you have an older Mac, like a Plus or anything earlier, you have to turn off the Mac, take the battery out, and wait for about twenty minutes or so. Then put the battery back in, turn the Mac on, and reset the time and date in the General Controls control panel. If you have a Classic, SE, portable, or II of any kind, it's time to take the Mac to a qualified repair shop.

FIGURE 1.13
The Sad Mac icon

Startup sound is weird.

Some models of Mac, including all IIs and the LC, make a C major chord sound instead of a beep when they start up. If the chord sounds disharmonious, or if one note does not sound at the same time as the others, or if there is an arpeggio (running up a scale, instead of all notes at once), then there is probably something wrong with the memory of your Mac. It may just be that one of the memory chips is loose in its socket, or it may mean that a chip has failed. Take your Mac to a qualified technician for a checkup and repair.

If the memory chips are OK, there are two other rare problems you may have. If you have a Mac II, there may be a problem with one of your NuBus expansion cards. Take your Mac to a qualified technician for help. If you have an external SCSI hard drive, there may be a problem with the driver software that controls the hard drive. Reinstall your driver software. If that doesn't help, take the Mac and the hard drive to a qualified technician.

Hard disk icon doesn't appear.

You have a hard disk, either an internal or an external one, and when your Mac starts up, the desktop appears as in Figure 1.14, but there is no hard disk icon in sight.

FIGURE 1.14
Upper right corner of desktop with hard disk icon

The hard disk is not communicating with the CPU of your Mac. The Mac doesn't even know it's there. The solution to the problem depends on what kind of drive it is and how you are using it. If it's an internal hard drive, turn off your Mac and leave it off for a minute or so. Then turn it back on. If it's an external hard drive, make sure it is plugged in, turned on, and connected to the Mac correctly. Then choose Restart from the Special menu. If the hard disk is your startup disk, turn off the Mac and wait a minute. Then insert a startup floppy disk, and start the Mac again. If the hard disk icon appears, reinstall the system software on the hard disk.

If you have more than one hard disk, check the ID number of any external hard disk to make sure it is not the same as the internal hard disk or the computer. For more information on hard disks, see Chapter 6.

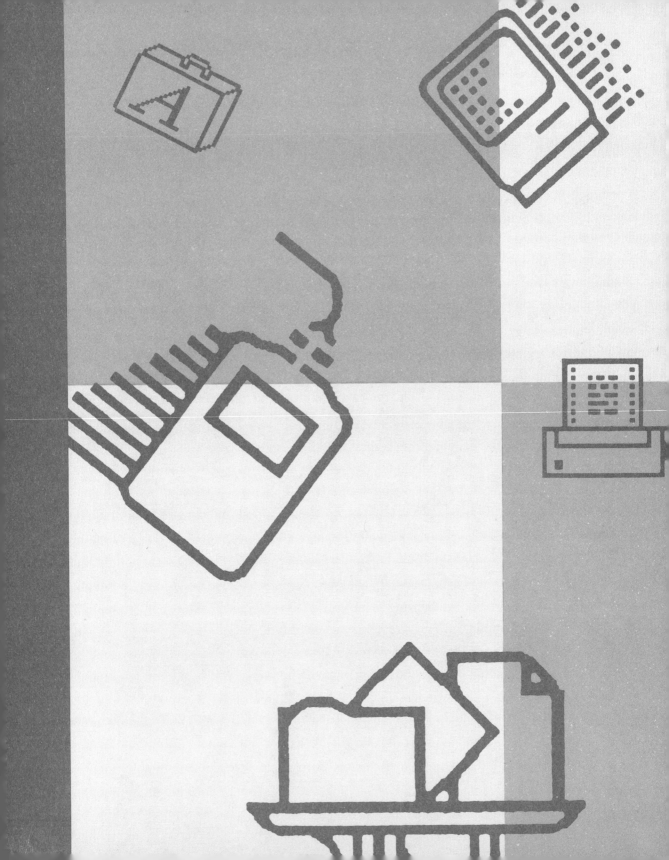

CHAPTER

2

Meet the Mouse and the Desktop

The mouse and the desktop (what you see on your Mac's screen) are the fundamental parts of the *interface*, which is nothing more than the means you have of talking to the computer. You can also use the keyboard, but if you have done any typing at all, it is pretty self-explanatory.

It is the mouse and the desktop that separate the Mac from most other computers. Other computers began by depending on the keyboard and clumsy, hard-to-remember commands. Some have made interfaces that imitate the Mac, but even these are relatively clumsy. The Mac mouse and desktop were designed to work beautifully together, from the start. They make it easy to choose commands and make settings that tell the machine what to do.

This chapter tells you how to use the fundamental tools of the Mac interface. It's worth the trouble to really get the basics right, because you use the same tools all the time on the Macintosh, no matter what application you work with.

If you are new to Macs and have the Macintosh Basics disk (it is in the Number 2 kit included with every new Mac), insert the disk before you turn your computer on. You will be treated to a leisurely, clear introduction to the mouse, the desktop, and the basic techniques for using them. If you don't have the Basics disk, or if you lost it and want a quick reminder of the fundamental Mac tools and techniques, here they are.

Meet the Mouse and the Desktop 33

 Introducing the Desktop

The *desktop* is what you see when you turn the Mac on and it is ready to use. It is called a desktop because you do things with it that you would normally do on a desk. Figure 2.1 shows a sample desktop and its basic elements. Although your desktop may look somewhat different from this one (if you start up from a hard disk, for instance, you won't see a floppy disk icon until you insert a floppy disk), the menu bar, icons, and the pointer are always there. These elements of the desktop have clear, practical purposes and uses:

- The *menu bar* contains the titles of the menus you can choose from.

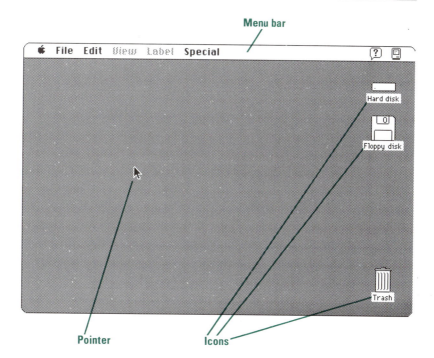

FIGURE 2.1
Key elements of the Macintosh desktop

- *Icons* tell you what places are available to you for storing things, what tools are available for you to work with, and what things your work has produced.
- The *pointer* points at things so you can choose them, move them, look inside them, start using them, or close them up and put them away. It's a very powerful little gadget.

The desktop is created by the Finder, which is the part of the Macintosh system software that helps you find whatever you need to do your work. Whenever you are looking at the desktop, you are "in" the Finder. If this book or some Mac guru tells you to go to the Finder, they don't mean anything deep or cosmic. They're really just telling you to change your view to the desktop.

If you are using a Macintosh that does not have at least 2Mb (megabytes) of RAM (random access memory) and a hard disk drive, your desktop will look different from Figure 2.1 and it will be different from other examples in this book. You will also notice minor differences in icons and titles for screen objects in the text of the book. This is because your Mac can only run on a version of the system software prior to System 7. Most procedures are similar, however, so you can still use the text and illustrations as guidelines.

Using the Mouse

The mouse is the primary tool you use to control the Mac. Fortunately, it's easy to use. Just hold the mouse with the cable pointing away from you. Grasp it gently with your thumb on one side and your other fingers on the other side, with your index finger hovering over the button, ready to click at any time.

Now move the mouse, and notice how the on-screen pointer moves that direction, too. You can move the mouse from side to side and up and down, but don't twist it; keep the cable pointing directly away

Meet the Mouse and the Desktop | 35

from you at all times. Twisting the mouse makes the pointer move in strange and unpredictable ways. As you move the mouse, slide the heel of your hand along the surface of the desk or mouse pad. A mouse pad with a firm, clean, textured surface improves the responsiveness of the mouse, in most cases. If you run the mouse off the edge of your mouse pad, just lift it and move it back to the middle of the pad.

Another tip about the mouse: The pointer or cursor that the mouse moves around on the screen has a "hot spot" that you have to place on or over any screen object you want to take an action on. The tip of the pointer arrow is its hot spot, for example.

Selecting, Dragging, and Opening Icons

To take an action on the Mac desktop, you often begin by selecting an icon. To select an icon, move the pointer tip over the icon, then hold the mouse still and press and quickly release the mouse button. The mouse button clicks and the icon becomes highlighted (the dark areas become light, and the light areas dark). For example, if you select the Trash icon in the lower right corner of the desktop, it turns dark, as in the left panel of Figure 2.2. In Macintosh manuals, selecting is often referred to as *clicking* or *highlighting*.

FIGURE 2.2
Clicking, dragging, and double-clicking the Trash icon

To move or *drag* an icon, you put the pointer tip over it, press the mouse button, and hold it down while you move the mouse. A *ghost* outline of the icon moves with the pointer as you move the mouse, as shown in the middle panel of Figure 2.2. When the icon is where you want it, release the mouse button.

To open an icon, you move the pointer tip over it, then click the mouse button twice, quickly, without moving the mouse. This is called *double-clicking*. In many cases, double-clicking an icon opens a *window*. The window shows what is inside the icon. For example, double-clicking on the Trash icon opens a window similar to the one shown in the right panel of Figure 2.2. To close the icon's window, you click in the *close box*, the small blank square in the upper left corner of the window.

Choosing Commands from Menus

To tell your Mac what to do, you choose a command from a pull-down menu. Put the tip of the pointer over one of the menu titles in the menu bar and press the mouse button to see the menu. Then hold the mouse button down and move the mouse toward yourself. You'll see a dark bar, a highlight, moving down through the commands in the menu. When the highlight is on the command you want, release the mouse button.

To see a simple example of how a menu command works, choose the New Folder command from the File menu (move the pointer to the word *File*, then pull the highlight down to the words *New Folder*). A new folder appears, with the name "untitled folder." You can drag the empty folder to the Trash if you don't want to leave it lying around. (See "Dragging Things to the Trash" later in this chapter for more information.)

In some menus you'll find that some of the commands are *dimmed* or *grayed*. This means that these commands cannot be used in the current situation. If you pull down a menu and find that the command you want to use is dimmed, just keep the mouse button pressed down and push the mouse away from you until the highlight has gone off the top of the menu.

If you use a command often, you can memorize the keyboard shortcut for the command. Each keyboard shortcut consists of the ⌘ key (the Command key) and a letter; each command's shortcut is displayed to its right on the pull-down menu. To use a keyboard shortcut, you just hold down the ⌘ key and press the letter key on the keyboard. For instance, to give the Open command, hold down the ⌘ key and press **O**. You don't have to reach over and grab the mouse, pull down the File menu, and select Open.

Using the Keyboard

Although you'll be using the mouse to perform most actions on your Mac, you still need to use the keyboard to create text. But before you can, you have to place a beginning point, or *insertion point*, so your computer knows where to display the text on the screen.

When you start word processing applications, the insertion point appears immediately, but you can place an insertion point on the desktop, too. For example, you can use the insertion point to change a folder name. Just follow these steps:

1. Click on the name of the untitled folder you just created, so it is highlighted as in the left panel of Figure 2.3. (If you threw the untitled folder into the Trash, create another by choosing New Folder from the File menu.)

2. Notice that when the text becomes highlighted, the pointer soon changes into a vertical line with sprouts at the ends. This is known as the *I-beam*, and it is the pointer you see whenever you can create text.

3. Click the mouse button; the I-beam becomes an insertion point. Move the I-beam out of the way, as shown in Figure 2.3.

4. Type in the word *text*. It appears at the insertion point, and if there is any text to the right of the insertion point, it moves over to make room for the new text. Whenever you are typing, the I-beam disappears. Do not type in too much text; icon labels can only be 31 characters long.

Now you've added to your icon title, but what if you want to replace it? You just delete what you don't want. To delete some text, you need to select it first. This is the most basic rule in text processing: *Select first, then operate.*

For example, to delete the word *untitled*, first double-click on the word, then press the Delete key to delete it. The word disappears, as in Figure 2.4. If you highlight some text, then decide you want to deselect it, just click somewhere else with the insertion point. The highlighting disappears.

To replace some text, first select it, then type in the new text. For example, to replace the word *folder* with the word *samples*, as in Figure 2.4, double-click on *folder*, then type **samples**.

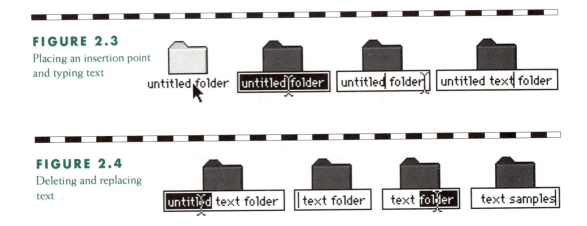

FIGURE 2.3
Placing an insertion point and typing text

FIGURE 2.4
Deleting and replacing text

If you want to select more than one word of text for deletion or replacement, drag the highlight over all the words.

Showing and Hiding Help Balloons

To see helpful information about items on the desktop and in windows, choose Show Balloons from the Help menu, which is under the cartoon balloon icon with a question mark in it (see Figure 2.5).

When balloon help is active, you can put the tip of the pointer on any object you need information about, and read the text that appears in a balloon. Many balloon help messages may seem a bit obvious to experienced users, but for an interesting example, choose the About This Macintosh command from the Apple menu at the left end of the menu bar, then put the pointer on the two-tone horizontal bars that show how much memory each application is using. A precise reading of the number of kilobytes of memory for each application appears in the balloon.

To turn the balloons off and go back to work, choose Hide Balloons from the Help menu. Notice how the Show Balloons command becomes Hide Balloons when the help balloons are showing. After you hide the balloons, you can pull down the menu and see the Show Balloons command again. This switching back and forth of a command depending on the situation is called *toggling*.

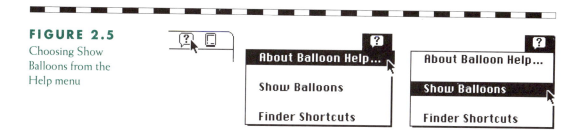

FIGURE 2.5
Choosing Show Balloons from the Help menu

Doing Things to Windows

Windows give you a view of what's in your Mac, or what's on your floppy and hard disks. If there are no windows open on the desktop, you can double-click on your hard disk or floppy disk icon to see a good example of a window. If you open a window or do something in it, it becomes the *active window*. The window titled "Hard disk" in Figure 2.6 is the active one. There are a bunch of horizontal lines running across the *title bar* of the active window. By contrast, the title bar, the side bar, and bottom bar of inactive windows are all blank. If windows overlap, like those in Figure 2.6, the active window appears in front.

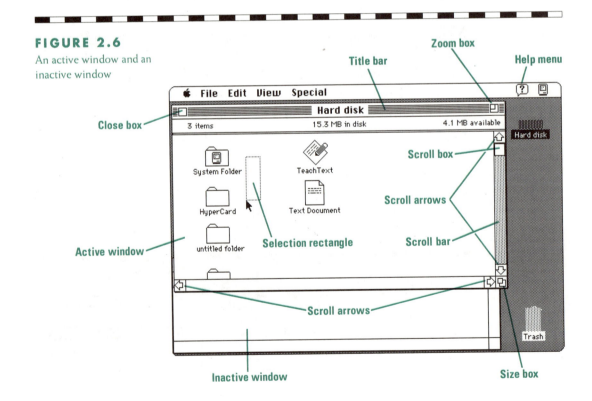

FIGURE 2.6
An active window and an inactive window

Here are the things you can do with the different parts of a window:

- To make a window active, click in it.
- To move a window around on the desktop, drag its title bar.
- To change the size of a window, drag the *size box* inward or outward.
- To zoom between the optimum window size and another size you have set, click the *zoom box*. The "optimum" size is shrink-to-fit around all the objects in the window. If there are more objects than will fit on the screen, the window zooms out as large as it can without covering the Trash and disk icons on the right side. To force a zoom to this large size, hold down the Option key and click the zoom box.
- To select multiple icons in a window, drag a *selection rectangle* across them; release the mouse button when the icons you want are highlighted.
- To add a single icon to a selected group, press the Shift key and click on the icon. This is called *Shift-clicking*. You can Shift-click to deselect one of a group of selected icons, too.
- To close the window, click on its close box.

If you have more things in a window than can be shown, *scroll bars* appear on the right and/or bottom edges. If you want to make a sample window with a scroll bar, place several files or folders along the left side of the window, then drag the size box in to shrink the window so an object is at least partially hidden, as the lowest folder is in Figure 2.6. The following actions are then possible using scroll bars:

- To move slowly, click on the scroll arrows.
- To move quickly, a section at a time, click in the gray scroll bar above or below the scroll box.
- To jump to a distant section, drag the scroll box.

In all cases, the window moves the way you tell it to. If you click the up arrow, for example, the window moves up, and the objects inside it move down. Practice will accustom you to these scrolling movements. If you want to practice in a window with lots of icons in it, and you don't have any crowded folders yet, just double-click your System Folder icon and shrink its window down so only a couple folders show at a time. Then you can scroll both sideways and up and down. (Just don't drag anything out of the System Folder!)

You can also scroll slowly by dragging an icon to the bottom or top of a window. Nudge the border of the window with the icon, rather than moving it up or down rapidly; if the icon is moving too fast, it zips right out of the window.

Dragging Things to the Trash

The Trash can in the lower right corner of the desktop is where you put things you want to delete or get rid of. If you are done with something you worked on and don't want to leave it around, or if you have an extra copy of something, you put it in the Trash.

You can drag an icon from anywhere on the desktop to the Trash can. The icon disappears and the Trash can bulges. If you ever want to see what is in the bulging Trash can, just double-click it; a Trash window opens, with all discarded items in it. Discarded items stay in the Trash until you choose Empty Trash from the Special menu. Even if you shut the Mac down and turn it off, when you start it up again, the Trash can will appear, bulging with your discarded items. Empty the Trash once a day or so, to keep stuff from piling up in there.

When you empty the Trash, an *alert box* tells you how much is in it and asks if you are sure you want to permanently remove it. Before you empty it, you should be *sure* there's nothing in there that you'll need again. Click the Cancel button and open the Trash window if you want to check the discarded items.

To recover a mistakenly discarded item, just drag its icon out of the Trash window and back to where it belongs. If you can't remember where it belongs, just select it in the Trash window and choose Put Away from the File menu. The Mac remembers for you!

If you know what is in the Trash and are sure you want to delete it permanently, press the Option key as you choose Empty Trash from the Special menu. The alert box doesn't appear. For more information on alert boxes, see the next section of this chapter.

Using Dialog and Alert Boxes

Dialog and alert boxes appear from time to time as you work with your Macintosh. These on-screen boxes help you make necessary choices, or warn you of risky actions, or prevent you from making destructive errors. Sometimes they seem like a bother, but if the Mac didn't have them, we'd all be a lot more bothered by the results of our own careless errors. They keep the environment we work in safe, sort of like warning signs on the handles of power tools.

A *dialog box* takes charge of the screen after you choose a command with three dots after it. Usually the dialog box will help you specify how the command should be carried out. For example, if you choose Print... from the File menu in an application, or if you choose Print Window... from the File menu in the Finder, a dialog box that looks something like Figure 2.7 appears.

Notice that the box has no title bar like windows have. When you see a dialog box like the Print one, you look at the choices in it, change any that you want to be different from default choices that have been made for you, and then click either the button with the bold double outline (Print in this case; OK in many others) or the Cancel button.

You *have* to click one button or the other to get out of this kind of dialog box. If you try to do anything else, like click in a window or choose another menu command, you just get a beep, and the dialog box stays there. For this reason, it is called a "must-do," or *modal*, dialog box. If you don't understand all the choices in a dialog box, it's usually safe to just leave things the way they are and click the bold outline button or press Return. If you want to see more information on the Print dialog box choices, see Chapter 3.

There are also dialog boxes that you can use or get out of without using. For example, in word processing applications such as Microsoft Word, you can choose a Find... command and a dialog box like the one in Figure 2.8 appears.

Once you've made your choices from this sort of dialog box, you have three options: You can go ahead with the action by clicking the button with the bold double outline, you can click Cancel to negate the command, or you can just click in another window.

If you click on another window the new active window will come to the front, but the dialog box will still be available; if part of it is showing at the edge of the active window, you can click the box and make it active again at any time. This makes dialog boxes like Find almost like windows. They even have title bars. They are officially called *modeless* dialog

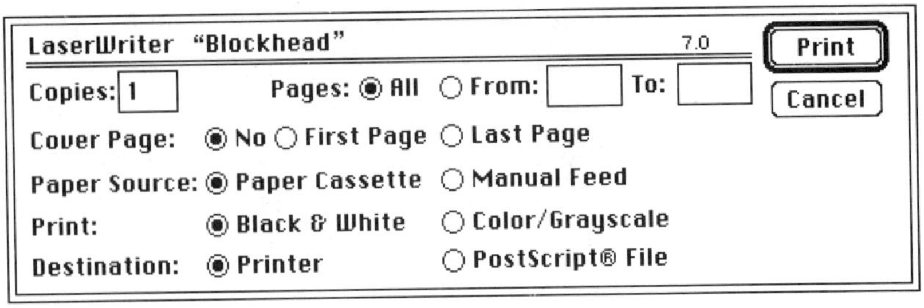

FIGURE 2.7
The Print dialog box

FIGURE 2.8
The Find dialog box

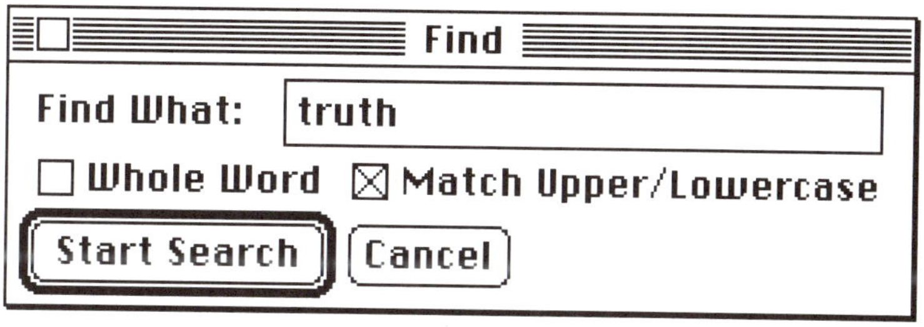

boxes. I call them window boxes, or "less-than-must-do" boxes, because I can never remember the difference between modal and modeless.

There is a third type of dialog box, which you can see if you choose the Open... or Save As... command from the File menu. It lets you choose files from lists. For more information on this special type of dialog box, see "Working with Applications and Documents" in Chapter 4.

Alert boxes are like must-do dialog boxes, but they appear when you try to do something you really shouldn't. For example, if you try to drag the Trash can into a window on your desktop, an alert box like the one in Figure 2.9 appears.

You can tell how serious an alert box is by the icon on its left side. The Stop icon means you can't do what you tried to do. The Caution icon means you can do it, but there might be some drawbacks, or you might have to take some special steps. The text in the alert box explains these things, and there are buttons to either go ahead or cancel the action. If you see an alert box with a Note icon, it is just telling you some added information about the action you are taking. Read the text, then click the OK button to go ahead with the action.

FIGURE 2.9
An alert box and alert icons

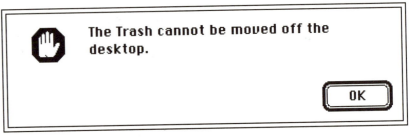

Stop   Caution   Note

 Troubleshooting Problems with the Mouse and the Desktop

The following subsections cover the most common problems you can have when using the mouse, the desktop, the icons on the desktop, and the Finder windows you see on your desktop.

Clicking doesn't work.

When you click the mouse button, the action doesn't take effect. This problem occurs most often when you're trying to click on something small, like a close box. The cause is usually that the tip or "hot spot" of the pointer is not over the thing you're trying to click on.

Move the mouse carefully to position the pointer, then try clicking again. In some rare cases, the Mac can be so busy thinking that it can't respond to the mouse click. Just repeat the clicking; it will surely work the second time. In *very* rare cases, static electricity or cosmic rays can freeze the screen: You can move the mouse pointer, but nothing else works. The only solution is to turn the Mac off, wait a few moments, then turn it back on.

If you get a beep when you try to click on something, or when you try to pull down a menu, it means you cannot do those things in the current situation. Most likely, there is a dialog box on the screen, and you have to click one of the buttons in it before you can do anything else.

Double-clicking doesn't work.

When you try to open something by double-clicking it, either nothing happens, or the thing just moves over a bit and doesn't open. The problem is that you moved the mouse a smidgen between the two clicks. Make sure you press down on the sides of the mouse with your thumb and other fingers as you tap lightly on the button with your index finger. And don't worry too much if you have trouble double-clicking on your first few tries; it takes a little practice.

Stuff hanging around the Trash.

Icons of documents or folders that you have dragged to the Trash don't disappear (see Figure 2.10). Instead, they loiter around it like teenagers around a video arcade. It's because you didn't drag them all the way to the Trash. Just drag each icon over the Trash until the Trash can is highlighted, then release the mouse button.

FIGURE 2.10
Stuff near the Trash can

Can't empty Trash because item is locked or in use.

You try to empty the Trash and you get an alert box that tells you such and so an item can't be deleted because it contains items that are locked or in use.

If you can't figure out why an "in use" item is stuck in the Trash, save your latest work and quit all applications that are running. If that doesn't work, you may have to restart the Mac to delete the item; the system software still has a hold on it.

If you can't empty a Trash file because it is locked, try holding down the Option key while you choose Empty Trash from the Special menu. If that doesn't delete the file, take it out of the Trash and choose Get Information from the File menu. Click the locked check box to unlock the file, then close the Information window, put the file back in the Trash, and empty it. If that doesn't work, restart the Mac and try again.

The mouse is squeaky and moves erratically.

If the mouse moves unevenly or squeaks at you (poor thing), or if the pointer doesn't move smoothly when you move the mouse, first turn off the computer. Then make sure that the mouse cable is connected firmly to the keyboard and the keyboard cable is connected firmly to the socket on the back of the computer. If that doesn't help, use the following procedure to clean the mouse:

1. Turn the mouse upside down in your hand.
2. Use two fingertips to press the ring that covers the ball. Then turn the ring counterclockwise, so the U mark moves from L for Lock to O for Open.
3. Tip the mouse over and catch the ring and the ball when they fall out.

4. Use a new cotton swab dipped in alcohol to clean off any lumps or ridges of grime on the three little plastic wheels inside the mouse, where the ball rolls.

5. Clean the ball with a lint-free cloth. If it's a little black ball, rather than a slightly bigger and heavier gray ball, get it *super* clean. Also, make sure your mouse pad or desk surface is clean all the time; quick, light mice are vulnerable to dust on the ball.

6. Ease the ball back into the mouse and replace the ring that holds it, starting with the mark pointing at the O and turning it clockwise until it clicks into place, pointing at the L.

If you have lots of trouble with your mouse, get a good mouse pad for it. Different mice scurry better on different pads, so ask the dealer who sold you the mouse which pad is best. If a good pad doesn't help, try a different mouse, or maybe even a track ball. I don't like track balls, but some people find them much easier to use.

Typing does not enter letters on the screen.

You may be in a situation that doesn't allow typing, or your keyboard may be disconnected or not working. Make sure you are in the window of an application that allows text, or in the text box of a dialog box. Click with the mouse pointer in the application's window or the text box. If you are in a situation that allows entering text but the keyboard does not do it, turn off your Mac and make sure the keyboard cable is firmly connected to the socket on the back of the computer. Try cleaning it as described in the next section. If that does not help, see your dealer to find out if the keyboard or your computer needs repairs.

The keyboard isn't working right.

If nothing happens when you do things with both the keyboard and the mouse, turn off the Mac and make sure the cables are plugged in all the way. If you have trouble with a certain key sticking or not making its letter appear on the screen, try cleaning the keyboard. Turn off the Mac and then unplug the keyboard and mouse. Turn the keyboard upside down and blow up in between the keys; clear the saliva out of your mouth so you don't spray moisture up in the works. Shake the keyboard up and down gently between breaths. If that doesn't help, or if you got something wet or sticky in the keyboard, like spilled root beer or peanut butter, you have to take the thing to a qualified repair shop.

The screen is frozen, or you are stuck in a bomb alert box.

Either the screen is frozen so neither typing nor moving the mouse has any effect, or there is a bomb alert box on the screen and nothing is working. People call this being "hung," as in "hung up." Sometimes it's more dramatic; if the software has really crashed, you might see bizarre patterns of dots and lines rippling across the screen. Sometimes you even hear dreadful dut-dut-dut noises as the Mac gags on screwed-up code. But much more often, you just see an alert box like the one in Figure 2.11.

The first thing to do is keep calm. Don't let the icon mislead you; there isn't a little bomb that will go off inside the Mac unless you do the right thing *now*. So keep cool; take a moment to gather a little information about what has happened. Try to recall the actions you took leading up to the error. Jot them down on a piece of paper. If an error message or a bomb alert box is on the screen, write down the message

FIGURE 2.11
Bomb alert box

Sorry, a system error has occured.

ID = 02

and the ID number if there is one. The message is usually a little more informative than the one in Figure 2.11 (by the way, system error 02 is an address error; usually caused by a bug in your application software).

Look for other screen clues as to what has gone wrong. If there is text left on the screen that you typed in, but didn't save, write it down on paper so you can reenter it later. If you work on a network or in an office with other Macintosh users, ask them to look at your screen and see if they are familiar with the problem. If you have to attack the problem on your own, try the following suggestions, starting with the ones that apply most clearly to your situation:

- Start afresh, if possible. If you are stuck in an application, try pressing ⌘-Option-Esc to quit the application you were using (press and hold down the ⌘ and Option keys, then press Esc). If this works, save any documents you were working on with other applications, then restart the computer. If the screen is no longer frozen and you are in the Finder, choose Restart from the Special menu. If you are stuck in a bomb message box, click the Restart button. If that does not work, press the Reset button on the left side, right side, or front or right rear corner of your Mac (there are two buttons; the Reset button is closer to the front or top). If you don't have a Reset button, such as on an LC, hold down the ⌘ key and the Ctrl key, then press the big left-arrow key at the top of the keyboard.

- If the computer fails to restart, try again, using a floppy disk with a System Folder on it as your startup disk. If this works, reinstall the system software on your hard disk as explained in Chapter 1.

- If you have an external hard disk or a printer connected to your Mac and there is any chance that the peripheral device is causing your problem, turn it off for a minute or so, then turn it back on and restart your Macintosh.

- If you are not sure what the exact problem is, think of all the possible causes you can, focusing on what actions you took recently. Then try fixing the possible causes one at a time, beginning with the easiest possibility and working up to the hardest one. For example, if the printer isn't working, try adding paper and turning the printer off and on before you try to figure out how to install a new printer driver. If you just added a new control panel (a program that lets you adjust a Mac feature, such as sound) or extension (a program that expands the Mac's system software capabilities), remove it. For more information on control panels and extensions, see Chapter 8.
- Still no luck? You may need outside help.

Before you call Apple or your software manufacturer's support department, do a little preparatory work. Narrow down the problem as much as you can. Get out your product registration number so you can tell it to the support people and jot down the version of the system software on your Mac. Then find out how much memory you have allocated to the disk cache and your applications (see Chapter 7), and determine the version of your problematic software. Also, jot down a list of the special customizing files (control panels, extensions, INITs or CDEVs) on your computer; these are often the source of problems when they aren't compatible with each other, the system software, or your applications.

Icon lost on desktop behind another icon.

You have a lot of icons on your desktop and one is lost behind one of the others. To find it without going around and moving all the others, just click in the window's open space and choose Clean Up Window. The icons will all sort out and you'll see your lost one.

Window lost under many others.

You let your desktop get all cluttered, and now you can't find a window because it is buried by others you opened later. The best solution is to press the Option key and click a close box in any window. All the windows close. Then start opening things in the hard disk window. It may be quicker to change to a list view of an upper level window, then just open the lists for the folders to work your way down to your lost folder. When you get to the folder you want, double-click it to open its window.

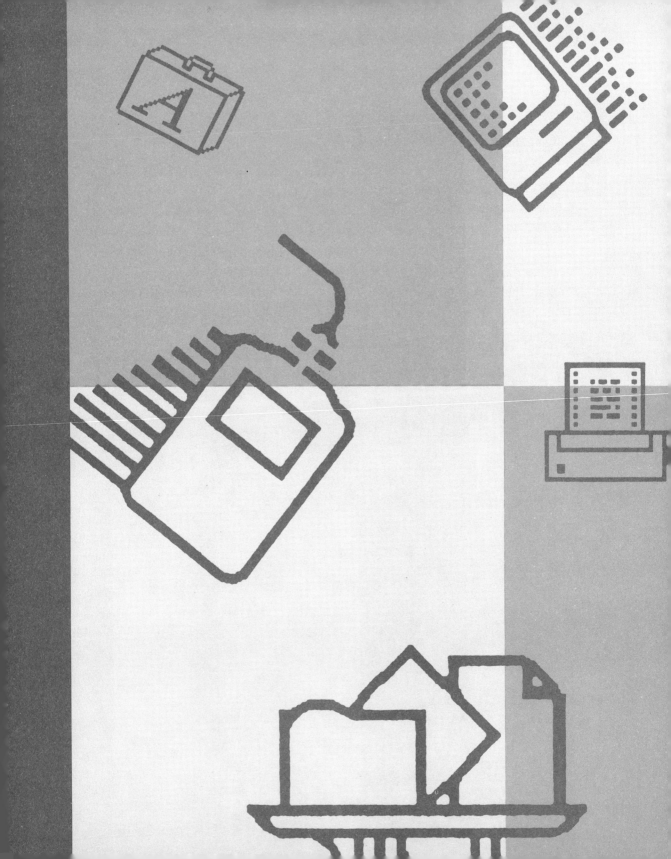

CHAPTER 3

Printing

Printing is making copies of your work on paper. Paper copies are called *hard* copies. Printing out copies of your work is a vast improvement over typing documents on a typewriter, or writing out budgets on accounting paper, or making freehand drawings, because you can make your work look any way you want. If you print out a copy, then discover that it isn't quite right, you can change either its contents or its appearance, and print out a new copy. No fuss, no muss, no white-out or retyping.

One thing you need to remember about the ease and speed of computer printing: It uses up paper. To save paper and the trees that are cut down to make it, you should proofread and edit documents carefully on the Mac before you print them. If you find that you still create piles of first-draft hard copies that you don't want to use, recycle them; you can use the back sides for other rough drafts, and when you have used both sides, you can take the used paper to a recycling center.

Which Printer for You?

Printers can cost a lot of money, but you don't necessarily have to buy a top-of-the-line laser printer to produce acceptable hard copies. Just buy a printer that prints what *you* need to print, at a rate and a price that you can live with. If you don't have extensive printing needs now, but plan to increase your use of the printer, buy one that will meet your foreseeable needs.

The following paragraphs describe the types of printers available for the Mac and list their strengths and weaknesses. The specific printers covered are not the only ones on the market, and new printers appear all the time. Take the recommendations as guidelines, and find the printer that works best for you. I tend to favor Apple printers because they have such a great reputation for reliability, and because they are sure to work with the Mac system software, even if it changes significantly. Other printers may work fine today, but not so well with future versions of the system software.

Inkjet Printers

If you only need to print short documents with either standard text formats and fonts or standard graphic formats such as black-and-white MacPaint or PICT, you can use an inkjet printer such as the StyleWriter or DeskWriter. Inkjet printers aren't as fast as laser printers, and their output isn't quite as lovely, but they are cheap and reliable. They are easy to use and care for, too.

Inkjet printers make images by spraying ultra-fine streams of ink onto the paper. They are relatively quiet and fast, in comparison to the ImageWriter and other dot-matrix printers that were once the low-budget printers of choice for Macs. The StyleWriter is more portable than the DeskWriter and prints some types of images more clearly; but if you want to print a larger number of documents, the DeskWriter is faster. The DeskWriter can also be connected to an AppleTalk network of several Macs; the StyleWriter has to be plugged directly into a single Mac. In addition to the StyleWriter and DeskWriter, there are other inkjet printers that can print more fonts and some that even print in color.

Laser Printers

If you need to print lots of complex documents with different text formats and fonts, or if you want to print desktop publications or graphics in PostScript format, buy a PostScript laser printer such as the LaserWriter NT or LaserWriter IInx. These printers use photocopying "engines" to crank out your documents much more quickly than other printers can. Their output is clean and crisp, and they give you a wide range of font and format options. Laser printers are suitable for almost any task, from rendering complex graphics to quick printouts of simple memos.

All this flexibility comes at a high price, of course. Fortunately laser printers come in many models, from less expensive ones with no memory, slow engines, and only a few fonts, to expensive models with many megabytes of RAM, twenty-page-per-minute engines, and dozens of built-in fonts.

Dot-Matrix Printers

If you need to print carbon copies of documents, or if you want to use fanfold (continuous-feed) paper for things like data printouts or labels, buy a dot-matrix printer like an ImageWriter II. The ImageWriter forms letters by impact on a type ribbon, like a typewriter, so it can be used on carbon-copy or multiple-layered business forms, unlike inkjet and laser printers.

The ImageWriter is noisy and much slower than either a StyleWriter or a LaserWriter, and it cannot produce text or images that are as sharp as those of the other printers. However, it is cheap and it prints well enough for many simple home and office needs.

 ## Setting Up Printing in the Chooser

Before you can print out your first Macintosh document, you have to connect the printer and select it in the Chooser. First make sure your printer's cable is connected to the proper port on the back of the computer. Then make sure the printer is properly configured, supplied with paper, and turned on. Install the necessary printer software that is correct and up-to-date for your specific printer. If you need help with these printer preparations, check your printer's owner's guide (the LaserWriter and StyleWriter guides are particularly clear and helpful), then see the section on the care and feeding of your type of printer later in this chapter.

To begin the process of setting up your Mac for printing on a connected printer, you select the Chooser from the Apple menu (click on the apple at the left end of the menu bar, and select Chooser). The Chooser window opens. What you see in it depends on whether your Macintosh is connected directly to a printer, or to a network with one or more printers on it.

Setting Up a Direct Connection to a Printer

If your Mac is connected directly to a printer, the Chooser window should look something like Figure 3.1. Your Chooser window may show different printer types, or only one type of printer. The AppleShare icon may not appear, either. That's fine, as long as the Chooser shows an icon for your type of printer. Take these steps to set up your computer for printing:

1. Select the printer icon for the type of printer you have. A choice of printer ports appears in the box on the right side of the window.

2. Select the port you connected your printer cable to. In most cases, this will be the printer port, although some printers may be connected to the modem port.

3. If your printer is an ImageWriter or StyleWriter, click the Inactive radio button for AppleTalk. If your printer is a LaserWriter or something compatible, it will be connected to your Mac via AppleTalk (LocalTalk or LocalTalk-compatible connectors).

FIGURE 3.1
The Chooser window

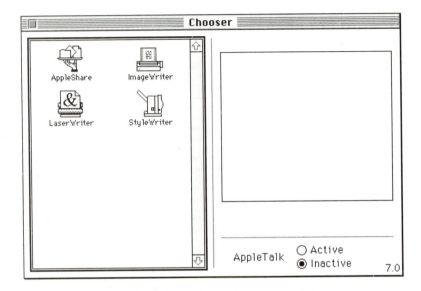

Click the Active button for AppleTalk so your Mac can talk to the printer over the cables. As soon as you make AppleTalk Active, buttons for Background Printing appear. Click the On button if you want to be able to keep working as your documents print on a LaserWriter.

Close the Chooser by clicking in the close box.

Setting Up a Network Connection to a Printer

If you are connected to a network and will be printing over it, the Chooser window will look something like Figure 3.2. Before you can arrange things in the Chooser, you must find out the following things from the person who administers your network:

- What type of printer you are going to use (LaserWriter, ImageWriter, or other)

- The name of your network zone if your network is divided up into zones
- The name of the printer you are going to use if your network has more than one printer of the same type

Once you have the network information you need, take the following steps to set up printing:

1. Click the Active button for AppleTalk if it isn't selected already.
2. Select the icon for the type of printer you are going to use. If you select a LaserWriter and want to keep working while your documents are printing, click the On button for Background Printing.
3. If your network has zones, select the zone of the printer you are going to use. Find the name of the zone in the AppleTalk Zones list box; use the scroll bars if the name is not in view. The list box does not appear if your network does not have zones.

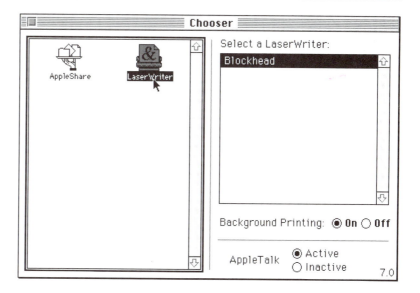

FIGURE 3.2
The Chooser with a LaserWriter selected

4. Select the name of the printer in the list box on the right side of the Chooser window. In Figure 3.2, the printer "Blockhead" is selected.

5. Close the Chooser.

Once you make these choices in the Chooser, you are ready to send documents to the printer. It seems odd to me that the Mac doesn't give you any message telling you that things are all set, but that's the way the Chooser works; you make your choice, then just close the window (by clicking the close box in the upper left corner) to finalize things. You don't have to open the Chooser again until you need to use a different printer.

Taking Care of Your Printer

Once you've purchased and set up a printer, you need to give it proper care, to ensure that it lasts and that it performs at its best for you. The following sections tell how to care for some of the most common types of printers. If you have a different printer from the ones covered below, just use the information as a guideline and fill in any details you need with the help of your owner's guide.

Care and Feeding of a StyleWriter

To turn on a StyleWriter after plugging it in and connecting it to your Mac, you press the Power button. The green Ready light glows, telling you that the printer is warming up; it stays on as long as the printer is ready to print. If you want to make sure everything is ready, just hold down the Form Feed button and press the Power button once, then release both buttons. The StyleWriter prints out a test page.

To add paper to the StyleWriter, first make sure the sheet feeder and paper support are firmly in place, sticking up from the back of the printer. Then press the center of the feeder panel so the feeder opens. Load a stack of about 40 sheets of paper into the sheet feeder, making sure the stack is not higher than the point of the arrow on the left side-rail of the feeder panel. Also make sure the right edges of the sheets of paper are all lined up flush against the right side-rail of the feeder panel. Then press the release button at the top of the right side-rail so the feeder snaps forward.

To change the ink cartridge, you open the access door at the front of the printer: Pull the two half-round tabs that stick out near the top corners of the access door and flip the door down out of your way. Then pull the blue lever next to the ink cartridge up and pull the cartridge (the small, almost cube-shaped black plastic box) straight out towards you.

Carefully remove the head cap and the sealing tape from the business end of the new ink cartridge. Avoid touching those areas as you slip the new cartridge into place on the blue post inside the printer. The new cartridge sits a little slanted to one side until you flip the blue lever down; that makes it click into a vertical position. Close the access door firmly, and you're ready to print. You can run a test page or two to make sure the ink is working right.

Care and Feeding of a DeskWriter

To turn a DeskWriter on after you plug it in and attach the connector to your Mac, reach under the front left corner of the printer and flip the power switch to On. If you haven't run the printer for some time, it's a good idea to press the Prime button; this runs a tiny bit of ink out of the jets so the ink cartridge gets cleaned out and ready to print.

To add paper, you simply pull out the drawer at the front of the printer and slide a block of paper in. Try to arrange the stack so the edges of the sheets are lined up; this keeps paper jams to a minimum.

To change the ink cartridge on a DeskWriter, you just open the plastic cover at the front of the printer, then pull the cartridge (the little black box with the green arrow on top) toward the front of the printer and up. Remove the cover from a new cartridge and push it in firmly where the old one came out. Push the Prime button once or twice to get the jets running, and you're ready to print.

Care and Feeding of a LaserWriter

LaserWriter printers are easy to use and care for. You can turn on your LaserWriter, add paper to the paper cassette, and even change the toner cartridge without any help from a printer expert. You can also complete the simple cleaning procedure that is the only maintenance a LaserWriter normally needs. Many other laser printers such as the Hewlett-Packard LaserJet are quite similar in design and just about as easy to operate and care for; just see the owner's guide for details about the care and feeding of your particular laser printer.

To turn on your LaserWriter after plugging it in and connecting the cable to your Mac, you reach around to the back and click the power switch; it is usually near the lower left corner as you face the back of the printer. The LaserWriter hums up to speed, and in a moment you hear the engine take a test run. If you haven't turned off the test sheet option as explained later in this section, the printer spits out a test page to prove that it's ready to go to work.

To add paper to the paper drawer, or *cassette* as it is called, all you have to do is reach under the front of the printer and pull the drawer out, just like pulling out a desk drawer, except that you pull it all the way out. If the drawer has a plastic cover, take it off.

Get a block of paper (the number of sheets depends on your printer) and clunk the edges on your tabletop so all the sheets line up in a nice smooth stack. Then hold one end of the block in your right hand and slide the other end of the stack down into the back end of the drawer, under the two retainer tabs that stick out towards you. The block of paper will slide down in there easily if you push the little wall spring on the side of the drawer back with your left thumb. Push the front corners of the block of paper down gently, past the metal corner brackets. On most LaserWriters' paper cassettes, there are pictures that show you how to slide the paper in.

Check to make sure the stack of paper isn't taller than the dotted line with an arrow that is on the side of the drawer. If the stack is too tall, take some sheets out. If the front end of the stack is uneven, tip the back end of the drawer up and jiggle the drawer until all of the sheets' edges are in line—this will keep the paper from jamming. Put the lid back on the drawer if there is a lid, then slide the drawer back into the printer all the way. When it's in there right, the yellow paper-out light goes off and the green ready-to-print light goes on. That's all there is to it.

To change the toner cartridge, turn the printer off, then pull up the cover release lever or press the cover release button and open the access door to the LaserWriter. On the NT and LS, the front opens; on others the top lifts up. If there is a little plastic flap on a spring at the top of the cartridge, hold it firmly with your thumb and fingers, then gently pull the cartridge up and out of the printer. If there is no little flap on your toner cartridge, just grip the body of the cartridge and slide it out and up.

Put the used cartridge down on a piece of newspaper. Remove the new cartridge from its package and pull the tape tab so the plastic tape slides all the way out of the cartridge and breaks off. Throw that messy tape thing away. Rock the new cartridge end-to-end in order to spread the toner around inside there (some models need to be rocked fore-and-aft).

Then hold on to the plastic tab on the top of the new cartridge and slip the cartridge into the same place the old one came out of. Most cartridges have little pictures on top of them that make it all very clear. When the new cartridge is in place, close the cover of the printer. Then wrap up the used cartridge in the new one's wrapper and contact a cartridge recycler such as the American Cartridge Recycling Association, at (305)539-0701. Recycling cartridges saves money as well as natural resources.

To run a cartridge through its paces and see that it's working OK, you simply find the document called Cleaning Page (it's on the Installation Disk you got with your LaserWriter) and select it in the Finder. Then choose Print from the Finder's File menu. The printer puts out a test page with a broad diagonal black line across it. Set your printer up for manual feeding of paper, then put the test sheet into the manual feed slot, face up so the printer can write on the back side of it. Select the Cleaning Page document and choose Print from the Finder's File menu again. This time, click the Manual Feed button in the Print dialog box. Your test page disappears into the printer and comes out with the big diagonal line across the back side of the paper. Check the quality of the black on the back-side diagonal line. It should be evenly dark throughout. If there are bands of faded gray or thin lines of white, it's time to replace the cartridge.

If you are using a LaserWriter and do not want the start page (the test page with the LaserWriter letterhead) to spit out every time your printer starts up, here is a way to stop those start pages:

1. Find the LaserWriter Font Utility. If you don't have it on your hard disk, you can find it on one of the Tidbits disks you received with your system software. Double-click on the LaserWriter Font Utility icon to open it. A dialog box tells you what the utility can do with fonts.

2. Click OK in the Font Utility dialog box. It goes away and a message box tells you that the utility is checking the characteristics of your printer. Then a new menu for the utility appears.

3. Choose Start Page Options from the Utilities menu. A small dialog box displays On and Off buttons for the printer start page.

4. Click the Off button and the OK button. The box goes away after the command has been sent to your printer.

5. Quit the Font Utility.

The start pages will no longer come out of the LaserWriter every time you start it up. If you need to see a start page, just follow the procedure above and click the On button in the Start Page dialog box.

Care and Feeding of an ImageWriter

To turn the ImageWriter on after plugging it in and connecting the cables to your Mac, you press the Power button on the right part of the printer's lid, then press the Select button.

To insert the first page of the paper roll, you pull off the vented cover at the top of the printer, then pull up the flaps that cover the tractor-feed poles. Place the first perforations on the paper over the poles. If the paper doesn't lie flat, adjust the width of the tractor-feed poles: Pull up the little black lever behind the right set of poles, then move those poles to match the distance between the perforations at the edges of the paper.

To change the ink ribbon in an ImageWriter, you have to open the cover on the top of the printer (squeeze the sides in to release the latches). Then pull the little latch on the right side of the ribbon cartridge and tip the cartridge up and to the left to remove it. Put the new cartridge in place, making sure the ribbon passes behind the black plastic post. Press the cartridge down until the little latch clicks into place. Close the cover down and press it until it snaps into place, and you're ready to print again.

If you need to print out something on a single sheet of paper, but don't want to remove and reengage the fanfold paper on the feeding pins, just back the paper up as far as it will go without coming off the pins. Do your manual feed of the single sheet. Then roll the fanfold paper back into the works again. If the fanfold paper is only engaged on the first pair of pins and none of the others, the ImageWriter doesn't know it's there.

Printing Documents

To get a hard copy of a document from a printer after you have connected it and set things up in the Chooser, you open the document with the application you used to create it, then choose Print from the File menu (or press ⌘-P; that is the keyboard short cut in most applications). The Print dialog box opens. It will have different options depending on what type of printer you have and what application you are using. Some of the most common options for a LaserWriter are shown in Figure 3.3.

The default settings are usually the ones you want to use. You can, however, make the following changes to the LaserWriter settings for special print jobs.

- Copies: Set the number of copies you want of each page of the document. Keep in mind that it is much cheaper and more energy-efficient to photocopy documents than to print multiple copies, as long as a photocopier is available.

- Pages: Enter numbers in the From and To boxes to print only a portion of the document. This is the most-used option in the dialog box. If you want to print the last few pages of a document, just enter the From page number and leave the To box blank.

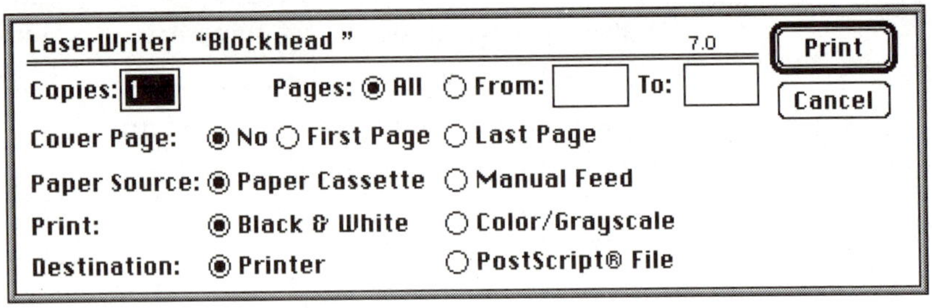

FIGURE 3.3
Print dialog box

- Cover Page: Click the First or Last Page button to add a cover page to the beginning or end of your print job. This lets others using the printer see whose it is and what it is.
- Paper Source: Click the Manual Feed button if your paper cassette or fanfold paper-feeding mechanism is broken, or if you want to feed nonstandard paper into the printer.
- Print: Select Color/Grayscale only if you have a color printer.
- Destination: Click the Postscript File button to make a PostScript format file on your current disk rather than a hard copy. Be aware that this process can often take much longer than printing.

When you have made your choices, click the Print button. Message boxes tell you how printing is going.

Using the PrintMonitor

If you are printing to a LaserWriter over an AppleTalk network and you have the PrintMonitor extension in your System Folder, you can continue work while printing is going on in the background. If you don't have the PrintMonitor in the Extensions folder in your System Folder, you can drag its icon there from the Printing disk. This disk is included with the system software disks you received with your Macintosh.

Make sure you have turned on Background Printing in the Chooser so the PrintMonitor is ready to work. Then, when you send a document to the printer, choose PrintMonitor from the Applications menu (that's the menu under the little application icon in the upper right corner of your screen) to see the status of your printing job, as shown in Figure 3.4. If there are other jobs being printed, yours appears in a waiting list.

You can click buttons to cancel your printing job or set a time for it to print later. When your job is finished, the PrintMonitor quits automatically. If you no longer see the PrintMonitor listed in the Applications menu, you can assume that your job is finished. If the printer cannot finish your job due to printing problems, such as running out of paper, the PrintMonitor icon flashes at the right end of the menu bar.

One odd quirk about the Print Monitor is that you don't have to close its window. When the print job finishes, the PrintMonitor disappears from the Applications menu, all by itself. This can be a bit confusing if you are looking at the window, see your job finish, then try to close the window; the PrintMonitor menu refuses to go away until you switch to another application.

Using Page Setup for Special Printing Needs

If you use the Chooser to change to a different printer while you are running an application, you must choose Page Setup from the File menu before you try to print documents again. When the dialog box

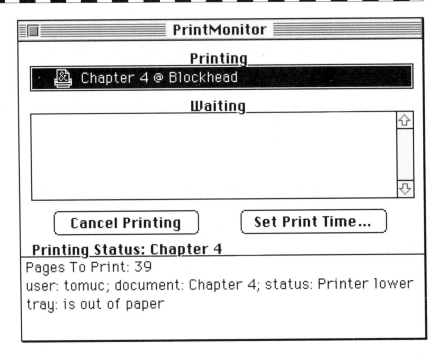

FIGURE 3.4
The PrintMonitor window

shown in Figure 3.5 appears, just click OK and you can print on the newly chosen printer.

You can also use the Page Setup dialog box to achieve a number of special printing options. The options vary depending on your printer. For example, if your Mac is connected to a LaserWriter printer, you see a dialog box like the one in Figure 3.5. You can make the following settings for a LaserWriter:

- Paper: Choose paper sizes and business envelope settings. The choices are these: US Letter (8.5" × 11"), US Legal (8.5" × 14"), A4 Letter (8.5" × 11.7"), B5 Letter (7" × 10"), Tabloid (11" × 17"), A3 Tabloid (11.7" × 16.5"), and two envelope choices.
- Reduce or Enlarge: Change the size of the printed output.
- Orientation: Change to horizontal printing for spreadsheets and other wide images.
- Printer Effects: Turn enhancements on or off for special effects or speed.
- Options: Click this button for image enhancement features, such as flipping, inverting, and precision-smoothing.

For more information on these options, choose Page Setup from the File menu in the Finder, then turn on balloon help and point at the options you want to know more about.

FIGURE 3.5
The Page Setup dialog box

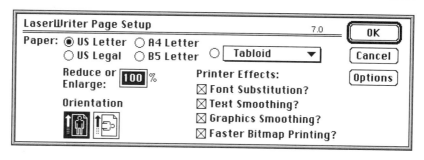

Printing a Window in the Finder

When you are in the Finder you can print the contents of the active window by choosing Print Window from the File menu. The Print dialog box opens. Click the Print button and the total contents of the window (including items in scrollable lists that aren't showing at the time) will be printed out by the current printer. This is a good way to make a hard copy of a long list of folders and files, so you can look at the list all at once rather than scrolling up and down it in a window. Just keep in mind that a very long list (like one that shows every item on your hard disk) can take quite a while to print out.

Printing a Snapshot of the Screen

If you'd like a hard copy of whatever is showing on your screen at a given moment, you can take a snapshot (screen dump) of it. Then you can print the snapshot. To start the process, press ⌘-Shift-3 (hold down the ⌘ and Shift keys and press 3). This Command-key short cut requires two hands unless you are a concert pianist with long fingers. It produces a graphic file in PICT format, names it Picture 1, and places it on your current startup disk. Picture 1 is listed among the files and folders at the top level of the hierarchy on your disk.

To look at the snapshot, you must open Picture 1 with TeachText or any graphics application that can read PICT files. To print the snapshot, choose Print from the File menu of the application you are using to look at Picture 1. Click OK in the Print dialog box. (If you don't understand some of these details about files, folders, and graphic formats, don't worry. Files and folders are explained in Chapters 4 and 5, and graphic formats are explained in Appendix A.)

You can also copy a snapshot to another document. First select a portion of the snapshot in TeachText or your graphics application.

Then choose Copy from the Edit menu to place the selection in the Clipboard. You can then paste the selection from the Clipboard into other documents. For more information, see Chapter 15.

Using the Right Fonts for Your Printer

A font is a particular design of letters that are all used together to print text. In printing jargon, a font is just one set of characters (a typeface) in one size and style only. For example, Helvetica 18-point bold refers to Helvetica type that is 18 points in size (a point is approximately 1/72 of an inch) and in the bold style. It looks like Figure 3.6.

In the Macintosh environment, a font has come to mean all the different sizes and styles of a typeface: the name *Times* refers to bold, italic, and plain type of the Times typeface, in sizes from 9-point to 48-point or more. So all of the styles and sizes in Figure 3.7 are considered parts of the Times font.

Kinds of Fonts

Your Mac has at least a basic set of three standard TrueType fonts. These are Courier, which looks like typewriter type, Times, which looks

FIGURE 3.6
Helvetica 18-point bold

Helvetica 18-point bold

FIGURE 3.7
Varieties of Times

Geneva **bold**, *italic*, 9-point, and 18-point

like the type in a magazine, and Helvetica, which is a *sans serif* font, meaning that it has no ornaments at the tips of the letters. Figure 3.8 shows an example of the difference between a serif font and a sans serif font.

Sans serif fonts make good headlines and short call-outs that you want people to see and grasp quickly. In fact, the "Kinds of Fonts" heading you see above is in a sans serif font. They are also clear and legible on the Mac screen. Serif fonts are better for long stretches of printed text, like the text of this book; most readers find them easier on the eyes. So you may well want to do your word processing work on the Mac using a sans serif font like Helvetica, then change all the text to a serif font like Times before you print it out for others to read.

Along with the three serif and sans serif fonts, you get Symbol, which is included for scientific notation like that in Figure 3.9.

These basic fonts are adequate for most word processing and spreadsheet applications. If you use them fully, varying sizes and styles, you can create documents with a fine, professional appearance, even if you are not printing them out on a LaserWriter. For example, you can mix larger bold Helvetica headings with smaller plain Times text in a report or a resume. Fonts like Times and Helvetica look fine when printed out on almost any printer. If you stick to these fonts, you will be able to print

FIGURE 3.8
A serif font and a sans serif font

Times font, with easy-to-read serifs

Helvetica, a legible sans serif

FIGURE 3.9
Symbol font

ωHνt Tλς Hεςκ?

any document you create on almost any printer that can handle your application's output.

If you want, you can buy and install a number of other fonts for your Mac. There are *bit-mapped fonts,* which are good for screen viewing and printing on dot-matrix printers like the ImageWriter. At the other extreme, you can purchase and install publication-quality PostScript *outline fonts.* Outline fonts are composed of programmed instructions for drawing the precise outline of each letter, then filling it in. They are used typically on a PostScript printer like the LaserWriter, but they can also be used on the highest-quality commercial printers, such as the Linotronic.

If you venture out from TrueType fonts into the world of bit-mapped or Postscript outline fonts, you can create documents with more variety of appearance, but remember that many special fonts may look good when printed on one kind of printer but awkward or even illegible when printed by other printers. Some may look strange on your screen, too. For example, if you use bit-mapped fonts with city names, such as New York, Geneva, or Monaco, they print out quite nicely on dot-matrix printers such as the ImageWriter. Each bit in the bit map is assigned to a dot in the dot-matrix printout. These same fonts will not look good at all if you print them out on a LaserWriter that does not have the exact bit map for the font, size, and style you are using. The Laser-Writer has to make up a bit-map estimation of what the font should look like, and it often comes out with jagged edges and weird lumps.

On the other hand, some high-quality PostScript outline fonts that make beautiful 24-point letters on a LaserWriter produce jagged jibberish on an ImageWriter and on your screen, unless you use a type-management utility such as Adobe Type Manager. ATM, as it is fondly called by font-folks, comes with the Macintosh system software, in all versions above 7.2. It allows you to use a vast selection of fonts, because it can either convert PostScript outline fonts to TrueType (which is really just another type of outline font) or adapt outline fonts to bit-mapped ones, so they look as clean as possible on your screen and in ImageWriter printouts. However, if your computer does not have much memory, if its CPU is slow, or if your printer doesn't have any memory, the printing process may become extremely slow, and you can even get weird, gratuitous changes of font in the middle of a print job.

You must also keep in mind, when you are working with converted or adapted fonts, that they change the spacing that you had with the original font, so that the line and page breaks in a document often change. For example, if you have been using a PostScript outline Times font and you begin using TrueType Times, the lines and pages will not always break the same. If you experiment with different fonts of varying quality, you can have difficulty finding a printer that will print all of the different fonts well. With that in mind, make the best possible use of the fonts you have, and add fonts to your System file judiciously, keeping to well-known outline fonts if possible. If you must change fonts often, obtain a font-juggling utility from a software vendor to keep them all straight. For more information on font-juggling utilities, see Chapter 8.

Installing Fonts

To install a font that you have on a floppy disk, use the following procedure:

1. Quit all applications and exit to the Finder. Pull down the Applications menu to make sure you have left no applications open.
2. Open the window for your hard disk and the window for the floppy disk that contains the new font.
3. Drag the font icon to the System Folder on your hard disk. Do not open the System Folder window and drag the font into the window. A dialog box asks if the font should be placed in the System file. Some outline fonts other than TrueType fonts are

stored in the Extensions folder; the dialog box will inform you if this is the case for the font you are installing.

4. Click the OK button in the dialog box.

If you are installing a bit-mapped font, you need to drag all available sizes of the font to the System Folder. You only need to drag one icon for an outline font to the System Folder, because the font is a scalable or variable-size font.

Removing Fonts

To get rid of a font that you no longer use or that has been replaced by a new font of the same name, use the following procedure:

1. Open the System Folder on your hard disk.
2. Find and double-click the System file; it is a suitcase icon with a little picture of a Macintosh on the side. In a few moments, the font icons appear.
3. Locate the font you want to remove and drag the icon out of the System file window. If you do not find the font there, look in the System Extensions folder. Some outline fonts are stored there instead of in the System file. You can copy the font to a floppy disk or throw it in the Trash. Do not leave the font in the System Folder, though.

If you have removed a set of fixed-size outline fonts from your System file so that your Mac and printer will use the TrueType font of the same name, you may have to adjust the format of documents that were created using the fixed-size outline fonts to keep the line and page breaks where you want them. If you have both TrueType and fixed-size fonts of the same name on your Mac, it will use the fixed-size fonts first.

Using Key Caps To Compare Fonts

If you are considering a change in font, you can use the Key Caps desk accessory get an idea of what a new font will look like before you put it in your document. This is especially useful if you are using True-Type fonts, or if your fonts have been adapted by a type managing program to look their best on your screen. The TrueType and adapted fonts you see in Key Caps closely resemble the fonts as they appear on the printed page. Bit-mapped fonts may not look the same on the screen as they do in print.

To see how a font looks before you use it, follow this procedure:

1. Choose Key Caps from the Apple menu. The keyboard window appears, as shown in Figure 3.10.

2. Choose a font from the Key Caps menu. The fonts listed are those installed in your System file.

3. Type characters or click on them in the keyboard window. They appear in the text box at the top of the window.

4. Press the Shift key, the Option key, and the Option and Shift key together to see all the special characters that are available with a font. If a rectangle appears in the place of a key cap, it means that there is no character for that keystroke.

FIGURE 3.10
Looking at a font in the Key Caps window

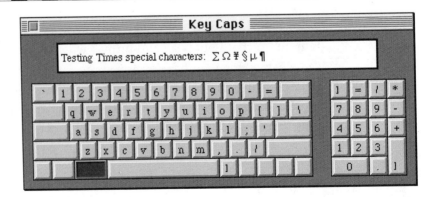

If you find a special character or a font that suits your needs, do a test printing to make sure it comes out looking the way you want before you create a large document using it. There are often slight differences between the way characters appear on the screen and the way they print out, and there are often variations of the printed characters between different printers. You have to experiment to find the best combination for your work.

Using Accented Characters

No matter which font you use, you will have trouble creating certain characters that are used in languages other than English. These include accents, tildes, and other special marks that appear over standard characters. To use accents and other special marks when you are using a Domestic U.S. Keyboard file, enter the following keystrokes:

ACCENT MARK	KEY COMBINATION
Grave accent (`)	Option-`, then the accented character
Acute accent (´)	Option-e, then the accented character
Circumflex (^)	Option-i, then the accented character
Tilde (~)	Option-n, then the accented character
Umlaut (¨)	Option-u, then the accented character
Cedilla (¸)	Option-c

If you type an accent with a character that does not accept it, the accent mark appears, then the character appears in the next space.

Chapter 3

 Troubleshooting Problems with Printing

The following subsections describe solutions to the problems that can occur when you are trying to print out documents from within Macintosh applications or from the Finder.

Your printer's icon does not appear in the Chooser.

When you open the Chooser to set up printing to your printer for the first time, the printer's icon is not in the left panel of the Chooser window. You probably have not installed the printer software you need for your printer. Make sure you have the latest version of the printer software (the printer *driver*, as it is called) and that you have installed it correctly, either by using the system software installer, or by dragging the icon of the printer software to the closed System Folder on your hard disk.

Your Mac refuses to talk to the printer.

You have chosen the icon of your printer in the Chooser, but either the name of the printer doesn't appear (if it's a networked printer), or nothing prints and you see a message box telling you that there is no printer or the printer could not be found. Either the printer is off or unplugged, or it is not ready to print (on a StyleWriter, the Ready light is off; on an ImageWriter, the Select button is off).

Fix the plugs, turn the printer on, and press the Select or Ready button. If the printer is on, it may be hung; turn it off and back on again. If the printer is on a network, make sure the network is functioning, and check to make sure nobody has changed the name of the printer. If none of those efforts help, contact a qualified technician.

Jagged text.

You wrote some great text, and converted it to a font that looks fine on the screen, but when you print it out, it is all ugly and jagged around the edges. Here are the most common causes and their solutions:

- You are using a city-name (bit-mapped) font and printing on a LaserWriter, and you do not have the bit map for that particular font in your System Folder. Change the font, or install the bit-mapped font for the one you want.
- You do not have Font Smoothing and/or Font Substitution selected in the Page Setup dialog box for the application you are using. Select them.
- You are using an ImageWriter or StyleWriter and you haven't selected Best Quality in the Print dialog box. Select it.
- You are using PostScript outline fonts on a non-PostScript printer, and you aren't using Adobe Type Manager, or you haven't turned it on in its control panel. Install ATM and turn it on.

Right-justified paragraphs have ragged right margins.

You are getting varied spacing with the font you are using. If your application has a fractional-width spacing option in the Page Setup dialog box, select it. If the application does not support fractional-width spacing, you have to install all of the bit-mapped font sizes you are using.

Characters overlap on ImageWriter printouts.

When you print out documents to an ImageWriter, the characters are too close to each other, and some overlap others. You must choose Page Setup from the File menu in the application you are printing from, and deselect the Fractional Widths option.

You can't remember the keystroke for a special character in your current font.

If you need to enter a special character, like a *u* with an umlaut, or a little heart, or some mathematical symbol, and you can't remember which key does the trick, you can use Key Caps for a reminder. Just choose Key Caps from the Apple Menu. If you want to keep referring back to Key Caps for different special characters, move the Key Caps window down to the bottom of your screen, then use the size box in your application window to resize the window, so you can see the Key Caps window under there. If any other windows are open, you have to resize or close them to get them out of the way.

Text switches to Geneva font for no apparent reason.

This is a spooky problem. You are working along, not thinking about fonts at all, and you either print a large document out, or do some memory-intensive process like a big spell-check or a repagination, and suddenly, your text starts converting from whatever font you chose to Geneva font.

The problem is that the Mac has run out of memory, so it can't use the outline font you chose. You have to free up some memory for your work in the application. You may be able to quit other applications, or cut down the number of special startup customizing files in your System Folder. You may have to reduce your RAM cache in the Memory control panel. (See Chapter 7 for details on adjusting the RAM cache.) Or you may just have to bite the bullet and go to your Apple dealer and install some more RAM.

Text in a particular font size is jagged.

Text in most of your document looks fine when you print it out, but if you change to an unusual font size for some of the text, it comes out jagged. This is because the size you changed to is not installed on your Mac, and it is having to do a bit-mapped approximation of that size. Either change the text to a font size that appears in outline form in the menu (see Figure 3.10 for samples) or install the font in your System Folder so it is available. If you are using ATM and PostScript outline fonts, check the troubleshooting chapter in the ATM *User Guide* for more information.

PrintMonitor window won't go away.

You look at the PrintMonitor window to see how your print job is doing, and pretty soon the print job is finished and disappears from the window. Then when you try to quit the PrintMonitor, or you close the window, you find there is no Quit option in the Find menu and the menu and the icon in the Application menu refuse to go away. This is because the PrintMonitor appears and disappears automatically. To get rid of it, you need to choose another application from the Applications menu. The moment you get into that application, the PrintMonitor disappears from the Application menu. If it doesn't disappear, it means that a print job is waiting in the background for enough memory to begin printing.

Paper jammed inside printer.

You sent a job to the printer and only half of the pages came out. If your printer has a little light with a jammed-paper icon next to it, the light is blinking merrily. No matter which kind of printer you have, press the Release button and open the cover of the printer. Find one end or the other of the paper and pull it out gently. For good hints on how to get jammed paper out, see your printer's owner's guide—all the Apple printers have great descriptions of how to get jammed paper out.

If you have a StyleWriter and the paper feeder won't feed the paper, make sure the Release button on the feeder is pushed down so the feeder panel has snapped forward. Then make sure the release lever on the front of the printer is pushed all the way in. Finally, make sure the two halves of the printer, the engine half and the feeder half, are pushed firmly together, and slide the latches at the sides toward the front of the printer.

Paper won't feed into printer properly.

The paper jams or gets skewed or crumpled as it leaves the paper tray and goes into the printer. If the paper feeder is overloaded, take out the extra paper and try printing again. If there are still problems, flip the whole stack of paper over; some types of paper have a slick side and a textured side, and if the slick side is up, they don't feed well. Make sure the edges of the paper are not dog-eared, and that they are all lined up so the stack is smooth-sided.

Printer status lights blinking or off.

The status lights on different printers mean different things. On all printers, though, a blinking paper light means it's time to add paper, and a blinking Ready light means that the printer is working on a job. If all the lights are off, the printer isn't getting power. Check to make sure it is plugged in, and that the outlet has power. If the Ready light on a LaserWriter blinks, pauses, and blinks again, over and over, there is something wrong with the PRAM that controls printing from the Mac. Choose Restart from the Special menu and hold down ⌘-Option-P-R until startup. All control panel settings go back to the default, so you may have to reset yours.

Text or images print off-center on page.

The text or images of a document you printed run off one side of the page. First check the margin settings in the application that made the document. You may have to select all of the text or all of the images, then set the margins. If that doesn't help, check the paper size that is selected in the Page Setup dialog box; if you select a larger paper size than the paper you are using, the printed matter runs off the bottom of each page.

If the margins and paper size are correct, check the paper feeder to make sure it isn't overloaded. Check to see that you are using good quality paper (16- to 24-pound cotton bond), and see that the stack of paper is lined up right, too.

Ink smudges on back side of pages printed on LaserWriter.

There are gray blots and clouds on the backs of pages you print out of your LaserWriter. The insides of the printer engine are getting coated with excess toner. You need to clean things out. See the "Care and Feeding of a LaserWriter" section for information on running a Cleaning Page.

Page prints all black, or with white streaks through letters.

The quality of your printed pages is going downhill. Either they come out all black, or white streaks run down the pages, or lines appear on the paper, running through the text or images. Your ink or toner cartridge is almost empty, or it has been sitting still for a long time and needs to be fiddled with.

Remove it as described in the "Care and Feeding" section for your type of printer earlier in this chapter. LaserWriter owners, rock the cartridge side to side or forward and back. StyleWriter owners, clear the ink cartridge, turn off the Power button, then hold the Ready button down while you press the Power button. Finally, release both the Power and Ready buttons. DeskWriter owners, just press the Prime button for a few seconds.

If fiddling with your ink or toner cartridge doesn't help your print quality, it's time to replace the cartridge. See the "Care and Feeding" section for your printer type.

If you are using an ImageWriter and the paper gets misaligned so the page breaks don't appear between the sheets of paper, use the following procedure to realign your paper properly:

1. With the printer turned on and the Select light off, press the Line Feed button until the page-break perforation is exactly lined up at the top of the printer head.
2. Do your printing. When printing long documents, you may have to pause the printer and adjust the paper to make up for any inaccuracy of the page breaks.
3. When the printer finishes a document, turn the Select button off and press the Form Feed button. This advances the paper to the next page and aligns the page-break perforation correctly.
4. Turn the Select button back on, then tear off the last page of your document, leaving the extra sheet sticking out of the ImageWriter.
5. Use extra sheets for children's art or scratch paper. Or add them to your collection of perforated edge-strips, and recycle them.

PART two

System 7 for Anybody

The second part of this book tells you how to get the most out of System 7. You'll learn how to use the software that runs the Mac to your best advantage. You'll also learn how to get to your work easily and quickly, how to keep your work well-organized, how to store it on hard and floppy disks, and how to make good use of the Mac's memory to help process your work. Once you've mastered these basics, you'll learn to customize the Mac to serve your own special needs.

CHAPTER 4

Working with Applications and Documents

Now that your Mac and your printer are set up, and you're comfortable with the mouse and the desktop, you're ready to get down to work with applications and documents. No matter what specific tasks you do with your Mac, and no matter which applications you use to do those tasks, you need to learn the basic techniques for using applications and documents. This chapter shows you how to install your applications, how to open applications and documents, and how to save the work you've created with your Mac.

Introducing Applications and Documents

Applications are the tools you use on the Macintosh to do your work. As you work, you and the applications produce *documents*. If your task is writing text, you will use a word processing application and produce text documents. If your task is creating art or illustrations, you will use drawing, drafting, or painting applications that create graphics documents. If your task is financial reporting or forecasting, you will use applications that create spreadsheets or database documents. If your task is fooling around, you will use games like Tetris and Dark Castle, and you will create high scores by making little shapes fit together and by escaping the flaming eyeball. But sooner or later you'll get back to work with applications and documents.

Applications and documents are different kinds of *files*. These electronic files are much more versatile and powerful than the files you stuff in a file case. In fact, everything your Mac does relies on files like applications and documents.

On the desktop, you see icons for applications, documents, and folders. You can put documents and applications inside folders by dragging the icons over the folder icons. Then, when you open up folders by double-clicking them, you see the icons of the applications and documents in each folder's window. Folders can also be put inside other folders; this nesting of folders is further explained in Chapter 5.

Applications have icons that indicate what they do. For example, a painting application may show a hand painting on a diamond-shaped piece of paper as in Figure 4.1. By convention, most documents look like a rectangular sheet of paper, often with one corner bent over. Text documents have text on them, graphics ones have some sort of artwork.

There are also application and document icons that look very different from the conventional ones. However, you can usually tell what an application does by looking at its icon, and you can get some sort of hint about the nature of a document by looking at its icon.

FIGURE 4.1
Application and document icons

TeachText

Text Document

Word doc

MacSplot

Graphics Document

Kid Pix doc

Chapter 4

 Installing an Application

To install an application on your Mac's hard disk, you insert the floppy disk that contains the application (often called the *program disk* or *setup disk*) into your computer's floppy disk drive. If you want to play it safe, make backup copies of the application and its supplemental items, as described in "Backing Up System and Application Disks" in Chapter 6. When you're done copying, insert your working copy of the application disk, and double-click the disk icon when it appears on the desktop. If you see an icon in the window called Install or Setup, double-click it.

With some applications, a dialog box then asks you to personalize your copy of the program. Enter your name and the name of the organization you work for in the text boxes. You have to click in the organization box with the mouse to move the insertion point into it. Click OK when you are done.

If a dialog box opens asking you what you want to install, choose the program and the essential supplemental files that go with it, such as Help, Dictionary, Plug-in, and Preference files. Figure 4.2 shows a few icons of these files. If you are familiar with the program, you can leave out any Tutorial files and Samples files on the floppy disk.

See the application's user guide if you need help deciding what is essential and what isn't. Click the Install or OK button when you have

FIGURE 4.2
Supplemental files for Word, SuperPaint, and Excel

MS Dictionary   Plug-in Tool   SuperPaint Prefs   Add-in Functions decided what to install. The installer program does its work. The screen usually displays a sliding bar that indicates how copying is going. The installer may put up a message box asking you to insert another disk (if two or more are required to install the program). Feed the Mac the disks it asks for.

Some programs are a bit more primitive: When you put the program disk into the computer and open the disk icon, all you see is the icon for the application and maybe a sample document or two. Open your hard disk icon, then resize the two windows so both can be seen at the same time. Find the icon for the application in the floppy disk window. Drag this icon to the hard disk window. If there are icons for supplemental files in the floppy disk window, find out from your application's user manual if you need to copy them onto the same disk as the application.

If you want to install some supplemental files onto your hard disk along with the application, it's good to create a new folder on the hard disk for them. (If you don't know how to create a folder, see Chapter 5 for more information.) Then drag the application and all its supplemental files into the folder. Name the folder after the application, so you don't lose it.

For example, if an imaginary application called MacSplot had a Custom Patterns file, you could create a new folder in your hard disk window and name it MacSplotters. Then you could drag the application icon and the Custom Patterns icon into the MacSplotters folder. If you have lots of applications, you can create an Applications folder and put all of the folders for the different tools inside it. When you finish copying an application off a floppy, you can drag the application's disk icon to the Trash so the disk ejects.

Opening an Installed Application

To open an application, you double-click on the icon for it. Some applications (especially ones that take some time to open up) display an opening message, but soon you see the application's document window. There are other visual clues that you are "in" an application now instead of in the Finder; the most obvious is the application's special icon in the upper right corner of the screen. The menu options are also different from the ones on the Finder's desktop, and the application's pointer, insertion point, or cursor is often different from the arrow seen on the desktop.

Once you have installed an application, you can make an *alias*, or copy, of the application's icon. This allows you to keep copies of the icon in places where they'll be convenient. Since an alias is only a copy of the icon, very little storage space is used up by the alias. This is better than keeping several copies of an application in different folders, which wastes large amounts of disk storage space, and which can lead to confusion if each version is set up differently.

To make an alias, select the original icon and choose Make Alias from the desktop's File menu. Then drag the alias to the folder where you keep your current documents created by that application. Or you can put an alias onto the desktop with your hard disk icon. If you double-click the alias it opens the application quickly.

Opening a Document

The most direct way to open a document is to double-click its icon. If the application that made the document is not open, it starts up, opens a window, and displays a page or section of the document you double-clicked on. There is another simple way to open a document from the desktop if you are looking at a Finder window containing both the document icon and the icon of the application that made it. Drag the document icon over the application one, and the document will open. This works with the alias of an application icon, too.

You can even drag a document onto the icon or alias of a different application from the one that created it, and if that application can read the format of your document, it will open the document. This avoids problems you can run into when you try to double-click an imported document that you don't have the application for. For example, if you drag a TeachText document onto the Microsoft Word icon, the document opens in Word. Or if you have several different types of graphics documents, all of which can be opened by SuperPaint, you can put an alias of SuperPaint in the same folder with all the different documents, then drag each one onto the SuperPaint alias to open it.

If you have opened an application, you can open a document from inside it. Choose the Open command from the application's File menu. A dialog box appears; find the name of the document in the current folder list and double-click it. You can look in folders other than the current one by pulling down the folder hierarchy menu as shown in Figure 4.3. Just move the pointer to the title of the current folder list and press the mouse button.

The hierarchy of folders in the folder hierarchy menu is inverted; this means that for the sample shown in Figure 4.3 the memos folder is inside the Correspondence folder, which is on the Hard disk. Figure 4.4 shows a picture of the hierarchy of folders, with the desktop at the top.

If you are not sure how to get to the document you want, choose Desktop from the folder hierarchy menu, or click the Desktop button in the dialog box. Then start your search by double-clicking on the name of your hard disk in the list box. It helps if you have a simple, clear hierarchy, so you don't have to hunt down through five layers of folders. The one shown in Figure 4.4 is over-simplified, but if you can limit yourself to about five to ten folders on any one level, and keep your

FIGURE 4.3
Pulling down the folder hierarchy menu in an Open dialog box

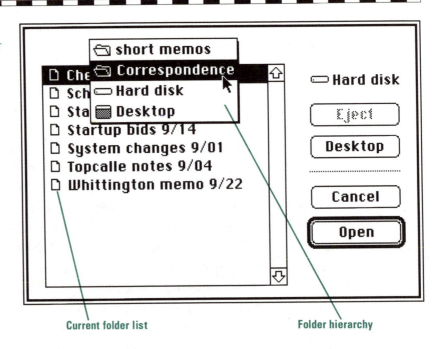

FIGURE 4.4
Hierarchy of folders with short memos inside Correspondence on Hard disk

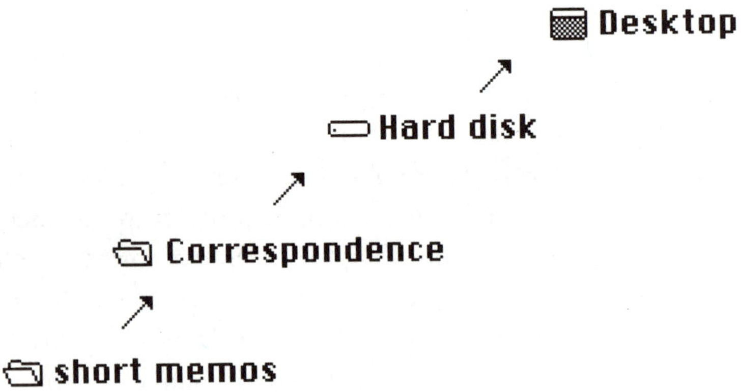

most-used documents just one or two levels down from the hard disk, you'll be happier and more productive. For more information on organizing files and folders, see Chapter 5.

If you bury a file way down in some obscure folder and then can't remember how to get to it, just cancel out of the Open dialog box, go to the Finder, and choose Find from the File menu. When you find the file, double-click it.

Saving Your Work on a Document

When you have found and opened a document you can either create new work in it, or edit the work you have done before. Either way, you want to make sure you don't lose that work. If you save your work as you go along you never have to worry about a power outage destroying everything you've done that day.

The key lesson is: *Save often*. If you are creating a text or graphics document, save at least every half hour. If you are making lots of changes at a high rate of input, save every fifteen minutes. Save before you leave your Macintosh even if you do not intend to be gone for long; if you are switching between two applications, save before you leave each of them to go do a little something in the other one. And make backup copies of your work at least once a day, especially if there is any chance of power fluctuations or hard disk trouble. For more information on backing up your work, see Chapter 6.

Saving a Document for the First Time

The first time you save a document you are creating, you have to name it and tell your Mac where to put it. When you open a new document, either by starting an application without choosing an existing document, or by choosing New from an application's File menu, the new document has a generic name, such as Untitled, or Document 1. If you see a generic title in the title bar of the window you are working in, use the following procedure to save your work:

1. Choose Save from the File menu. A dialog box opens, as in Figure 4.5. It displays a list of the contents of your hard disk or your current folder (the folder you are working in). There is a text box for naming the document, with the generic title highlighted in it, and buttons for saving, canceling, opening a new folder, and switching to the desktop. For more information on these features, see the "Special Saving Techniques" section that follows.

2. Type in a name for your new file. The new name replaces *Untitled* in the text box.

3. Click the Save button. The disk drive whirrs as it writes your document onto the disk, and then the document window returns, with the new name in the title bar.

Saving as You Edit

As you work on a document, the changes you make are stored in the temporary memory of your Mac. To put this work in a permanent storage place, choose Save in the File menu, or, in most applications, press ⌘-S. If you save often, each save takes only a moment, so your work pace is not interrupted.

There is only one situation in which you should not save your work. If you realize that everything you have done since the last time you saved is all a big mistake, *do not* save your work. Instead, close the window, and when you see a dialog box asking if you want to save changes before closing, click the No button.

FIGURE 4.5
The Save As dialog box

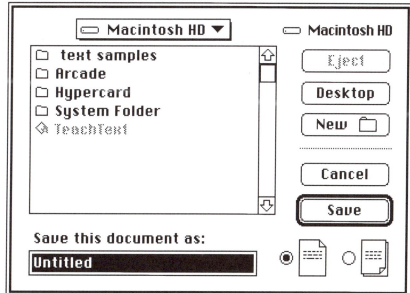

Special Saving Techniques

There might be times when you make changes to a document and want to keep both the original and edited versions of that document. For situations like this, choose the Save As command from the File menu and use the dialog box shown in Figure 4.5. These are the different possibilities:

- Click the New Folder button, enter a folder name, and click Save to save the document in a new folder inside the current folder.
- Click Desktop if you want to save the document on the desktop instead of inside your current folder. If you want to save a

backup copy of a document to a floppy disk, click Desktop, then click the floppy disk name in the list box and click the Open button.

- Click Eject if you want to save a document to a different floppy disk from the one in the floppy drive. You must click Desktop before this button becomes active.
- Enter a new name for the document if you want to have two copies of it: the previous version, and a new version with your latest changes.
- Pull down the folder hierarchy menu if you are inside a folder and want to save the document to the desktop or another folder. Choose the Desktop from the folder hierarchy menu if you are not sure where the desired folder is. You can start seeking it from the desktop down.

Managing Your Applications

Once you've acquired a few applications, you'll find yourself casting about for quicker and easier ways to open and move among them. By using the Apple and the Applications menus judiciously, you can make sure your applications are right where you need them.

Opening Applications from the Apple Menu

You can set up your Mac so you can open your most-used applications from the Apple menu. You have already learned in this chapter about double-clicking the icon or an alias of the icon of an application. You can also put an alias of an application icon in the Apple Menu Items folder in your System Folder. The alias will appear in the Apple menu, which is accessible any time, just like the Applications menu. The advantage to having an application's alias in the Apple menu is that you can use it to open the application. The Applications menu only shows applications that are already open.

There are minor drawbacks to using application aliases in the Apple menu. If you use them to switch between applications you see the desktop blink on and off as the switch occurs. Also, if you work with a number of applications and have lots of other things in your Apple menu, the thing can get so long it's a pain to use. In this case, switching between applications with the Applications menu can be less clumsy and more direct.

For seasoned Mac users who are in the habit of opening applications via the Apple menu, there is a trick you can do to put the aliases of your most-used applications at the top of the menu. Just add a space before the first letter of an alias title, and it will go to the head of the menu. In Figure 4.6, the Microsoft Word and SuperPaint aliases have spaces in front of them, and the TeachText alias does not. You can add an apostrophe to the front of a title, and it will move to the end of the list. Double spaces and double apostrophes give you even more possibilities for putting items in order.

Switching between Applications

If your Mac has enough internal memory (RAM), you can open more than one application at a time and switch quickly between applications. You need at least 3 megabytes (3 Mb) of RAM to run the system software and two large applications on top of it.

To open two applications, start by opening the most-used one. Then choose Finder from the Applications menu, which you pull down from the first application's icon at the far right end of the menu bar. Then you find the second application's icon on your desktop. If the desktop is cluttered with windows opened by the first application, choose Hide Others from the Applications menu. When you find the second application's icon, double-click it. You can also double-click the

FIGURE 4.6
Application aliases in the Apple menu

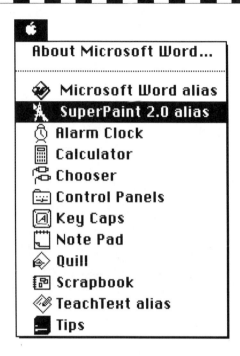

icon of any document created by the second application, and it will open a window for that application with the document displayed.

To switch between two or more open applications, you choose the one you want from the Applications menu. If you arrange the windows of the different applications carefully, you can also switch from application to application by simply clicking in the different windows. For example, if you open a TeachText window in the lower left portion of the screen and have a paint or draw application window open in the upper right part of the screen, you can click in the corners of the windows to switch back and forth between the applications.

If you want to hide one application's windows when you switch to another one, just hold down the Option key as you choose the second application from the Applications menu. The other application's windows are hidden, but you can get at them by choosing the dimmed name and icon of the application from the Applications menu.

 ## Managing Your Documents

The Mac also gives you several ways to find, open, and move among your documents. These are described in the following sections.

Finding Misplaced Documents

If you have a large number of folders and you can't remember where a document is, you can use the following Finder procedure to seek out your document and select it for you.

1. Choose Finder from the Applications menu. This menu is under the application icon on the far right end of your menu bar.
2. Click in the window for your hard disk to make it active. If you can't find the hard disk window, choose Hide Others from the Applications menu, then double-click your hard disk icon to open its window.
3. Choose Find from the File menu on the desktop.
4. Type the name of the document you want to open, or as much of the name as you can remember.
5. Click on the More Choices button if you want to be more specific about the document you are searching for. For example, if you know the name of the document starts with the letters *Sche*, you can enter those letters in the Find dialog box, click More Choices, then pull down the menu under "contains" and change it to "starts with."
6. Click the Find button when you have narrowed your search as much as possible. A dialog box tells you how the search is

going, then the Finder opens the window that contains the document and selects it for you. Double-click it to open it.

7. If more than one document matches the pattern of characters you are searching for, choose Find Again from the File menu on the desktop. The Finder runs around your folder hierarchy again until it finds another document that fits the pattern you specified.

Switching between Documents

Many applications let you open more than one document at a time. To find out if opening multiple documents is allowed in an application, you open one document and pull down the File menu. If the Open command is dimmed, you cannot open another document. If the command is dark, choose it, then double-click a second document in the Open dialog box. The second document appears in its own window, and in most cases, the two document windows are staggered in such a way that you can see the edge of the inactive one behind the active one.

To switch from one window to the other, so you can work on one document and then the other, you just click on the edge of the inactive window. It becomes active, and you can go to work immediately.

When working with multiple documents make sure you save your work in each one. If you do some work in a document and go on to another one without saving, it is easy to forget all about the first document until there is a power surge or a system problem that makes you restart and lose your work. The best policy is to save your work in each document before you leave it to work in another one.

Changing Your Desktop View of Documents and Folders

There are a lot of ways to look at the documents and folders in a window on the desktop. Each view of the items is useful for different reasons; don't use the same view for all situations. Here is a list of the views as they appear in the Views menu, and the most obvious situation called for by each:

- by Small Icon: Shows little icons and titles for files and folders. Good for showing lots of different types of files and folders in one window.
- by Icon: Shows a full-size icon and title for each file or folder. Good for showing a few icons of different kinds, especially if kids or other less dextrous users are going to be using the window.
- by Name: Lists folders and files with the names sorted alphabetically. Good for long lists of documents you want to sort alphabetically.
- by Size: Lists folders and files sorted by size, largest first. Good for finding out which folders and documents need cleaning out when you are running short of disk space.
- by Kind: Lists folders, applications, and documents in separate, alphabetized groups. Good for finding and listing documents; gives you a clear view of your hierarchy of folders and documents. In Figure 4.7 you can see a listing by kind of a simple folder and file hierarchy.
- by Label: Lists folders and files sorted by the labels you assign to them. Good for organizing long lists of similar files, so you don't mix them up.

- **by Date:** Lists folders and files sorted by last modification date, most recently modified first. Good for determining which documents need to be backed up.

If any of these views are not available in the View menu, you probably need to make an adjustment in the Views control panel, as explained in "Views Control Settings" in Chapter 8. Only the by Name view is always available.

Using List Views

To get the most out of list views, you may need to expand and collapse the lists of what is in the folders. Sometimes you want to see what is in a folder, and sometimes you want to hide the contents of a folder so they don't fill the screen and prevent you from seeing the top levels of your folder and file hierarchy. The more complex and extensive your

FIGURE 4.7
A list by kind of a simple file and folder hierarchy

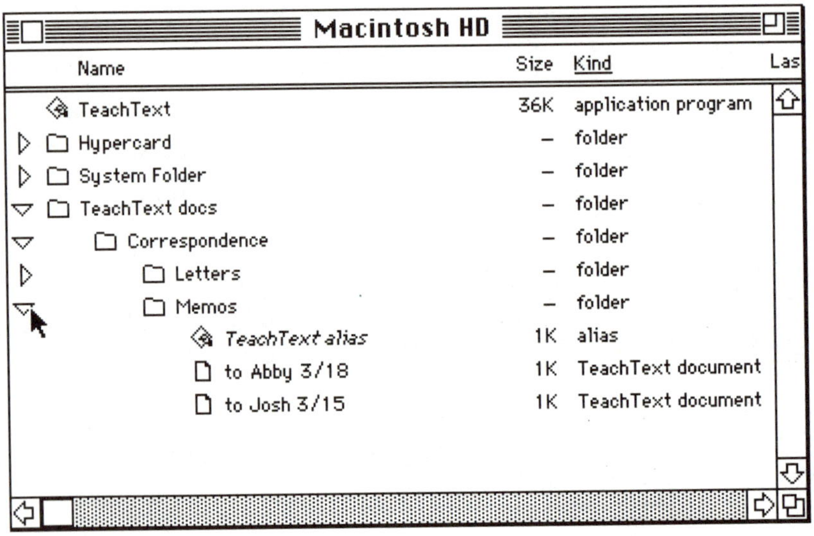

Name	Size	Kind
TeachText	36K	application program
▷ Hypercard	—	folder
▷ System Folder	—	folder
▽ TeachText docs	—	folder
▽ Correspondence	—	folder
▷ Letters	—	folder
▽ Memos	—	folder
TeachText alias	1K	alias
to Abby 3/18	1K	TeachText document
to Josh 3/15	1K	TeachText document

hierarchy is, the more you need to manipulate the lists. Here are a few of the most useful techniques:

- To see as much information in a list window as possible, expand the window with the size box in the lower right corner of the screen (not the zoom box in the upper right corner) until it fills the whole screen. Also, use the Views control panel (see "Views Control Settings" later in Chapter 8) to hide any column of information you don't need, such as the Label column.
- To display the contents of a folder in the list, click the triangle in the left margin of the list. To hide the contents, you click the triangle again. When the triangle points down, the contents show, when it points to the right, the contents are hidden, as shown in Figure 4.7.
- To display *all* the contents of a folder, including the contents of folders inside it, select the folder, then either press ⌘-Option-→ or hold down the ⌘ and Option keys and click the triangle. To hide all of the contents of a folder, you select it (click on the folder's icon up at the top of the whole list of contents), then either press ⌘-Option-← or press ⌘-Option and click the triangle. The next time you display the contents of this folder, you will see only the immediate contents of it; the contents of enclosed folders will be hidden.
- To move a selected icon to a folder that is listed in a remote part of the hierarchy, use the previous techniques to hide as much as you can between your selected icon and the folder you want to put it in. Then drag the icon *slowly* to its destination, scrolling the window. If you drag it too quickly, it will zip right out of the window to some other window or the desktop.
- To select widely dispersed icons, hide as much of the list between them as you can, then click on the first icon and Shift-click the others. This technique is great for selecting documents

in a bunch of different folders; you don't have to open and close all those windows.

- To select a file or folder from a long list without having to scroll until you find it, just type the first few letters of its name, without any pause between letters. Presto; the icon of the file or folder appears, selected.
- To select several icons in one folder, start a selection rectangle in the left margin and drag a bit to the right and then down through the list of icons. You can keep dragging down a long list, even if it runs out of sight at the bottom of the window.
- To change the way items are listed, click on the column header for the listing you want. For example, if the items are listed by kind, you can click the Last Modified column header and the window will change to a by Date listing. The column header of the current list type is underlined.
- To adjust the list view display and to show additional information in list views, see "Views Control Settings" in Chapter 8.

Troubleshooting Problems with Applications and Documents

These are the problems you may have in working with your applications and documents and using the System 7 Finder.

Lost in FinderSpace, or, "What view am I looking at?"

You switch to the Finder and either no windows are open, or you are looking at a window that doesn't make any sense to you at all.

To get away from the blank desktop, you just double-click your hard disk or floppy disk icon.

To figure out what kind of a list view you are looking at in a window, you just check out the column titles up near the top of the window, and see which one, Name, Size, Kind, Label, or Last Modified, is underlined.

If you are looking at a window with a title you don't recognize, and you can't figure out what folder you're in, just press the ⌘ key and use the mouse to pull down the hierarchy menu hidden under the title of the window. This trick doesn't work in application windows, but all you have to do in an application is choose Open from the File menu, then pull down the folder hierarchy in the title of the list box. See "Opening a Document" earlier in this chapter for details.

An application is not available.

You see an alert box that looks like Figure 4.8. In most cases, this means you double-clicked a document icon, and your Mac can't find the application that created the document.

The solution is to open the application first, then open the document, but that only works if you have the application that created the document. If you don't, try opening the closest application you have, then opening the document from inside that application. For example, if you are trying to open a MacWrite document but don't have MacWrite, you can open Word, then open the MacWrite document. Word will convert the MacWrite document to Word format as it opens the document. Similarly, you can use SuperPaint to open all kinds of paint and draw documents. If you have PageMaker, you can open almost anything with it.

Application won't quit as expected.

You try to quit an application after finishing work in it, and either the screen hangs, or the Mac puts you right back in the application. The cause of the problem is that you still have a utility or desk accessory

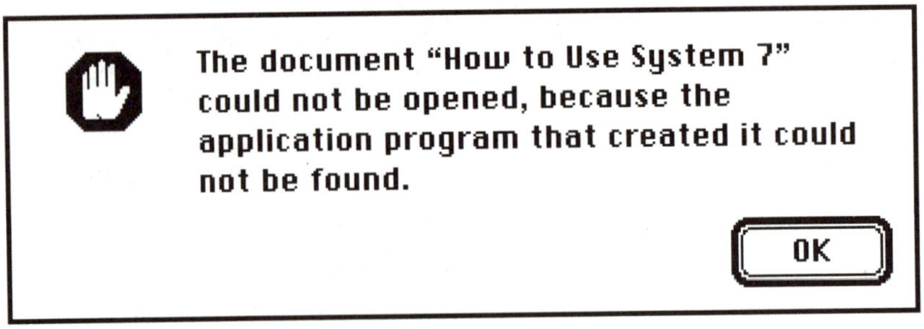

FIGURE 4.8
Application Not Available alert box

The document "How to Use System 7" could not be opened, because the application program that created it could not be found.

OK

open. Check the items in your Apple menu. When you find the open utility or desk accessory, close it, then quit your main application.

File lost after moving in a list view.

You moved a file to a folder in a window that was displaying a list view, and now you can't find that file. Use the Find command in the File menu to find the lost file, then move it carefully, making sure that the target folder is highlighted before you "drop" the file. It is easy to miss a target folder in a list view, especially if you are using the small icons of files and folders in order to squeeze as long a list as possible into the window.

CHAPTER

Using Folders to Organize Your Work

This chapter tells how to keep your work organized on your Macintosh. A Mac can store a lot of documents and applications on its hard disk. But it is up to you to organize your files so you can use the computer efficiently. Remember, all applications and documents are just files, as far as the Mac knows. And as long as you don't mess with its System file, it doesn't care *what* you do with all the other ones. But it can slow both you and the Mac down if files are scattered all over and neither of you can find them when they are needed. So you need to organize your files.

You organize files by putting them in *folders*. That's simple enough; it's just like when you accumulate a bunch of related papers on your real-world desk and then store them in a folder. However, when you have several folders of stuff cluttering up your desk, you put them in a pile or stick them in an alphabetized file case.

On the Mac, it's a little different. You put related files in a folder, but when you accumulate lots of folders, you can put some of them inside another folder.

Now, you *could* do that with real-world folders, but the folder holding the other folders would get unwieldy. By contrast, the Mac can handle folders inside folders with ease. The folders inside folders create a nice organization of layers; you can put a document file or an application in any folder, at any level of the folder organization.

Apple calls the whole thing the Macintosh hierarchical file system, or HFS for short. The *hierarchy* refers to the layers of folders. Folders inside other folders are at "lower" levels of the hierarchy. Folders you see when you open your hard disk are near the top. The desktop itself is at the peak of the pyramid, above the hard disk and any floppy disks that appear on it. Whenever you work with the hierarchy of files and folders, remember that "up" is toward the desktop, and "down" is deeper into the layers of folders inside other folders. Figure 5.1 shows a picture of how the hierarchy is set up.

There aren't any names for the folders in the picture; but naming is an important part of organizing your work, and it is explained later in this chapter.

Creating Folders

OK, so folders are the basic building blocks of the hierarchical file system. To make them, you need to be in the Finder with your hard disk window open. If you aren't already there, choose the Finder from the Applications menu. Choose Hide Others from the Applications menu if the desktop is cluttered with open windows. If, when the clutter clears, you find that your hard disk window isn't open, double-click the hard disk icon. If the hard disk window is inactive, click in it to make it active.

To make a folder in the active window, you choose New Folder from the File menu. The folder appears, highlighted, with the name

FIGURE 5.1
Hierarchy of folders on disks under the desktop

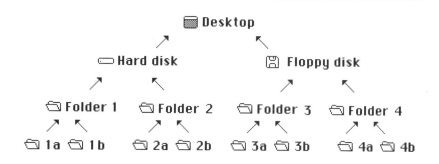

"untitled folder." There is a frame around the name of the folder, indicating that it is selected so you can type in a better name.

You can also put folders on the desktop. However, the folders and the stuff in them have to be stored on a disk *somewhere*, so I prefer to build all hierarchies inside disk windows. Besides, it's confusing to clutter up the desktop with stuff that is of uncertain origin. Better to put each folder that holds a hierarchy in the window of the disk where it is stored.

Naming and Nesting Folders to Make a Hierarchy

To name a newly created folder, you just type in the new name when you see the frame around "untitled folder." To change the name of an existing folder or file, you click on the name (*not* the folder) and wait for the frame to appear around it. Then either type in a new name, or select part of the old name and replace it. For more information on selecting and replacing text, see "Deleting and Replacing Text" in Chapter 9.

To put a file such as a document into a folder, you drag the icon of the document to the folder. When the folder becomes highlighted, release the mouse button, "dropping" the document into the folder. To put several files in a folder, you drag a selection rectangle through them, then drag one of the icons to the folder. The others follow.

To put a folder into another folder, or "nest" it, you drag the icon of the "egg" folder to the icon of the "nest" folder and drop it in. Open up the nest folder and the egg one will be inside there.

For an example of the basic techniques of nesting folders to make a hierarchy, create a few new folders, such as those shown in Figure 5.2. If your computer is new and you haven't rearranged things on your hard disk, you'll probably already have a System Folder (remember, you *do not* nest it anywhere or move stuff in or out of it unless you know exactly what you are doing), a HyperCard folder, and TeachText. If you do not have any documents in your hard disk window, create and save two with TeachText or your word processing application of choice. (If you don't know how to create and save a word processing document, see Chapter 9, "Word Processors.")

The names of the files and folders in this sample are simple, clear, and easy to organize into a logical hierarchy. The two memos, "to Cory" and "to Kira," belong in the Memos folder. The Memos and Letters folders belong in the Correspondence folder, since they are for two different kinds of correspondence files.

The HyperCard folder, which contains the HyperCard application, belongs in the Applications folder. TeachText, another application, goes there too.

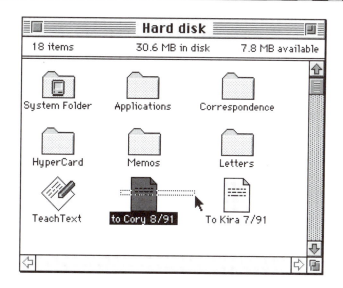

FIGURE 5.2
Some folders and files in a hard disk window

So, to create the hierarchy shown in Figure 5.3, just follow these steps:

1. Select the two memos and drag them to the Memos folder.
2. Select the Memos and Letters folders and drag them to Correspondence.
3. Select the HyperCard folder and TeachText and drag them to the Applications folder.

Now all you see in the hard disk window is three folders: Applications, Correspondence, and the System Folder.

This simple hierarchy would be adequate to organize 20 or 30 memos and letters in the Correspondence folder, and 10 or 15 applications. To help you remember when you created a particular file, you can add a date after it, as shown for the memos above. You don't need to add a last modification date; you can see that in a list view, as explained below.

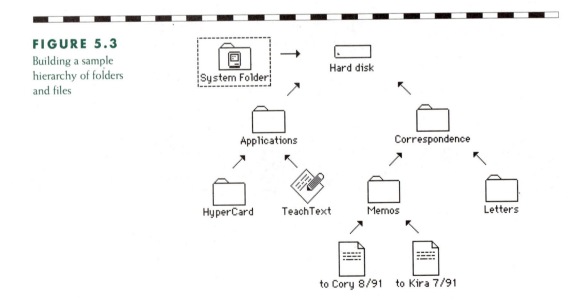

FIGURE 5.3
Building a sample hierarchy of folders and files

If you build up a large number of files in any folder, you can split them into subfolders. Although there is almost no limit to how many layers and folders you can nest, it is best to keep each level to less than ten folders, and to limit the hierarchy to three or four levels, so you can find things easily. You would never have trouble finding files down inside a sample hiearchy like the one in Figure 5.3, because the names of all the folders describe what is in them.

Keeping things in a clear, simple hierarchy doesn't mean you have to be rigid. For example, it's OK to have both files and folders in a folder, like having the HyperCard folder and TeachText (an application file) in the Applications folder.

Using List Views to Work with Folders

If you want to see several layers of your folder hierarchy at once, in order to find out if the naming and nesting is clear and logical, just open the window for your hard disk and choose by Name or by Kind from the View menu. You'll see something similar to Figure 5.4. The sample shows the name, size, and kind of each file or folder. If you scroll the list to the right, you can see the time and date that the files and folders were last modified.

This view gives you an outline of the files and folders; the logic of the naming scheme is obvious when you see it in outline form. This is the key to good organization of your folders and files. If the folder names make a clear outline in a list view, you won't lose things in the hierarchy. If the names of the folders don't make a sensible outline, or if files are in folders that don't make sense, the hierarchy needs work. If you don't fix it up, and if you add more and more files and folders, higgledy-piggledy, the thing will soon become such a mess that you can't locate anything without using the Find command in the File menu.

Chapter 5

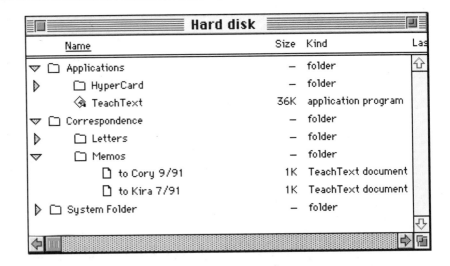

FIGURE 5.4
List view of a sample folder hierarchy

For example, if you wrote a short letter one day, and decided to put it in the Memos folder, even though it wasn't really a memo, you might forget that it was there later, and go looking for it in the Letters folder. And if it turned out to be a very important letter, you would go through some anxious moments before you found it in the Memos folder. Or if you named the folders Shrtntes.B52 and Lngstff.B17 instead of Memos and Letters, you might forget what in the world those names meant.

Save yourself the trouble. Build your hierarchy with clear, simple names, and put files in the appropriate folders. If you can tell that a name is wrong in a list view, you can select and change it. If a file is in the wrong folder, you can move it, even if the folder where you want to put it is not in view. Just drag the icon of the file to the top or bottom of the screen, then drag it slowly to scroll the list view. For more information on list views, see "Using List Views" in Chapter 4.

If you want to change the order in which files are listed in a folder, you can put special characters (things other than letters or numbers) in front of the files' names. To move a file to the front of a list, you can put a space or exclamation point in front of the name. To move a file to the end of a list, you put an accent (`) or caret (^) in front of the name. This technique is good for straightening out the way numbered files are listed.

For example, if you list some files named File 1 through File 12, you'll find that files 10, 11, and 12 appear between File 1 and File 2. Not cool. To move those two-digit files to the end of the list, you put an accent in front of the number for each file, so they become File `10, File `11, and File `12. If you have a long list with many two-digit numbers (like File 1 through File 37), just put a space in front of the one-digit numbers so they go to the front of the list. If you have a HUGE long list, like File 1 through File 325, you can put a space in front of the single digits and an exclamation point in front of all those two-digit numbers. But a file list that long should be broken up into a bunch of smaller folders.

 ## Troubleshooting Problems with Files and Folders

The following sections cover the problems you can have when using files and folders to build your file hierarchy.

Can't determine where current folder fits in hierarchy.

You are looking at a window that shows the contents of a folder, but you can't figure out what folder the current one is inside (the *parent* folder, as they say). Press the ⌘ key and click on the title of the current window. A menu like the one in Figure 5.5 pops down, with the layers of the hierarchy above your current folder, listed in reverse order. That means the parent folder is listed first, then the parent of that folder, and so forth, to the hard disk.

FIGURE 5.5
Folder hierarchy pop-up menu

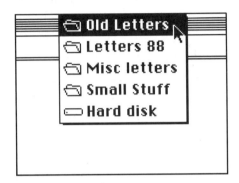

File or folder is lost.

You can't remember where a file is. Or you just dragged a file or folder into a window with a list view, and it disappeared. Choose Find from the File menu at the desktop (you have to be in the Finder to find stuff). A dialog box opens, with a text box ready for you to enter the name of the file or folder you want to find. You don't have to enter the whole name; all the Finder needs is enough letters to distinguish the item you've lost from all the other ones.

If you enter only part of the name and the Finder turns up a different file or folder from the one you want, just choose Find Again from File menu or press ⌘-G to find the next item that matches the pattern of letters you entered in the Find text box.

If you want to find and list a group of files that share something in common, you can use an expanded Find dialog box. First choose Find from the File menu, then click the More Choices button in the small dialog box. A larger dialog box appears, with three boxes containing pop-up menus across the top. Click on the boxes to see the choices in each pop-up menu. Choose limiting categories from all three pop-up menus, always working from left to right.

For example, if you want to find and list all of the files you modified yesterday (you *know* you want some information out of one of those files, you just can't remember which one), first choose "date modified" from the left pop-up. Leave "is" for the center pop-up, and select the day part of the date and use the down arrow to change it to yesterday's date. Click the Find button, and the files appear, highlighted in a list view. If they are inside a folder, the folder's list opens automatically so you can scroll down the list and see all of the files. This is a slick way to list related files. Just check out the different choices in the left pop-up menu to see all the ways you can limit the search.

Can't find a buried folder window.

You have about ten windows open on your desktop, and they are completely covering the window of a folder that you want to see. The simple solution is to close all the other windows, but this means switching between programs and it may also mean closing up something you want to get back to soon. Not to worry; there are alternative paths to your buried window.

First, choose Hide Others from the Applications menu. That gets all your open document windows out of the way. Then, if the window you want is partly in view, just click on it to bring it to the front. If it is still completely hidden, see if you can find an icon for it quickly, then just double-click the icon to bring the window up front. For instance, if your hard disk icon is in view (and you should set things up so some edge or corner of it is *always* in view) and the folder you want has an icon in the hard disk window, double-click on the hard disk icon. If the folder is down inside the hierarchy, you can choose by Kind or by Name from the View menu, then quickly open the folders you need to in order to get at your desired folder. When you get to the folder, its icon will be highlighted if its window is open.

Can't change a file's name.

If you try to select the name of a file and the frame doesn't appear around it, so you can't edit the name, the file or disk that contains it is locked. To unlock a file, you need to choose Get Info from the File menu, click the Locked check box to uncheck it (thereby unlocking the file), then close the Info window. Now you can select the name of the file and change it when the frame appears around it.

If the file is unlocked and you still can't select the name, it must be on a locked floppy disk. Eject the disk and slide the lock tab over the hole. Then reinsert the disk, open it, and select the name of the file you want to change. See Chapter 6 for more information on locking and unlocking floppy disks.

New file or folder is selected when you try to change a file or folder's name.

You select a file or folder, but when you start to type characters to change its name, a new file or folder becomes selected. The problem is that you selected the item, but didn't select the title. You have to click on the title itself and wait for the frame to appear around it. *Then* edit the title. When the item is selected rather than its title, you are telling the Mac to find and select a new item when you type in letters.

CHAPTER 6

Storage: Hard and Floppy Disks

Disks are what you store things on when you use the Mac. They contain the tools you use and they give you space to save the work you produce. Your work is stored in the form of electronic blips on the surfaces of the disks, somewhat like music is stored on magnetic cassette tape. You need disk storage because the main portion of your computer's memory, the *random access memory* (RAM), is lost when you turn the computer off. So if you do not store your hard-earned blips on disks, you lose them.

This chapter describes the two different types of disks, hard disks and floppy disks, and tells how to prepare and use them, how to make backup copies of them, how to lock and erase them, and how to check the amount of space you have to store things on them. It also tells you how to solve the most common problems you can have with disks.

 ## Introducing Hard Disks

A *hard disk* consists of one or more platters for storing information. The platters are sealed inside a disk drive, either inside your Mac or inside a separate, external hard disk drive that you connect to your computer. You can't get into the drive and look at the platters, but the computer can read things off of them and write things to them. On the desktop, the icon for your hard disk drive, or "hard drive," is a horizontal rectangle with a name under it, like the one in Figure 6.1. The icon appears in the upper right corner of the desktop. You can move it, but when you shut down or restart the Mac, it goes back to its corner.

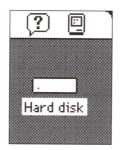

FIGURE 6.1
Hard disk icon

You cannot drag the active hard disk (the one with your system software) to the Trash. If you have other hard drives connected to your Mac, either by direct cables or by network connections, you can drag their icons to the Trash and undo the logical connection to them.

Introducing Floppy Disks

A *floppy disk* is a thin, round, floppy piece of plastic. The plastic disk behaves somewhat like the magnetized plastic used for cassette tape. It is inside a sturdy plastic case with a metal door. You can put floppy disks into your Macintosh and take them out; the computer reads things off a floppy disk and writes things onto it. On the desktop, the icon for a floppy disk looks like Figure 6.2. It appears under your hard disk icon when you insert the floppy disk in the disk drive. You can move the floppy disk icon anywhere you want on the desktop, but it's easiest to leave it over there on the right side, so you can find it when you have windows open.

FIGURE 6.2
Floppy disk icon

You can drag a floppy disk icon to the Trash to eject the disk from the floppy drive, unless the floppy disk is your startup disk (the one with the system software that is running the computer). The first time you eject a floppy disk by dragging it to the Trash you may feel a twinge of fear; you can't help wondering if throwing a disk in the Trash might delete things on the disk, or at least get them a little messy around the edges. Fear not. Throwing a floppy disk in the Trash is merely a symbolic act. The actual disk pops out of the disk drive, without any coffee grounds or bad odors clinging to it.

Bytes, Kilobytes, Megabytes

Different types of disks can store different amounts of data. For instance, hard disks can store much more information than floppy disks. Information in computers comes in tiny units called *bytes*: 1024 bytes make a kilobyte (K), 1024 kilobytes make a megabyte (Mb). A standard 3.5-inch floppy disk can hold either 800K or 1.4Mb of information. Hard disks can store 40Mb or more, and they are getting larger all the time. One gigabyte (1000Mb) hard disks are becoming common.

To put these figures in more concrete terms, a floppy disk can store about a book's worth of information; a hard disk can store a hefty encyclopedia or more. In terms of graphics, a floppy disk can hold one or two complex color photographs, and a hard disk can usually hold more than a hundred.

To distinguish 800K from 1.4Mb floppy disks, you look at the corners. If the disk has a single little square hole in the upper right corner of the case, it's an 800K disk. If it has two little square holes, one in each upper corner of the case, and an HD symbol in the lower left corner, it's a 1.4Mb disk. Figure 6.3 shows examples of both kinds of disk.

FIGURE 6.3
Two different 3.5-inch floppy disks

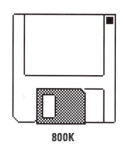
800K

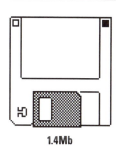
1.4Mb

Some Macs have the SuperDrives that accept 1.4Mb disks, while others can use only 800K floppies. If you work with two or more Macs and some have SuperDrives and others don't, you should buy and use 800K disks and use them on all machines. You can't transfer data on 1.4Mb disks from a Mac with a SuperDrive to a Mac without the Super-Drive, unless the 1.4Mb floppy is formatted as an 800K disk. And what's worse, if you format a 1.4Mb floppy as an 800K disk on a non-SuperDrive Mac, then put lots of important data on it and stick it in your SuperDrive Mac, it asks you if you want to reinitialize the disk and erase all the data. This is not good. What's worse, even if you *do* want to re-initialize a 1.4Mb disk that you formatted on an 800K drive, the Super-Drive often can't manage it!

Which Disk for You?

If possible, purchase a Mac with a built-in hard disk, or purchase an external hard disk drive that connects to the SCSI socket (or "port") on the back of your Macintosh. It is best to use floppy disks only for storing backup copies of the work you produce and the applications you use. Keep your working tools and the things you create or modify daily on a hard disk. Your Mac can write things to and read things from a hard disk much more quickly than a floppy disk, and you can keep so much more on a hard disk that you shouldn't try to get along with just floppy disks unless your work requires using only one application and you create only a few small documents. If you try to do more than that without a hard drive, you'll go nuts switching floppies in and out of your Mac. You can use two floppy drives, and keep your startup disk in one of them, but you'll still have to do a lot of disk swapping.

So, you should get a hard disk if you possibly can. But do you want an internal or an external hard disk? If you have a compact, portable, or PowerBook Mac, you want an internal drive, to keep the machine portable. On the other hand, if you have two Macs in different locations and you have to run data back and forth a lot, get an external drive, so that it is the only thing you have to transport.

There are many small, light, fast, and quiet external drives on the market. Another advantage to an external drive is that if you have trouble with it, you can take it to a shop without having to turn over your whole Mac. On the downside for external drives, the service can be poor, and if the Mac system software changes, you can have problems with getting compatible driver software to run your external drive properly. So if you buy an external drive, get one from a company that has a reputation for good service and perfect compatibility with the Mac system software.

There are other features you want in any hard drive. Large capacity is the most critical; you will *always* need more disk space in the future, no matter how much is in a drive you buy. Fast access and data transfer are important too. Any good hard drive will also have automatic head parking, so the little heads that read and write on the disk move a safe distance away from it when you aren't using them.

Care and Feeding of a Hard Disk

Hard disks don't require much care, normally. All you have to do is make sure you shut down properly before you switch off your Mac; see Chapter 1 for more information. If you avoid dropping your hard disk down the stairs or pouring cleaning solvent into it, it should give you many years of carefree service.

However, if you do have major problems with a hard disk, they can cause real nightmares, like losing all your data and applications. So you should follow a few basic rules and precautions.

Connect and Initialize the Hard Drive Properly

If you are using an internal hard drive, all you have to do is make sure the disk is initialized before you start using it. Most disks are initialized by the factory or shop that installed them; but if yours isn't, the system software will ask you to initialize it the first time you access the disk. Click Initialize to finish the job.

If you are connecting an external disk drive to your Mac, connect the SCSI (Small Computer System Interface) cable as described in the drive's documentation. Make sure you set the ID number to something other than 0 (zero) or 7. Many people set their SCSI drive ID at 6, which makes it the first thing the Mac accesses after its own memory and internal hard drive (if there is one).

Some SCSI drives require a terminator. Plug the terminator into the hard drive's cable socket, then plug the connector cable into it.

Some hard drives have the terminator built into the hardware; your owner's guide will tell you if the drive needs a terminator or not.

Once a new external hard drive is connected to your Mac, turn on the hard disk, then the Mac, and see if the hard disk icon appears on the desktop. If it doesn't, initialize the disk by running the Apple HD SC Setup program, which is on the Disk Tools disk you received with your system software. If this program cannot format your particular brand of hard disk, you should have received a floppy disk with the hard disk, and this floppy should have a utility on it that can initialize the hard disk. Follow the instructions for the utility in your hard drive's documentation.

When you have connected and initialized an external hard drive, the icon appears on the Mac desktop. You can double-click it to open the drive's window and use it for all your storage needs.

Turn the External Drive On First, and Turn It Off Last

You have to turn your external hard drive on before you turn your Mac on, and you have to leave the external drive on until after you shut down the Mac and turn it off. It's usually OK to turn on the drive and the Mac simultaneously, unless the hard drive is extremely slow in coming up to speed. Just make sure you shut down and turn off the Mac before you turn the hard drive off. The one exception to this rule is that you must use the Mac to park the heads of a few oddball SCSI drives. I recommend that you avoid these oddball drives, however.

Although you must shut down your Mac and turn it off before turning off the hard drive, you must also make sure you never turn off the Mac while the hard drive is reading or writing data. This can't happen as long as you make sure you shut down before you turn the Mac off. See Chapter 1 for more information on shutting down.

Be Kind to Your Hard Disk

Don't slide, move, tip, punch, or bump your hard disk while it is at work. If the heads bump the disk while it is spinning, they can cause major damage (known as a "head crash").

Use the hard drive at comfortable room temperatures only. If you move the drive from a hot or cold place to a comfy-temperature place, let it acclimatize for an hour or so before you turn it on.

Keep only one System Folder and one copy of the system software on your hard disk at a time. The Mac system software is not good at competing with itself. The Finder tends to get lost and race around in wild, endless loops looking for things that aren't there, or things that are at two different addresses at the same time. Kafkaesque situations like that are tough on hard disks, just as they are tough on humans.

Clean the filter screens in the vents to your hard drive. You can do it yourself with a strong vacuum that has a narrow mouth, like a Dust Buster. Or you can take the hard drive to a qualified technician once a year or so and have it cleaned professionally.

Rebuild your desktop once a week or so. All you have to do is hold down the Command key (⌘) and the Option key as you start up or restart the Mac, then click OK when it asks if you want to rebuild. Just keep in mind, as the dialog box tells you, that any comments in Info boxes for files and folders on the hard disk will be erased.

Check the hard disk's window now and then to see how many megabytes of data are on the disk, and how much space still remains. See "Checking Disk Capacity" later in this chapter for more info on the subject. Don't trust the advertised capacity of the drive; in reality, most drives hold about 5 to 10 percent less than they claim. When your disk gets to about two-thirds full, see if you can save some data to floppies, or copy off some applications or games that you don't or shouldn't be using much. If you have been running the disk at more than two-thirds full for some time, and moving lots of things onto it and off it, consider defragmenting, as explained later in this chapter.

Keep an eye out for little warning signs, like the Mac taking a long time to switch from an application to the Finder, or unexplained appearances of the message, "The application is busy or missing," or unexplained appearances of bomb boxes. These things call for rebuilding the desktop, as explained above. After you rebuild, check to see how full the hard disk is, and if you still need space.

Save and Back Up

I know, I know, you've been told before. I also know that you are human, like me. We tend to overlook things like saving and backing up, especially when we are in a hurry, and when we are in a hurry we tend to push the Mac a little bit too hard, just the way we tend to pull shoelaces a little too hard when we are rushed.

But shoelaces are cheap. Your applications and all your data are much more valuable. Save your work every ten or fifteen minutes, so you never have to redo much in the event of an electrical surge or a system software crash.

Back up your work at least once a week if your hard disk is less than half full, and back up your work once a day if your hard disk is more than two-thirds full. If your hard disk gets more than three-quarters full, or if it starts giving you "Out of Space" messages when you do things like save, or if you notice that it takes more time than usual to switch to the Finder, or if the Finder takes a long time to find things, BACK UP RIGHT NOW!!!!! Don't stop to tie your shoes or hurry up to finish the file you were working on.

Backing up your work can be either very simple or very complex, depending on how paranoid you are. If you are just working on one project at a time, and you just want to make sure you have a copy of your latest work on the project, all you have to do is copy the whole project once a week or so, then back up the last chapter you did major work on once every day or so. If you have trouble remembering to do this, you can automate the process with a utility such as FastBack or Redux. See Chapter 18 for more information on these utilities.

If you can afford to put some extra money into your Mac, you can buy an inexpensive second hard disk drive and do your backups to it. Copying files from one hard disk to another is much faster than copying to floppy disks, and you can keep all the backups for each project in one nice, big folder, rather than scattered among a bunch of floppies. Some people even back up their applications on a second hard drive, but I think it's safe enough to keep a backup copy of the original program floppy.

Whether you use a hard disk or floppies for backup, make sure you have a large amount of memory set aside in your Mac's disk cache. The rule of thumb is to allot at least 32K of memory to the disk cache for each megabyte of RAM your machine has. Allot much more if you use memory-hungry applications or ones that create huge (200K+) documents. The larger the disk cache, the faster you can copy things, and the easier it will be for the Mac to do the copying in the background, which allows you to go on working in your current application.

Defragment the Hard Disk Before It Fills Up

When you have filled your hard disk to three-quarters of its capacity, or if you have been running it at about two-thirds full for a few months, it will be fragmented. This means that the individual files on the disk are scattered all over it, rather than kept all together.

Fragmenting happens because the disk's driver software places data on the disk wherever it can find space, and the space on the disk is divided up into small units. As a disk gets near to full, files are put into all the little leftover units of space between other files. As you add and delete more new files, the little leftover units of space get more and more scattered, so your files wind up in little fragments all over the disk. Then when the Finder comes looking for a file it has to do a lot of hunting around and collecting fragments to make the whole file. This is hard on the Finder, and it means the disk has to do a lot more spinning to get your work done.

If it takes a long time for the Mac to open an edited file, or if you see the message "The application is busy or missing," even though you know the application is right there in front of you and not busy at all, then you can bet you need to defragment your hard disk.

The simplest way to defragment a hard disk is to copy all of it to another hard disk or to floppy disks. Then initialize the fragmented disk, and copy everything back onto it. If you can rent or borrow a hard disk that is the same size as yours and copy everything over to it and back again, this is not only simple, but quick. Copying everything to floppies takes quite some time and effort, especially if you haven't been backing up your work regularly.

You can also get a utility, such as Speed Disk or DiskExpress II, that can take what is already on your hard disk and defragment all the files without moving them off the disk. These utilities can also keep your files in order in the future, so fragmentation doesn't creep back in. The only problem with some of them is that they take a lot of time to do their work, especially if you start using one on a nearly full disk. For information on defragmenting utilities, see Chapter 17.

A good compromise is to copy everything off your disk to a borrowed or rented hard disk, then install the defragmenting utility, then copy everything back. Once the disk is in good order, the utility doesn't get in your way much as it prevents future defragmentation. You can even divide up your hard disk into partitions, which further prevents fragmentation (see your hard drive documentation for more information on partitioning). I prefer to keep everything in one partition, but use the utility to guard against fragmentation.

Care and Feeding of Floppy Disks

The main things you do with floppy disks is insert them, eject them, name them, and copy things onto and off of them.

To "feed" or insert a floppy disk into your Mac, you hold the disk label side up, metal part away from you, and slide the disk into the drive. It clicks firmly into place, and if the Macintosh screen is displaying the desktop, the icon for the inserted floppy disk appears.

To eject (or spit out, as some say) a floppy disk when you can see its icon on the desktop, you drag the icon to the Trash. This does not delete or erase anything on the floppy disk. It just tells the computer to spit out the disk. You can also select the disk icon and choose Put Away from the File menu.

To change the name of any floppy or hard disk, you select the name under the icon on the desktop and type the new name, which replaces the old name automatically. Give each disk a distinct name that reflects what is on it. You can use any character exept the colon (:) in a disk name, and you can use spaces as well.

To copy things onto a floppy disk, you just drag their icons to the floppy disk icon on the desktop, or into the floppy disk's open window. To copy things from a floppy disk, open the disk's window and drag the icons to the window of the folder or disk you want to copy them to.

Floppy Disk Precautions

Floppy disks don't require much care, but keep them away from the following things:

- Magnets: Toy magnets, paper clip holders, telephones, TV or computer-monitor magnets, stereo-speaker magnets, and electric motors. If you have an external disk drive and a compact Mac, keep the drive away from the left side of your Mac; there are strong magnetic fields by the power supply on that side. Keep disks away from the left side of ImageWriters, too.

- Heat and cold: Use floppies and the floppy disk drive only when both are at room temperature.
- Static Electricity: Avoid touching the metal door on a floppy disk with your fingers, and don't put disks in plastic bags.
- Grease, dust, water: Never open the metal door and touch the floppy itself. Don't store floppies in damp or dusty places.

Preparing a Floppy Disk for Use

Before you can use a brand-new blank floppy disk, you have to format it so your Macintosh can write to and read from it. Use the following procedure to prepare a disk:

1. Insert the new disk in the floppy disk drive. A dialog box tells you that the disk is unreadable and asks if you want to initialize it.
2. If you inserted a 1.4Mb disk, click the Initialize button. If you inserted an 800K disk, click Two-Sided. An alert box warns you that the initialization process will erase everything on the disk.
3. As long as you are sure you did insert a new, blank disk, click the Erase button. A message box tells you how formatting is going. The box closes and the disk's icon appears on the desktop when formatting is complete.

Floppy Disks for Different Uses

The following sections describe the different types of disks that you use to start up your Mac, to run it, and to do your work.

The Startup Disk

A startup disk can be either a hard disk or a floppy disk. It must contain the System Folder, and it must be in your Macintosh or in an external drive that is properly connected to the computer, before you turn on the Mac. When you switch the Mac on, it starts up the system software and presents the desktop to you.

System Disks and Application Disks

When you purchase a new Mac, you receive a number of floppy disks with the system software on them. When you purchase applications software for your computer, you receive one or more floppy disks that contain the application program and any additional software you need. You often receive floppy disks with installation software, to help put all the other stuff on your hard disk.

If you lose or damage your system or application disks, then lose or corrupt the system or application software on your hard disk, you are stuck. You have to purchase and install new software before you can go back to work. Avoid this fiasco; make backup copies of the system disks and any application disks you have purchased. See "Backing Up System and Applications Disks" later in this chapter.

Data Disks

Data disks are the disks you use to store your work. If you have no hard disk, you must save all your work to data disks as you create it. If you have a hard disk, save your work to it, and use data disks or a second hard disk to back up your work once a day or so.

Chapter 6

 Backing Up System and Applications Disks

Back up your valuable software disks to prevent loss of the tools you need most for your work. You can also back up data disks by the same method. If you know you want to copy *all* of the files on a system or application disk, you can use the procedure in "Copying an Entire Floppy Disk" later in this chapter.

1. Insert the system or application disk in the floppy disk drive.
2. Double-click on the disk icon to open a window displaying its contents.
3. Double-click on the hard disk icon to open its window. Resize and arrange the two windows so they fit on the screen.
4. Click in the hard disk window, then choose New Folder from the File menu to create an untitled folder in the hard disk window.
5. Click in the window of the system or application floppy disk, then drag a selection rectangle across all of the files and folders you want to back up.
6. Drag all of the files and folders to the untitled folder in the hard disk window. A message box tells you how copying is going.
7. Rename the folder to reflect the name of the system or application disk.
8. If there is more than one windowful of files and folders in the system or application disk window, repeat the selection and copying process.
9. Close the window for the system or application floppy disk. Drag the disk icon to the Trash to eject the disk.

10. Insert a new disk and initialize it. See "Preparing a Floppy Disk for Use" earlier in this chapter for more information.

11. Drag the newly named system or application folder from the hard disk window to the new floppy disk icon. A message box tells you how copying is going.

12. When copying is complete, open the floppy disk icon and check the contents. Then close the window, drag the floppy disk icon to the Trash to eject it, and label the floppy disk.

13. Store the backup disk in a safe but handy place, preferably not the same place where you store the original system or application disk.

Copying an Entire Floppy Disk

If you have two floppy drives in your Mac, or an external and an internal floppy drive, it is quite simple to copy the entire contents of one floppy disk to another floppy disk. You just put the two disks in the two drives, and when the two floppy disk icons appear on the desktop, you drag the source disk icon to the target disk icon. The source disk is the one with the stuff you want to copy, and the target is the empty disk you're aiming to fill. A dialog box appears, asking if you want to replace the contents of the target disk with those of the source. Just click OK, and the Mac does the copying. Anything that was on the target disk is erased.

It's a bit more of a trick to copy a whole floppy to another one if you have only one disk drive. Use the following steps to limit disk-swapping to a minimum.

1. Insert the target floppy disk and make sure it has nothing on it that you want to keep.

Chapter 6

2. Close the disk's window, but leave the icon selected.
3. Choose Eject Disk from the Special menu. The target disk spits out of the disk drive, but a ghost icon remains on the desktop.
4. Insert the source disk. When its icon appears, drag it to the ghost icon of the target disk, as shown in Figure 6.4.
5. Click OK in the message box that asks if you want to replace the contents of the target disk with those of the source disk.
6. Switch disks when the Mac asks you to.

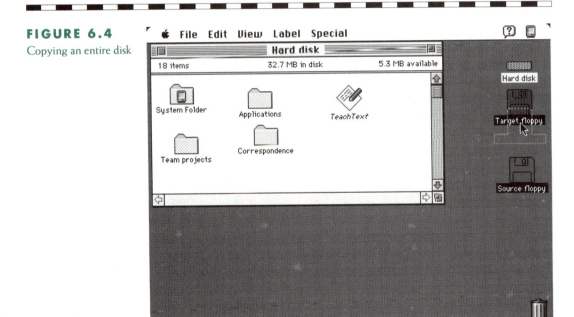

FIGURE 6.4
Copying an entire disk

Locking and Unlocking a Floppy Disk

To lock a disk so you cannot add to, change, or delete anything on it, use the following procedure:

1. Eject the disk from the computer if it is inserted.
2. Hold the disk face down, with the metal end away from you, and look closely at the locking tab in the lower right corner.
3. Use your fingernail or the tip of a ballpoint pen to slide the locking tab toward the edge of the disk cover, as shown in Figure 6.5. A small hole opens.
4. To unlock the disk, use your fingernail or pen tip to slide the tab back over the hole.

It is wise to lock all system and application disks, and data backup disks for projects that you have finished working on. Unlock a data disk if you need to add information to it.

FIGURE 6.5
Locking a floppy disk

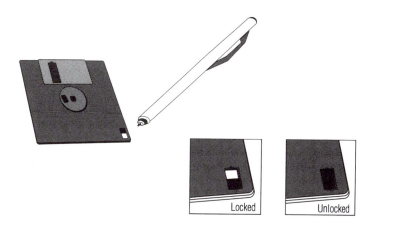

Erasing a Floppy Disk

If you have a disk with old information on it that you no longer need, you can erase it and reuse the disk. Insert the disk in the drive and open the icon to make sure there's nothing you want on the disk. Then close the window and choose Erase Disk from the Special menu. A dialog box asks if you want to completely erase the disk. If you are erasing a 1.4Mb disk, click the Initialize button. If you are erasing an 800K disk, click the Two-Sided button.

 ## Checking Disk Capacity

To see how much storage space you have used and how much is left on any hard or floppy disk, open the icon for the disk and look at the information bar (shown in Figure 6.6) that is just under the title bar of the disk's window.

In this bar you can see how many items are on the disk, how many bytes they take up, and how many bytes are left. The example in Figure 6.6 is an 800K floppy disk with 3 items taking up 34K of space, leaving 752K available. Notice that the two figures don't add up to 800K. About three percent of each disk is used up by hidden files that the Mac needs to keep tabs on what is in the disk and what you have done with it. Similarly, on a hard disk, about five percent to ten percent of the disk capacity is taken up by formatting and hidden files.

FIGURE 6.6
Information bar for a floppy disk

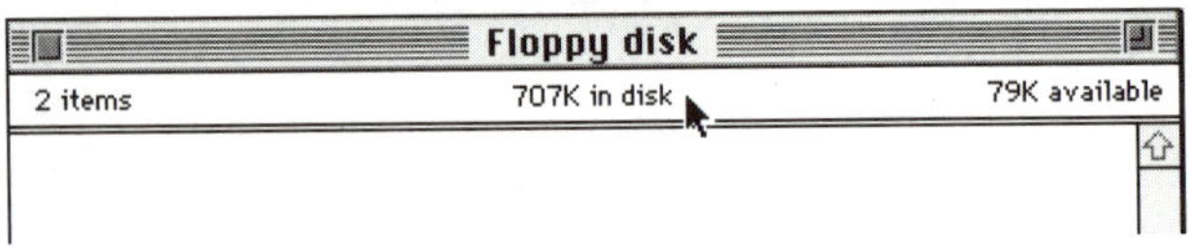

Troubleshooting Problems with Hard and Floppy Disks

These are the problems you are most likely to have with hard and floppy disks, and how to solve them without causing damage to the applications and data you have stored on disks.

Hard disk icon does not appear on desktop.

The problem is that either the Mac can't communicate with the hard drive, or that the hard drive isn't working.

First, try turning everything off and checking the power plugs and cable connections; then turn everything back on. If the hard drive is an internal one, all you have to do is turn the Mac off and wait about a half minute or so, then turn it back on.

If the hard disk is your startup disk, you'll just get a question mark disk icon. Turn the Mac off and start it with a startup floppy disk. If the Mac starts OK and the hard disk icon appears, you need to reinstall the system software on your hard disk. If the hard disk icon still does not appear, and it is an external drive, you probably have it set to a bad SCSI ID number. Find the dial or thumb-wheel for setting the ID number on the back of your hard drive, and set it to be something other than 0 (zero) or 7, and something different from any other SCSI device you have attached to your Mac. For more information, see "Connect and Initialize the Hard Drive Properly" earlier in this chapter.

If you try all of the above and still don't see the hard disk icon, you may have to rebuild the desktop. See "Be Kind to Your Hard Disk" earlier in this chapter for help with rebuilding your desktop. If that doesn't help, it's time to take the Mac to a qualified technician for service. If you have an early Mac Plus and you experience lots of trouble with an external SCSI drive, you might have a faulty ROM chip; have the technician check out your ROM.

You can't remember what disk your current folder is on.

If you are looking at the window of a folder in the Finder and you can't remember if the folder is on your hard disk or a floppy disk, or you can't remember the name of the floppy disk in the floppy drive, just press the Command key (⌘) and pull down the menu under the window's title. The name of the disk will be the bottom item on the menu.

A disk is too full.

You are trying to move or save a file to a hard or floppy disk, and you get an error message box that says the item could not be moved because the disk is full. If you are trying to move something to a floppy disk, you can open the disk's window and delete items to make more room. If you are trying to move or save a file to your hard disk and you get this message, WATCH OUT!!!! You are putting your hard disk and your system software at risk. You need to clear a lot of stuff off of your hard disk (until it is only about ⅔ full) and you need to defragment the hard disk if you have not already done so. See the section, "Defragment the Hard Disk Before It Fills Up" earlier in this chapter.

Hard disk has crashed.

You bumped the hard disk or the electricity surged or something, and the Mac is hung up or making weird noises. Keep calm. The first thing to try is just turning off the Mac, then the hard drive (if it is external). Wait a minute or two, then turn the hard drive (if it is external) and the Mac back on. Hold down the ⌘ key and Option as you turn on the Mac.

This rebuilds the desktop. If the hard disk refuses to start up, take the following steps:

1. If it is an external hard drive, make sure the cables are connected firmly. If the drive has a terminator, make sure it is firmly connected, too.
2. If the hard disk is your startup disk, start the Mac with a floppy disk such as Disk Tools (which you got with your system software) or the Norton Utilities Application disk.
3. Use Disk First Aid or the Norton Utilities Disk Doctor to check and repair the hard disk (see Chapter 18 for help using the Disk Doctor).
4. If that didn't help, reinstall the system software on your hard disk.
5. Still no go? Reinstall the hard drive's driver software (see your hard disk documentation for help).
6. If all else fails, you have to zap your Mac's PRAM. If you are still running on a floppy disk, press the ⌘, Shift, and Option keys and choose Control Panel from the Apple menu. Click Yes when asked if you want to zap the PRAM. This resets the Mac so it should work with your hard disk.

If *none* of these solutions work, take your Mac and hard disk to a qualified technician.

The Mac is slow to load an edited file, or it tells you wrongly that an application is busy or missing.

These two problems may just mean that you are loading a big file, or that an application is not where the Mac expects it to be, but if you notice the two symptoms cropping up often, and without obvious reason, you can bet your hard disk is fragmented. See the section "Defragment the Hard Disk Before It Fills Up" earlier in this chapter for information on how to fix the problem, before it starts causing crashes and data loss.

The Mac can't read or write a file you're trying to copy to a floppy disk.

When you try to copy a file to a floppy disk, you see an error message that says the file couldn't be read or it couldn't be written and it was skipped. Before you do anything else, look closely at the error message. If it says the file cannot be read, then you have a problem with the source file or the hard disk. If it says the file cannot be written, there is a problem with the target floppy disk.

First just try copying the file again. If that doesn't work, and the problem is with the source on your hard disk, use a utility such as Disk First Aid, or the Norton Utilities Disk Doctor, to see if you can save the file (for more information on disk repair utilities, see Chapter 18). If the problem was with the target floppy disk, eject it, reinsert it, and copy something else to it. Then try copying the file you want. If you keep getting the same error message, or you get a message that says the disk is damaged, back up everything on the floppy disk, then erase it and try to copy something to it again. If it still acts up, discard it. It is damaged, and you may lose data you put on it.

The Mac can't read from or write to a disk because of a disk error caused by bad media.

You are trying to open a file on a hard or floppy disk, or you are trying to copy a file to or from a disk, and you see an error message that says there is a disk error due to bad media. Either there is something like a piece of dust on the disk, or it has been damaged in some way. If it is a floppy disk, try this low-tech procedure first: Eject the disk, tap its edge on your palm, reinsert it, then try the read or write action you wanted.

No luck? Use a disk repair utility, such as Disk First Aid (which comes with your system software, on the Disk Tools disk), or the Norton Utilities Disk Doctor, to check the disk for errors that can be fixed easily. Usually, media errors can't be fixed by these utilities. There is one other thing you can try, though. If you have a disk defragmenting utility, such as Norton's Speed Disk, it may be able to move things around and save the file. Just use the optimizing or defragmenting feature to defragment the disk with bad media error. (See Chapter 17 for information on Speed Disk and Chapter 18 for information on the Disk Doctor.)

If you do manage to fix the disk error or work around it, save any important data you have on the disk to a backup disk, immediately. If the media problem was on a hard disk, and it crops up more than once, see a qualified technician to see if your hard disk can be repaired or at least reformatted in such a way that the media problem doesn't come back and haunt you.

The Mac thinks it can't read a floppy disk.

If you insert a floppy disk that you know has information on it, you may nonetheless see an error message that says:

This disk is unreadable:
Do you want to initialize it?

There may be a bit of dust on the disk. Click the Eject button in the error message box, then grasp a corner of the disk and tap the edge of the case against your palm briskly. Slide the metal door open and shut a couple times (without touching the floppy inside), to make sure it works. Put two fingertips on the metal hub in the middle of the back of the floppy and turn the thing a bit. Reinsert the disk.

If you get the "unreadable" message again, the disk is probably damaged. One last-ditch effort you can make is to hold down the ⌘ and Option keys as you insert the faulty disk. Click the Yes button when a message box asks if you want to rebuild the desktop file. Sometimes a disk has a glitch in its desktop file code. If you still get the "unreadable" message, you can try to reinitialize the disk, erasing all the contents, but initialization may fail. Even if it doesn't, the disk is a poor risk; the best thing to do with it is throw it away.

If there are files on the disk that you need, you can use a utility such as Disk First Aid, which is on the Disk Tools disk you received with your system software, or the Norton Disk Doctor Utilities. Place the recovered files on another disk, then throw away the damaged disk so you don't lose any more data on it.

A floppy disk you want to eject is hidden by open windows.

If open windows on your desktop hide the icon of a disk you want to eject, choose Put Away from the Finder's File menu or press ⌘-Y. Don't eject the hidden disk by choosing the Eject Disk command from the Special menu or you may have problems later with floppy disk ghosts, like the one in Figure 6.7.

Disk ghosts can haunt you with problems, so don't leave them on the desktop unless you are *sure* you are going to put the indicated disk back in the drive very soon.

The Mac demands a disk you ejected.

You ejected a disk with the Eject Disk command from the Special menu in the Finder. Although this seems like a logical way to eject a disk, it leaves a ghost behind (as explained in the previous problem), and

FIGURE 6.7
Floppy ghost

when you perform some other Finder action later, the Finder asks for the disk that belongs to the ghost. Eject disks by dragging them to the Trash, or by selecting their icons and choosing Put Away from the File menu.

Floppy disk icon does not appear on desktop.

You have inserted a floppy disk, but its icon does not show up on the desktop. To kick the floppy disk out, press ⌘-Shift-1 (for an internal drive) or ⌘-Shift-2. If that doesn't work, use the paper-clip method described in the next problem. When you get the floppy disk out, restart the computer and try again. If the problem recurs, take your Mac to a qualified technician; the Mac or disk drive is sick.

Floppy disk stuck in disk drive.

No matter how you try to eject a disk, whether you drag it to the Trash or choose the Put Away or Eject Disk command, the thing just sticks in there. Often the drive will make painful choking and hacking noises, but to no avail. First, try pressing ⌘-Shift-1 (for the internal floppy drive) or ⌘-Shift-2 (for an external floppy drive). If that doesn't spit it out, try shutting down and turning the Mac off, then turning it on with the mouse button held down.

Still no luck? To dislodge a really stuck floppy, use the custom-made power-user's tool: a straightened paper clip. Seriously, you have to get a paper clip (the large, heavy-duty ones are best) and straighten one end of it out. Stick that end into the tiny hole to the side of your disk drive, and press straight in on the button that's in there. It takes a firm, but gentle push, and you have to make sure the end of the paper clip is pushing directly against the little lever in there. If the disk won't come out all the way when you press that lever repeatedly, don't try to yank the disk out with pliers or your bare hands; you could destroy the disk drive by yanking it. Take the Mac to a qualified technician instead.

Can't find a seldom-used file on a forgotten floppy.

You forgot which floppy a file is on, and you can't even remember the name of the file for sure. Use the Find command with More Choices in the Finder's File menu, and use any clues you can remember, like the last modification date or any part of the name. Search through your floppies one at a time, and when you find the dumb file, make an alias of it and put the alias in some logical place on your hard drive. Then, if you need the file again and forget what floppy it's on, you can just double-click the alias and the Mac will ask you for the floppy by name.

You are switching floppy disks over and over.

You keep seeing a little message box that asks you to insert a floppy disk; at the same time, the Mac spits out the floppy that is in the drive. What a pain. People call this problem a switch-disk nightmare. To stop it, try pressing ⌘-. (period) at least once, and several times if that doesn't work the first time.

CHAPTER 7

Checking and Adjusting Memory

This chapter explains how to make the best use of the memory in your Mac. A computer needs memory to retain information temporarily; it keeps data and applications on its memory chips as it uses them. When you start an application or open a document, the information is brought out of storage on your hard disk (or a floppy disk) and the computer puts the parts it needs into the memory chips. When you save your work on a document or quit an application, your Mac puts the information that is in its temporary memory back into the more permanent storage space available on your disk.

There are several different types of memory on different chips in the computer, but the most important type for your purposes is *random access memory* (RAM). The Mac can access the different parts of this memory in any order, and can therefore use the memory to do whatever an application requires.

The more RAM you have, the more you can do with your computer. This chapter tells you how to make the most of what you have, but there is no substitute for having enough RAM to start with. If you have 2 megabytes (2Mb) of RAM in your Macintosh, for instance, you can only open one program that requires 1Mb of RAM to operate. In fact, you have to use a small-sized version of the system software to leave 1Mb for an application. You may be able to open a small desk accessory or a second application that doesn't use much RAM, but even this can cause problems when your major application tries to do a memory-intensive operation such as repaginating a text document, cutting or pasting a complex graphic image, or recalculating a large spreadsheet.

If you have 4Mb of RAM, you can open at least two applications and keep a desk accessory open on the side, if none of the three require excessive amounts of memory. Or you can use one application and let it take over a large portion of the computer's memory, so it works as efficiently as possible, without having to "hit the disk" (access the hard disk) for information.

When you have enough RAM, your Macintosh works silently and quickly. When you hear the hard disk whirring often during your work, you know you need to install more memory or adjust the allocation of the memory you have. Before adjusting your computer's memory, give serious consideration to increasing the RAM to 4Mb or as much as you can afford. See your Apple dealer for a memory upgrade. The memory chips, or SIMMS (Single In-line Memory Modules), are becoming less and less expensive, so the upgrade may cost you less than five percent of the cost of your computer. Once you have installed as much memory as you can afford, or as much as your Mac can support, use the remainder of this chapter to make the most of the memory you have.

Monitoring Your Memory Use

To see what your memory needs are and how you should adjust for them, use the About This Macintosh window. To open the window, go to the Finder (chose the Finder from the Applications menu at the right end of your menu bar), then choose About This Macintosh from the Apple menu. A window more or less like the one in Figure 7.1 appears. The applications and memory figures will vary according to how much memory you have and how you have allocated it.

FIGURE 7.1
About This Macintosh window showing memory information

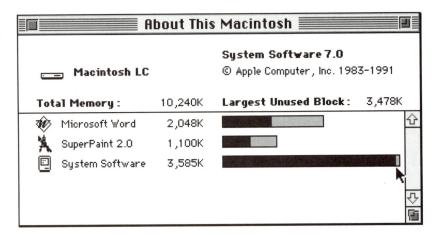

Use the About This Macintosh window to learn the following things:

- To determine how much memory your Mac contains, see the Total Memory amount (10,240K in the example).
- To see how much memory is available to open another application, see the Largest Unused Block amount (3,478K in the example).
- To see how much memory is allocated for the use of each open application, see the amounts listed next to them (2,048K for Microsoft Word and 1,100K for SuperPaint in the example).
- To estimate how much of its allotted memory an application is using, look at the black bars and the white spaces (Word is using just about half of its alloted memory in the example).

If you want to know exactly how much memory the system software or an application is using, just choose Show Balloons from the Help menu (the menu with a question mark in a balloon), then hold the pointer on the bar of the system software or an application in the

About This Macintosh window. A balloon appears; text in it tells you about the bar and tells you how much memory the application or system software is using. To get rid of the balloons, choose Hide Balloons from the Help menu.

Adjusting Application Allocations

If you want to open an application that needs more memory than the largest unused block, you may be able to do it by adjusting memory. For example, if you have a situation like the one shown in Figure 7.1 and want to open an application that needs 3,500K of memory (whew, what a memory hog), you can reduce the memory allocated to Microsoft Word by 100K or so, freeing up enough memory to open your third application. In the example, Microsoft Word is only using about half of its allocation; it seems to have plenty of memory to spare. Just remember that if you open a number of large documents in an application, or if you invoke some memory-intensive processes such as repaginating, recalculating, or checking spelling, you might run out of memory.

There is another situation that calls for adjusting the amount of memory allocated to your applications. If you have opened all the applications you need, but in the About This Macintosh window your application memory bars are all almost full of black, you should see if it is possible to increase their allocations. Look at the size of the largest unused block of memory. Is there more than 1 Mb (1,000 K) of RAM available? If so, you need to increase the allocations for your applications.

Use the following procedure to increase or decrease the amount of memory that is allocated to an application:

1. Quit the application if you are using it.
2. In the Finder, select the icon for the application. If you have trouble finding it, select the icon for an alias of it, choose Get

Info from the File menu, and click the Find Original button in the Info window. If there are no aliases, choose Find from the File menu and enter the name of the application.

3. When you have selected the icon for the application, choose Get Info from the File menu. The Info window opens, as shown in Figure 7.2.

4. Select the number in the Current size box in the lower right corner of the Info window.

5. Enter a new number. Do not enter a number lower than the suggested size unless you have tried all other methods of memory

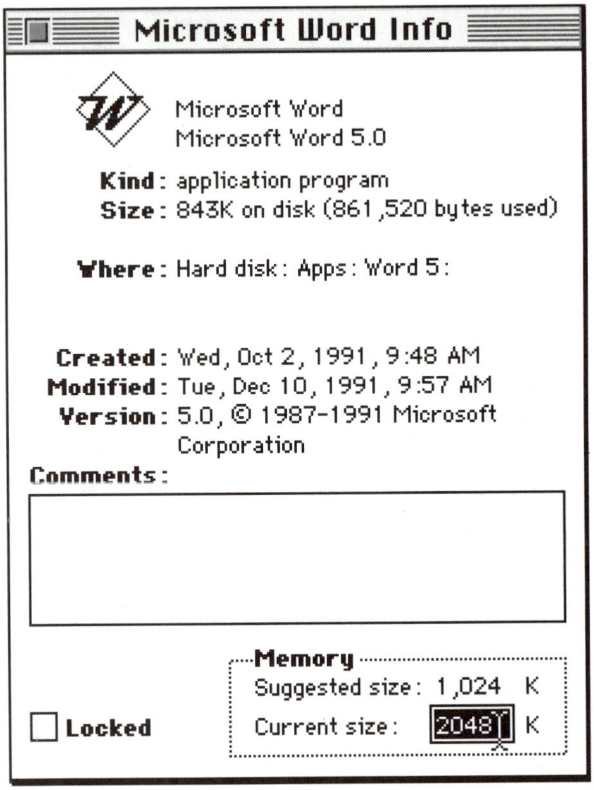

FIGURE 7.2
Changing an application's memory allocation

Microsoft Word Info

Microsoft Word
Microsoft Word 5.0

Kind: application program
Size: 843K on disk (861,520 bytes used)

Where: Hard disk : Apps : Word 5 :

Created: Wed, Oct 2, 1991, 9:48 AM
Modified: Tue, Dec 10, 1991, 9:57 AM
Version: 5.0, © 1987-1991 Microsoft Corporation
Comments:

☐ **Locked**

Memory
Suggested size: 1,024 K
Current size: 2048 K

adjustment. If you set the allocation even slightly lower than the suggested amount, save your work often and avoid memory-intensive procedures when using the application.

6. Close the Info window. If you have entered a current size that is smaller than suggested, a dialog box asks you to confirm that you want to do this. Click Cancel unless you are sure you want to take the risk.

The next time you start the program it will set aside the amount of memory you have allocated for its use.

Adjusting the Disk Cache

The *disk cache* (or RAM cache, as it is often called) is a portion of your Mac's RAM set aside to speed up frequently used operations such as opening, quitting, and switching between applications. Some operations inside applications can run from the disk cache rather than the hard disk, too. The disk cache holds an image of often-used items on the hard disk. Whenever the Mac needs to read an item from the hard disk, it checks the disk cache first. This all happens behind the scenes, without requiring you to do anything except increase the size of the disk cache for it.

You should set the disk cache to be as big as possible, depending on how much RAM you have and how much of it you require to open applications. Even if the disk cache is a relatively small portion of your total RAM, it can improve your Mac's performance greatly, as long as you keep it at least up to the default settings. To manage your disk cache setting, use the following procedure:

1. Quit any applications you are using.
2. Choose Control Panels from the Apple menu. The Control Panels window opens.

3. Double-click the Memory icon in the Control Panels window. The Memory control panel shown in Figure 7.3 opens, showing the current size of your disk cache.

4. Click the Use Defaults button to see what the default setting is. If your setting is different than the default, the number in the Cache Size box changes.

5. Click the up and down arrows, as shown in Figure 7.3, to adjust the disk cache size. Set the cache to be larger than the default if possible.

6. Close the Memory control panel and close the Control Panels window.

7. Choose Restart from the Special menu. Your Mac shuts down and starts up again. When the desktop returns, the new disk cache setting will be in effect.

The setting you choose for your disk cache size should reflect how much memory you have and how much of that memory you need to open applications. For example, if you have 4Mb of RAM and normally use only one or two applications, increase the disk cache size to 192K

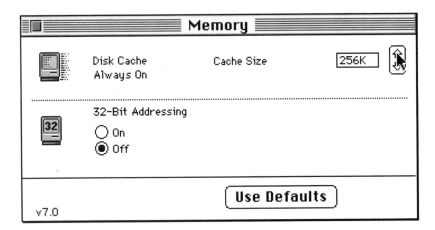

FIGURE 7.3
Increasing the disk cache size

or 256K. If you use a spreadsheet application, you can improve performance with even higher settings. On the other hand, if you have only 2Mb of memory and want to use every bit you can for opening two memory-hungry applications, you can lower the disk cache size one setting below the default (32K instead of 64K). This may slow down your Macintosh, however.

Troubleshooting Problems with Memory

The following sections cover the most common problems you can have with memory and memory allocations in your Mac. Although different solutions are suggested for each problem, keep in mind that the first and often the best solution to memory problems is to install more RAM.

Out of memory messages, or memory bars full.

This is a common problem, and a very unpleasant one. If you see messages telling you your Mac can't do things like recalculating, repaginating, or opening applications because it doesn't have enough memory, you have a RAM shortage. You may not get "Not enough memory" messages. You may notice, when you look in the About This Macintosh window, that your application memory bars are all close to full and the largest unused block of memory is less than 1Mb. This is a warning sign; if you don't take care of the memory shortage, you will soon start getting "Not enough memory" messages. You might even start getting bombs and freeze-ups of the screen. Before things get that bad, try one or more of the following solutions. The easiest solutions are listed first.

- If you can get along without having so many applications open, close one.

- If you are sure you should have more available memory than the largest unused block indicates, quit all your open applications and start them again; you may have isolated bits and pieces of unused memory (fragmented memory, as it is called). Restarting the applications will free the whole block of unused memory. To prevent this fragmentation, always start your largest, most-used applications *before* starting others.
- If you have a huge item such as a complex graphic or a long spreadsheet in the Clipboard, remove it. Select a small item, like a dot or one letter of text, and copy it twice into the Clipboard to flush out the large item (the second copy flushes the large item from the Undo memory, too).
- If you only have 2Mb of RAM, upgrade to 4Mb, or more if possible. That's easy to say, but it may be hard for you to afford. One thing is for sure; you will never regret adding more RAM to your Mac. The more RAM the merrier, as they say.
- If you have lots of extra sounds and fonts in your System file, or if you are running lots of unimportant special customizing files (INITs), delete them to reduce the amount of memory your system software uses. You can also quit any background desk accessories and turn off File Sharing (in the Sharing Setup control panel) if it is on. It always makes sense to keep your System file as small and unencumbered as possible, but if you need to use File Sharing or some special customizing file, you have to make a compromise.
- If you have no other choice, you can reduce your disk cache. Do this as a last resort, especially if it means reducing the cache size below the default setting. See "Adjusting the Disk Cache" earlier in this chapter for details.

If you need to do things that require more memory than you have, the only sure-fire solution is to install more RAM. Even if you don't use every bit of it all the time, you will find that the Mac works better and faster with the extra memory.

You see a message that says your application has unexpectedly quit.

This problem is almost always due to the fact that there is not enough memory alloted to the application. See "Adjusting Application Allocations" earlier in this chapter, and increase the allocation so there is enough for the application and enough extra to hold the largest possible document. If the application has plenty of memory for itself *and* any document you were trying to work with, then the error is due to an internal problem in the application. If you get the same message every time you try to use a certain feature or carry out a certain task, contact the customer support people for the application.

The Mac bombs at startup or as a screen saver or other control panel takes over.

There can be a number of reasons for these bombs, but the most common is that some special customizing files (INITs) or control panels (CDEVs) are overtaxing the specific portion of the Mac's RAM that is set aside for the system software. This portion of RAM, the *system heap*, can expand and contract as needed; you can watch it grow and shrink in the About This Macintosh window. But sometimes special customizing files and control panels can make concurrent demands on the system heap, causing crashes and bomb messages.

To prevent these problems, you can try increasing the size of the system heap with a system heap repair utility, but this may provide only temporary relief, depending on what is causing the memory overload. In some cases, increasing the system heap can actually interfere with the system software's ability to grow and shrink the heap, which will hurt the Mac rather than helping it.

Chapter 7

The more permanent solution to system-heap overload is to remove all of your special customizing files and non-Apple control panels. Then reinstall them one at a time, testing each addition to find out which is the lemon. Some types of control panels just don't get along together, because they are both trying to customize the same elements of the system software. For example, screen capture programs and screen savers are often incompatible, as are menu-customizing programs and macro or keystroke-shortcut programs.

For more information on the compatibility of utilities such as special customizing files and control panels, see Chapter 8.

CHAPTER 8

Customizing Your Mac

This chapter is about customizing your Mac to make it a comfortable, efficient environment to work in. The system software lets you change many aspects of your Mac's operations—from your screen colors to your mouse's double-click speed—by altering the settings in its *control panels*. You can change these settings at any time, or you can leave them at the default settings selected by Apple at the factory.

If you want to customize your Mac even more than you can using the system software alone, you can add various special customizing files that run automatically at startup time. Special customizing files go by several names (INITs, CDEVs, extensions, control panels), and they perform any number of functions, from preventing your screen from "burning in" to organizing your fonts.

Looking Around Your System Folder

You customize your Mac from within the System Folder, so it pays to learn a bit about it before you start fooling around. To open your System Folder, double-click on your hard disk icon, then double-click on the System Folder in your hard disk window. You should see a window that looks like Figure 8.1. The following list describes the different items inside your System Folder, and what goes inside each item:

- System file: Contains fonts and sounds. If you want to use different fonts or different sounds, see "Utilities that Organize Your Resources" in Chapter 17.
- Finder: Contains the system software that makes the desktop work. You can't get in there to look at it. You can't add to it or change it, unless you are a programmer with special programming tools. So leave it alone.
- Apple Menu Items folder: Contains any items you want to have easy access to. You can reach the contents of the Apple Menu Items folder at any time by pulling down the Apple menu. The things that make the most sense to add to this folder, in addition

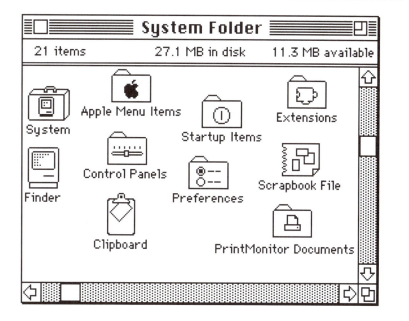

FIGURE 8.1
System Folder contents

to the standard items such as the control panels and the Alarm Clock, are other handy desk accessories, aliases for much-used applications and control panels, and small, much-used documents, such as tips you want to remember.

- Startup Items folder: Contains the items you want to have start up automatically each time you turn the Mac on. You can put applications or their aliases in it, or you can put in documents or special customizing files that do things like automatically empty the Trash at startup.
- Control Panels folder: Contains small programs that change the look, sound, and behavior of the desktop, monitor, mouse, and keyboard of your Mac. You can also add special customizing files to the Control Panels folder.
- Preferences: Contains the preferences files for applications, so that each time you start one, it comes up looking like it was when you left it.
- Scrapbook and Clipboard files: Contain the things you save in the Scrapbook and the last thing you cut or copied to the Clipboard.
- PrintMonitor Documents folder: Holds documents for printing in the background (for LaserWriters and other compatible printers with memory only).

Specifying Startup Applications and Documents

If you use the same application every day, you can tell your Macintosh to open it for you automatically when you start the computer up.

You can even pick a document to open at startup. Use the following procedure to specify items for startup:

1. Open the System Folder. The files and folders inside it are displayed.
2. Open the folder containing the application or document you want to specify for startup.
3. Drag the item you want to specify for startup into the Startup Items folder. If you want to open an application at startup, it is usually best to make an alias of the application and place this in the Startup Items folder. This saves memory in the System Folder and allows you to leave your applications in folders that have the supplementary files they need to run.

The item or items you put in the Startup Items folder will be opened automatically the next time you start up your Mac.

If you ever want to stop an item from opening at startup, open the Startup Items folder in the System Folder and drag the icon for the startup item out of both the Startup Items folder *and* the System Folder. The next time you start up your Macintosh, the item will not open automatically.

 ## Using Special Customizing Files

You can add special utilities to your System Folder to do a number of valuable chores as you start up your Mac and use it. These files are sometimes referred to as special customizing files, or *INITs*, because they become part of the initialization process the computer goes through when you start it up. These files do *not* belong in the Startup Items folder. They belong in either the Extensions or Control Panels folders, depending on how they work.

Special customizing files that work in the background and never need adjusting are usually *system software extensions.* There are extensions that do simple things, such as Quote Init, which substitutes curly quotes for the standard Macintosh vertical ones. There are also extensions that perform complex jobs, such as Disinfectant, which guards against viruses.

Any special customizing file that you can control or adjust by making settings is a *control panel.* You can look through your control panels at any time by choosing Control Panels from the Apple menu. You can add control panels that do many different jobs, and adjust them to do their jobs in ways that suit your needs.

You can obtain the more common extensions and control panels from software dealers, or by ordering them from the catalogs that post listings in popular Macintosh periodicals such as *Macworld* and *MacUser.* New and more esoteric utilities of this kind can be obtained from electronic bulletin boards of user groups, or from online information services such as CompuServe and America Online. Once you have obtained a special customizing file that is either an extension or a control panel, use the following procedure to install it:

1. Check the file to make sure it is compatible with your system software. Either contact the maker of the special customizing file, or use the Compatibility Checker you received with your system software. It is critical that you have special customizing files that are updated to work with the version of the Macintosh system software you are using.

2. Insert and open the disk. If necessary, open the folder with the icon of the special customizing file you want to install. Then open your hard disk window.

3. Drag the special customizing file icon to the *closed* System Folder (do not open the System Folder window and drag the special customizing file into it). A dialog box appears, telling you that

the file you are installing must be stored in the Extensions or Control Panels folder.

4. Click OK in the dialog box. The file is copied into the appropriate folder inside your System Folder.

Some extensions do not work properly if they are inside a folder in the System Folder. If your Macintosh does not start after installing an extension, or if the extension does not work properly, hold the Shift key down while starting the computer (this disables all extensions), and then move the extension from the Extensions folder to the System Folder itself. Restart the computer and try out the extension. If you still have trouble, see the "Troubleshooting" section at the end of this chapter.

If you find that you do not need a particular special customizing file, or if one causes system problems or problems with an application, you can remove the special customizing file from the System Folder. If you are not sure which folder the file is in, choose Find from the File menu and search for the file. When you find the file, drag it out of the System Folder completely. You cannot throw the file in the Trash until you have started your Mac again; startup files remain in use until you shut down and start up again.

 ## Using Control Panels

You can change the way your Mac looks, sounds, and behaves at any time by choosing Control Panels from the Apple menu, then changing the settings in any of the different control panel windows.

You follow the same basic procedure to open a control panel window for any setting:

1. Choose the Control Panels command from the Apple menu at the far left end of your menu bar. The Control Panels window

opens and displays the icons for all the things you can customize on your Mac.

2. Double-click the icon for the item you want to change.
3. When the panel's window opens, make the settings you want. Close each panel's window before opening another.

For example, you can double-click the General Controls icon in the Control Panels window to see settings for basic desktop items. The General Controls window displays several panels, which contain dialog boxes for the different settings. In Figure 8.2, the hour setting in the Time panel is selected.

The following sections cover all of the most commonly used control panels and their settings. The Labels settings are covered in Chapter 5, "Using Folders to Organize Your Files." For information on specialized settings such as Easy Access and Sharing Setup, see the *Macintosh Reference* manual you received with your Macintosh.

FIGURE 8.2
The Control Panels window and the General Controls window

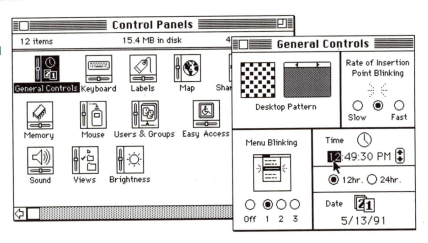

General Controls Settings

You can make the following adjustments to your Macintosh environment by changing settings in the dialog boxes of the General Controls window:

- Change the desktop pattern by clicking the small white bar above the unenlarged pattern, or by modifying the enlarged pattern. Click in the unenlarged pattern to see your choice take effect on the desktop immediately. *Recommended setting:* Leave gray or solid color pattern.
- Change the rate of insertion point blinking by clicking in the *radio buttons* for either Slow or Fast blinking. *Recommended setting:* Medium blinking rate.
- Change the number of times a menu command blinks when you select it by clicking in the radio buttons. *Recommended setting:* 1 or 2.
- Set the time by clicking on the various time increments, then clicking or pressing on the up and down arrows to correct the time.
- Choose the 12- or 24-hour clock by clicking in the appropriate radio button.
- Set the date by clicking on the various time increments, then clicking or pressing on the up and down arrows that appear.

Of all the General Controls settings, the time and date are probably the only ones you need to adjust. Experiment with the desktop pattern if you want, but you will probably find that a simple, shaded background causes the least eye strain.

Brightness Control Settings

This control panel appears on Macs that do not support color and do not have a brightness control knob built into the monitor. If you don't see the control panel icon, adjust the brightness of your monitor with the knob that is either on the side of the monitor or under the front of the screen. To use the control panel, you double-click the Brightness icon in the Control Panels window; a horizontal slider for brightness adjustment appears in a dialog box.

Drag the slider to the right for a brighter screen, to the left for darker. *Recommended setting*: Barely bright enough so your screen is slightly brighter than whatever is behind the computer; a strong contrast between screen brightness and ambient light can strain your eyes.

Color Control Settings

If your monitor (display screen) and your Mac are capable of showing colors, there will be a Monitors control panel (shown in Figure 8.3) and a Color control panel. First double-click the Monitors icon to see a dialog box that lets you switch your monitor from shades of gray to color. If you have more than one monitor, click the icon for the one you want to adjust in the lower part of the dialog box.

To see black and white only, you click the Grays radio button, then click Black & White in the list box. If your monitor can display shades of gray, click the number of shades you want to see.

To see color, you click the Colors radio button, then, in the list box, click the number of colors you want displayed. In most cases, 256 colors works best. If you have a special high-resolution monitor and a color expansion card, you may want to display more colors, but some applications will not be able to take advantage of the colors anyway. If you have a Mac with a slow CPU, you may want to choose fewer colors; the more colors, the slower the Mac runs when doing graphic-intensive work.

FIGURE 8.3
Monitors control panel, set for black and white

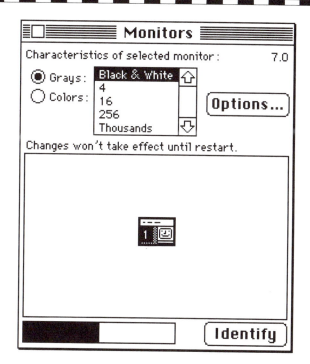

After turning on color in the Monitors control panel, open the Color control panel shown in Figure 8.4 to select highlight and window trim colors. Press on the little triangles in the Highlight and Window color pop-up menus to see the choices of color, gray, or black and white.

If none of the colors suit you, choose Other from either pop-up menu and use the color wheel to come up with your own custom color. You can get anything from hi-liter yellow to chocolate brown, but remember that it's hard to read text inside a dark or deeply saturated color. *Recommended setting:* Gray highlight, and whatever window trim

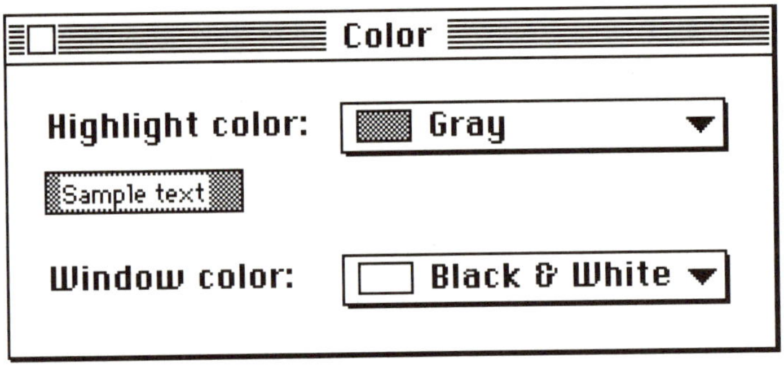

FIGURE 8.4

The Color control panel

you like (I prefer black and white to flashy colored window trim, because my eyes do better with the plain vanilla shapes you get if you choose black and white).

To change the color of your desktop, you open the General Controls panel after turning color on in the Monitors control panel. You'll find a color bar under the desktop patterns (see Figure 8.5). You click a color to select it, then drag the pointer around in the magnified view of the desktop pattern to fill in all the dots. Then click in the nonmagnified view of the desktop on the right side of the panel and the new desktop color will go into effect.

If you want to make a custom color, double-click any of the color squares in the color bar, then click a color in the color wheel that appears (see Figure 8.6). Drag the scroll box up and down to change the brightness of the colors.

When you have the color you want, click OK, then drag the pointer around in the magnified view of the desktop pattern to fill in all the dots. Click in the unmagnified view to put your new color into effect.

FIGURE 8.5
Color bar in General Controls panel

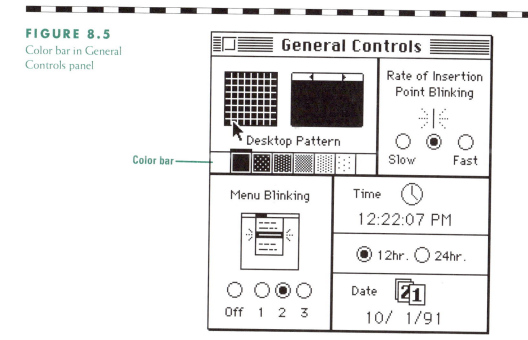

Keyboard Control Settings

Double-click the Keyboard icon to see the settings for your keyboard. Boxes appear with settings for key repeats and domestic or international keyboard designs. You can make the following adjustments:

- Change the rate at which a key repeats if you hold it down. Click in the radio buttons for a slower or faster rate. *Recommended setting:* Second fastest.
- Set how long you have to hold down a key before it repeats, or turn the repeat feature off. Click in a radio button to make a choice. *Recommended setting:* Second shortest.
- Set the keyboard to Domestic or International; if there are other options, they appear in the central panel of the window.

FIGURE 8.6
Color wheel

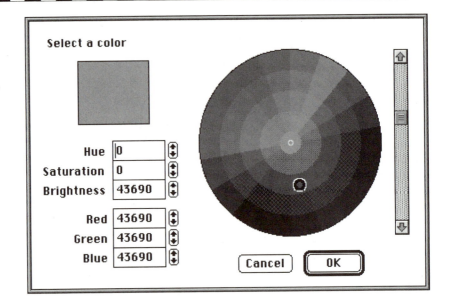

If you are a seasoned typist but tend to rest your fingers on the keyboard, turn off the repeat feature.

Mouse Control Settings

Double-click the Mouse icon to see the settings for double-clicking and tracking on your mouse. Click in the appropriate radio button to select the speed at which you want the mouse to track, and the speed required for double-clicking. *Recommended settings:* Second fastest for both.

Sound Control Settings

Double-click the Sound icon to see settings for speaker volume and the type of sound you hear when the Macintosh alerts you (normally a beep). Set the Speaker Volume slider so the volume of the alert sound suits you. Scroll through the list of possible sounds and click on the one that bothers you the least.

If you want other sounds, anything from laughter to fierce growls, you can obtain a sound-installing utility and add whatever alert sound you want. If your Mac has a microphone, you can even record your own sounds and add them to the list. You can also remove sounds when you get sick of them. *Recommended settings:* Volume at 1 or 2. The alert sound is up to you, but keep in mind that anybody else using your computer has to put up with the sound you select.

Views Control Settings

Double-click the Views icon to see a dialog box (shown in Figure 8.7) for changing the look and the types of information in list views

FIGURE 8.7
The Views control panel

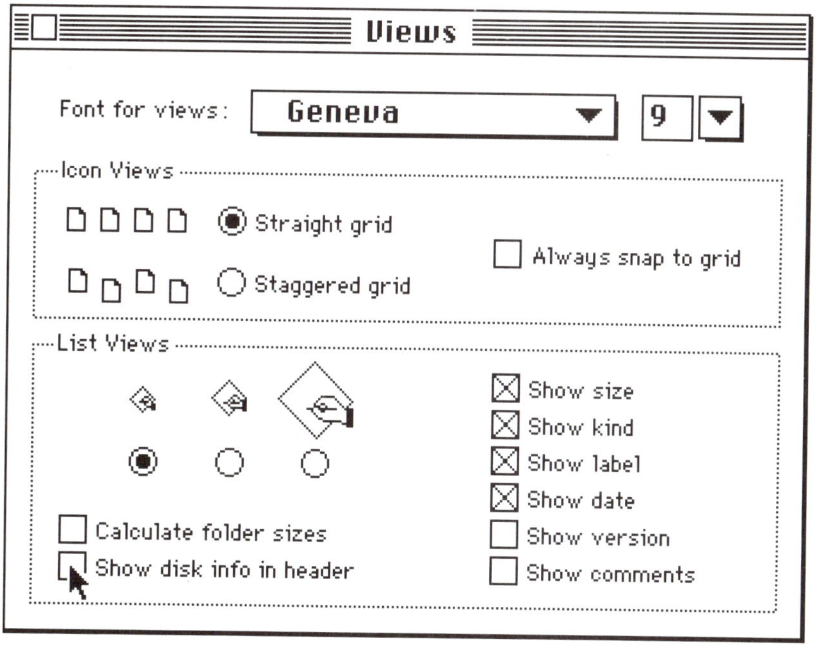

that appear in Finder windows. For more information on views, see "Changing Your Desktop View" in Chapter 4.

You can make the following settings in the Views control panel:

- Font for views: Allows you to set a font and font size for all views. *Recommended setting:* Geneva 9-point, because it is the clearest font at the smallest standard size, allowing you to see the maximum information in a window at one time.

- Icon Views: Allows you to set for staggered or straight grid and turn snap-to-grid on or off. *Recommended setting:* Straight grid, snap-to-grid off. If you use full icon views in most windows, opt for staggered grid so you can pack more icons with large titles into each window.

- List Views: Allows you to set size of icons displayed, set which information you want listed, turn folder size calculation and disk information header on and off. *Recommended setting:* Smallest icons in lists (allows maximum information in window at one time). Turn on Show size, kind, and date. Turn on disk info header if you are running short of disk space; turn on folder size calculation only when you are short of disk space and you want to see which folders need cleaning out. Folder size calculation slows the Finder on older, slower Macs.

Of course, if you have special needs or tastes, you can use settings other than the recommended ones. For example, if you have dozens of similar documents in a folder and you want to distinguish between a few "hot" ones you are working on and all the "cool" ones that aren't important anymore, you can click the Show label box in the Views control panel, then select the documents in the Finder, and choose Hot or Cool from the Label menu to tag them. If you list these documents in a window and choose the by Label option from the View menu, the Hot documents will be neatly separated from all the Cool ones, and listed first. You can even open the Labels control panel and make up new labels of your own.

Memory Control Settings

Double-click on the Memory icon to see a dialog box for setting the RAM cache, which is the amount of random access memory (RAM) reserved for used operations and much-used data. It speeds up your work considerably. Click the up and down arrows to raise or lower the number of bytes. *Recommended setting:* 32K per megabyte of total RAM in your Mac. For more information, see Chapter 7, "Checking and Adjusting Memory."

Closing Control Panels

When you have made all the adjustments to your environment that you want, click in the close box in the last control window, then click the close box in the Control Panels window. You do not have to do anything else for the settings to take effect. All settings are stored in a special part of the Macintosh's memory (PRAM) that is not lost at shutdown, and so they remain in effect even when you turn the computer off and turn it back on.

Customizing Icons

If you want, you can make your own icon for a folder or file you use often, so it will stand out on the desktop. Just use the following procedure:

1. Create or copy a small image in a paint or draw program (for information on graphics applications, see Chapter 10). Images that are a size of about 35 by 40 pixels work best.

2. Select the image and copy it to the Clipboard by choosing Copy from the Edit menu.
3. Go to the desktop and select the folder or file you want to assign the new icon to.
4. Choose Get Info from the File menu. The Info window opens.
5. Select the file or folder's old icon in the upper left corner of the Info window.
6. Choose Paste from the Edit menu. Your new icon appears.

You can also copy an icon from another file or folder's Info window and paste it into the Info window of your target file or folder, but remember that you may confuse the icons of the target and the source on the desktop.

Troubleshooting Customization Problems

The following subsections are the problems you may have when customizing your Mac.

Just started the Mac, and everything looks different.

You just turned the Mac on, and when the desktop came up, it didn't look right. The things you have customized, like the desktop pattern, the location of windows and icons, and the list views inside windows, are different. The problem is that your Mac is running different, outdated system software. Unless you have just installed new system software and removed all the preference files from your previous system software, you must have gotten two System Folders onto your hard disk, or you must have started from a floppy startup disk.

To remove an extra System Folder from your hard disk, you must start up from a floppy disk such as the Disk Tools one that you received with your system software. Then you look at the contents of the two System Folders on your hard disk and remove the one that is not set up the way you want it. Drag the whole folder to the Trash, or copy it to a floppy disk. Then restart your Mac without inserting the floppy start-up disk.

The screen went dark.

If you have a screen saver, just press any key or move or click the mouse. If that doesn't help, see "Screen stays dark" in the "Troubleshooting" section of Chapter 1.

A control panel is missing.

Either your Mac is not capable of doing the things that the control panel deals with (you won't have a Color control panel if your Mac is black and white, for example) or you have not installed the software for the feature that the control panel deals with (network software must be installed, for example, before the Sharing Setup and other networking control panels show up).

A column is missing from a list view window.

You are looking at a list view, and one of the columns is gone, such as the Label column, or the Size or Kind column. To bring back the column, you open the Views control panel and click on the appropriate check box. If you want to see the sizes of folders as well as files, you have to click on the Calculate folder sizes check box.

New control panel or extension causing problems.

Your Mac won't start, or you have numerous unexplained problems (anything from lost functions to bombs) in applications and in the Finder after installing a control panel or an extension. If an extension causes problems in both the Extensions folder and the System Folder, or if a control panel causes problems, try changing its name. In some cases, just changing the name of an extension so it begins with *A* or *Z* will solve the problems. During initialization, two extensions may be clashing; if you change the name of one, it will start earlier or later than the other.

If neither moving an extension nor changing its name solves your problems with it, you have to remove the extension or control panel from the System Folder, as explained in "Using Special Customizing Files" in this chapter.

If you are installing several extensions, it is best to install one at a time. Then test your most-used applications and the Finder between installations, so if you have problems, you can remove just the last-installed extension.

If you want to use more than two or three extensions and control panels, obtain a utility to help you manage them, such as INITPicker or Extensions Manager. Such utilities let you select the files you want to run either at startup or in a control panel. Some also tell you how much memory each file is using and protect against clashes between extensions.

PART three

Applications for the Mac

The third part of this book describes the major tools you can use for your work on the Mac. Each chapter introduces one type of tool and tells what features make it especially useful. Taken together, the different chapters cover the full range of types of work that you can do on a Macintosh, from writing a memo to drawing a logo, from creating a spreadsheet to laying out the pages of a newsletter.

In each chapter, there are guidelines to help you find the best application for your specific needs and some recommendations of specific products that are well-known and well-liked. For each type of application, one or more examples are given of how to do the basic tasks of opening a document, entering things, correcting things, saving your work, and printing. Using the basic principles from the examples, you can quickly master the application that's best for your specific type of work.

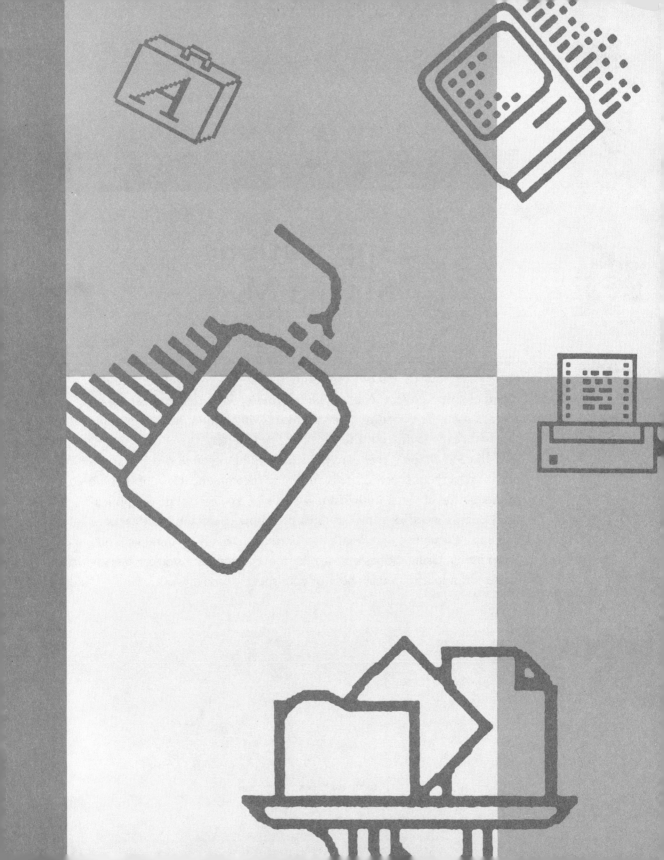

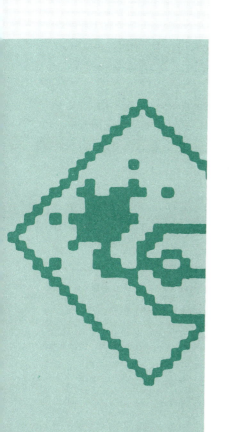

CHAPTER 9

Word Processors

Word processors are tools you use to write text and format it so it looks right. Good word processing applications make it easy to write what you want to, whether you want to write something simple or complex, and they make it easy to change the format and style of the text so it looks just like you want it to.

Since none of us writes porfectly, a word processor should also help you to select, edit, move, and remove text. Fortunately, the Mac interface makes all these jobs easy. All the application has to do is use the Mac to good advantage.

Some word processors can do much more, though. They can check your spelling, for instance, and tell you that *porfectly* should be *perfectly*. They can let you change the format of your text with a single command. They can show two separate parts of your text in split windows. They can let you put in things like pictures, tables, and lists. Some can let you transfer graphics files into the text, or let you translate text into formats used by other word processing applications, like DOS ones, for example. They can let you outline your work, and change the outline as you work. Similarly, they can let you keep a running index, a table of contents, or even footnotes that move with the text that they refer to.

If you're lucky, you can get one that lets you make custom commands and keystrokes to use as shortcuts for the tasks you perform most often. It's a happy day when you discover a word processor that takes the drudgery out of repetitive work.

Which Word Processor for You?

There are so many word processors that you can go crazy trying to shop for one, so it pays to do a little thinking before you wander down to the local software shop. First, decide what you expect to be writing, then look at the recommendations below and decide which kind of word processor comes closest to filling your needs.

Word Processors for Big Writing Jobs

If you write long documents with changing formats and lots of lists and tables, try Microsoft Word; it has the power to do all kinds of writing tasks, and it is fast and reliable. Some of the powerful features are a bit hard to use, but in the newer versions of Word, the power is more accessible. There are great ways to change the style of your text as you write, and ways to customize text in a given style after you have finished the writing. There are handy ways to find text, move text, and change the font style and size of text. You can also put text into tables, around pictures, and just about anywhere else on the page you want it. And there are always shortcuts, shortcuts, shortcuts.

Microsoft Word has been the leading word processor for Macs for so long that many other applications, including DOS ones, can accept files from it. Word can import data from lots of other applications, too.

If you work on a network with lots of DOS machines and people who write with WordPerfect, you can use WordPerfect for the Mac, too. It is powerful and fairly easy to use, but it doesn't let you do as many different things as Word, and it is noticeably slower when carrying out some common tasks.

A Word Processor for Everyday Jobs

If you write mostly short letters and reports, and you don't have to compose long or complicated documents with lots of style changes, consider MacWrite II. It is wonderfully easy to use, and the features it has are all readily available, so you don't have to wander around in a maze of menus and dialog boxes looking for the option you need. You just write, edit, and format your text with the tools that are right at hand, and MacWrite II never gets in your way.

MacWrite II was one of the first applications for the Mac, and it has a fresh, clear feel to it that is still hard to beat. Since it formed the first standard for Mac word processing, you can transfer many types of data and translate many different documents into and out of it.

The only problem with MacWrite II is that there are definite limitations to the features. You can't change most of the formatting with styles commands, and you can't make tables easily, for instance. And there is no way to create shortcuts for often-repeated tasks.

Bargain Word Processors

If you only need to do a few simple jobs with a word processor, you don't have to spend hundreds of dollars on an application. For writing letters and short memos or reports, you can use WriteNow; it is fast, easy to learn, and powerful enough to take care of a surprising number of basic writing needs. It also has a number of features you normally expect in more complicated applications, such as a spelling checker and a word finder that can search forwards and backwards.

If you are really a penny-pincher you can use TeachText, which comes with your system software. It has almost no features, but you can write a simple letter and edit the text in the most basic fashion. Just don't expect to do any fancy formatting, spell checking, or much of anything else. There are other small word processing applications that you can use for notes, letters, and address lists, but they are a far cry from Write-Now or MacWrite II.

The bargain word processors are not covered in the rest of this chapter, but you can use the sections on Microsoft Word and MacWrite II as guidelines, and read your application's user manual for details.

Using Microsoft Word

The following sections describe how to create a simple document using Microsoft Word. You can follow the procedures just as they are written and make a document like the example, or you can use them as guidelines to create your own document. The basic steps of opening a document, creating and editing text, and saving and printing your work are the same for all kinds of documents, from short memos like the sample to full-length manuscripts. Once you have become familiar with the basic steps, see the Microsoft Word *User's Guide* for details about the application's specialized features.

Opening a Document

Take one of the following actions to open a new document in Microsoft Word, depending on your situation:

- If you have not started Microsoft Word, double-click the Word icon, as shown in Figure 9.1, or an alias for it.

FIGURE 9.1
The Microsoft Word icon

Chapter 9

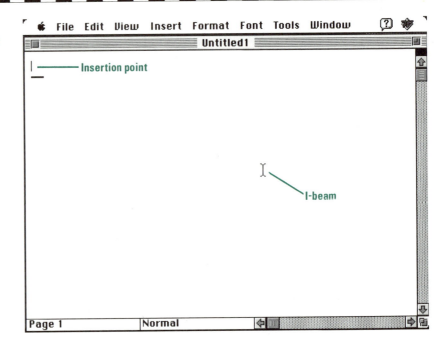

FIGURE 9.2
The Microsoft Word document window

- If you have started Microsoft Word and are looking at an existing document, choose New from the File menu.

The Word document window, shown in Figure 9.2, opens with menu titles in the menu bar and the Word icon at the right end of the menu bar. In the title bar of the window is the name "Untitled1." This name will change the first time you save the document and give it a title.

Nothing appears inside the window but a vertical line blinking near the top left corner and a thick horizontal line beneath the blinking one. The blinking vertical line is your *insertion point*. The thick horizontal line marks the end of the document. You may also see a vertical line with sprouts at the end; this is the *I-beam*, a special kind of pointer you will soon learn to use in Word.

Entering Text

To enter text at the insertion point, you just start typing. Use the following hints to help you write the example memo shown in Figure 9.3.

1. After each short line at the top of the memo, press the Return key to go on to the next line.
2. Press Return to create a blank line between lines of text.
3. When typing a paragraph of text, do not press Return at the end of each line; Word *wraps* the text for you, breaking each line at the right margin.
4. You do not need to enter two spaces between the end of each sentence and the beginning of the next. Word spaces the sentence breaks for you when it prints the file.

FIGURE 9.3
An example of a memo written in Word

July 5

To: Shotput Development Team
From: Big Al
Subject: Design Considerations

Why do all of you keep griping about the shape of the new product? It seems perfect to me, and it has a track record. Besides, it is the most efficient shape for a heavy product. Forget Matt's shape. Power putters will never buy a 16-pound shot shaped like a quiche; it's just too skinny.

Let's meet at Basta Pasta for lunch at one. Bring your ideas for alternate shapes. Just don't bring up quiche again. The designer and I haven't settled on a color yet. I'm willing to consider anything but pastels.

Chapter 9

Editing Text

You use the special *I-beam* pointer, the vertical line with sprouts at the end, to add to and edit the text you have entered. To edit existing text, you need to select it first. This is the most basic rule in text processing: *Select first, then operate.*

- To add text, as shown in Figure 9.4, move the I-beam pointer to where you want to add the text and click. Then type the text in.
- To replace text, as shown in Figure 9.5, first select it by dragging the I-beam over it. Then type in the new text.
- To delete text, as shown in Figure 9.6, first select it by dragging the I-beam over it. Then press the Delete key.
- To move text to a nearby location, use the drag-and-drop method shown in Figure 9.7. First, select the text by dragging the I-beam over it, and move the I-beam into the selected area so it turns into a pointer, as shown in the top panel of Figure 9.7. Then drag the pointer and the flickering insertion point that comes with it to the place where you want to insert the text. Release the mouse button to drop the text into place. (To move a block of text to a distant location, see the next section of this chapter.)
- To copy a block of text, use the drag-and-drop method, but hold down the ⌘ key as you drag the selected text.
- To increase the size of a block of selected text, move the I-beam to the new endpoint for the block you want to select. Then Shift-click (hold the Shift key down and click the mouse button) to extend the selection.
- To select lines of text, move the I-beam to the left of the text, until it becomes an arrow pointing to the right. Click to select a single line, double-click to select a paragraph.

- To undo a small typing or spelling mistake, you back up over it and retype the text. Use your Delete key to back up. To undo larger mistakes, choose Undo from the Edit menu. The command in the menu changes to reflect your last action. For example, if you just entered some text, the command is Undo Typing.

FIGURE 9.4
Adding text

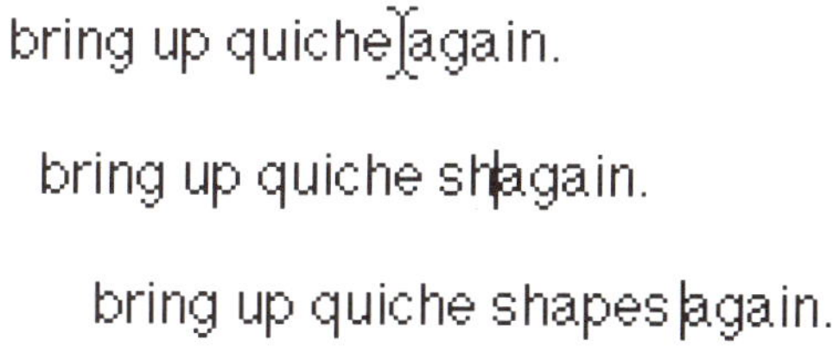

bring up quiche]again.

bring up quiche sh]again.

bring up quiche shapes]again.

FIGURE 9.5
Replacing text

just too skinny].

just too fl].

just too flat].

FIGURE 9.6
Deleting text

lunch]at one.

lunch at one].

lunch].

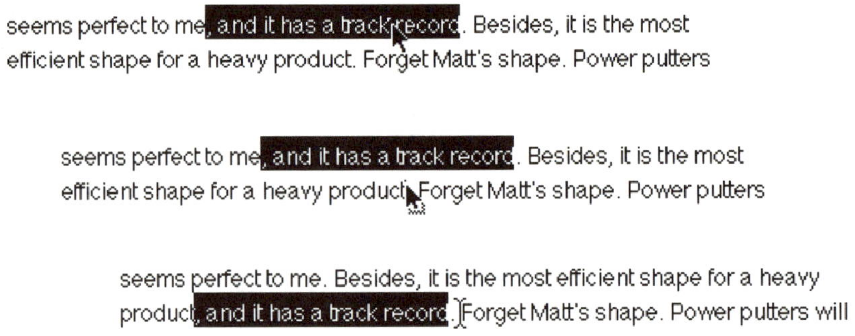

FIGURE 9.7
Dragging and dropping selected text in Word

seems perfect to me, and it has a track record. Besides, it is the most efficient shape for a heavy product. Forget Matt's shape. Power putters

seems perfect to me, and it has a track record. Besides, it is the most efficient shape for a heavy product. Forget Matt's shape. Power putters

seems perfect to me. Besides, it is the most efficient shape for a heavy product, and it has a track record. Forget Matt's shape. Power putters will

Moving and Replacing Text via the Clipboard

Word provides several commands in the Edit menu to move and replace blocks of text that are not near each other. These commands take text out of your document, hold it temporarily in the *Clipboard*, a special storage place in the Macintosh's memory, and put it back into your document. Use the following Edit commands to handle any large block of text you have selected:

- To remove a selected text block from a document and store it temporarily in the Clipboard, choose Cut from the Edit menu.
- To make a duplicate of a selected text block and store it temporarily in the Clipboard, choose Copy from the Edit menu.
- To replace a selected text block with a block you have just cut or copied into the Clipboard, choose Paste from the Edit menu.
- To move a selected text block to a different place, choose Cut from the Edit menu. Then scroll to the location where you want the text to appear, place the insertion point, and choose Paste from the Edit menu.

- To delete a block *without* storing it in the Clipboard, choose Clear from the Edit menu. This is the same as pressing the Delete key.

When using the Clipboard, keep in mind that it can only hold one item at a time. For example, if you copy a large text block into the Clipboard so you can paste it somewhere else, but then cut two words of text before pasting the large block, you lose the large block of text. On the other hand, if you copy text into the Clipboard, you can paste it into your document in several different places; text stays in the Clipboard no matter how many times you paste. The only ways to lose the text in the Clipboard are cutting and copying new text or shutting down your Mac. For more information on the Clipboard and how to cut and paste things, see Chapter 15.

Using the Ruler to Format Text

The Word ruler allows you to make formatting changes to your documents visually. By dragging and clicking on the markers and icons shown in Figure 9.8, you can set or change your document's indents, tabs, and line spacing. If you make settings with the ruler before you type a block of text, the block will show all your ruler settings. If you want to change the format of a block of text you have already typed, select the whole block, then make your ruler settings.

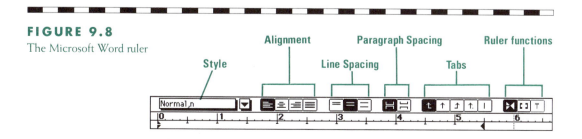

FIGURE 9.8
The Microsoft Word ruler

To get a sense of how the ruler works, let's change the first-line indent of our shotput memo:

1. If the ruler is not showing at the top of the document window, choose Ruler from the View menu.
2. Select both paragraphs of the memo.
3. Drag the upper left indent marker to the half-inch mark to set the indent for the first line of each paragraph. Your memo should now look like Figure 9.9.

The other settings on the Word ruler work much like the one we just experimented with. The following list tells how to make each setting:

- Drag the lower indent marker in or out to change the indentation of the left edge of the text. The large triangle marker at the right end of the ruler sets the indentation of the right edge of text. With all the body text of the memo selected, move the indent markers in and out and watch what happens to the body

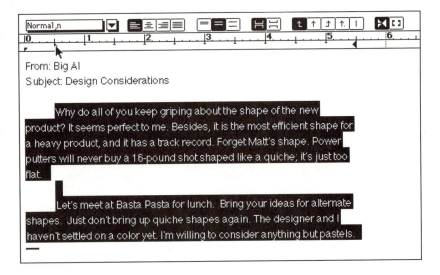

FIGURE 9.9
Changing the first-line indent

text. When you move the left indent marker, notice that the first-line indent marker always moves too, so you keep your first-line indent.

- Drag a tab marker to each point on the ruler where you want to set a tab. There are left align, center, and right align tabs, as well as a tab for entering a decimal point. To remove tab settings, drag the marker off the bottom of the ruler. In the sample memo, you can set a tab for a sign-off at the end, as shown in Figure 9.10. Place the insertion point after the last word in the memo and then drag a left align tab (which is selected by default) to about the 4-inch mark on the ruler. Then press Return to start a new line, press the Tab key, and type a sign-off, like **Yours, Big Al**.

- Click on the different alignment icons to align the text at the left margin (as shown), or to center the text, or align it on the right margin. Try selecting the date at the top of the memo and clicking the icon for centered text (the second alignment icon from the left).

- Click on the different line spacing icons to select narrow, medium, or wide spacing between lines of text. Typically, with 12-point fonts, the choices are 12, 18, and 24 points. To see what the memo looks like with narrow spacing, select all of the body text and click the narrow spacing icon (the one on the left).

- There are buttons at the right end of the Word ruler that change the ruler's functions. Click on the fat parentheses button and you can drag two margin icons to change the limits for the margins. Click the fat T button to change the margins and column widths for a table. See your Word documentation for details on tables; they work well in Word.

- There is also a text box at the left end of the Word ruler that shows the style you are now using. Press on the little down-pointing triangle next to the box to see a list of other styles. You can choose a style and see its ruler; at the same time, the current paragraph changes to that style. See the Word *User's Guide* for more information on styles.

If you select a large block of text and notice that the ruler becomes grayed, it means that there are different formats mixed in the selected text block. To find out where the exceptions are, reduce the size of the selected block by Shift-clicking. If you reduce the block by a few lines

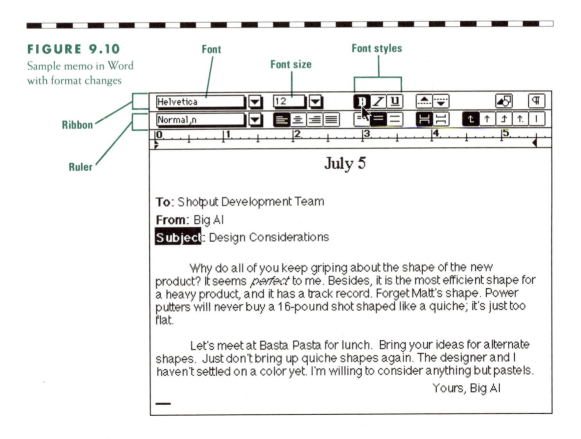

FIGURE 9.10
Sample memo in Word with format changes

at a time and watch for the ruler to change, you can quickly locate the problem. Word has hidden formatting characters that you can see if you need them to find a formatting change. Just choose Show ¶ from the View menu in order to display the hidden characters.

Changing Text Style

To change text from a plain appearance to bold or other styles, first select the text, then choose the style you want from the Format menu. Make sure you don't confuse the Style command in the Format menu with text styles; you can change all kinds of things with the Style command, as explained in the Word documentation.

For an example of a style change in the sample memo, let's give emphasis to the word *perfect* in the first paragraph.

1. Select *perfect* and the space before it.
2. Then choose Italic from the Format menu. The word becomes italicized.
3. If the end of the word leans over and runs into the next one, just select the last couple of letters and the space, type the letters over, and hold down the Option key as you press the spacebar. That makes a bigger space on the screen, like the one shown in Figure 9.10.

To deitalicize a selected word if you change your mind about emphasizing it, choose Plain Text from the Format menu.

You can change the font or font size of text by using the same method and selecting the new font or size you want from the Font menu.

You can also use the *ribbon* (a band that goes across the top of the window like the ruler) with buttons for changing font, font style and size. Press ⌘-Option-R to see the ribbon at the top of the document window, as in Figure 9.10. Let's use the ribbon to make some changes to the memo.

1. Select the date.
2. Click on the downward-pointing triangle next to the font box and choose Times from the drop-down list.
3. Click on the triangle next to the font size box and choose 18 point from the list.
4. Select each of the first words of the header lines (*To*, *From*, and *Subject*) and click the Bold button in the ribbon. Your memo should now look like Figure 9.10.

These are all little touches, but they can add strength and clarity to your work. For more information on them, and on the other icons in the ribbon and ruler, see the Microsoft Word *User's Guide*.

After you have changed the text style, font, or font size of a word, keep in mind that any text you enter immediately after that word adopts the changed text style. So if you put the insertion point at the end of an italicized word, all new text you enter will be italicized, too. To prevent this, choose Plain Text from the Format menu after placing the insertion point.

Saving and Printing a Word Document

To protect your work, save it often, like every ten to fifteen minutes. All you have to do is choose Save from the File menu, or press ⌘-S. The first time you save a document, you must name it and choose where to place it in your folder hierarchy. For more information on this, see "Saving Your Work on a Document" in Chapter 4.

To print a hard copy of your document, first save it, then choose Print from the File menu, or press ⌘-P. The Print dialog box opens. Unless you want to do something special, leave all the settings as they are and click the Print button (or just press the Return key) to start printing. If you have a LaserWriter or compatible printer that allows background printing, the PrintMonitor will take over your print job in a moment or two, and you can go right back to work while printing proceeds. For more information on printing, see Chapter 3.

 ## Using MacWrite II

Using MacWrite II is a lot like using Word. If you've worked through the exercises in Word, you'll notice that many procedures are identical in the two programs. As before, you can follow the procedures just as they are written and make a document like the example, or you can use them as guidelines to create your own original document. Once you have become familiar with the basic steps, see the MacWrite II *User's Guide*. It is a superb manual, a shining example of clarity and good organization.

Opening a Document

Take one of the following actions to open a new document in MacWrite II, depending on your situation:

1. If you have not started MacWrite II, double-click the MacWrite II icon, as shown in Figure 9.11, or an alias for it.
2. If you have started MacWrite II and are looking at an existing document, choose New from the File menu.

A window opens with the MacWrite II menu titles in the menu bar and the MacWrite II icon at the right end of the menu bar, as shown in Figure 9.12. In the title bar of the window is the name "Document1."

FIGURE 9.11
The MacWrite II icon

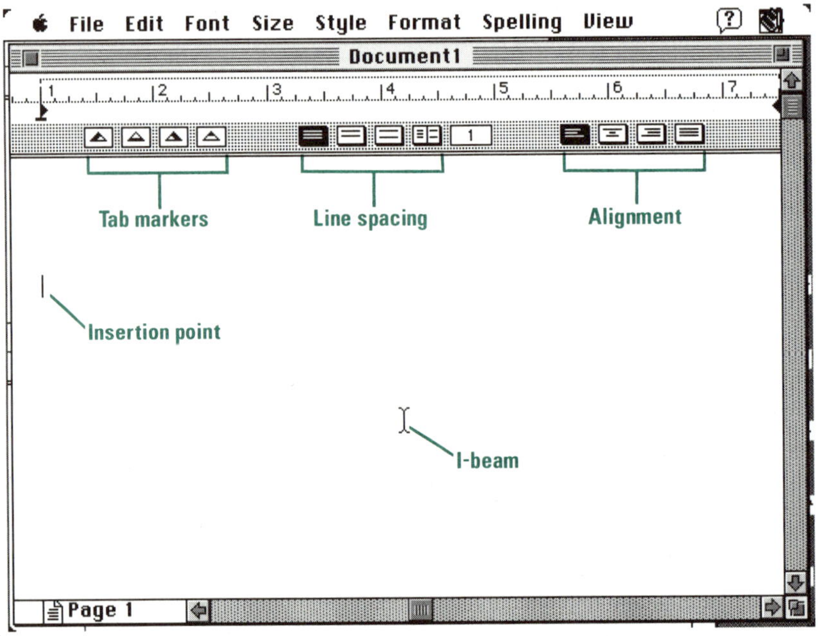

FIGURE 9.12
The MacWrite II document window

[Screenshot of MacWrite II document window showing menu bar with File, Edit, Font, Size, Style, Format, Spelling, View; Document1 window with ruler, Tab markers, Line spacing, Alignment controls, Insertion point, and I-beam cursor labeled; Page 1 indicator at bottom]

This name will change the first time you save the document and give it a title.

When the window first opens, all you see in it is a vertical line blinking near the left side and a cursor that is a line with sprouts at the end. The blinking vertical line is your *insertion point*. The line with sprouts is a special kind of pointer you will soon learn to use in MacWrite.

Entering Text

To enter text in MacWrite, simply type at the keyboard, and your text appears at the insertion point. Write the example memo shown in Figure 9.13; the following hints may help.

FIGURE 9.13

An example of a memo written in MacWrite II

July 5

To: Shotput Development Team
From: Big Al
Subject: Design Considerations

Why do all of you keep griping about the shape of the new product? It seems perfect to me, and it has a track record. Besides, it is the most efficient shape for a heavy product. Forget Matt's shape. Power putters will never buy a 16-pound shot shaped like a quiche; it's just too skinny.

Let's meet at Basta Pasta for lunch at one. Bring your ideas for alternate shapes. Just don't bring up quiche again. The designer and I haven't settled on a color yet. I'm willing to consider anything but pastels.|

1. After you type each short line of the memo header, press the Return key to go on to the next line.
2. Press Return to create a blank line between lines of text.
3. When you type a paragraph of text, do not press Return at the end of each line. MacWrite II *wraps* the text for you, ending each line at the right margin and starting a new line below.
4. You don't have to enter two spaces after the period at the end of each sentence. MacWrite II will make spaces at the sentence breaks for you when it prints the file.

Editing Text

MacWrite II has many of the same editing features as Word, so as you work through this section, you can look back to Figures 9.4 to 9.6 for guidance. As with Word, you use the special *I-beam* pointer, the vertical line with sprouts at the end, to add to and edit the text you have entered. And, of course, to edit existing text, make sure you *select it first*.

- To add text, place the I-beam pointer and click where you want to begin adding text. Then type the text in, as shown in Figure 9.4.

- To replace text, first drag the I-beam over it to select it. Then type in the new text, as shown in Figure 9.5.
- To delete text, first select it by dragging the I-beam over it. Then press the Delete key, as shown in Figure 9.6.
- To increase the size of a block of selected text, place the I-beam at the new endpoint you want to select. Then Shift-click (hold the Shift key down and click the mouse button) to extend the selection. To decrease the size of a selected block of text, Shift-click at the new endpoint within the selection.
- To extend a selection to the end of a line, press ⌘-Shift-→. Use ⌘-Shift-← to extend the selection to the beginning of a line.
- To undo a small typing or spelling mistake, you back up over it and retype the text. Use your Delete key to back up. To undo larger mistakes, choose Undo from the File menu. The command in the menu changes to reflect your last action. For example, if you just entered some text, the command is Undo Typing.

You can also use the commands in the Edit menu to move and replace blocks of text. These commands take text out of your document, hold it temporarily in the Clipboard, a special storage place in the Macintosh's memory, and put it back into your document. MacWrite's commands for working with the Clipboard are identical to those in Word, so for more information, turn to the section on "Moving and Replacing Text via the Clipboard" in Word, earlier in this chapter.

Using the Ruler to Format Text

MacWrite also has a ruler you can use to make formatting changes quickly and easily. Figure 9.12 shows the icons and markers. To see how the ruler works, let's change the first-line indent of the shotput memo.

1. If the ruler is not showing at the top of the document window, choose Show Ruler from the Format menu.
2. Select both paragraphs of the memo.
3. Drag the first-line indent marker (the one that looks like an upside-down T) in to set the indent for the first line of text in each paragraph. Your memo should now look like Figure 9.14.

The other settings on the MacWrite II ruler work a lot like the first-line indent. The list below tells how to make each setting.

- Drag the left margin marker (the triangle at the left margin) in or out to change the left margin of the text. The triangle marker at the right end of the ruler sets the margin for the right edge of text. With all the body text of the memo selected, move the margin markers in and out and watch what happens to the margins. When you move the left margin marker, notice that the first-line indent marker always moves too, so you keep your first-line indent.

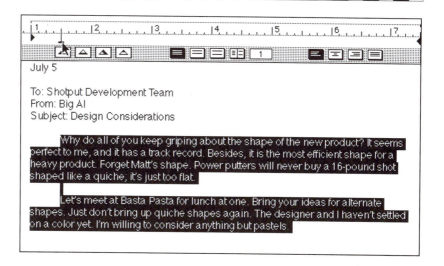

FIGURE 9.14
Changing the first line indent with the MacWrite II ruler

- Drag a triangular tab marker to each point on the ruler where you want to set a tab. There are left align, center, and right align tabs, as well as a tab for entering a decimal point. The dark part of each tab triangle tells you the alignment. Ain't that cute? To remove tab settings, drag the marker off the bottom of the ruler. In the sample memo, you can set a tab for a sign-off at the end, as shown in Figure 9.14. Place the insertion point after the last word of the memo, and then drag a left align tab (the triangle with the dark left side) to about the 5-inch mark on the ruler. Then press Return to start a new line, press the Tab key, and type a sign-off, like **Yours, Big Al**.

- Click on the different alignment icons to align the text at the left margin (as shown), or to center the text, or align it on the left margin. Try selecting the date at the top of the memo and clicking the icon for centered text (the second alignment icon from the left).

- Click on the different line spacing icons to select narrow (single), medium (1.5), or wide (double) spacing between lines of text. Typically, with 12-point fonts, the choices are 16, 24, and 32 points. To see what the memo looks like with medium spacing, select all of the body text and click the middle icon. The text box changes to show that you went from single spacing to one and a half. If you select something in the header of the memo, as in Figure 9.15, the spacing goes back to one.

If you select a large block of text and notice that there are different formats mixed in the selected text block, just make the setting you want for the whole block, and the parts that are different will straighten themselves out. Sometimes you have to change the setting and change it back to have it take effect. If you need to see hidden formatting characters to figure out what formatting is where, choose Show Invisibles from the View menu.

Changing Text Style

If you want to change text so it has a different style, such as bold, first select the text, then choose the style you want from the Format menu. For example, let's emphasize the word *perfect* in the first paragraph of the memo.

1. Select the word and the space before it.
2. Then choose Italic from the Style menu. The word becomes italicized.
3. If the end of the word leans over so far it runs into the next one, just select the last couple of letters and the space, type the letters over, and hold down the ⌘ key as you press the spacebar. That makes a bigger space on the screen, like the one shown in Figure 9.15.

FIGURE 9.15
Sample memo in MacWrite II with format changes

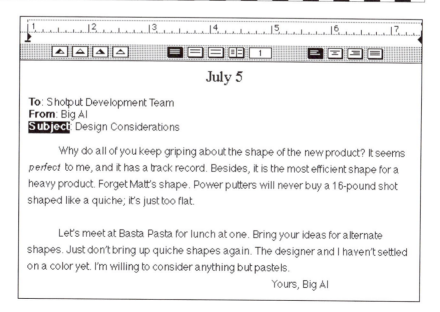

To deitalicize a selected word if you change your mind about emphasizing it, choose Plain Text from the Style menu.

To change the font or font size of text, use the same method and select the new font or size you want from the Font and Size menus. In the sample memo, select the date and use the Font and Size menus to change it to Times 18-point. Then select each of the first words of the header lines (*To*, *From*, and *Subject*) and either choose Bold from the Style menu or press ⌘-B.

These font style changes are minor, but they can make a difference in the overall effect of your document. For more information on them, see the MacWrite II *User's Guide*.

After you change the text style, font, or font size of a word, keep in mind that any text you enter immediately after that word adopts the changed text style. If you put the insertion point at the end of an italicized word, for example, all new text you enter will be italicized, too. To prevent this, choose Plain Text from the Style menu after placing the insertion point.

Saving and Printing a MacWrite II Document

Save your MacWrite documents every ten to fifteen minutes as you work on them. Just choose Save from the File menu, or press ⌘-S. The first time you save a document, you must name it and choose where to place it in your folder hierarchy. For more information on this, see "Saving Your Work on a Document" in Chapter 4.

To print a hard copy of your document, first save it, then choose Print from the File menu, or press ⌘-P. The Print dialog box opens. Unless you want to do something special, leave all the settings as they are and click the Print button or just press the Return key to start printing. If you have a LaserWriter or compatible printer that allows background printing, the PrintMonitor will take over your print job in a moment or two, and you can go right back to work while printing proceeds. For more information on printing, see Chapter 3.

Troubleshooting Problems with Your Word Processor

The following subsections cover the problems you are most likely to have while working with word processing applications. The solutions given in some of these sections apply specifically to Microsoft Word and MacWrite II. If you use a different word processing application, you can still use the suggestions as general guidelines.

Not enough memory.

You get the message "Not enough memory to open the application" when you try to open your word processor. If you have auxiliary tools you don't use with your application, see if you can remove or disable them. For example, if you have Microsoft Word, take the Grammar file out of the Word Commands folder that is in the same folder as the Word application. Take out any converter files that you don't need for converting files to other formats, too.

If you still do not have enough memory, try increasing the memory allocation in the application's Info box; Chapter 7 contains information on how to do this. If you cannot give the application enough memory because there is not enough RAM in your Mac, then you have to take the Mac to a qualified technician to install more.

Text appears in wrong style.

You have a paragraph of text in one style, and you place the insertion point on the next line after the paragraph, and when you type in new text, it appears in the wrong style. The problem is that the invisible paragraph mark on the line below the existing text has a change of style embedded in it.

To keep the style of the paragraph above, first choose Show ¶ from the View menu. Then select the paragraph marker on the line below the existing text and change the style to the one used for the preceding paragraph. To change the style, you can either choose the one that's right from the list at the left end of the ruler, or choose Style from the Format menu and choose the style from the list there.

Text disappeared.

The most likely problem is that you have deleted the text or replaced it with a space or a single letter. Before you do anything else, choose Undo from the Edit menu. If that doesn't bring the text back, scroll up and down to see if the text has simply been pushed out of view. If it is really gone, you can choose Save As from the File menu and give the document a temporary name. Then open the original document, and if the text is in it, copy it out and paste it into the temporary version. Finally, use Save As to replace the old version with the updated temporary one.

If even that method fails to turn up your missing text, you have no choice but to type the text in again. Save often to avoid problems like this in the future.

Indents not printing as expected.

You created a document without using the ruler to make indents at the beginning of each paragraph, and when you print out the document, some of the indents are different sizes than others. To make sure your indents are consistent in size, you must make them all with tabs, or set the first-line indent in the ruler and use the Return key to start each new paragraph.

Mixed formatting.

You have typed in a long paragraph that is all supposed to be in the same style, but parts of it have strange formatting that you don't know how you put there. The simplest solution is to select the whole block of text and apply a single style to it. Then go through the text and select any pieces that still have incorrect font styles or other attributes and correct them.

Phrase split by word wrap.

A phrase that you want to keep together (Something like St. Nick or Henry VIII) gets split at the end of a line. Just select the space between the two words and press Option-spacebar. This makes a nonbreaking link between the two words.

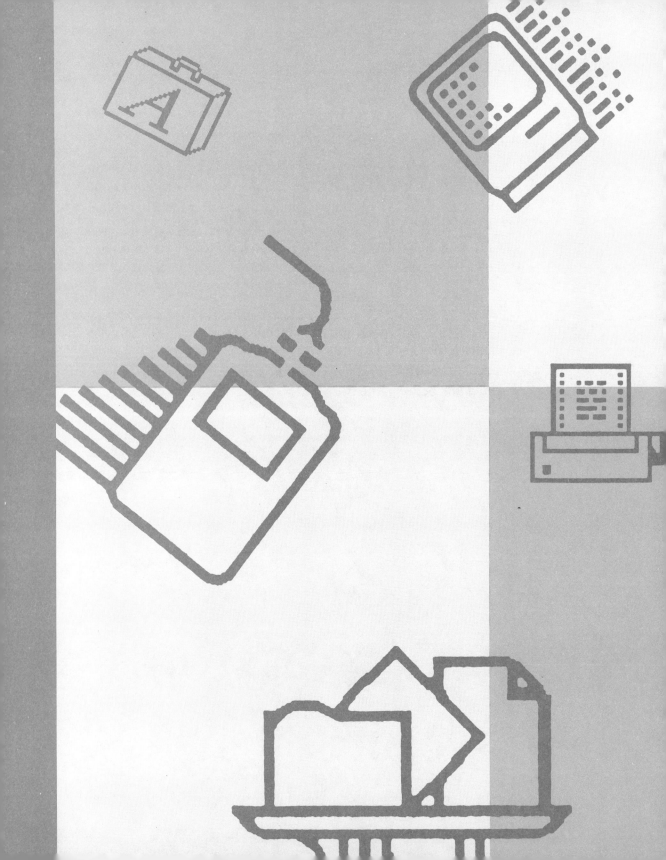

CHAPTER 10

Graphics Applications

Graphics applications are the tools you use to create images. Good graphics applications make it easy and fun to be creative, whether you are doodling with a spray can or making three-dimensional engineering plans.

All graphics programs should make it simple for you to revise and manipulate the images you have created. The greatest advantage the computer has over other art media is the ease with which you can undo and redo your work. If a graphics application takes advantage of the Mac's mouse, menus, and dialog boxes, it can make revision almost as much fun as the original creative effort.

The better graphics applications let you draw straight and curved lines, shapes, patterns, and shades of gray. They usually give you a way to copy public domain *clip art* and alter it according to your taste. Some graphics applications allow the use of color, if your Mac supports color. Others specialize in certain types of graphics, such as paintings, drawings, or photographs.

Look through the applications listed in this chapter and find the one that seems best suited to your needs.

■ Which Graphics Application for You?

You can choose from several distinct types of graphics applications. There are bit-mapped painting programs, such as Kid Pix and MacPaint, and there are object-oriented drawing/illustrating programs such as MacDraw, Illustrator, and Freehand. Some applications, such as SuperPaint and Canvas, can handle both bit-mapped and object-oriented graphics.

A Great Beginner's Graffic Application

If you are new to computing with a Mac, or you are just starting to work in graphics, there's one program that is miles ahead of all the others. It's called Kid Pix. It costs much less than other basic painting or drawing applications, but it lets you do a lot of fun things with bit-mapped painting tools. It is great for anyone new to the Mac, because it encourages you to use the mouse, menus, and the basic elements of Mac windows, and it shows you right away how easy it is to get things done on a Mac. For an example of how to make a picture with Kid Pix, see the "Using Kid Pix" section later in this chapter.

Workhorse Applications that Paint and Draw

If you want to sketch out simple bit-mapped images *and* create fine object-oriented images that require precision and control, you should choose a graphics application that allows you to work with both types of graphics. SuperPaint and Canvas are the two leaders in the field. If your Mac has a monochrome monitor, less than 4Mb of RAM, and a relatively slow CPU (if it's a Plus, for instance), you should use SuperPaint 2.0. If you have a high-powered Mac, like a IIci, and lots of RAM and a color monitor, it makes more sense to use SuperPaint 3.0 or higher, or the more expensive Canvas.

These applications can churn out good quality artwork, and they let you either paint or draw, as your needs dictate. You can create illustrations that are suitable for publication in either application, but each has its limits. SuperPaint has problems with several file formats that are often used in the publishing industry, and Canvas is relatively hard to learn. For an example of how to combine bit-mapped and object-oriented graphics to make a simple illustration, see "Using SuperPaint" later in this chapter.

High-Power Drawing Applications

If you want to create complex illustrations for publication, ones that require precision and fully controlled use of lines, shapes, shading, and color, then you should buy an object-oriented drawing program such as Illustrator or FreeHand. These applications allow you to manipulate lines in very sophisticated ways. Every straight line has endpoints, and every curved line has a number of points that define the *path*. These points act as handles, which you can adjust to a very fine degree. If the path of a line begins and ends at the same point, it becomes a *closed path*, which you can fill with shades of gray or color. You can also specify the stroke width, color, and pattern of a path, whether it is an open or a closed one.

The business advantage of Illustrator and other high-end drawing programs is that they produce graphics that can be reproduced at any resolution, from 72 DPI (dots per inch) on a Mac Classic screen to 2540 DPI on a Linotronic printing press used for publishing. The graphics are usually EPS (encapsulated PostScript) files, which means that they can be exported to many page layout applications, both for Macs and other computers, and they can be printed on most high-quality printers in the publishing world. EPS files can also be printed directly to negative or positive film for printing or silkscreening.

Illustrator can handle text in all kinds of ways, too. You can type in text, then change the font, shape, size and color. You can also align text to a curved path, or make it fit inside a closed path so it conforms to the shape. Graphs are no problem for Illustrator, either; you can create six different kinds of graphs from data you enter or import from other programs.

Learning to manipulate curves and layered images in an application like Illustrator is tricky at first, and it may seem that it takes you too long to get your idea into a workable form. Once you do have the basic form of a graphic in place, however, you will be amazed at how easily and precisely you can edit and develop it into a polished work of art. Your initial time investment can lead to huge payoffs as you build more and more complex graphics. For an example of a simple illustration, see "Using Illustrator" later in this chapter.

 ## Using Kid Pix

Kid Pix is the Macintosh dream come true. It's so simple it begs you to play around and be creative. In fact, I recommend Kid Pix to anybody who has just bought a Mac. Using Kid Pix is the easiest and most entertaining way to learn about the mouse and the other basic elements of the Mac interface. The following procedures will give you a peek at the many joys of Kid Pix, but you'll have to explore on your own to find all of its wonderful little tricks, jokes, and funny noises.

Opening a Document

Take one of the following actions to open a document in Kid Pix, depending on your situation:

- To open a new document if you have not started Kid Pix, double-click the Kid Pix icon, as shown in Figure 10.1, or an alias for it.
- To open a new document if you have started Kid Pix and are looking at an existing picture, choose New from the File menu.

A window opens with the ultra-simple set of Kid Pix menu titles in the menu bar, the Kid Pix icon at the right end of the bar, the tools palette on the left side of the window, and the options for the selected tool at the bottom of the window, as shown in Figure 10.2. Since the pencil tool is selected by default, the cursor looks like a short, fat pencil, and the pencil tool box in the tools palette is highlighted.

If this is the first time you have ever used a Mac, or if you are helping a young or uncoordinated user learn about the Mac, you can make the experience almost fool-proof by pulling down the Goodies menu

FIGURE 10.1
The Kid Pix icon

FIGURE 10.2
The Kid Pix window

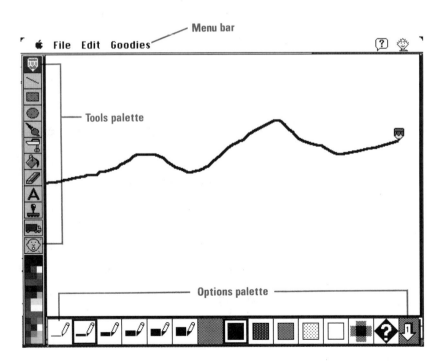

and choosing Small Kids Mode. This hides most of the menus and sets the screen so you can't run off the edge of the Kid Pix window and switch into the Finder or another application by mistake. You can always get the menus back by choosing Show Menu Bar from the Kid Pix menu.

Drawing Lines

To draw a line, just press the mouse button and drag the fat pencil around on the screen. It makes a scratchy noise as it draws. To make wider, thinner, or textured lines, just move the fat pencil down to the boxes at the bottom of the screen (it turns into an arrow down there) and choose a different box. Fool around a little. Then go on to the section "Undoing and Erasing Mistakes" and erase your experiments. When you have a clean window, draw a nice horizon with some mountains, as shown in Figure 10.2.

Undoing and Erasing Mistakes

To undo the last line you drew, choose Undo from the Edit menu, or click the undo guy (the guy with his mouth open) at the bottom of the tools palette. To erase things, move the pointer to the tools palette on the left side of the screen and click on the chalkboard eraser tool (it looks more like a short board; it's under the paint can and above the letter A). A whole set of eraser options appear in the boxes at the bottom of the screen. The ones on the left can be dragged around the screen like erasers. There are different sizes and shapes, but they all erase white swaths across the screen when you drag them. The other eraser options are for either clearing the screen completely, or for creating mysterious images as you erase.

Chapter 10

Placing Stamps

To add preformed images of things to your Kid Pix graphic, click the rubber stamp tool in the tools palette on the left side of the screen (it's below the letter *A*). Then browse through the stamps that appear on the bottom of the screen. To see stamps other than the ones shown, click the down arrow at the right end of the palette. Click on your stamp of choice, then click with the stamp pointer wherever you want the image to appear in your picture. To make an image larger than the standard one, like the house in Figure 10.3, hold down the Option key while you click with the stamp pointer. Use the rubber stamp to put a cactus, a horse, some palm trees, or whatever you want into your mountain scene.

FIGURE 10.3
A Kid Pix graphic

Painting with the Wacky Brush

To add a tree to your picture, use the wacky brush. When you click on it (it's the one with a blobby end, just below the round shape in the tools palette) you see a bunch of new options at the bottom of the screen, many of which don't make sense until you try them.

1. Click on the wacky brush to make it the active tool.
2. Click on the tree icon in the second set of options (click the down arrow at the right end of the palette to see the two sets of options).
3. Then click in the picture. Kid Pix paints a fractal tree (every one is different than the last) and makes a wonderful chime sound.
4. To put foliage on the tree, as shown in Figure 10.3, use the bubbly option for the wacky brush (it's the fourth option from the left in the first set of options) and drag the wacky brush around in the upper branches of the fractal tree.

Painting an Area with the Paint Can

To fill an area with a pattern, click on the paint can in the tools palette, then click on a pattern in the palette that appears across the bottom of the screen. Then move the paint can pointer to the space you want to fill (the tip of the pouring paint is the hot spot, if you have to fill a small area) and click.

You can fill an area with graded bands of gray, like the sky in Figure 10.3.

1. Choose the paint can from the tools palette.
2. Click the question mark option in the pattern palette.
3. Move the paint can to the area you want to fill, hold down the Option key, and click the mouse button.

Shades of gray look best on a color monitor, and they print out best on a high-resolution printer, but you can get some interesting effects with grays on a monochrome screen and a 72 DPI or 300 DPI printer.

Saving and Printing a Kid Pix Document

To protect your priceless Kid Pix art, save it often, about every fifteen minutes when you are working on it. All you have to do is choose Save from the File menu. The first time you save a document, you must name it and choose where to place it in your folder hierarchy, or it will be called "Untitled Kids" and placed in the same folder with the Kid Pix application. For more information on using the Save command, see "Saving Your Work on a Document" in Chapter 4.

To print a hard copy of your graphic, first save it, then choose Print from the File menu. A print dialog box opens. Unless you want to do something special, leave all the settings as they are and click the Print button or press the Return key to start printing. If you have a LaserWriter or compatible printer that allows background printing, the PrintMonitor will take over your print job in a moment or two, and you can go right back to Kid Pix while printing proceeds. For more information on printing, see Chapter 3.

Using SuperPaint

SuperPaint has a painting layer that works much like Kid Pix, but it also has a drawing layer that creates objects you can deal with as units. For example, if you make a hill shape and put a house shape on it in Kid Pix or in the paint layer of SuperPaint, you can't select the house and move it around to different places on the hill to see where it looks best. If you try to select the house, you select the part of the hill that is behind it, too. This is because the whole graphic is a single bitmap—a collection of dark and light bits, exactly as you see them on the screen. To move something on a bit-mapped graphic, you have to erase it, fix the background, then recreate the erased object in a new place.

However, if you make a hill shape in a draw application or in SuperPaint's draw layer, then create a house shape in the draw layer too, you can select the house and move it around on the hill. It's more like the shapes are cut-outs that you can place on a board and then play with. The following procedures show how to create a paint image with SuperPaint, and then add a framed text object. See the SuperPaint *User Manual* for more information on the tools and how to use them.

Opening a Document

Take one of the following actions to open a document in SuperPaint, depending on your situation:

- To open a new document if you have not started SuperPaint, double-click the SuperPaint icon, as shown in Figure 10.4, or an alias for it.
- To open a new document if you have started SuperPaint and are looking at an existing graphic, choose New from the File menu.

A window opens with the SuperPaint menu titles in the menu bar, the SuperPaint icon at the right end of the bar, the tools palette on the left side of the window, and the line and fill palette at the top of the window, as shown in Figure 10.5. In the upper left corner of the window, between the palettes, there are two icons, for the paint and draw layers

FIGURE 10.4
The SuperPaint icon

Chapter 10

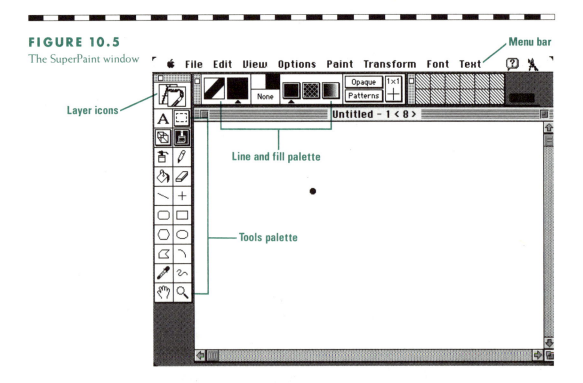

FIGURE 10.5
The SuperPaint window

of SuperPaint. The paint icon is in front, indicating that you are in the paint layer.

The window has the name "Untitled - 1" in the title bar, and there is an 8 in brackets, indicating that this is an 8-bit color or grayscale document. The name of the document will change the first time you save it and give it a title. Since the paint brush tool is selected by default, the cursor looks like a large black dot, and the paint brush tool in the tools palette is highlighted.

In general, the way you create images in SuperPaint is to go through the following steps:

1. Choose a layer (either the draw layer or the paint layer) to work in.
2. Choose a tool that will do what you want.

3. Choose the line and/or fill you want.
4. Create the image you have in mind.

In the sections that follow, we'll use SuperPaint to create another desert scene. If you follow the procedures to create this graphic, you will make the same general choices over and over. In the draw layer, after you have created an object, you may have an added step; before you edit an object, you must select it so the handles (little squares) show up at the ends or corners.

Creating a Shape

To create a shape in the paint layer, first you choose the shape tool for the shape you want to create from the tools palette. Then you choose a fill to fill in the shape with a pattern; or if you want to leave it empty, choose None for no fill. To finish the shape, you choose a line width for the border of the shape. Then drag diagonally to make the shape.

To see how this works, let's have the first shape for our desert scene be a nice rectangular frame to contain the picture. Follow these steps:

1. Choose the rectangle tool from the tools palette (the one under the plus in the tools palette).
2. Since we're making a frame, we want the shape to be empty. Go up to the line and fill palette shown in Figure 10.6, make sure the little black triangle is under the area fill box, and click on None.
3. Now let's choose a line width from the frame. Go over to the line width box, which says 1×1 at the top, and pull down the menu.
4. Choose a thicker line, like the fourth one down, which is 3×3 (three pixels by three pixels).
5. Move the cursor down into the window; it becomes a fat plus.

Chapter 10

FIGURE 10.6
The line and fill palette

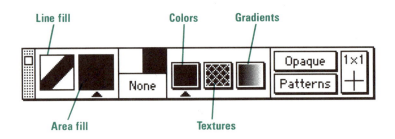

6. Drag diagonally from upper left to lower right to draw a rectangle near the middle of the screen. Make it big enough to draw a little picture in.

Now you've got a frame. Ain't it fun? Especially if you are the kind of person who has never been able to draw a good rectangle with a pencil and paper. By the time you're done, you'll have a desert scene like the one in Figure 10.7.

FIGURE 10.7
A SuperPaint desert scene

Drawing Freehand Outlines

To draw an irregular shape in the paint layer, first you click the pencil tool. Then choose a line width for the shape. When you're ready to draw, drag the pencil around the window.

For example, to make some hills and ridges for a simple desert scene, follow these steps:

1. Click on the pencil tool.
2. Pull down the line width menu and choose the thin line, which is 1×1.
3. Sketch some nice hilltops and a horizon with mesas for your desert scene, like those in Figure 10.7. Don't worry if your hills and ridges look a little too jagged, or if your lines don't meet, or if they overlap in nervous little squiggles. You'll get a chance to fix stuff like that in the next section. If you start a line and find that it is invisible, it means you started on top of another line; when the pencil points at a black pixel, it erases, when it points at white space, it draws a black line.

OK, you have put a fair amount of work into your graphic. Save it by choosing Save from the File menu or pressing ⌘-S. For more on saving, see "Saving and Printing a SuperPaint Document" later in this chapter.

Drawing and Refining a Detailed Shape

This where you really start to flex your artistic muscles. To make a detailed shape that looks just like you want, first make a rough sketch with the pencil tool, then zoom in to look at the shape up close, so you can refine it pixel by pixel. You do all of this in the paint layer.

For example, draw a rough outline of a cactus for your desert scene. Don't worry if it looks funny; just get the general shape and size of the thing on the screen. Then point the pencil at any part of the cactus that

Chapter 10

needs fixing, press the ⌘ key, and click the mouse button. The screen divides into two panels, one that shows the cactus at normal size, and another that shows the magnified part, as in Figure 10.8.

Use the pencil to erase pixels that are out of place and to draw new lines that look right. If you want to see how the whole cactus is turning out, look at the left panel of the window, or ⌘-click with the pencil to zoom out to the whole graphic. If you want to draw straight vertical or horizontal lines with the pencil, hold down the Shift key while you drag the pencil. The Shift key *constrains* the pencil tool to straight lines. This sort of constraining action works with many tools; see the SuperPaint documentation or just try using each tool with the Shift key.

If you need to move the magnified image around, press the spacebar. The grabber hand appears and you can use it to drag the whole graphic any way you want. This works better than scrolling with the scroll bars, especially in the magnified view.

If there were lines you drew for hills and ridges that need refining, use the same techniques you used on the cactus to fix them. Make sure the ends of the lines meet other lines. Any spaces will let your fill colors leak out.

FIGURE 10.8
Revising a bit-mapped image in magnified view

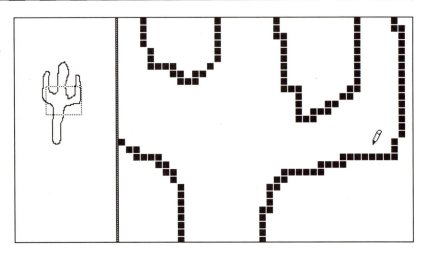

When you get done with all that, save your work again. It's a pain to redo that detail work if there's a power surge or something.

Filling Closed Areas with the Paint Can

The paint can is a powerful little tool. You have to be in the paint layer to use it. To fill an area or a closed shape with a pattern, texture, graded shades of gray, or color, all you have to do is click the paint can tool, click your choice of fill, and click once in the area you want to fill up. If the fill doesn't look right, you just choose Undo from the Edit menu.

For example, you can fill the shapes you've made for your desert scene by following the tree procedures below:

To fill in the cactus with black, and the mountains with some nice grays:

1. Choose the paint can in the tools palette.
2. Pull down the colors menu from the line and fill palette and choose black.
3. Click the paint can when the tip of the pouring paint is inside the cactus.
4. Pull down the colors menu again and choose a medium light gray.
5. Click in the mid-distant mountain area to fill it with a gray like the one back in Figure 10.7.
6. Pull down the colors menu once more and choose a slightly lighter gray for the far-distant mountain area.

To fill the foreground with a texture:

1. Leave the paint can tool selected.
2. Pull down the textures menu from the line and fill palette, and choose the texture that seems suitable, such as the mottled gray one shown in Figure 10.7.

3. Click the paint can in the foreground shape.

   To fill in the sky with a nice sunset:

1. Leave the paint can tool selected.
2. Pull down the gradients menu and choose the linear type gradient (the box on the left; it is chosen by default) and the grays gradient bar.
3. Click in the sky with the paint can. A funny texture fills the area and a rubber-band thingie stretches from the center of the area to the pointer.
4. Move the pointer so the rubber band is pointing straight up from the center point, then click the mouse again. Presto. A sunset appears.

Adding Text in the Draw Layer

To add text to a graphic, you first change from the paint layer to the draw layer. Then you type in text and draw a frame around it. Both the text and the frame automatically become objects in the draw layer. When you're satisfied with the way the text looks, you can join it with the frame to make a single object, then place the object where you want it.

Let's add a title to your desert graphic:

1. Start by clicking the draw icon in the upper left corner of the SuperPaint window. Notice that most of the tools go dim, and a couple of the menus change.
2. Click on the text tool, which is the large A.
3. Go to the line and fill palette and choose the black line fill and the black area fill, too.
4. Click anywhere in the open space below your graphic and type in a title, like **Desert Scene**.

5. Select the title by dragging the I-beam over it.
6. To change the font for your title, choose 18 from the Text menu and choose Times from the Font menu.

Now let's put a frame around the text:

1. Choose the rounded rectangle tool (just to the left of the rectangle tool in the tools palette).
2. Place the crosshair pointer above and to the left of the title and drag down and to the right to make a frame around it. When you release the mouse button, the frame gets handles.
3. To resize or move the frame to fit the title better, just click in the pointer tool in the tools palette, then click on a corner handle to resize the frame, or a side of the frame to move the whole thing.

When the title and frame look good, leave the frame selected and Shift-click in the middle of the title, so both objects become selected. Then drag the whole unit to a nice place, or center it under the graphic. That's the wonder of the draw layer; you can move those objects around and fix their size so easily.

That's it. You've created a masterpiece.

Saving and Printing a SuperPaint Document

Save your SuperPaint art often, around every fifteen minutes when you are working on it. All you have to do is choose Save from the File menu. The first time you save a document, you must name it and choose where to place it in your folder hierarchy, or it will be called "Untitled - 1" and placed in the same folder with the SuperPaint application. For more information on using the Save command, see "Saving Your Work on a Document" in Chapter 4.

To print a hard copy of your graphic, first save it, then choose Print from the File menu. A print dialog box opens. Unless you want to do something special, leave all the settings as they are and click the Print button or just press the Return key to start printing. If you have a Laser-Writer or compatible printer that allows background printing, the Print-Monitor will take over your print job in a moment or two, and you can go right back to SuperPaint while printing proceeds. For more information on printing, see Chapter 3.

Using Adobe Illustrator

Illustrator doesn't have a paint layer like SuperPaint, but what it lacks in the quick-sketching arena it makes up for with precision and control. Every image you create becomes an object that you can resize, move, and fiddle with until it is just the way you want it. You can build graphics by carefully constructing objects and layering them so they make a composite that is far more controlled than anything an artist could sketch using a bit-mapped paint program.

The following procedures show how to create a simple illustration such as might be used at the front of a small newsletter. Even though it is a relatively simple example, it may be hard for you to get through unless you have had some experience with other Mac graphics applications. See the Adobe Illustrator *Tutorial* and the *User Guide* for more detailed information on all the powerful features this application offers.

Opening a New Document

Take one of the following actions to open a new document in Illustrator, depending on your situation:

- To open a new document if you have not started Illustrator, double-click the icon of the application, as shown in Figure 10.9, or double-click an alias for it. The Illustrator menu

FIGURE 10.9
Illustrator icon

titles appear in the menu bar, but no window opens; choose New from the File menu.

- To open a new document if you have started Illustrator and are looking at an existing graphic, choose New from the File menu.

A dialog box opens, asking you to choose a template for your document or click None. Click the None button.

Finally, the Illustrator window opens with the Illustrator tools palette on the left side, as shown in Figure 10.10. Although there do not appear to be many tools available, if you point at some of them and hold down the mouse button, alternate tools appear in pop-up menus. The window has the name "Untitled Art 1" in the title bar. The name of the document will change the first time you save it and give it a title. Since the pointer or *selection tool* is active by default, the cursor looks like a standard arrow pointer and the selection tool in the tools palette is highlighted. In the bottom left corner of the window there is an information bar that tells what tool you have selected or what you can do with it; when the selection tool is active, it says "Selection."

In general, the way you create images in Illustrator is to go through the following steps:

1. Choose a tool that will do what you want.
2. Create the path you have in mind, either an open or closed one (paths are explained in the sections below).

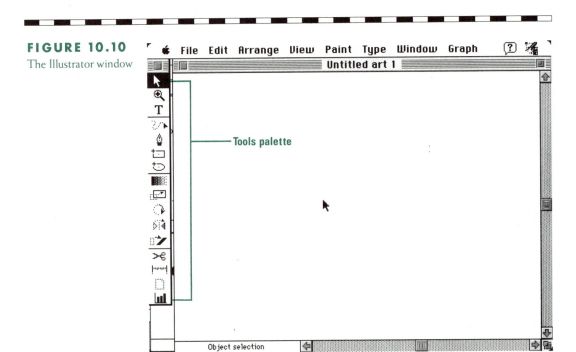

FIGURE 10.10
The Illustrator window

3. Choose the fill and/or stroke you want for the path.
4. Adjust the path and reset the fill/stroke in order to get the precise effect you want.

In the sections that follow, we'll create a graphic that would make a nice logo for a desert newsletter. If you follow the procedures to create this sample graphic, you will make the same general choices over and over. Keep in mind that before you edit a path or its style, you must select it so the handles (little squares) show up at the ends or corners.

Although the process seems simple as described above, it can get very complex. You do things in layers, and after you have created two or more layers of objects, you may have to hide one layer to work on the one under it. And you have to plan ahead a lot, so that your layers will fit together the way you want when you are done. It's a bit like chess; you have to think several moves ahead, or you can get trapped in your own layers.

Starting Off with a Sketch

Before you begin to create a graphic in Illustrator, it's a good idea to do a sketch, so you know what your goal is and you can plan out how to attain it. You can do the sketch with a pencil or a simple paint program like Kid Pix or MacPaint. For example, let's do a sketch of a logo for a newsletter that has a cactus in the foreground, a mountain range in the background, and lettering running across it, as shown in Figure 10.11. To really show off the power of Illustrator, let's plan on making a sunset effect by doing a blend of grays in the sky.

To make this logo in Illustrator, you need to make a rectangular frame to hold the logo. In Illustrator, shapes like rectangles and circles are called *closed paths*. Then you have to make the horizon. To make the blend in the sky, you have to split the rectangular closed path in half at the horizon, making two open paths. After creating the blend for the

FIGURE 10.11
A sketch for a newsletter logo

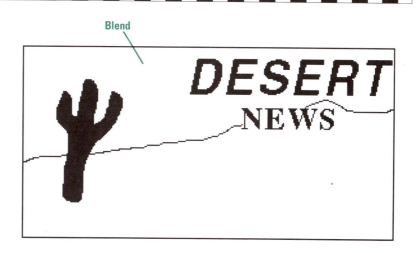

top half, you can put the two halves back together again, and add your cactus and lettering.

Creating a Closed Path

You'll start creating the logo by making the frame for it. You can create a rectangular closed path by dragging the rectangle tool diagonally. If you want to make a rectangle of a specified size, you can measure it with the rulers at the right side and bottom of the Illustrator window.

To see how this works, let's make a 4" by 2" frame for the logo graphic.

1. Choose Show Rulers from the View menu. If the ruler shows units other than inches, choose Preferences from the Edit menu, then click the Inches radio button and click OK in the Preferences dialog box.

2. Select the rectangle tool (just below the pen tool in the tools palette). The pointer becomes crosshairs.

3. Place the crosshairs so the dotted lines are at the 7" mark on the vertical ruler and the 2" mark on the horizontal ruler.

4. Drag the rectangle down until the dotted lines are at the 5" mark on the vertical ruler and the 6" mark on the horizontal ruler, and release the mouse button. A rectangular closed path appears. Notice that there is a black square in the center of the rectangle and black squares at all four corners. These are selected handles and they indicate that the whole object is selected and *grouped*.

5. Choose Ungroup from the Arrange menu so you can work on the different parts of the *ungrouped* object.

Splitting a Closed Path into Two Shapes

To make the logo into two parts, a sky that you can fill with a sunset, and a foreground that isn't blended, you need to divide the whole logo in half. One of the great strengths of Illustrator is that you can divide an object and take different actions on each part, so that you can later build a composite that has more variety. Use the following procedure to make two matched halves out of the logo frame, one for the sky and one for the earth. The halves will meet at the horizon.

First you need to snip the rectangle in half.

1. Make sure the rectangle for the whole graphic is selected (click it with the pointer tool), so the handles are dark on all four corners.
2. Select the scissors tool from the tool palette. The pointer becomes crosshairs.
3. Click the crosshairs to cut the sides of the rectangle; cut the right side two-thirds of the way up, and the left side one-third of the way up. These are the points where your horizon meets the frame; look back at Figure 10.11 to get the idea.

Next you need to set up *ruler guides*, which are nonprinting dotted horizontal and vertical lines used for alignment. You want ruler guides on the sides and bottom of the rectangle, so you can move parts of it around and bring them back into perfect alignment later. To place your ruler guides:

1. Click the selection tool and move the pointer into the vertical ruler. Then drag a dotted vertical line out of the ruler to the right edge of the rectangle. It snaps to the line.
2. Drag a second vertical guide to the left edge of the rectangle.

3. Drag a third ruler guide up from the bottom ruler to the bottom edge of the rectangle. The sides and bottom of the rectangle change to fine dots when each ruler guide is lined up right.
4. If you drop a ruler guide in the wrong place, just press the Control and Shift keys, then drag the guide to the correct place.

Ruler guides set? Good. Now you can select the bottom half of the logo and move it down so you can make the horizon on it.

1. Select the selection tool if you haven't already.
2. Hold down the Option key and click the lower open path. Notice that the selection pointer gets a plus when you hold down the Option key. This means that it's become the object-selection tool, so clicking the lower open path selects that part, making four black squares appear.
3. Move this lower shape straight down by putting the pointer on the bottom line, pressing the mouse button, then pressing the Shift key and dragging downward an inch or so, as shown in Figure 10.12. The Shift key *constrains* the movement to vertical or horizontal.

Now you can draw the line that will be common to both shapes: the horizon.

1. Click in the blank space outside the graphic with the selection tool. This deselects the shape you just moved.
2. Click on the high endpoint of the left side of the lower open path. The square at that endpoint turns black; the other three are open.
3. Choose the freehand tool (the one under the T) from the tools palette and move the pointer to the selected endpoint.

Graphics Applications

FIGURE 10.12
A split closed path

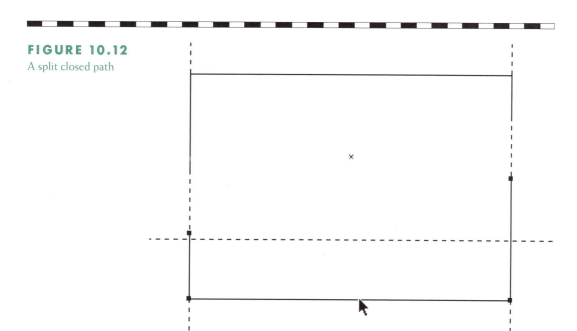

4. Drag an undulating line across the top of the lower shape (this will be your finishing horizon), ending at the upperend point of the other side.

5. To make sure the horizon line joins the end of the right side there, as shown in Figure 10.13, select the zoom-in tool and click on that corner a couple of times to get a close look. The line endpoints must meet *exactly*.

6. Choose Actual Size from the View menu to get things back to normal.

7. Save your work. See "Saving and Printing an Illustrator Document" later in the chapter for details about the Save dialog box; there are several different ways you can save a document, and each is best for a particular situation.

FIGURE 10.13
A horizon line for a desert scene

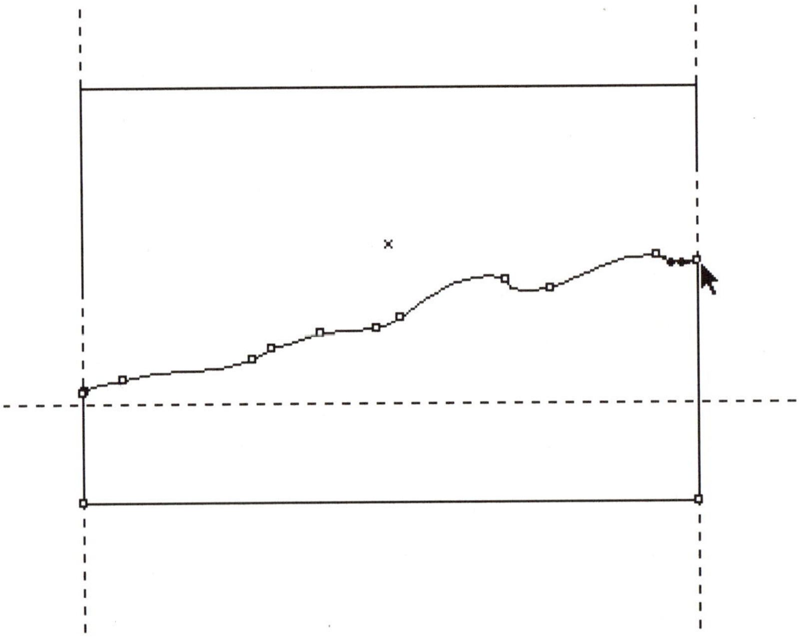

Matching Two Closed Paths

Now you have the bottom half of the logo with the horizon. But you need a top half to match. To get one, you have to make a closed path for the sky. Then you can put the blend in the sky and put it all back together. To put two closed paths back together after you have split them from a single shape, you must copy the joining line from one path and use it to make a joining line for the other path.

So before you put the two halves of your desert logo back together, you must copy the horizon from the bottom half and add it to the top half, the sky. First you have to make a copy of the whole bottom shape and cut away everything but the horizon:

1. Click on the select tool, then press the Option key and click on one of the sides of the bottom shape, so the whole object is selected.

2. Press the Option key again and drag a copy of the shape down about two inches. Keep the sides lined up on the ruler guides. Now you have three objects, the upper open path, the lower closed path, and a copy of the lower closed path.

3. Select the scissors tool and click on the the square at the corner of the horizon and the left side of the frame.

4. Click again on the right end of the horizon. If the horizon line missed the frame, a message box appears, telling you that you can't split an open path. Click OK. Then cut a bit to the left along the horizon.

5. Choose the selection tool, hold down the Option key, and select the lower part of the shape. Press the Delete key to erase everything but the horizon, as shown in Figure 10.14.

Now you have to select the horizon and drag it up to meet the top or sky half of your logo.

1. Select the whole horizon by pressing the Option key and clicking on the line.

2. Now you're going to do a mouse-Shift trick that is unusual. Release the Option key and keep the pointer on the line. Then press *first* the mouse button and *then* the Shift key, and drag the horizon straight up, with the ends lined up on the ruler guides. It seems odd to press a key after pushing the mouse button, but it sure is nice to constrain that move so the horizon doesn't drift to one side or the other.

3. Place the horizon line so the left end matches the lower end point of the top half of the rectangle shape.

4. Click with the zoom-in tool at the line junction if you have to, in order to make sure the left ends of the two lines meet. You can even select and move the ruler guide out of your way, with the Control and Shift keys held down. Just make sure you move

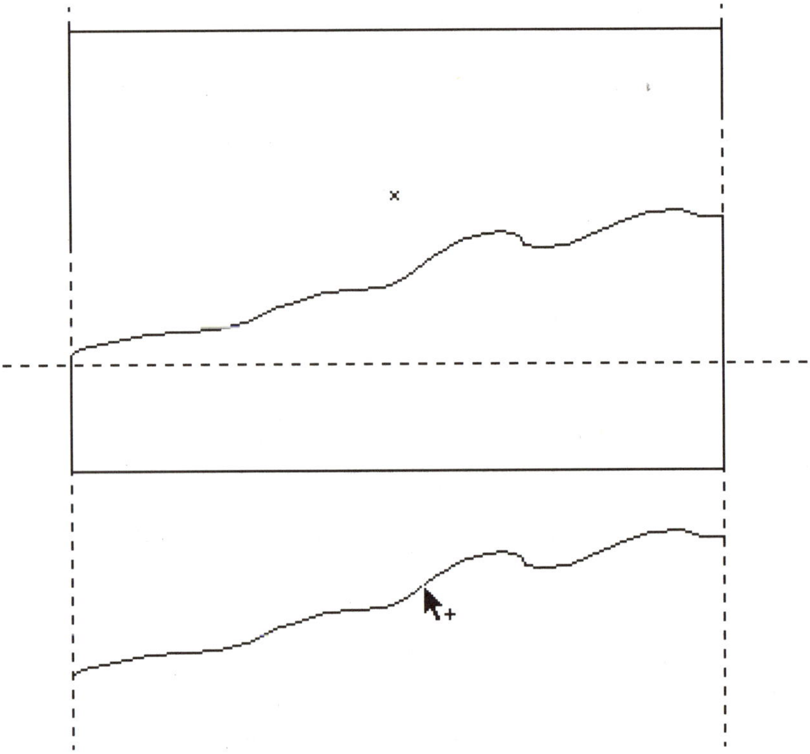

FIGURE 10.14
A copy of the horizon

it back when you're done. When you're sure the line ends meet, choose Actual Size from the View menu to see the whole picture again.

5. Drag with the selection tool to make a marquee (a selection rectangle) that encloses the area where the right end of the horizon line and the right end of the top half of the rectangle look like they meet. They probably don't meet, if you cut a bit to the left along the horizon.

6. Choose Join from the Arrange menu. If Illustrator asks you whether you want a smooth point or a corner point, select

corner point. This completes the upper shape, as shown in Figure 10.15.

You now have two matched closed paths. You need to mask the sky (this makes sure it will show up later after you cover it with things) right now, before you join it with the bottom half.

1. Select the top half of the logo with the Option key down, so the whole object is selected.
2. Choose Style from the Paint menu. The Paint Style dialog box opens. It has a Fill box on the left, a Stroke box in the middle, and a Weight box at the bottom. For information on the other choices in this dialog box, see the Adobe Illustrator *User Guide*.

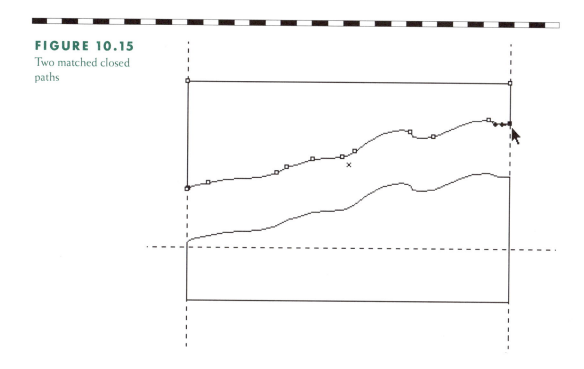

FIGURE 10.15
Two matched closed paths

3. In the dialog box, select None from the Fill box and None from the Stroke box. (We'll talk more about these things in the next section.)
4. Click the check box for Mask, then click OK.

The upper part of the logo is now prepared to become the sunset-shaded sky. You can put the two halves of your graphic back together.

1. Option-select the bottom half of the logo.
2. Release the Option key, then press *first* the mouse button and *then* the Shift key (that unusual mouse-Shift again), and slide the shape straight up between the ruler guides until the bottom half of the logo matches the horizontal ruler guide and the two horizon lines become one.
3. If parts of the horizontal line look thick, Option-select and nudge the upper half of the graphic up or down with the arrow keys until the match is perfect.

Aah. You did it. It took some time, but now you can do all kinds of magic with the two halves of your logo. For instance, you can fill the earth part of the logo with a plain shade, and then make a gorgeous sunset in the sky. Save your work now. You'd hate to do that all over again.

Filling a Closed Path with a Shade of Gray

To change the color or shade of a closed path, like the bottom shape of your logo, you select it, then use the Paint Style dialog box to define the shade inside it, the *fill*, and the shade of the border, or *stroke*.

Use the following steps to fill the desert mountains with a nice gray.

1. Option-select the whole lower half of your logo.
2. Choose Style from the Paint menu. The Paint Style dialog box opens.

3. Click on the Black radio button in the Fill box, then change the percentage of fill from 100 percent to 20 percent by typing **20**.
4. Leave the setting in the Stroke box at None, and click the OK button.

The shape does not change color on the screen, but it has the fill attribute attached to it. You'll get a chance to preview it after the next step.

Creating and Hiding a Blend

Now you can do the sunset in the sky. To make a shaded area, or *blend*, in a graphic, with gradients of color or grays, you have to make starting and ending points for the blend, and then use the blend tool to fill in the area with the gradients. To make a blend of grays that looks like a sunset in the sky of your desert logo, use the following procedure:

1. Select the rectangle tool and make a long, narrow rectangle that encloses the top edge of the upper shape of your logo, like the upper skinny rectangle in Figure 10.16.
2. While this rectangle is still selected, choose Ungroup from the Arrange menu.
3. Choose the select tool, then hold the Option key down and drag a copy of the long skinny rectangle down until it encloses the lower left corner of the sky shape, as shown in Figure 10.16. These rectangles will define the start and finish of the blend.
4. While the lower rectangle is still selected, choose Style from the Paint menu. Then select Black from the Fill box and set it to 80 percent by typing **80**. Click OK to close the Paint Style dialog box.
5. Option-select the upper rectangle.
6. Choose Style from the Paint menu again, then select Black from the Fill box and set it to 20 percent. Then click OK.

7. Click with the selection tool in blank space outside the graphic to deselect the rectangles.
8. Select the *upper left* corner of the upper rectangle and Shift-select the *lower left* corner of the lower rectangle, so both points are selected (filled in black), as shown in Figure 10.16. Make sure you have those two corners selected, and no others.
9. Select the blend tool (the shaded bar under the oval tool) and click on the two selected corner points. Illustrator shows you a dialog box telling how many steps it is going to take to do the blend. Whoosh; that seems like a lot. But it goes fast.
10. Click OK. The blended area appears as a black box on the screen.

That black box doesn't look much like a sunset, does it? But the sunset is in there, believe me. You'll get a sneak preview soon. Before you do anything else though, you need to group the blend elements so they don't blot out things you add to your logo later.

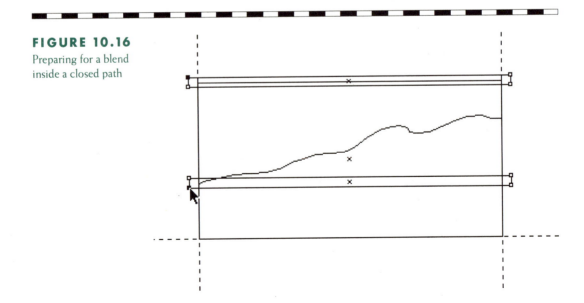

FIGURE 10.16
Preparing for a blend inside a closed path

1. Option-select the lower half of the logo.
2. Do the mouse-Shift-drag trick to drag the bottom half straight down until it is away from the big black area.
3. Drag the select tool over the black blend area to marquee-select the blend, shape, and rectangles, but *not* the lower half of the logo.
4. Choose Group from the Arrange menu. *This is important.* If you don't group the elements of the blend, the mask that you applied earlier will mask out anything else you draw later.
5. Move the lower half of the logo back up, using the same method you used to move it down, and lining it up with the bottom and side ruler guides so it will join the top half under the blend. Then save your work again.
6. Choose Preview Illustration from the View menu to see how the blend worked. Aaah. Aren't sunsets grand?
7. To go back to your working view, choose Artwork Only from the View menu.
8. To get that big black area out of your way so you can continue work, Option-select the area, then choose Hide from the Arrange menu.

All that you can see is the lower half of the logo now. That will be enough to add the last elements to the logo, the cactus and the text.

Adding a Freehand Drawing to a Graphic

Let's add a cactus. Not just a funky cactus, a really nice one. To put a freehand-drawn object into an Illustrator graphic, you draw it first with the freehand tool, then edit it to perfection by adjusting the Bezier curves that make it up. Then you can fill it and set the stroke. Here's how it goes.

1. Select the freehand tool from the tool palette; it's the squiggly dotted one under the T.
2. Draw a rough sketch of a cactus near the left side of the scene, as in Figure 10.17. Don't worry if it isn't perfect on your first try. If it is really a mess, you can just choose Undo from the Edit menu and start over.
3. When the cactus sketch is decent, you can edit it. Start by using the zoom-in tool to zoom in on any area that needs work.
4. Select a curve and drag the *pivot points* (the hollow squares along the line) to change the basic shape.
5. When the line is in the right place, move the *direction points* (the black squares with straight lines attached) to flex the curves into the shapes you want. It takes a little fooling around, but you soon learn to control the curves very precisely.
6. When you have the cactus drawn the way you want it, Option-select it.

FIGURE 10.17
Adding text to a graphic

7. Choose Style from the Paint menu. Then select black fill at 100 percent, and black stroke at 100 percent too, with a weight of .5 point. Then click OK.

The cactus doesn't look like it's filled in black. To see it in black, just select Preview Illustration (⌘-Y) from the View menu to get a look at it, then select Artwork Only (⌘-W) from the View menu to get back to work.

Adding Text to a Graphic

To add a title to your logo, you use the type tool and manipulate the text blocks as objects. This is how it works:

1. Select the type tool and click in a blank area somewhere in the window far from the logo.
2. Type **DESERT** in all capitals.
3. Drag the text tool over the type to select it, then choose Style from the Type menu.
4. Select Other from the font pop-up menu. The Font dialog box appears. Choose Helvetica and the Bold Oblique option. Then click OK.
5. Enter 48 for the size, and click OK.
6. Choose Style from the Paint menu and select white fill, black stroke at 100 percent, and 1 point weight. Click OK again.
7. Choose the select tool and click in blank space somewhere to deselect *DESERT.*
8. Select the type tool again, and click with it in a free space.
9. Type **NEWS** in all capitals.
10. Select the word and use the same method you used on *DESERT* to make the type style Times Bold, 36-point size.

11. Make the paint style 100 percent black fill, and choose None for the stroke.
12. When you have finished with *NEWS*, click in open space with the select tool to deselect it. Then select each of the words with the select tool and drag it to where you want it on the logo, as shown in Figure 10.17. Then save your work again.

Using Layers for Depth Effects

For a fancy little touch, you can use the layers of an Illustrator graphic to create a three-dimensional effect by moving some of the text behind the hills. The blended shape at the top of the logo must be hidden, as described at the end of the "Creating and Hiding a Blend" section. The following steps tell you how to move the word *DESERT* behind the horizon.

1. Drag the selection arrow across the bottom half of the graphic to select the landscape, the cactus, and the word *NEWS*. Make sure no part of the word *DESERT* is touched by the marquee.
2. Choose Bring To Front from the Edit menu. The word *DESERT* is now set behind the hill.
3. Choose Show All from the Arrange menu.
4. Choose Preview Illustration to see your masterpiece, as shown in Figure 10.18.

Good work! Now all you have to do is go on to the next section and save and print that puppy out, and you can start a newsletter.

Saving and Printing an Illustrator Document

To protect your hard-earned Illustrator art, save it every ten or fifteen minutes when you are working on it. All you have to do is choose

FIGURE 10.18
Finished sample
Illustrator graphic

Save from the File menu or press ⌘-S. The first time you save a document, Illustrator gives you the Save as dialog box. Follow these steps:

1. Type a name for your graphic in the Save illustration as box. If you don't name it, it will be called "Untitled art 1" and placed in the same folder with the Illustrator application.

2. Then choose Black & White Macintosh from the Preview popup menu. This will let you or anybody see the graphic in Preview mode. Don't use the None choice; no matter which monitor you have, your graphic will show up as a gray square if you place it in a page layout application.

3. Leave the compatibility setting at Adobe Illustrator 3 unless you have some special need for compatibility with another graphics application.

4. Click Save.

For more information on using the Save command, see "Saving Your Work on a Document" in Chapter 4.

To print a hard copy of your graphic, first save it, then choose Print from the File menu. A print dialog box opens. Unless you want to do something special, leave all the settings as they are and click the Print button or just press the Return key to start printing. If you have a LaserWriter or compatible printer that allows background printing, the PrintMonitor will take over your print job in a moment or two, and you can go right back to Illustrator while printing proceeds. For more information on printing, see Chapter 3.

Troubleshooting Problems with Graphics Applications

The following subsections cover the most common problems you may encounter when working with graphics applications.

Paint or a fill spread beyond intended area.

You poured paint or a texture into what you thought was a closed area, but the stuff escapes and goes all over the place. The problem is that there is a leak somewhere: a space between the ends of two lines, or a corner where the sides don't meet. First, choose Undo from the Edit menu to clean up the mess instantly. Then look for the leak, using a magnified view at any points where holes are likely. When you find the leak, close it off, then try your paint-pour or fill over again.

Text in a bit-mapped graphic is jagged.

Bit-mapped graphics can only make approximations of outline fonts; if you copy text from a word processing application into your graphics, or if you use fonts that you don't have a bit map for, the text will look jagged in the printed graphics. The solution is to stick to fonts that print well as bit maps, such as those with city names. Otherwise, use an object-oriented application for all text work.

Objects disappear under other layers.

The problem is that something you made is hidden by either another object, or a mask that was not grouped, or (in SuperPaint) by being in the draw layer behind the paint layer. In most cases, you can either move the covering object, select the hidden one and move it to the front, or in the case of SuperPaint, move the hidden object from the draw layer into the paint layer. If you forgot to group the parts of a blend in Illustrator and the mask is hiding all later work, select the blend and delete it, then redo the mask and blend. Make sure you group all the parts of the blend before continuing work.

Printed graphic looks bad.

This usually means the printer is not capable of printing with good enough resolution to show the effects you have created. If you are using an object-oriented application, try saving your graphic in PICT or MacPaint format and printing it. If your application and monitor can show grayscale, you may be able to print graphics in black and white (choose Black & White in the Print dialog box), but the results may be pretty dotty and muddled. The best solution is to print the grayscale graphics on a high-resolution printer.

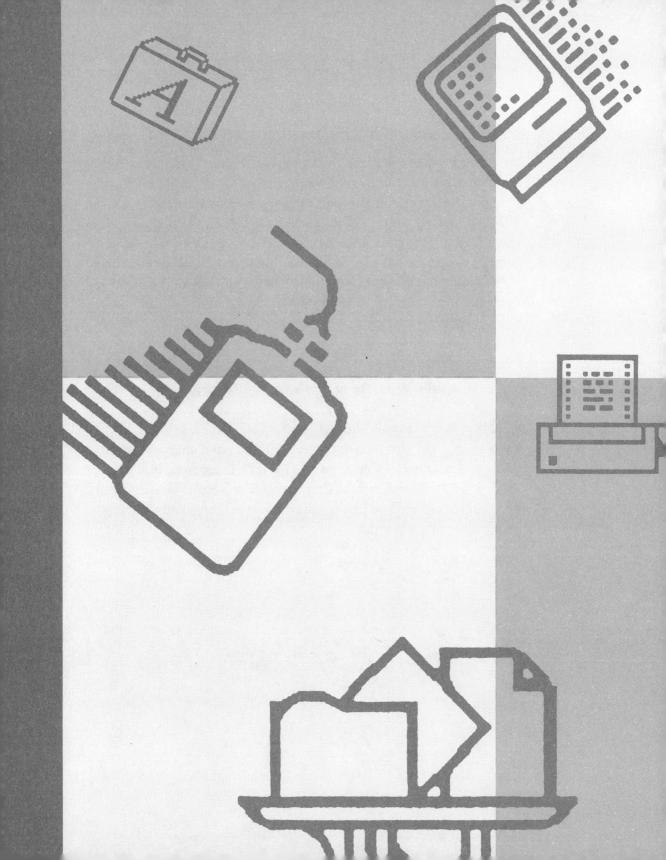

CHAPTER 11

Page Layout Applications

Page layout applications are tools for putting together text and graphics to make nice-looking documents. But that doesn't really tell the whole story of page layout on the Mac.

Page layout is what put the Mac on the map. When PageMaker for the Mac came out, a revolution in publishing began. It is called desktop publishing, and it has succeeded because you can do page layout much faster, cheaper, and more creatively on a Mac than you can by cutting up pieces of paper and sticking them on big pasteboards. You waste a lot less paper, too, unless you do dozens of test printouts.

The effects of desktop publishing have been amazing. Instead of dozens of people slaving away to create pasteups, now there are single individuals, often working at home, creating the page layouts for everything from church calendars to major periodicals and full-length books. Desktop publishing is a major cottage industry, and the Mac is the desktop publisher's computer of choice.

The growth of this cottage industry is not just due to the economics. It's also due to the fact that it's fun. A desktop publisher can collect a bunch of graphics files that have been created by a gifted artist or illustrator, and a bunch of text files written by talented writers, and shape them into a document that has even more impact than the ingredients that went into it. This is highly satisfying work. Even if the document is just a newsletter made up of corny articles and clip art (public domain cartoons and simple graphics), the process of creating pages is a gratifying one; you can watch a page take shape before your eyes, and you have great power to manipulate the different elements to make it look the way you want.

You can use page layout applications to do simple things like writing letters and adding letterheads, or you can do huge, complex jobs like full-color professional publications. You have complete control of all phases of the production, from editing text to the final printout. The feeling of power you get from this control is downright exhilarating, especially when the printout actually looks just like you wanted.

Which Page Layout Application for You?

There are only a few serious contenders in the world of page layout applications. There are inexpensive page layout applications such as Personal Press that are good for simple, short documents. Then there are the big applications, such as PageMaker and QuarkXPress, for all kinds of publishing needs, and there is FrameMaker, which is especially good for long technical documents.

An Inexpensive Page Layout Tool for Small Jobs

If you don't want to do all kinds of fancy publishing tricks, and you have a low-end Mac and a tight budget, try Aldus Personal Press. It works great for short documents like newsletters, fliers, and business cards. Aldus made this application to take care of all the people who don't want to learn about automatic kerning and such things. To make a layout, you just choose a template and fill in the text and graphics where you want, and you're done. You can crank out your weekly newsletter without having to relearn the whole art and science of page layout each week. Personal Press can make nice-looking documents on low-cost printers such as the StyleWriter, too. You can play around with the elements as you lay them out, but you don't have the freedom or the power to create a look completely unique to your documents.

Publish It Easy is another low-end layout tool that gives you much more flexibility and power, but it is often confusing and non-intuitive, which are the last things you want if you are new to the page layout game.

Page Layout Applications for Big Jobs

QuarkXPress versus PageMaker: the battle has been raging since the conception of the two leading page layout programs. Discussing these programs with a user from another camp can be like discussing religion with your Aunt Maude. You can both give strong arguments for your side, but no one leaves satisfied that they have discovered the one and only truth.

PageMaker is easier to learn and you can change your layout easier than you can in Quark. PageMaker also has the ability to link separate documents and create an index and table of contents for the entire linked group. This is an important feature for producing multichapter books. Quark, however, lets you open more than one document at a time and lets you drag elements from one document to another. Quark is also known for its precision in handling text and graphics.

You can group, lock, and align elements in Quark, but you can't in PageMaker. Quark lets you set up multiple master pages; PageMaker only gives you two. Quark is the alleged leader in handling color files, but PageMaker is very close behind. However, Aldus, the manufacturer of PageMaker, has better technical support, judging from what Quark users have told me; and Aldus has never let me down. PageMaker has better online help and a better manual. PageMaker also has a broader user base, and therefore you are more likely to find someone to advise you on PageMaker than on Quark. I could go on and on but Aunt Maude is getting tired.

What it boils down to is this—if you are doing mostly high-end color work, demand precision typographic control, and have the time to invest in learning Quark, then go for it. Otherwise, I would choose PageMaker mostly for its ease of use and Aldus' outstanding technical support.

One other application is worth mentioning: FrameMaker. It is a powerful and well-integrated page layout tool that works best on long technical documents. It is not too easy to learn, however; and it requires a powerful Mac and a lot of memory and storage to run at a reasonable speed.

Using PageMaker

This section and the subsections that follow tell how to create a newsletter with PageMaker, from opening the document to printing the finished publication. The procedures are arranged in the same order you would go through them to create any publication, but the example is short and relatively simple so you can get through it quickly.

The basic steps of the procedure are:

1. Make a rough sketch and locate text and graphics files.
2. Create master pages that serve as templates for all other pages.
3. Place text and graphics on page one.
4. Refine the format of text and graphics on page one.
5. Place extra text on page two.
6. Print.

Of course, you will be saving your work frequently during the whole procedure. PageMaker encourages and often requires lots of creative effort. Losing the product of your creativity is especially frustrating, so save often.

Making a Rough Sketch and Collecting Files

Before you start in on the layout procedures in PageMaker, you should make at least a rough sketch for your newsletter and get the necessary text and graphics files together. There are a lot of choices you have to make as you set up your page design, and if you make a sketch before you start and know what the pieces are going to be, the pieces all fall into place much easier.

For instance, if you know you want a newsletter that looks something like the one in Figure 11.1, you can plan for three columns of text on standard letter-size paper, with some graphics and a logo at the top. You can make the margins and page numbering standard, plain vanilla.

FIGURE 11.1
A rough sketch of a newsletter layout

To keep the page from being too boring, you can plan for part of one story to span a couple of columns, like the one in the lower right corner of the sketch.

To build up a newsletter like this, you'll need some text files and some graphics files. You can use the practice files in the PageMaker Tutorial folder that you received with the application. Make sure the Tutorial folder is installed on your hard disk; it should be in the same folder with PageMaker. When you prepare to do an original PageMaker document of your own, you will have to get the text and graphics files together, preferably in one or two folders on the same hard disk with PageMaker, and check to make sure they are compatible with PageMaker and the printer you plan to use. See Appendix A for details on graphics file format compatibility.

Opening a Document

Take one of the following actions to open a new document in PageMaker, depending on your situation:

- To open a new document if you have not started PageMaker, double-click the application's icon, as shown in Figure 11.2, or click an alias for it.
- To open a new document if you have already started PageMaker, close your previous document, then choose New from the File menu.

FIGURE 11.2
The PageMaker icon

No matter which action you take, the Page setup dialog box appears, as shown in Figure 11.3.

Making Preliminary Page Settings

Before you even get into PageMaker, it asks you to make some settings for page size, margins, and orientation. Make these settings according to the basic look you decided upon when you made your sketch. Although the settings are not really part of the page layout, they set limits within which all the page layout decisions must fit, so don't take them lightly. The following steps describe how to make page setup settings for the newsletter I sketched in Figure 11.1.

1. Leave Page set to Letter. That's a good standard size for a newsletter.
2. Leave Page dimensions set at 8.5 by 11 inches.
3. Leave the Tall radio button selected for orientation.

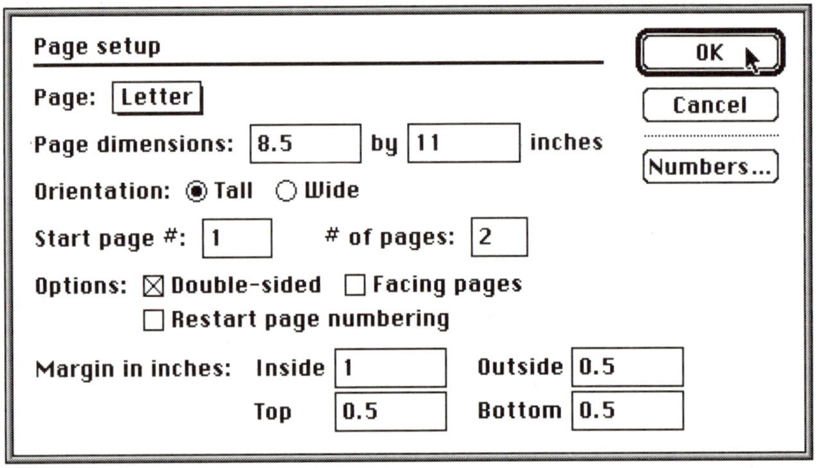

FIGURE 11.3
The Page setup dialog box

4. You want your document to start with page 1, but change the number of pages to 2 so the sample newsletter can be two pages long.
5. In the Options boxes leave Double-sided selected. The newsletter will be printed on both sides of one page.
6. Uncheck the Facing pages box. This lets you see more of your page, especially if you are working on a small-screen Mac.
7. Leave the Inside margin at 1 inch so newsletter readers can punch holes for binder rings.
8. Change all the other margins from 0.75" to 0.5" wide. This gives you more room for text
9. Click OK. The PageMaker document window opens, as shown in Figure 11.4.

FIGURE 11.4
The PageMaker document window

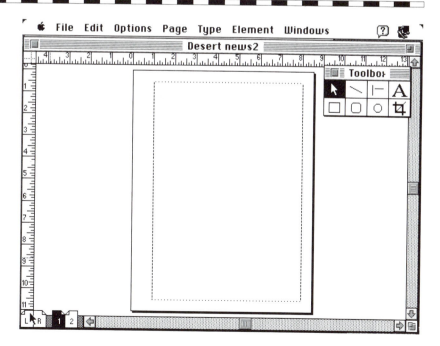

The PageMaker Document Window

The PageMaker document window displays a small Toolbox and a number of helpful features around the borders.

The Toolbox is a *floating palette,* which means it can be dragged with the pointer by the title bar to the position that's most convenient for you. It contains icons for tools you can use to do graphic work and select elements of the page you're creating.

- The pointer tool (the arrow-shaped tool) is for selecting text blocks and graphics.
- The tool to the right of the pointer is the diagonal-line tool. This tool draws straight lines at any angle.
- The next tool to the right is the perpendicular-line tool for drawing vertical and horizontal lines and lines at a 45-degree angle.
- The tool represented by the letter A is the text tool for selecting and editing text.
- The tool below the pointer tool is the square-corner tool for drawing squares or rectangles. Hold down the Shift key to draw a square.
- The next tool to the right also draws squares and rectangles, but with rounded corners.
- The circle-shaped tool is for drawing circles and ovals. You get circles by holding down the Shift key when you draw with this tool.
- The odd tool under the A is a cropping tool; you can cut graphics down to smaller sizes with it.

The document window can also display two other palettes. Choose Style palette from the Windows menu if you use styles to speed up formatting, or choose Color palette if you use Color. See the PageMaker *Reference Manual* for details on these palettes.

There are a number of other key elements of the document window:

- There are rulers on the top and left sides of the window. You can set the units of measurement for rulers by choosing Preferences from the Edit menu and making choices in the dialog box.
- The menu bar is above the window. Take a minute to explore the menus by clicking on the words and holding down the mouse button while you read.
- Scroll bars appear on the right and bottom of the window. Click on the arrows, move the scroll box, or just click in the scroll bar to move the document up or down in the window.
- Page icons appear in the bottom left corner of the window. You can click on the L and R icons to get to your left and right master pages (pages you set up as templates for all the rest). Click on the numbered pages to get to your actual working pages.
- The margins of your page are indicated by a magenta rectangle if you have a color monitor, or by dashed-line rectangle if you have a black and white monitor.
- The area outside of your page is called the pasteboard. This is where you place things you don't want showing on the current page but may want to get later for another page. Sometimes I put notes to myself here so I remember to check something later; the note doesn't show up on the page when I'm printing.

Creating Master Pages

Now that you know your way around the document window, you're probably champing at the bit, just itching to slap some text and graphics into that first page. Rein in. Remember that this is *page layout*, not just page fill-up. You need to set up master pages, so things that repeat on every page don't have to be placed over and over. Whatever you place on the master pages will show up on all the other pages in your document.

Master pages can save you lots of time. This is especially true if you plan to use the same format for a whole bunch of documents, like issues of a newsletter. When you start a new issue you can paste in your master pages from a previous issue, and you'll have a lot less work to do. So take a few moments and use the following procedures to create master pages for the sample newsletter.

To create three columns as in the sketch, take these steps:

1. Click on the L in the page icon in the lower left corner of the document window. The L stands for Left. Your left master page appears in the middle of the window.
2. Choose Column guides from the Options menu. The Column guides dialog box appears.
3. Change the number of columns to 3.
4. Leave the space between columns as it is and click OK. Column guides appear, dividing the area inside your margins into three equal vertical spaces.
5. Click the R page icon and repeat the above steps for the right master page.

Now that you have your columns, you can add page numbers. Even though the newsletter document only has two pages, number them. The newsletter may grow in the future and you'll want the numbers included in the design. If you set up the numbering on the master pages, all pages of your newsletter will be paginated, no matter how many you add.

1. Click in the L to get back to the left master page.

2. Select the text tool in the Toolbox and drag a little text block (a dotted rectangle) just outside the lower left hand corner of the margin area.

3. Look at your rulers as you drag. The dotted lines there show where your cursor is. If you start dragging at 10½" on the vertical ruler and 7/16" on the horizontal ruler, the block should come out about right.

4. If you are working on a small screen, press ⌘-1 to get a closer look at the placement of the text block. When you release your mouse button after dragging the text block, an insertion point appears.

5. Press ⌘-Option-P. On the left master page you'll see LM for left master page. The L should wind up just below the left margin guide, as shown in Figure 11.5.

6. Click on the R page icon and drag a text block just outside the lower right margin corner.

7. Type ⌘-Option-P. RM for right master page appears in the text block; the R should be under the right margin guide line.

The correct page numbers will automatically replace the LM and RM on the actual pages of the document.

When you are satisfied with your master pages, choose Save from the File menu or press ⌘-S. Save your work often in PageMaker; there

FIGURE 11.5
A page number symbol placed on the left master page

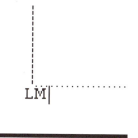

is nothing more frustrating than working out some great solution to a formatting problem, only to lose it to a power surge. For more information on saving, see "Saving and Printing a PageMaker Document" later in this chapter.

Placing Text

The following procedure tells how to place text in the sample newsletter columns, but it is the same basic procedure you use no matter what kind of document you are creating. In this case, you will place the text in all of the three columns, but you will leave some space at the beginning for your newsletter logo.

1. Click the page 1 icon in the lower left corner of the window. A right page appears with nothing on it but the column and margin guides and the page number. Books normally start each chapter with a right page; that's why PageMaker makes the first page a right one.

2. Choose Autoflow in the Options menu. This will place all of the text you bring in from someplace else, filling your column guides to make three nice columns. Even if it overflows onto another page of your document, it will *all* flow in.

3. Choose Place from the File menu or press ⌘-D. The Open dialog box appears. You probably see a list of folders in the Aldus PageMaker folder.

4. Double-click the Tutorial folder, then double-click the Basic Lesson folder.

5. Select the Practice text file and click OK.

6. Your cursor becomes a "loaded" text icon. It looks like a carpenter's square with a curvy arrow in it. If you ever select the wrong file, click in the Toolbox to unload the icon.

7. Line up the left side of the icon with the left margin guide, about half way down the left column. This will leave space for your logo.

8. Click the mouse button. Your text flows into the columns until the entire text file is placed.

Your page will now look like it's filled with three columns of gray bars, with some blank space at the top of the left column, and some at the bottom of the right column, as in Figure 11.6. It isn't too exciting, but it's a good start. It gives you a clear idea of how much room you have for graphics and a second story.

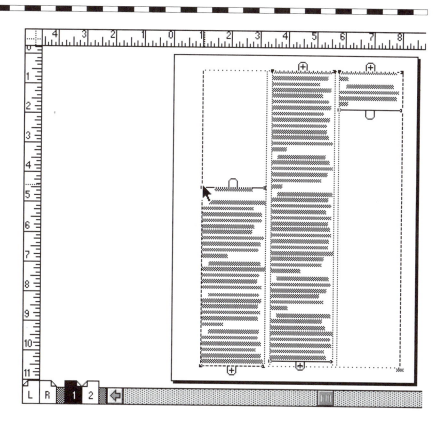

FIGURE 11.6
Text placed on the first page

Placing a Graphic

Placing graphics in PageMaker is just like placing text. The following procedure is for putting a nice graphic title at the head of your sample newsletter. You will place and size a graphic in the available space, but you won't be able to put it in the place you want it until you adjust the text layout.

1. Press ⌘-D and select the Anchor.TIF file in the Lesson 4 folder, then click OK.
2. Click with the loaded pointer at the top left corner of your newsletter, in the left column where you left some open space. The graphic appears at the same size and shape it was created. This isn't the size and shape you sketched, so let's change it.
3. Drag the handle (the little square) in the lower left corner of the graphic to the left, to make a long rectangle like the logo in the sketch. When you are done, it should look like Figure 11.7.
4. Select the sized graphic and move it as close as you can to where you want to place it. In the sample, you can't put the graphic at the top right corner of the page yet, so just line up the top edge with the top margin guide.
6. Save your file.

So how do you place that graphic where you want it? You have to move the text out of the way, but first you need to learn how to look at things up close.

Changing Your View of the Page

Once you have placed something, you will need to look at it up close to make sure the text reads correctly and is placed so the paragraphs break nicely at the ends of columns. In the Page menu, there are commands for making the current page fit in the window, appear at

FIGURE 11.7
A placed graphic

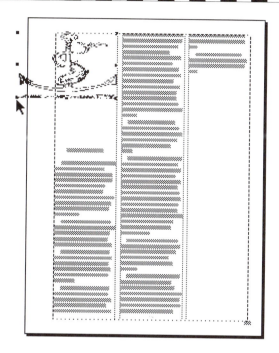

actual size, or appear at 25%, 50%, 75%, 200% or 400% of the actual size. There are also a couple of great tricks for zooming in and out of magnified views in PageMaker.

For example, let's take a closer look at the text you just placed. Choose Actual size from the Page menu or press ⌘-1 (for 100%) to see your text at the size it will print at. To get back to the default view, choose Fit in window from the Page menu, or press ⌘-W. To zoom in and out even faster, hold down the ⌘ and Option keys on the keyboard and click the part of the page that you want to see up close. Presto change-o. Now you can read your text!

If you want to see a part of your page at 200% (twice actual size) hold down ⌘-Option-Shift and click where you need to zoom in. Use the ⌘-Option-Shift-click action again and it toggles your view back to

100% size. These view-shifting commands work no matter which tool is selected at the time you use them.

Adjusting Text Blocks

After placing a graphic, you often need to adjust the text blocks to fit around it better. The following procedure tells how to adjust for the title graphic you added to the newsletter document. First you need to make an open space across the top of the page, and fit the text onto the page below that space. This will make room for the graphic, so it doesn't have to be squeezed into the upper left corner of the page. Then, to line the text and graphic up, you use ruler guides. These guides look like column and margin guides, but you can move them around easily.

1. Drag a ruler guide down from the top ruler. Just move the pointer into the top ruler and drag a horizontal dotted line down. Align the ruler guide with the bottom of your graphic. Now drag another ruler guide ¼" below that.

2. Adjust the three text blocks in the three columns by dragging them. Select a block by clicking it with the arrow tool, then put the pointer tool in the little windowshade handle at the top and drag the top line of the text block down to the lower of the two ruler guides.

3. If you have long columns of text, they will run off the bottom of the page. To adjust the text, first click on the long block, then drag the bottom windowshade handle up to the bottom margin of the page. To check the text for bad line breaks, zoom in by pressing ⌘-1. The shortened text block looks like the one in Figure 11.8.

When you shorten a text block, PageMaker keeps track of the text you just hid. It either flows into the next column, or it is loaded into the bottom windowshade handle to place elsewhere. If your selected text

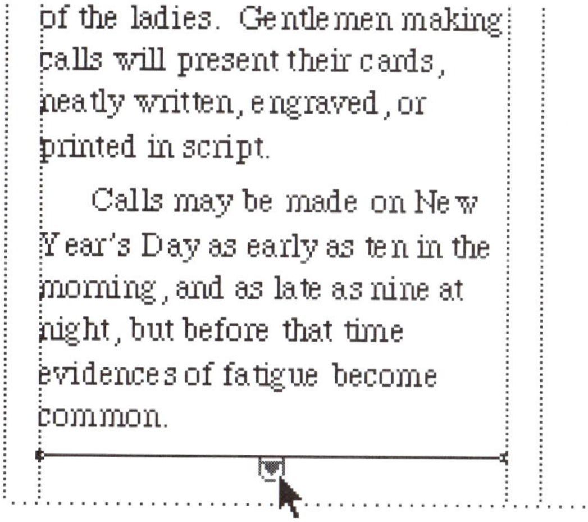

FIGURE 11.8
Adjusted text block with handle

> of the ladies. Gentlemen making calls will present their cards, neatly written, engraved, or printed in script.
>
> Calls may be made on New Year's Day as early as ten in the morning, and as late as nine at night, but before that time evidences of fatigue become common.

block has a plus sign in the windowshade handle, it means that there is text from the same story after this text block, in the next column or on the next page. If the windowshade handle has a triangle in it, as shown in Figure 11.8, then you know that there is more text from that story yet to be placed in your document. Click in that loaded windowshade handle, then move to a new column or a new page and use the loaded pointer to place the leftover text. The page should look like Figure 11.9.

Adjusting the Layout of a Document

OK, you've gotten your feet wet moving those text blocks. It's time to really start dragging things around, so you can achieve the layout in the sketch shown in Figure 11.1. This section tells how to move elements of text and graphics around on a page to improve the page's appearance and impact. The techniques used for the example newsletter can be used on any document; the key thing is to use the layout to give your material more impact.

FIGURE 11.9
The newsletter with its text adjusted

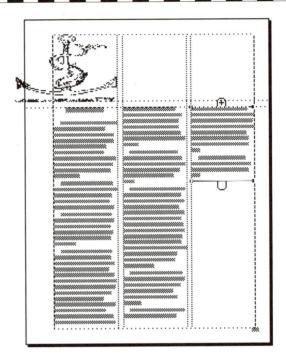

To get the look of that sketch, you need to add a thick line across the top of the page. Then you'll move all of the text up so you can add a little graphic to the lower left column and create a new text block that spans the two right columns down at the bottom.

You should be looking at your page in Fit in window view. Start your layout work by moving the graphic and raising the bottoms of the three columns of text:

1. Select the graphic and move it to the right side of the page. Keep it inside the ruler and margin guides.
2. Select the left column text block and drag the lower windowshade handle up about an inch. This will make space for your little graphic.

3. Shorten the text block in the center column up about a third of the page to make room for your two-column story. You may have to raise the right column text block now to match the center one.

4. If you wind up with a loaded windowshade handle, as shown in Figure 11.10, select it and click with the loaded text icon on the page 2 icon. Then place the extra text in the first column of that page. Come back to page 1 when you're done.

Now that you have moved the text out of the way, you can put in the new story that spans two columns.

1. Press ⌘-D to give the Place command.
2. Use the file list title of the Basic Lesson folder to move to the Tutorial folder, then open the Lesson 4 folder and select Story 2. Click OK.

FIGURE 11.10
Adjusting the layout

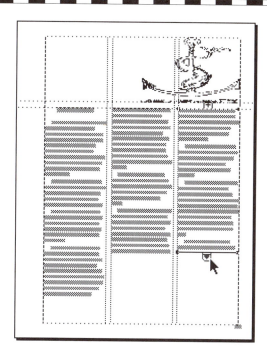

3. Drag a text block across the open space in the two left columns, starting at the column guide in the upper left corner of the space, about a half inch below the bottom of the existing text. The story fills in the two-column space.

4. If there is extra text, click the loaded windowshade handle, then click the page 2 icon and place the extra text in a different column from the other leftover text block.

Now that you have all your text in place, you can work on the graphic. Use the following procedure to add a thick line, or *rule*, across the top of the newsletter, running into the graphic there.

1. Click on the perpendicular-line tool. Draw a line by clicking next to the graphic and dragging to the left.

2. When your line is long enough, release the mouse button. The line should still be selected (you can tell by the selection handles on either end).

3. Choose Line from the Element menu. A submenu appears.

4. While still holding down the mouse button, drag to the right and down until 8 pt line is selected, then release the mouse button.

5. To run the line into the graphic, select it with the pointer tool and move it to the right until it touches the end of the anchor.

Go back to Fit in window view (⌘-W). Does your page look like Figure 11.11? If everything looks good so far, save your work by choosing Save from the File menu or pressing ⌘-S.

Changing Font Size and Style for Headings

To make the headings for the stories in your newsletter look good, you need to work on the fonts. The following steps show how to make the headings stand out and still fit in the format you have set up.

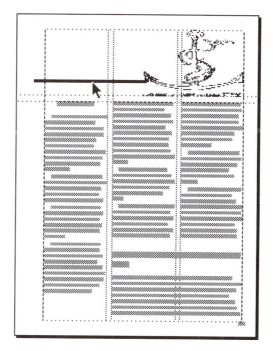

FIGURE 11.11
Adding a two-column story and adding a rule to the logo graphic

1. Hold down the ⌘ and Option keys and click on the first line of type in the first (far left) column. You see the heading, which looks puny.
2. Click on the text tool.
3. Select the heading.
4. To make it stand out, pull down the Type menu and choose Type style. Then go into the Type style submenu and choose Bold.
5. Use ⌘-Option-click to get back to Fit in window view, then use it again to zoom in on the heading for the two-column story. That heading is too big to fit in its space.
6. Select the heading with the text tool.

7. Pull down the Type menu and choose Size. Choose 14 from the Size submenu. The heading shrinks to fit.

Now let's add a nice dividing line between your two-column story and the rest of the text. Just take these steps.

1. Click on the perpendicular-line tool.
2. Pull down the Element menu, go into the Line submenu, and choose the medium-thick dashed line.
3. Drag a dashed line between the heading of the two-column story and the text of the other story.

Finally, you can add a title to your newsletter by following these steps:

1. Select the text tool from the Toolbox and type **Anchor News** somewhere on the pasteboard.
2. Select the title, then go through the Type menu to the Size submenu and choose 24 points.
3. Go through the Type menu again to the Type style submenu and choose Outline. If the font isn't Times, choose that from the Font submenu of the Type menu, too.
4. Select the pointer tool from the Toolbox and select the title.
5. Drag the title to the open space to the left of the newsletter logo. Move it around until it looks right.

Hey, that front page is looking pretty good. For a really classy touch, though, you can go on to the next section and see how to add a little graphic and wrap text around it.

Wrapping Text around a Graphic

The following procedure tells how to add a graphic and form the body text to fit around it. This can be a good way to add interest and clarity to your layout, and not use up too much space. You may want to use more informative graphics than the one in the sample, but the method is always the same.

Start with these steps to place the graphic:

1. Press ⌘-D for the Place command.
2. Select the Anchor.TIF file in the Lesson 4 folder and click OK.
3. Click with the loaded icon just below the text on the left margin of your page.

The graphic probably extends down too far, but don't worry, you'll move it up soon. First, follow these steps to turn on text wrap:

1. While the graphic is still selected, choose Text wrap from the Element menu. You see the Text wrap dialog box.
2. Click on the middle wrap option, as shown in Figure 11.12. The Text flow setting changes to Wrap-all-sides, which means that the text will flow around all sides of the graphic, wherever it will fit. In this case, it will only fit on the right side of the graphic. PageMaker automatically selects the standoff dimensions.
3. Click OK.

The dialog box goes away and now your graphic has two sets of selection handles. One set controls the graphic and the other controls the text wrap. The text wrap boundary looks like a dotted line with handles (little black boxes) at the corners.

1. Use ⌘-Option-Shift click to zoom up close to the graphic.
2. Move the pointer into the middle of the graphic and drag it up until the bottom is lined up with the bottom margin guide.

FIGURE 11.12
The Text wrap dialog box

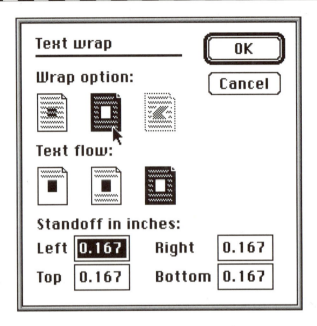

3. Drag the bottom windowshade for the text block down to the bottom margin.
4. Click anywhere on the dotted text wrap boundary and you get another handle.
5. Drag a point or a segment of the boundary to change the wrap. When you finish a boundary move, the text fills in for you.
6. Create a boundary that closely resembles the graphic, as in Figure 11.13.

If you notice that the text that's fitting into the new spaces you've made disappears after each redraw, you have to choose Send to back from the Element menu while the graphic is selected. Also, make sure you check the text that follows your new graphic on the page. Part of your story may have flowed to another column or a heading may have been pushed out of place. Fix any text problems, then save your work

FIGURE 11.13
Text wrapped around a graphic

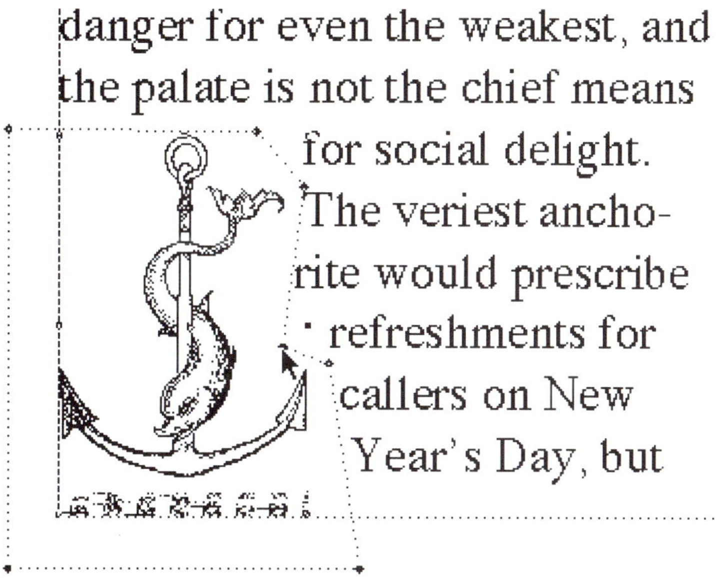

> danger for even the weakest, and the palate is not the chief means for social delight. The veriest anchorite would prescribe refreshments for callers on New Year's Day, but

by pressing ⌘-S. The front page should look like Figure 11.14. Happy with how your newsletter looks on screen? If you are, you can go ahead with printing.

Saving and Printing a PageMaker Document

To protect your PageMaker work, save it often, about every fifteen minutes while you are working on it. All you have to do is choose Save from the File menu or press ⌘-S. The first time you save a document, you must name it and choose where to place it in your folder hierarchy, or it will be called "Untitled" and placed in the same folder with the PageMaker application. For more information on using the Save command, see "Saving Your Work on a Document" in Chapter 4.

To print a hard copy of your document, first save it, then choose Print from the File menu or type ⌘-P. The Print to dialog box appears.

FIGURE 11.14
Finished sample
PageMaker document

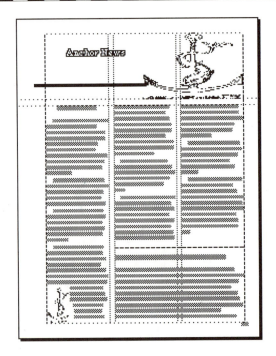

Select your printer type from the Printer box menu at the bottom of the dialog box. If this box is blank, printing will not start. If you want one copy of page one only, press the Tab key twice until the second page range box is selected. Then type 1 in there. Click Print to begin printing. For more information on printing, see Chapter 3.

Troubleshooting Problems in PageMaker

The following subsections cover the problems you are most likely to have while working with PageMaker and other page layout applications.

Missing text.

Remember that text blocks in the same story are linked or threaded together. If you change one text block, it affects the others. If you are missing some text, look on the next page or next column; chances are it flowed from the text block you changed to another text block in that next column or on that next page.

Can't find the center of a page or column.

Want to find the center of the page or a column? Draw a rectangle the width (or height) of what you are trying to find the center of. The selection handles in the middle of the rectangle will be the center of the column or page.

Can't find an object left on the pasteboard.

You can't find some text you were sure you left on the pasteboard? Hold down the Shift key while you select Fit in window from the Page menu, or type ⌘-0 (zero). This fits the whole pasteboard in your window. When you find the text, move it near to the page you want to put it on, then zoom in to a closer view and drag the text to where you want it.

Can't calculate measurements in the middle of the page.

To measure something on your page, go up to the upper left corner of your PageMaker window where the two rulers meet and click on the space with the dotted lines in it. Then drag along one ruler or the other until the zero point is aligned with your graphic or whatever it is that you want to measure.

Can't select a hidden element.

To select something that is behind some other element, hold down the ⌘ key while you keep clicking, until the item you want is selected. This problem occurs most often when you place a large graphic or long text block and it runs right over a small block of text. After you ⌘-click to select the covered-up item, drag it out to the pasteboard, then place it where it won't get covered up again.

Added text doesn't thread to next text block.

You are trying to add text to the end of a text block with the text tool, but the text doesn't thread into the next text block; it just goes on down the page mindlessly. The problem is that you put the insertion point below the bottom or beyond the side of the text block you were trying to add to. Select the new text, choose Cut from the Edit menu, place the insertion point carefully inside the text block, then choose Paste from the Edit menu.

When you type in text, it is in the wrong font.

The default font is wrong. To change it, click on the pointer tool (not the text tool, as you might expect), then go through the Type menu to the Font submenu and choose the font you want to have as your current default. It will be the font you see when you type unless you change the font just before entering text. If you bring in text from an application with different defaults, you'll get those defaults inside the text blocks, however.

You can't move the ruler or column guides.

You probably want to get your guides out of the way so you can do some detail work, but they won't budge. Pull down the Options menu and see if Lock Guides has a check in front of it. Select it if it does, and the guides will come unlocked so you can move them. Move them back home after you're done with your detail work, and you can choose Lock Guides again to make them stay put for your other work.

Loaded icon appears when you try to drag a windowshade handle.

All you were doing was trying to move a windowshade up or down, for crying out loud, and now you've got this loaded icon on your hands. The problem is that you clicked in a windowshade handle with a plus or a triangle in it, when what you meant to do was drag the handle. Don't aim that loaded icon at anybody, whatever you do. Just move it up into the Toolbox and click the pointer (or any other tool). Then go back to that windowshade handle, and this time, hold the mouse button down firmly as you drag the handle up or down.

The story doesn't appear in the Edit story window.

You choose Edit story from the Edit menu so you can see the whole story you are working on, instead of all those pieces in text blocks. But instead of seeing the whole story, you see nothing, or just a little fuzzy patch. The problem is that no part of the story is selected. Close the empty window, click with either the text or pointer tool in any part of the story, then choose Edit story from the Edit menu again. There you go; it wasn't in the twilight zone after all.

Difficult to line things up on margin, column, or ruler guides.

You can't get anything to stick to those guides; things like text blocks and loaded icons just drift off the guides, right and left. The problem is embarrassingly simple; Snap to guides is off. Just choose Snap to guides from the Options menu, and all the text and graphics will get right in line for you, like obedient little soldiers.

Columns incorrect.

Either you have the wrong number of columns, or you want to change the spacing between your columns. You might think that you have to start all over to get back to the Page setup dialog box. Not to worry. Just choose Column guides from the Options menu and change the settings. Of course, changing the guides or spaces won't rearrange the text you have already placed. You have to do that yourself.

Can't find a file you want to place.

Don't feel bad. It happens to us all. You hit ⌘-D, the file box opens with a list of some obscure bunch of files somewhere in the bowels of your folder hierarchy, and you just stare at the screen, wondering where the heck you put that graphic you were ready to place. Click Cancel to get out of the dialog box, then use the Find command in the Finder to find your file.

PageMaker file will not print.

This can be due to many things. If the print job won't even start, there is probably something in the file that is not printable. The most likely candidate is a graphic that cannot be printed on your printer, such as an EPS (Encapsulated PostScript) file that you are trying to print to a non-PostScript printer, or a font that the printer can't handle.

If the file prints part way and then hangs up, you have a problem graphic in there, or the file is just too complex for the printer to take into its limited RAM all at once. Try compressing the whole file by using Save as to save it (click Yes when asked if you want to replace the existing item with the same name), then print it again. If that doesn't help, choose Proof print (print without graphics) in the Options dialog box (you get the Options dialog box by clicking the Options button in the Print dialog box). If the file prints without the graphics, then you can bet you have a graphic that is causing problems. If there are any uncompressed TIFF files in the document, replace them with compressed versions of the TIFF graphics. If there are some really complex TIFF, EPS, or PICT graphics, they can choke some laser printers. Print the document one page at a time to find out where the problem graphic is.

For some hints (sometimes very obscure, jargon-riddled hints) as to what is causing the problem, you can click the PostScript button in the Print dialog box, then click the check box for View last error message, and see the message generated by the mishap.

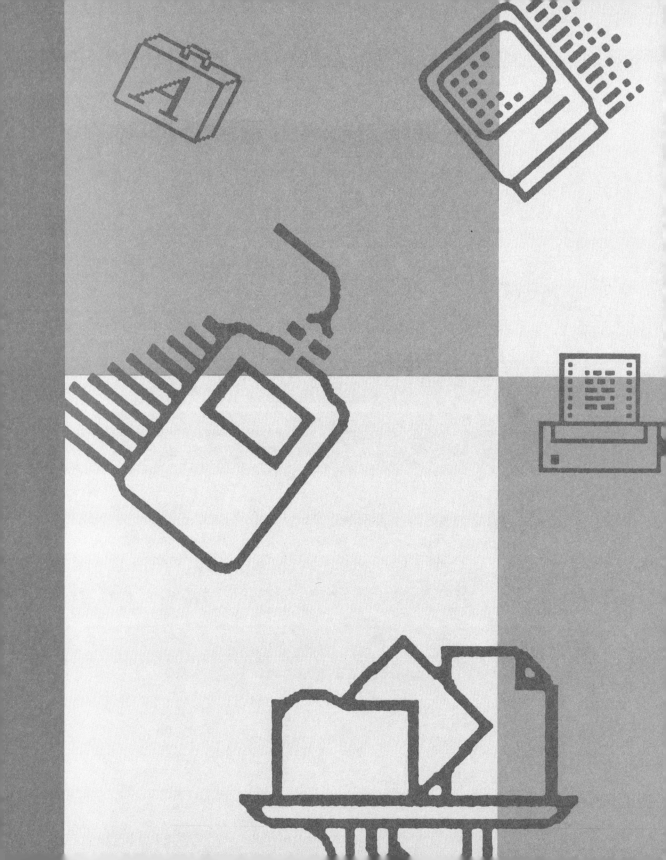

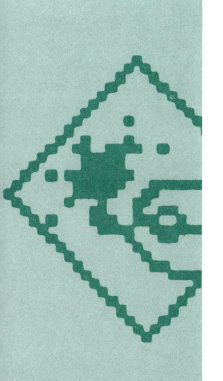

CHAPTER 12

Spreadsheets

The spreadsheet is the computer version of the accountant's ledger. Many businesses use spreadsheets to keep track of transactions, budgets, receivables, payables, and the like. You can create spreadsheets that will help you balance your own budget and plan your finances.

The key difference between an accountant's ledger and a spreadsheet is that a spreadsheet does most of the accounting automatically. You enter each figure only once and the spreadsheet does all the calculating for you—no more punching long lists of numbers into a calculator. What's even better, a spreadsheet can easily accommodate changes in your figures. You can make corrections, or explore "what-if" scenarios, without endless erasing and scribbling.

But modern spreadsheets do more than just make calculations; they can create graphs of your data and work as database managers. They can, with the swoop of the mouse, sum up an entire column. They have special formulas built in, even nasty ones like finding percentages. They can even change the color of the type in your charts so they look more interesting.

Which Spreadsheet for You?

It used to be that spreadsheet applications didn't have many features. You could make a spreadsheet, do basic calculations of items in the cells, and print out your results. Today the choices are far more complex, and as the Mac system software advances, spreadsheets such as

Excel and Resolve expand to take advantage of the new versions. On the other hand, there are less expensive spreadsheet applications that may not have every feature in the world, but that often can do what most people in business need: keep good records and help forecast financial developments.

High-Power Spreadsheet Applications

There are a number of powerful spreadsheet tools that are designed for the Mac, including Full Impact, Wingz, Resolve, and Excel, but the last two are far and away the most prominent. If you want to create spreadsheets and three-dimensional color graphs for presentation purposes, Full Impact is a good choice. Wingz also shines when it comes to 3D graphs, and if you like to use HyperScript you can customize Wingz to a great degree. But Full Impact has a very small base of users, and Wingz can be slow to draw its spiffy graphs. If you want to get quick access to spreadsheet power, the best choices are Excel and Resolve.

Excel has long been a leader in the features department, but Resolve has high-power features of its own, and it is relatively easy to learn. If you are an old hand at spreadsheets and macros, and you want raw power for customizing, calculating, or programming, Excel is probably the best choice. If you are looking for ease of use and a clear, intuitive interface that makes high-power spreadsheet work a breeze, try Resolve. If you have needs for specific features, such as a particular set of statistical functions or a certain type of graph, check out both programs and see which is best for you. They both have lots of power, and Excel is improving its usability, too.

Budget Spreadsheet Applications

If you just want to make a simple spreadsheet and don't need graphs, you can use a basic application like MacCalc. If you want to integrate a spreadsheet with another application such as a word processor or a database, you should look into Microsoft Works, BeagleWorks, or ClarisWorks. Of the three, Microsoft Works provides the most spreadsheet power, including fairly good graphing capability and most of the functions you need for business analysis. But it can't do anything with text in cells. Any low-cost spreadsheet will have limitations of this sort. So you might try one if you do only simple record-keeping and financial forecasting for a small business, but not if you need to develop complex, customized tables and sophisticated graphs. Low-budget spreadsheets also tend to lack programming tools, number-crunching power, and graphic finesse.

Using Excel

In the sections that follow, you can learn how to set up and use a simple worksheet with Excel (a worksheet is a spreadsheet in progress). The procedures guide you to understand the basic concepts of Mac spreadsheets in general, and some of the special powers you have when you use Excel. You can also use these steps to begin setting up your own spreadsheet, but for full use of the advanced features of Excel, see the *User's Guide* and *Functions Reference*.

The first step to take when you are making a new spreadsheet is to sketch out a rough plan. If you plot out the basic design and content of your spreadsheet, how many columns you'll need and how many rows, what kinds of titles will look best and what form of data will be presented, you can save yourself a lot of time and effort. However, not much planning is needed for the simple spreadsheet you'll create in this section. It will be very straightforward, and it will only take up about a half dozen rows and five columns.

Starting a New Document

Take one of the following actions to open a spreadsheet in Excel, depending on your situation.

- If you have not started Excel, double-click on the Excel icon, as shown in Figure 12.1, or an alias for it.
- To open a new spreadsheet if you have started Excel and are looking at an existing worksheet, choose New from the File menu, then click OK in the small dialog box.

You should now be looking at a blank page of a worksheet, like the one shown in Figure 12.2. It consists of small boxes, or *cells*, that are separated into rows and columns throughout the page. Each cell has a name; the cell in the upper left corner is in the A column and the 1 row, so it is called the A1 cell. The A1 cell should be highlighted when a fresh document is created.

At the top of the Excel window, there is a toolbar with some buttons in it. These are for Excel's graphics features. You'll learn how to use them as you work through the following sections.

You can highlight other cells by clicking on them with your pointer, which looks like a big plus sign now. Each cell can hold a single piece of information: either a number, a name, or a formula. The page of cells is expandable; you can scroll happily for quite some time either down or to the right. There is an end to the cells, but you probably won't fill them up for some time.

FIGURE 12.1
The Microsoft Excel icon

FIGURE 12.2
The Excel window

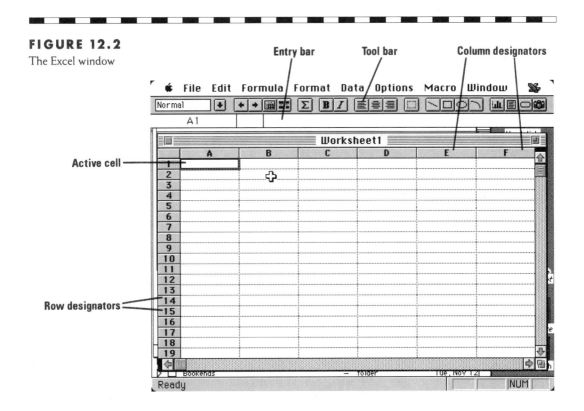

Entering Some Data

Start your worksheet by clicking in cell A3. Now type the word **Name**. Notice that the words appear in a bar near the top of the screen as in Figure 12.3. This bar is called the *entry bar*. If you make a mistake just use the Delete key to correct it or click on the X next to the entry bar near the top of the screen. This X is the *Cancel button*.

If you want to keep what you've typed, click on the check mark; this enters the word *Name*. You can also use the Return key on your keyboard instead of the check mark; this selects the next cell down.

FIGURE 12.3

Entering text in a cell

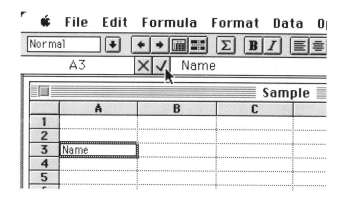

Now that you can enter data into a cell, go ahead and enter the data shown in Figure 12.4. Move from cell to cell by clicking in the cell you want to use or by using the arrow keys on your keyboard.

Now look over your worksheet to make sure all the figures are right. If you made a mistake, just click on the cell with the incorrect data, select the incorrect part of the data in the entry bar (up at the top of the window), and edit it. The entry bar works just like a little word processor. You can select, delete, or change the text in the entry bar just as you would if you were using Microsoft Word.

FIGURE 12.4

Entering more text and numbers

	A	B	C	D	E
1					
2		First Sale	Second Sale	Third Sale	
3	Name	Classic	LC	IIsi	
4	Macintosh	1199	1729	2898	
5	Monitor	0	475	699	
6	Printer	465	999	1749	
7	Modem	139	139	465	
8					
9					
10					
11					
12					

When all the data looks right, choose Save from the File menu. Save often in Excel; it can be hard to reconstruct a spreadsheet if you lose it to a power surge or something.

Changing Type Style and Format

Now that you have some data, you'll want to make it look a little nicer. The following exercise shows how to make bold and italic text, and how to center whatever you have in a cell.

1. Click on *First Sale* in cell B2.
2. Click on the B button located above the entry bar. Now cell B2 should be bold. This is a simple way to make a title stand out more.
3. Repeat these steps for *Second Sale* and *Third Sale* so that all the column titles are bold.
4. Names like Classic and LC are not column titles, but they should also stand out, so let's make them italic. Click on *Classic* in cell B3.
5. This time, we'll use a shortcut method to change all the names at once. Hold down the Shift key on the keyboard while clicking the mouse on cell D3. *Classic* should be highlighted normally, while *LC* and *IIsi* should now look highlighted in a new way. These cells are shown differently so that you know which one was clicked first.
6. Now click on the I button above the entry bar. All three cells should now be italic.
7. Finally, we'll create a title and anchor it. Click in the cell C1 so that it becomes selected.
8. Type **Macintosh Sales Price Comparison** and click the check mark. Don't worry if the text gets too long to fit inside the cell.

Excel knows what to do in situations like this. When you click the check mark, the text appears on the spreadsheet.

9. Make sure that you have clicked the check mark, and that cell C1 is still selected. Then click the Center button (two buttons to the right of the Italic button). Your spreadsheet should now look like Figure 12.5.

Using Insert

No matter how much planning you do, you'll almost always run into something that needs to be changed. For example, even though you have a nice title, now things seem a little squished. It would be nice if there was a blank row between the title and the rest of the table. Luckily, Excel is flexible; you can easily insert a blank row where you want it.

1. Click on the number two row label. This selects the entire row.
2. Select Insert from the Edit menu.

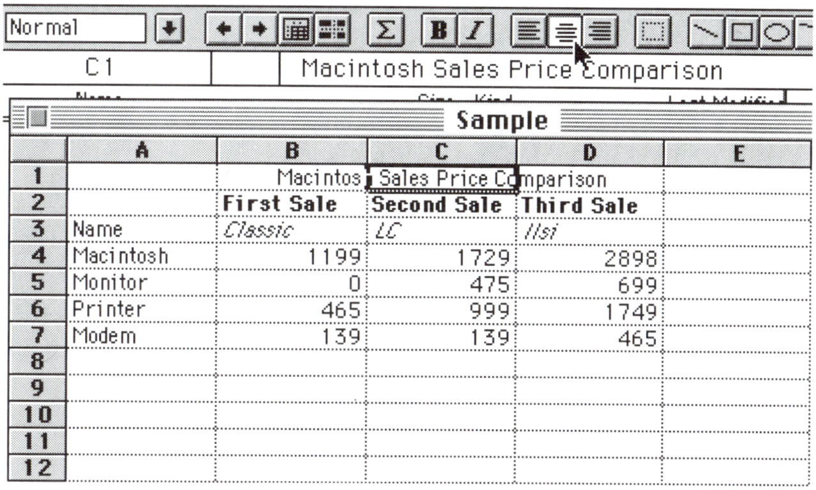

FIGURE 12.5
Formatting the spreadsheet

You should now have a new blank row in your table. This time, the insertion was not entirely necessary. In many cases, though, it can mean much more than aesthetics. For example, it can separate ranges on which you use different functions.

Using the Font Dialog Box

The title over the table is nice, but to my eye, it's not quite impressive enough. Let's use a bigger font for the title.

1. Start by clicking on cell C1; this selects the heading.
2. Choose Font from the Format menu to bring up the Font dialog box.
3. Click 18 under Size and click in the Bold check box.
4. If you have a color monitor you might try selecting a color as well.
5. Click in the OK button to finish up.

You now have a spreadsheet title that stands out clearly.

Range Selection and Changing the Number Format

For a last change in format, you can select all of the cells that contain numbers and force these numbers to look more like dollar amounts.

1. Select all of the cells with numbers in them. Start by clicking on the upper leftmost number, in cell B5. Don't let your finger up from the mouse button, though; drag the mouse to the lower rightmost number, in cell D8. Then release the mouse button. This highlights the entire *range*, or block, so you can work with it all at once.

2. Choose Number from the Format menu. This should bring up a dialog box with some very odd looking figures that may read like hieroglyphics if you've never seen them before. These lines of gibberish actually do have meaning. They are formatting characteristics that tell the computer how to display numbers. The default setting is General. This means that it displays numbers right-justified and without a decimal point in most cases.

3. Choose the third format down. This should be 0.00. This tells the computer you want all the numbers to look like dollars and cents with the decimal in the right spot.

4. Notice that the format you choose and an example of this format appear below. You might also note that this example is taken from the top leftmost cell that you choose. You should experiment with the other formats to try to get a feel for what they mean. When you've finished experimenting and you're back to 0.00, click in the OK button.

You now have a nice spreadsheet that shows how much each Mac, monitor, printer, and modem sold for.

Using Formulas

So far you've created the entire worksheet by typing the information in each cell. This is fine for making a short simple listing of prices, but if you want to show a value that's the sum of the sales figures, you should use a *formula*.

A formula is simply a mathematical equation relating the data in two or more cells of the spreadsheet. You can write formulas that perform a variety of mathematical operations, from addition and subtraction to finding percentages and averages.

The main reason you use formulas is because they'll change if you change the cells they refer to. This is because they use *variables* that refer to the cells containing your figures. For instance, the formula =*A1*A2* multiplies the figure in cell A1 by the figure in cell A2, regardless of what the actual figures in these cells are. This flexibility makes formulas the key time-saving feature of spreadsheets.

The following short procedure shows how to add up the amounts shown in a group of cells.

1. In cell A10, type **Subtotal** and click the check mark.
2. Click in cell B10 and type =. Typing = starts a formula.
3. Now type **B5+B6+B7+B8**, as in Figure 12.6, then click the check mark.

This formula tells Excel that the value to be put in this cell equals the sum of all the cells from B5 to B8. Another way to add up simple sums like this is to select the cell (B10), click the sum button (Σ) in the tool bar, then select the cells to be summed (B5 to B8). You can also write formulas that will subtract, multiply, or divide figures by using these mathematical operators: − for subtraction, * for multiplication, and / for division.

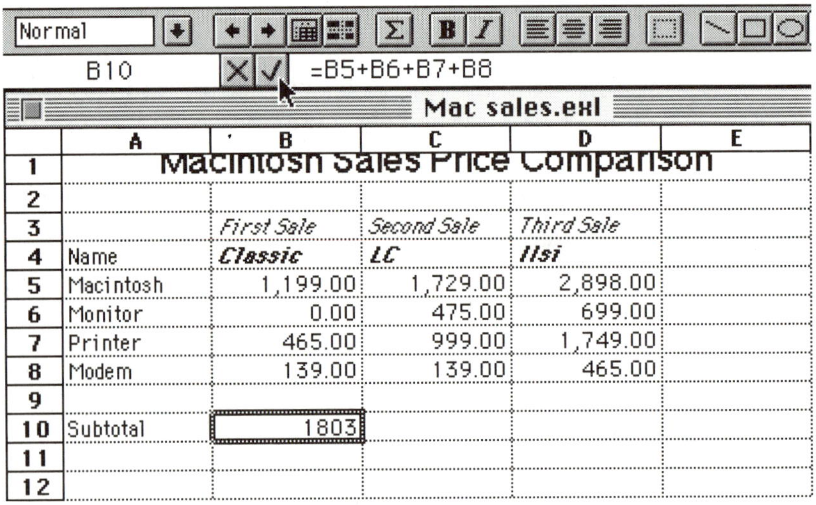

FIGURE 12.6
Using a formula to add up numbers

	A	B	C	D	E
1			Macintosh Sales Price Comparison		
2					
3		First Sale	Second Sale	Third Sale	
4	Name	Classic	LC	IIsi	
5	Macintosh	1,199.00	1,729.00	2,898.00	
6	Monitor	0.00	475.00	699.00	
7	Printer	465.00	999.00	1,749.00	
8	Modem	139.00	139.00	465.00	
9					
10	Subtotal	1803			
11					
12					

Whenever you type a formula, the entry bar displays what you typed, but as soon as you click the check mark, the cell will show the numerical value of the sum. The entry bar always shows the formula while the cell itself shows the value of the result of that formula.

Using the Fill Function

You can now add up the other two columns for Mac sales, but you can use a shortcut to do the task more quickly. You can tell Excel that you are going to do the same sort of calculation to get the results in cells C10 and D10, but you will be using the data in columns C and D to get the sums. Excel can fill in these similar formulas, basing them on the one you put in cell B10.

1. Click on cell B10 and drag to cell D10 so that all three are selected.
2. Under the Edit menu choose Fill Right.

Wow! If everything went well, you just got Excel to do a bunch of work for us. All three cells should now have the subtotals for their corresponding columns. Fill is one of the simplest, but most useful, functions of spreadsheets. You'll find that you can use it just about anywhere.

Absolute Cell Referencing

Sometimes Excel has a hard time knowing which cell you want it to refer to when you choose Fill Right or Fill Down. To help Excel, you can specify an *absolute cell reference*. To see how these absolute references work, use the following procedure to add a Tax row to the table.

1. To prepare for inevitable changes in the tax percentage, add a separate area for it. Select cell A15 and type **Tax %**.
2. Click in cell B15 and choose Number from the Format menu.

3. Select 0.00% and click in the OK button.
4. Now enter **0.065** (this is the tax rate) into cell B15. Notice that it displays as a percentage after you click the check mark. This is because you formatted cell B15 to display a percentage in steps 2 and 3.
5. Type **Tax** into cell A11.
6. Select cell B11 and enter the formula **=B10*$B15**. The reference to cell B15 is absolute because it has a dollar sign in front of it. If you fill the formula to other cells, it will always refer back to cell B15 for the second multiplier. Click the check mark, and the tax for column B appears.
7. By selecting cells B11 through D11 and choosing Fill Right from the Edit menu, you can extend the formula over all three cells.

The figures that appear in cells B11, C11 and D11 are the results of the formulas. They all refer to the tax number in cell B15, so if the tax rate changes, all you have to do is change the figure in B15 and all of the tax figures in cells B11, C11, and D11 will change automatically. This sort of setup (a bunch of formulas that have the same absolute cell reference) can save an awful lot of work if you have hundreds of figures that are dependent upon one variable like the tax rate.

Completing the Spreadsheet

You now have everything you need to make a Total row in the table. This will complete the table and review some of the steps you used previously.

1. Enter **Total** in cell A13.
2. In cell B13, type **=SUM(B10:B11)**. This is a shorthand way of totaling a column of numbers. It finds the total of the Tax and Subtotal for the B column.

3. Complete the other formulas for this row by using Fill Right.
4. Make the row bold by using the Bold button.
5. Lastly, choose Number from the Format menu to change the number format to represent dollar amounts.

Great. You are all done with the table. It should look like Figure 12.7. After it's all set up, you might try experimenting by changing some of the price entries. Notice that the values for the totals and the taxes change when you change the prices. After you have completed the chart in the next section, you will notice that the chart changes to represent the new figures as well.

Using Charts

Charts are surprisingly easy to create in Excel and they can look quite impressive. All you need to know is what data you want to chart. After you select the data, Excel does the chart work for you.

FIGURE 12.7
Completed sample worksheet

	A	B	C	D	E
1	Macintosh Sales Price Comparison				
2					
3		First Sale	Second Sale	Third Sale	
4	Name	Classic	LC	IIsi	
5	Macintosh	1199.00	1729.00	2898.00	
6	Monitor	0.00	475.00	699.00	
7	Printer	465.00	999.00	1749.00	
8	Modem	139.00	139.00	465.00	
9					
10	Subtotal	1803	3342	5811	
11	Tax	117.195	217.23	377.715	
12					
13	Total	1920.20	3559.23	6188.72	
14					
15	Tax %	6.50%			
16					

Chapter 12

You can make a meaningful chart for the sample table you've just completed, comparing how the price of each piece of each computer relates to the others. You shouldn't chart the totals, since they are so much larger they would throw off the scale. However, you will need to select the labels of the rows and columns since you have to tell Excel to put the names of each computer on the chart.

Use the following procedure to get the idea of how Excel can make a chart out of your spreadsheet data. Save your spreadsheet before you graph it. For more information on saving, see "Saving and Printing an Excel Document" later in this chapter.

1. Drag the mouse from cell A4 to cell D8. This selects the range of data you want charted.

2. Now scroll the spreadsheet to the left until H is the leftmost column so the chart can have a page of its own.

3. Click on the Chart button above the entry bar (it's the fourth from the right, with a little bar chart on it). Notice that the bottom help bar tells you what needs to be done to complete the chart.

4. Drag from cell H2 to cell M15 and release the mouse button. The size of this block only needs to be approximate; you can always adjust the size later. Click OK in the dialog box to create the chart. Now you have a chart, but it's pretty ugly and uninformative.

5. To spruce it up, double-click right in the middle of the chart. This should bring up a window exactly the size of the chart and should alter the menus a little. This is the charting mode of Excel.

6. First, try changing the type of chart you're working with. Choose Area from the Gallery menu.

7. A large dialog box appears. Click in the fourth picture and then click in the OK button. This should make the chart look a little more fancy.

8. The numbers seem to clutter the picture with zeros. Since this will be a qualitative chart you can delete them entirely. Double-click right on one of the numbers. This should bring up a big dialog box with all sorts of options. You don't have to learn them all right now. Just think of the possibilities, though, if you really want to get into charting.

9. Click the None radio button under Tick Labels and then click in the OK button. Not only do the numbers go away, but Excel readjusts the graph so that it still fits in the window. You can always take manual control of this adjustment, but it sure is nice to have Excel do it automatically.

10. Finally, the graph doesn't tell which color (or shade) represents which computer. You need to add a legend. Choose Add Legend from the Chart menu.

11. You might want to move the legend to a better spot, as in Figure 12.8. Just click and drag it to the spot you want it to go.

12. To place our spruced-up chart back into the Excel document, just choose Close from the File menu or click in the close box.

Saving and Printing an Excel Document

To protect your work in Excel, save it often, like every ten to fifteen minutes. All you have to do is choose Save from the File menu, or press ⌘-S. The first time you save a document, you must name it and choose where to place it in your folder hierarchy. There's also an Options button that allows you to password-protect your file and save in many different formats. For more information on this, see "Saving Your Work on a Document" in Chapter 4.

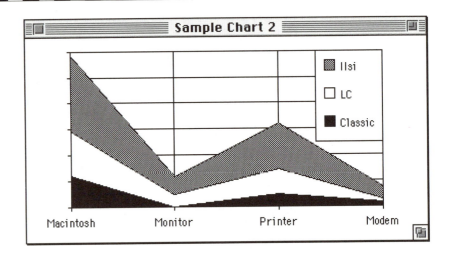

FIGURE 12.8
Chart for the sample spreadsheet

After creating your table and chart, you can print them out. Before you print, choose Print Preview from the File menu; you get a look at exactly what the printed pages are going to look like. It's always a good idea to preview before you print, because sometimes printing spreadsheets can take a while.

When you are sure your spreadsheet is ready to go, choose Print from the File menu and click in the OK button in the dialog box. The printer will chew on the spreadsheet and chart for a while, then give you a hard copy. Make sure you save before you print. Printing seems to be one of those times when programs lose data the most. When printing out the file you just created, the table and the chart should come out on different pages. You might try moving the chart under the table to get them on a single page. For more information on printing, see Chapter 3.

Using Resolve

The next few sections will outline the basic steps of using Resolve to set up a simple worksheet (a *worksheet* is a spreadsheet in progress).

You can follow the procedures as written, or you can use them as guidelines for setting up your own worksheet. For full use of Resolve's advanced features, see the Resolve *User Guide* and *Functions and Scripts*.

The first thing to do when setting up a brand new worksheet is to formulate a plan. The more planning you do before you start, the faster you'll set up your worksheet. Planning for a spreadsheet doesn't have to be complex, though; it can just be a thought. However, if your worksheet is complex, it's best to spend your time sketching out a picture first.

Starting a New Document

Take one of the following actions to open a new worksheet, depending on your situation:

- If you have not started Resolve, double-click on the Resolve icon, as shown in Figure 12.9, or an alias for the icon.
- If you are already looking at an existing worksheet, choose New from the File menu.

In either case a blank worksheet appears. It is made up of small boxes, or *cells*, that are organized into rows and columns that fill the window. Each cell has a name; the top left cell is in column A and row 1, so it is called the A1 cell. It is highlighted when you open Resolve. To highlight other cells so you can put things in them, click on them with the pointer, which is a fat plus sign, as shown in Figure 12.10. When you highlight a cell, you can put either a name, a number, or a formula in it.

FIGURE 12.9
The Resolve icon

FIGURE 12.10
The Resolve window

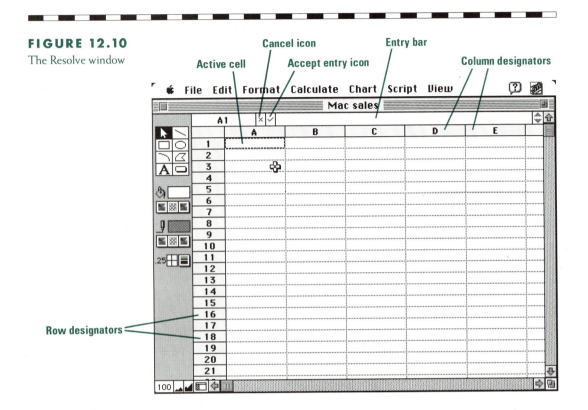

There are many, many more cells than those showing on the screen; you can scroll for miles either down or to the right.

To the left of all the cells there is a panel with some tools in it. These are for graphics features in Resolve. You will learn how to use these later in the chapter.

Entering Some Data

Click in cell A3 to start making your sample spreadsheet. Type in **Name**. The word appears in the bar at the top of the window, as shown in Figure 12.11. This is the entry bar. If you make a mistake while entering something, you can either press the Delete key to back up over the

FIGURE 12.11

Entering text in a cell

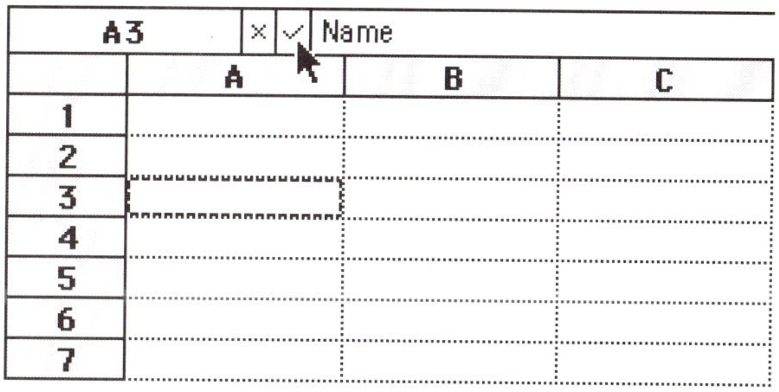

mistake, or click the X next to the entry bar. The X is a cancel icon; it lets you start over in the entry for the cell.

If you typed *Name* correctly and you want to put it in the selected cell, click on the check mark to the left of the entry bar. This is the accept entry icon. You can also just press the Return key to accept the word and move down to the next cell.

Now that you have entered a title in one cell, try entering titles and numbers in a few more. Enter the data shown in Figure 12.12, using the exact same cells. Click each new cell you want to fill by clicking in it with the pointer, or move from cell to cell with the arrow keys on your keyboard.

FIGURE 12.12

Entering more text and numbers

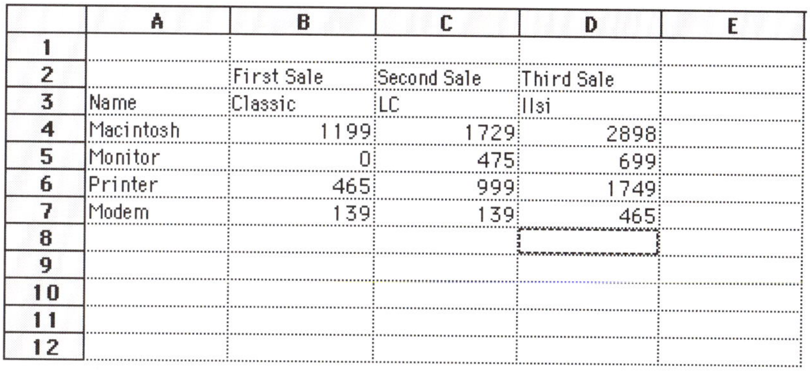

	A	B	C	D	E
1					
2		First Sale	Second Sale	Third Sale	
3	Name	Classic	LC	IIsi	
4	Macintosh	1199	1729	2898	
5	Monitor	0	475	699	
6	Printer	465	999	1749	
7	Modem	139	139	465	
8					
9					
10					
11					
12					

Chapter 12

As soon as you have entered all the data, choose Save from the File menu to save your work. You can also use ⌘-S to save. Do it often; it's hard to remember how you set up your worksheet if you lose it due to a power surge or hard drive crash.

If you have made a mistake and clicked the accept entry icon (hey, we're all human; I entered *Classic* twice by mistake), you need to know how to start a cell from scratch. Just click on the cell with the mistake, then select the incorrect part of the data in the entry bar (up at the top of the window) and edit it. The entry bar works just like a little word processor. You can select, delete, or change the text in the entry bar just as you would if you were using MacWrite II.

Changing Type Style and Format

To make things stand out and look different from each other in the worksheet, you can change the look of the text. This section tells how to make some of the text bold and some italic, and it shows how to center text you have written in a cell.

1. Click on cell B2, so *First Sale* is highlighted.
2. Choose Bold from the Style submenu in the Format menu. To do this, pull down the Format menu, drag to Style, then move the pointer sideways into the Style submenu and choose Bold.
3. Repeat the procedure for *Second Sale* and *Third Sale*, so that all the column titles are bold.
4. To make all of the names of the computers italic in one fell swoop, click on cell B3 to highlight *Classic*.
5. Hold down the Shift key and click cell D3. *Classic* becomes highlighted normally, and the *LC* and *IIsi* cells become highlighted in reverse video; this is so you know which cell you clicked first.

6. Choose Italic from the Style submenu of the Format menu. All three computer names become italic.
7. To make a nice big title that is centered over your data, select cell C1, which is over the center of your data columns.
8. Enter **Macintosh Sales Price Comparison** and click the accept entry icon. Don't worry about the text being too long; Resolve can handle it.
9. With the text entered and still selected, choose Bold from the Style submenu of the Format menu.
10. Choose Center from the Style submenu of the Format menu.
11. Choose 14 from the Size submenu of the Format menu.

Save your work. You've done some pretty nice formatting, and it would be a shame to have to do it over.

Inserting a Row

You can add a blank row or column to your worksheet any time you need one. This is fortunate, because no matter how well you plan it, the worksheet always seems to need another row here or a column there. To put a little breathing space between your nice big title and the rest of the worksheet, add a blank row by taking the following steps:

1. Click on the number 2 in the row label column at the left edge of the worksheet. This selects all of row two, sales titles and all.
2. Choose Insert from the Edit menu. A blank row appears above row 2, and the others all move down.

Although this insertion of a new row was merely for appearance, you will probably have times when you need a row for data or titles.

Selecting a Range and Changing Number Format

The worksheet is starting to look pretty clear and meaningful. Those numbers don't make much sense, though. Use the following steps to make them into dollar figures.

1. Place the pointer in cell B5 and drag diagonally to cell D8. Cell B5 becomes normally highlighted, and the rest of the cells in the block, or *range*, become highlighted in reverse video.
2. Choose Fixed from the Numeric submenu of the Format menu. The numbers all turn into dollars and cents, but without dollar signs, as in Figure 12.13.

You now have a nice spreadsheet that records a bunch of sales of computer systems. All you need to do is add the numbers up, and it will be in a useful form.

Using Formulas

So far you have been typing in data in each cell of the spreadsheet. To show a result of adding several cells together, you put a formula in the cell where you want the result to appear.

FIGURE 12.13
Changing the number format of a range of cells

	A	B	C	D	E
1		Macintosh Sales Price Comparison			
2					
3		First Sale	Second Sale	Third Sale	
4	Name	Classic	LC	IIsi	
5	Macintosh	1,199.00	1,729.00	2,898.00	
6	Monitor	0.00	475.00	699.00	
7	Printer	465.00	999.00	1,749.00	
8	Modem	139.00	139.00	465.00	
9					
10	Subtotal				
11					
12					

A formula is a mathematical equation relating the data in two or more cells of the spreadsheet. Formulas can perform many mathematical operations, from addition and subtraction to finding percentages and averages.

You use formulas because they'll change if you change the cells they refer to. This is because they use *variables* that refer to the cells containing your figures. For instance, the formula =A_1*A_2 multiplies the figure in cell A1 by the figure in cell A2, regardless of what the actual figures in the cells are.

Follow these steps to add up the prices of the items in each Macintosh system listed.

1. Select cell A10 and type **Subtotal**, then click the accept entry icon.
2. Select cell B10 and enter the formula =(B5+B6+B7+B8). Make sure the formula starts with an equals sign (this tells Resolve that it is a formula), as shown in Figure 12.14.
3. Click the accept entry icon.

The result of adding up cells B5, B6, B7, and B8 appears in cell B10. Notice that when the cell is selected, as it is now, the entry bar shows

FIGURE 12.14
Entering a formula in a cell

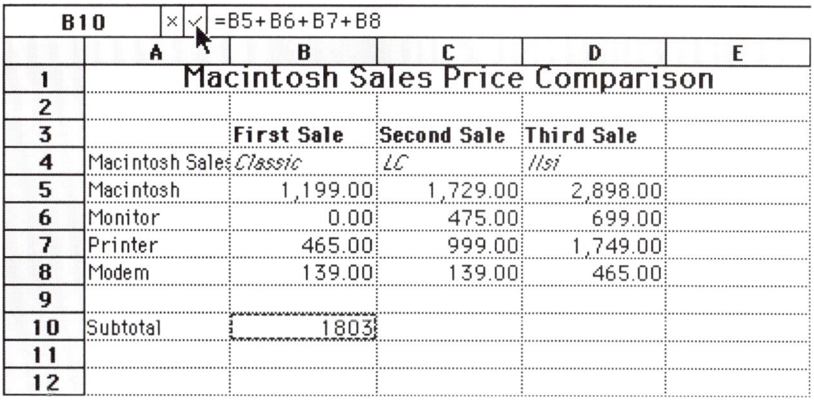

	A	B	C	D	E
		B10	×✓ =B5+B6+B7+B8		
1		Macintosh Sales Price Comparison			
2					
3		First Sale	Second Sale	Third Sale	
4	Macintosh Sales	*Classic*	*LC*	*IIsi*	
5	Macintosh	1,199.00	1,729.00	2,898.00	
6	Monitor	0.00	475.00	699.00	
7	Printer	465.00	999.00	1,749.00	
8	Modem	139.00	139.00	465.00	
9					
10	Subtotal	1803			
11					
12					

the formula you typed, but the cell itself shows the value of the result of the formula.

You can also write Resolve formulas that will subtract, multiply, and divide your figures. Use − for subtraction, * for multiplication, and / for division.

Using the Fill Function

Now let's add up the other two columns, but this time we'll use a shortcut. If you try to imagine how the formulas should appear for the next two you might notice that the only difference will be that the B's should become C's and D's. That is, $(B_5+B_6+B_7+B_8)$ will become $(C_5+C_6+C_7+C_8)$ and $(D_5+D_6+D_7+D_8)$. Resolve has a special function that can automate the task of creating all those formulas.

1. Place the pointer in cell B10 and drag to cell D10 so all three are selected.
2. Choose Fill Right from the Calculate menu. The results of the calculations appear in cells C10 and B10.
3. Click on C10 and D10 to see the formulas for each in the entry bar.

Ain't that cute? You just got Resolve to do a bunch of formula-typing for you. Fill is one of the simplest but most useful functions of spreadsheets; see the Resolve *User's Guide* for some of the great things you can do with fills.

Absolute Cell Referencing

Sometimes it is hard for Resolve to figure out which cell you want it to refer to if you choose Fill Right or Fill Down. To help the program out, you can enter an *absolute cell reference.* To see how these cell references work, add a Tax row to your worksheet by following these steps:

1. Select cell A15 and type **Tax %** and click the accept entry icon.
2. Now you can put a specific figure in the next cell for the current tax rate. Select cell B15 and choose Percent from the Numeric submenu of the Format menu.
3. Enter .07 (this is the tax rate) in the entry bar and click the accept entry icon.
4. Select cell A11 and enter the title **Tax** in it.
5. Select cell B11 and enter the formula **=B10*$B15**. The reference to B15 is absolute because it has the dollar sign in front of it. If you fill the formula to other cells, it will always refer back to cell B15 for the second multiplier. Click the accept entry icon; the tax for column B appears.
6. Drag from B11 to D11 to select those cells. Choose Fill Right from the Calculate menu. The tax figures for the C and D columns appear.

The figures that appear in B11, C11 and D11 are all a result of multiplying the column totals times the tax figure in cell B15. If the tax rate changes (as it is bound to), all you have to do is change the figure in B15 and the other tax figures will update automatically. This sort of setup can save you a heap of work if you have hundreds of figures that are dependent upon one variable like the tax rate.

Save your work to make sure you don't lose any of those carefully arranged formulas.

Chapter 12

Completing the Spreadsheet

You now have the data you need to make a Total row in the worksheet. This procedure will complete your worksheet and review some things you have learned already.

1. Enter **Total** in cell A13.
2. In cell B13 enter **=SUM(B10..B11)**. This is a short way of finding the total of the Subtotal and Tax for the B column.
3. Complete the other formulas for this row by using Fill Right.
4. Make the row bold by selecting the row and then choosing Bold from the Style submenu of the Format menu.
5. Finally, change the number format to dollars and cents by choosing Currency from the Numeric submenu of the Format menu.

Good work. You have completed the spreadsheet. It should look like Figure 12.15. After it is all set up and you have saved it, try experimenting with the spreadsheet; change some of the price figures. Notice that the values for the totals and the taxes update automatically.

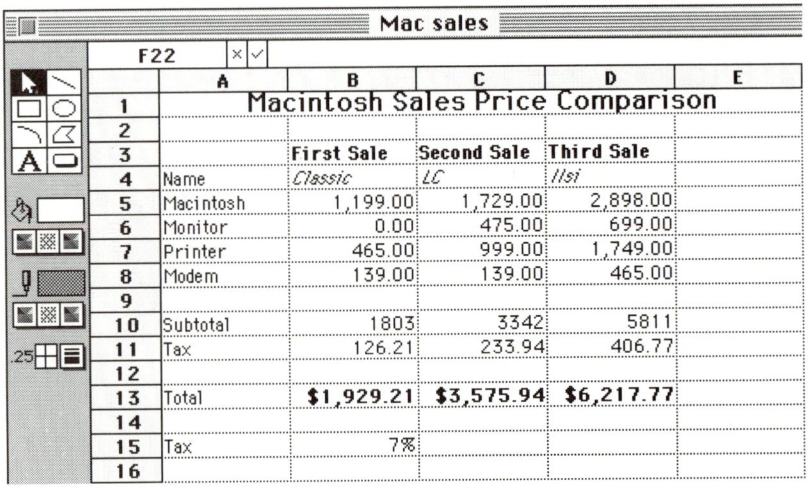

FIGURE 12.15
The completed sample spreadsheet

	A	B	C	D	E
1		Macintosh Sales Price Comparison			
2					
3		First Sale	Second Sale	Third Sale	
4	Name	Classic	LC	IIsi	
5	Macintosh	1,199.00	1,729.00	2,898.00	
6	Monitor	0.00	475.00	699.00	
7	Printer	465.00	999.00	1,749.00	
8	Modem	139.00	139.00	465.00	
9					
10	Subtotal	1803	3342	5811	
11	Tax	126.21	233.94	406.77	
12					
13	Total	$1,929.21	$3,575.94	$6,217.77	
14					
15	Tax	7%			
16					

After you complete the chart in the next section, you will notice that a single price change can ripple through the spreadsheet and the chart as well.

Using Charts

Charts are one of the strong points of Resolve. They can make your data much easier to grasp and more impressive. All you have to do is select the data you want to chart and you can let Resolve do the work.

To make a useful chart of the sample worksheet you've made, you can do one that compares how the price of each piece of each system relates to the others. If you select the part prices and the labels of the rows and columns, Resolve will put these into a simple chart form.

1. Drag the pointer from cell A4 to cell D8 to select the range that includes the row and column labels and the data.
2. Scroll the spreadsheet up so you are looking at empty cells in rows 20 to 35 or so.
3. Choose Make Chart from the Chart menu. A plain bar chart appears.
4. With the chart still selected, choose Gallery from the Chart menu.
5. Select the Layer icon in the Categories box. A sample of a layered graph appears, with options for types of layered graphs listed to the left.
6. Choose the Stacked option. A sample graph appears.
7. Click OK. Your graph appears, complete with a legend.
8. To add a title to the graph, click the Name box at the top of the graph and enter **Macintosh Sales**, then click the accept entry icon. The graph now looks like the one in Figure 12.16.

That's all there is to it. Save your spreadsheet and graph. If you would like to print them out, you can do that too. See the "Saving and

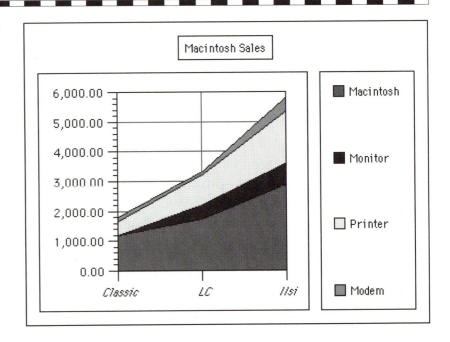

FIGURE 12.16
Graph for Resolve spreadsheet

Printing an Excel Document" earlier in this chapter for details; the instructions are just the same.

Troubleshooting Problems with Spreadsheet Applications

The following subsections cover the problems you are most likely to have while working with spreadsheet applications.

Not enough memory.

This problem will occur when you're trying to open a spreadsheet application. Spreadsheets have become huge in the past few years and now require a considerable portion of your RAM. The first thing to check when trying to cure this problem is any special utilities that you've loaded into the System Folder. These can be "turned off" by removing them from your System Folder and then rebooting your Macintosh. These programs are usually small utilities like virus checkers, screen savers, and print spoolers. They're usually not completely necessary and removing them temporarily won't hurt.

If things still don't seem to be working, you might try increasing the memory that's being allocated to your spreadsheet. See Chapter 7 for more information on memory allocation. Finally, if Excel still says you're out of memory, you'll need to increase the memory of your Macintosh by adding more RAM. This should only be done by a qualified technician.

Gridlines don't go away when printing.

The rule is, if you can see them on the screen, then they are going to come out on the printer. To turn them off in Excel, choose Display from the Options menu. You will get a dialog box with some interesting options. Just click on the Gridlines check box and they'll go away. In Resolve, choose Show from the View menu and uncheck Cell Grid check box. You might also want to preview your printing before you actually print. This can tell you in a few seconds what your printer will tell you in a few minutes.

*All a cell displays is ###### or ******

This is caused by having your column width set too small. Widen you column manually with your mouse. Place the mouse pointer on the right border of the column you want to widen, and when your pointer turns into two arrows pointing left and right, just drag your mouse to the right to make it wider. When you release the mouse button your numbers will come back.

Chapter 12

Formulas don't display the correct answer.

First, check your formula for mistakes. If you are using a built-in formula, check to make sure the name is spelled correctly. If you made up the formula yourself, make sure the parentheses are all in the correct locations.

If your formulas are correct and the numbers displayed don't change even if you change the cells they relate to, then your spreadsheet has been set to manual calculation. To set it back to automatic calculation in Excel, choose Calculation from the Options menu and select Automatic under Calculation. Click in the OK button and everything should be fine. In Resolve, choose AutoCalc from the Calculate menu.

In Excel, you see the "Cannot resolve circular reference" error message.

This means that a formula is relating to a cell that relates back to the original formula. There is almost no way to fix this problem other than by changing your formula. Look at each cell that the formula in question is referencing. Do any of these cells reference the original cell? Maybe one of these cells relates to another cell that relates to the original cell. The problem can be tricky to track down. Once you do find it, see if you can find an error in the logic used to set up the formula.

The Microsoft Excel *User's Guide* also gives some hints on how to use manual calculation to make circular referencing actually work. Intentional circular referencing should not be taken lightly, though. In most cases, it won't correct the problem, and the only way is to try a totally different approach.

In Excel, column labels don't appear in charts.

Some types of charts don't have enough space to add the labels of the columns. This can usually be resolved by choosing Add Legend from the Chart menu in Excel's charting mode. However, if you selected your data without selecting the labels, they will not appear. To remedy this situation, just start a new chart and make sure you select all the spreadsheet labels that you want to see on the chart.

After entering a formula and clicking the accept entry icon in Resolve, you see ERR 46 in the selected cell or an error message.

This just means that there is something wrong with the way you typed in the formula. Likely errors are an extra space, a forgotten parenthesis, a colon or comma instead of the two periods between the cell addresses, and a misspelled function. Fix the formula or check the Resolve *Functions and Scripts* book to make sure you are entering it correctly.

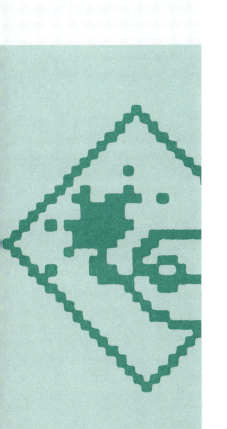

CHAPTER 13

Databases

Databases are tools that allow you to manage large amounts of information. A database is pretty much like a rolodex, one of those address-holders with all the cards attached to double rings. As each card in a rolodex holds one address, each *record* in a database contains a bunch of information on a single subject. The cards in a rolodex are all kept in order on the double rings; you can take out a card and change a person's address, then put it back. You can add cards or remove them. You can do the same things with records in a database, but you don't even have to take them out.

The big difference between a database and a rolodex is that with a database you can resort the records in lots of ways, and do it instantly, without winding up with a bunch of cards scattered all over your desk. You can ask the database to find a record or a bunch of records, and then tell it to display the data in any of a whole bunch of formats or *layouts*. You can also tell the database to pull certain bits of information off each record and make a neat report out of it. And a database can do all this easily, even if you put much, much more information in it than you can cram into a rolodex.

Databases are great for stores that need to have data on everything they carry at their disposal instantaneously. In fact, the machine that reads the bar code off your groceries at the supermarket is connected to a kind of database. You can make smaller databases to keep track of almost anything you are interested in. For example, if you are an audiophile, you can make a database to list your CDs, tapes, or records. If you love books, you can catalog your library. If you cook, you can make a personal cook book of favorite recipes, with your latest variation added to each one.

In terms of work, you can make a list of all the important business contacts you have, with their addresses and telephone numbers, and some important notes about your latest dealings with each of them. A rolodex would get real messy if you tried to put this much on it; a database can take it all in stride, and it doesn't mind if you change it every time you make a business contact. You can see an example of this type of database in "Using FileMaker Pro" later in this chapter.

Which Database Application for You?

Databases were the first applications that were developed for the consumer world, so there is a wide array of choices. There are complex databases that are designed to run large businesses and small ones that are made solely for the purpose of holding your address book. Most people will probably want something that's in between. Fortunately, this is the category that most databases fit into. You can choose between a simple flat-file database that puts all the information in one file, and a big, powerful relational database that keeps data in separate, connected files. The following sections cover each type of database, starting with the most expensive and working down.

Relational Databases

A relational database is a collection of related data that is stored in a structure made up of a number of files. Where a flat-file database stores all related information in one file, a relational one allows the sharing of information between many related files.

If you think of a flat-file database as a single rolodex with a bunch of phone numbers in it, you can think of a relational database as a magical rolodex that can call up some of the numbers listed in it and draw on other rolodexes at those numbers for information. But even that is too limited a view; it is as if each magical rolodex can contact not only other rolodexes, but all kinds of other data storage files—from price lists to personnel profiles, a single database file can make use of a tremendous scope of information. The key concept is that the database is not just the single file, it is the whole structure of related files.

Large databases like 4th Dimension from Acius and Foxbase Pro from Fox are difficult to get involved in, but they give you unmatched flexibility. You can collect many categories of information in different files, and have different people updating each file; the database automatically takes the updated stuff from one file and feeds it into the others so they all stay current. This is much nicer than a flat-file database, where you have to update changes in every record affected by any change in another record. But a relational database is much harder to set up. When a large business wants to have a database set up that requires the speed, size, and flexibility of a relational one, they often hire a consultant to do the designing for them. The database might track sales, customers, personnel, inventory, and overhead expenses, and relate all of these things to each other in a number of ways. Whew. Quite a feat of organization.

Not all uses of relational databases are so vast, though. Small businesses can use them to track sales and customers, for instance. And some are easier for nonexperts to set up. If you are interested in using a relational database with a relatively friendly Mac approach, 4th Dimension is definitely the prime candidate.

4th Dimension was designed by a couple of French Macintosh enthusiasts, specifically for the Mac. It makes excellent use of the Macintosh interface, so that you can quickly learn to design and implement a database that is made up of many indirectly related files storing different kinds of specific information. The whole structure is made up of simple connections that are represented graphically, so you know exactly what you are doing as you build the relationships between files.

For a commonly used example, if your business has one file called Invoices containing records of all the company's sales, and another file called Customers with information about each customer, you can set up a simple relation between the Invoices file and the Customers file, as shown in Figure 13.1. Now, if you want each customer's invoice to show the customer's name and address, you can use the Customer field in the Invoices file to access the Customers file; it finds the record for the customer and has access to his or her address.

The beauty of this setup is that it saves you from having to enter data in two places. You enter the customer address in the fields in the Customers file, and then, when you are making out an invoice, you just specify the customer, and your Mac fills in the address for you. Notice that the example in Figure 13.1 also has a subfile for Line items, so you automatically update your sales data for every transaction.

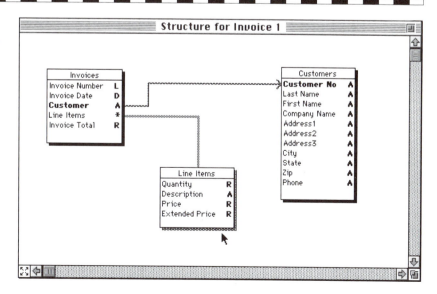

FIGURE 13.1
Graphic view of a 4th Dimension database structure

This simple use of a relational database can save huge amounts of time for a small business. If you are willing to pay the higher price for the application and take the time to set the database up properly, you won't regret it in the long run.

Flat-File Databases

Medium-scale, single-file databases may not have the features that the large databases have, but they are usually much easier to learn and much more affordable. A few, like FileMaker Pro from Claris or File Force from Acius, have some of the powers of relational databases. Others, like Panorama from ProVUE, are strictly flat-file databases. File Force is good for setting up a simple set of relationships between databases, and Panorama is a powerful flat-file tool that works well for users who are accustomed to spreadsheets.

The rest of this chapter focuses on FileMaker Pro, a leading Mac database application. It is a very straightforward database with a great deal of flexibility, and it's extremely easy to use. FileMaker Pro actually incorporates the rolodex concept into its graphic interface; you can flip through the records of your database just like you are flipping through the cards of a rolodex. But FileMaker Pro is no toy. It has a lot of power, including a lookup feature that works like a one-direction relationship in a relational database. As databases become more powerful and complex, it is a rare thing to find one such as FileMaker Pro with power that is easy to take advantage of.

Budget Databases

Small databases and address books are numerous and are more affordable than their heavy-duty cousins. They aren't relational and might not even give you the ability to create your own layout for your data. Don't let this lack of features scare you, though, they can be great for what they do. Many people like to keep an address book with a program like Touch Base by After Hours. Touch Base can print out your data on sheets that will fit in your daily scheduling book. For the technologically advanced, they can also upload information to other applications. Many business people find these to be essential for keeping track of all their contacts.

 ## Using FileMaker Pro

FileMaker Pro started as a simple database years ago and has become an easy-to-use yet powerful database. Databases are difficult to learn at best, but Claris has done a good job at making FileMaker Pro the easiest to get started with. It has the same type of interface that you might remember from MacWrite II and MacDraw. In the following sections, you'll use FileMaker Pro to create a small, familiar address book type of file that tracks your business contacts.

Designing a Database

Before you plunge into the building of a database, you should plan out its design. You may even want to make a rough sketch with a pencil and paper, so you have an idea of how you are going to organize things. Even if you just scribble the thing out on a napkin, any design is better than no design. After all, a database is just a way of organizing information. The better you organize it, the easier the information is to find and use.

The basic building blocks of database organization are *fields* and *records*. A field is an area that stores a single piece of information. It's like one line on a card of your rolodex. Each field of your address book will store a different type of information. You put together a bunch of fields to make a record.

A record is about the same as a single rolodex card. It contains all the information about a single item. You put the records into some kind of logical order, so you can zip through them and find things quickly. Alphabetical order works well for lists of names or objects.

If you are organizing a list of names and addresses, for example, you set up fields for the name, street number, city, state, and zip code for the records. Then you fill in the fields with data for each person, so each one has a separate record. Then you put the records in alphabetical order, so you can look up any person's information by going to their name. In the sample explained below, you'll see each step of the process in detail.

Opening a Document

You have to take different steps to open a new document in FileMaker Pro, depending on whether you have started the application or not. Use the following steps if you have not started FileMaker Pro:

1. To start the application, double-click on the FileMaker Pro icon, as shown in Figure 13.2, or double-click on an alias of it. A dialog box appears, asking you to open an existing document or create a new one.
2. Click on the New button. The New File dialog box appears.
3. Type in a name you like, such as **Business Contacts**.
4. If you want the file to be stored in a different folder from the one listed, use the menu under the folder title to move to a new folder.

FIGURE 13.2
The FileMaker Pro icon

5. Click the New button again. The Define Fields dialog appears, with the cursor in the Name box.

To open a new document if you have already opened FileMaker Pro and are looking at an existing database file, use the following steps:

1. Choose New from the File menu. The New File dialog box appears.
2. Type in a name you like, such as **Business Contacts**.
3. If you want the file to be stored in a different folder from the one listed, use the menu under the folder title to move to a new folder.
4. Click the New button again. The Define Fields dialog box appears, with the cursor in the Name box.

Setting Up the Fields

You are now ready to set up the fields of your address book. Follow these steps to make them:

1. Start by typing **First Name** in the Name box (if you make a typing mistake, use the Delete key to fix it). The Create button comes to life.
2. Click the Create button, as shown in Figure 13.3. Notice that the field name is displayed in the text box.
3. Repeat steps 1 and 2 to create fields for the following information:
    Last Name
    Street Address
    City
    State
    Zip Code
    Phone Number

4. Now look over your field names in the list box at the top of the dialog. If you created a field name that has mistakes in it, select the field name. Then select the typo in the Name box, type in the correction and click the Change button. This corrects the selected field name.

5. When the fields are all correct, click the Done button.

The Define Fields dialog box goes away and a blank record appears, with the fields you defined.

Entering Records

After you click the Done button, FileMaker Pro moves into *Browse* mode. This is the place you go when you want to enter or edit a record. Use the following steps to create your first record, beginning with the First Name field, where the cursor awaits you.

1. Type **Tracey**.

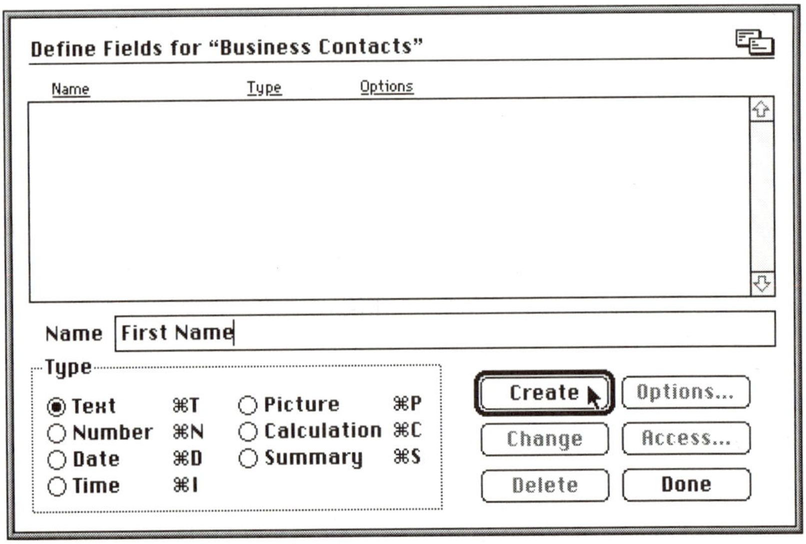

FIGURE 13.3
Defining fields for database records

2. Press Tab to advance to the next field.
3. Type **Smith** and press Tab again to advance.
4. Fill in the remaining fields for Tracey, using the information in Figure 13.4.
5. If you press Tab when you have filled in the last field, you will notice that you advance to the Name field again.
6. Choose New Record from the Edit menu. You now have a blank record and the cursor is still in the First Name field. You did not destroy the last record, you merely added another blank card to the rolodex-type stack.
7. Create the following records, using the same procedure you used for Tracey's:

   Adam Adams
   789 Some Blvd.
   New York, NY 12345
   (123) 555-0987

   Mike Mandel
   456 That Way
   Chicago, IL 76543
   (321) 555-4567

   Mark Mandel
   456 That Way
   Chicago, IL 76543
   (321) 555-4567

In most applications, you'd want to save after doing all this, but you do not have to save your work in FileMaker Pro; the application automatically saves your files to the FileMaker Pro folder. In fact, there is no Save command in FileMaker Pro's File menu.

FIGURE 13.4
Entering a record's data in the fields

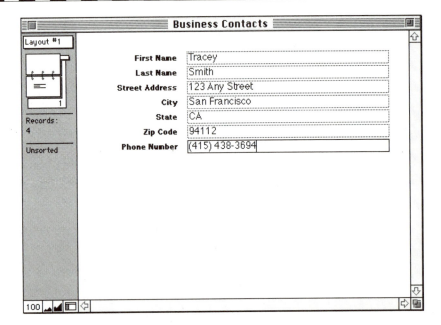

Using the Toolbar

Now that you have a little database to work with, you can manipulate it with the tools FileMaker Pro offers. Some of the most accessible and useful of these tools are located on the toolbar in the area to the left of your record.

- The title "Layout #1" at the top of the bar means that this is your first layout. You will create another layout later on.
- Just below the layout marker is a picture of a rolodex. This rolodex is a representation of your database file. If you click the bottom card of the rolodex, you advance to the next record. Clicking the top card moves you to the previous record. (If you are at the top card of the database, the previous card button will be blank; if you are at the bottom, the next card button will be blank.)

You can move quickly through the database by sliding the bookmark. Nifty, isn't it?

- The buttons at the bottom of the window let you change your view of the database. The number 100 tells you the magnification percentage that you are seeing. To magnify the card, click on the button showing a large mountain; to shrink the card, click on the button showing a distant mountain; and to get back to 100 percent, click on the current percentage number to the left of the mountains.

- The last button looks just like a little FileMaker Pro window with the toolbar highlighted. Clicking on this button makes the toolbar disappear. This can be great if you need a little more space to work with, especially if you are working on a small-screen Macintosh.

None of these lower buttons change your database; they just change the way you see it, so you should try them all out. Experimentation is the best way to make yourself comfortable, and a good program like FileMaker Pro encourages you to experiment.

Sorting Records

OK, so you've got an address book and you can flip back and forth between the records. So far, so good, but you may be wondering how this is any better than the rolodex on your desk. Well, for starters, it's a lot more flexible. If you want your records to be in a particular order, you can have FileMaker Pro sort them in just about any order you can imagine. For example, you could have FileMaker Pro do what you'd normally do with a rolodex—sort alphabetically by last name. Or you could sort the addresses by state, or by first name, if you have trouble remembering last names. Sorting is one of the most often used features of a database. Follow the steps below to sort your database by last name.

1. Choose Sort from the Select menu. A large dialog box appears with many choices in it. You can ignore most of them for now. The important things are the two list boxes. The box on the left represents each of your fields. The box on the right represents the sorting order.
2. Click on Last Name in the left list box.
3. Click on the Move button as in Figure 13.5.
4. Last Name appears in the sort order list. This means that the alphabetical (ascending from A to Z) sorting will start with the last name of each person, just like in a real address book. You still have a problem, though; the two brothers have the same last name.
5. To sort by first names too, click on First Name in the left list box, and then click the Move button again. Now when the computer gets to the brothers it will sort them by their first names.

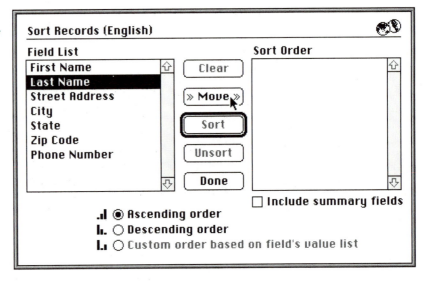

FIGURE 13.5
Setting up sorting order

6. Click the Sort button to put your address book in alphabetical order.

Finding Records

You can also use FileMaker Pro to find records or particular groups of records. Suppose you need to contact everyone in Chicago for a business convention. If you were using a real address book, you'd have to leaf through the whole thing page by page, looking for contacts that live in Chicago. This would be tedious. Using *Find* mode, you can easily select all the people from Chicago and separate them out, even if you have hundreds of contacts.

1. Choose Find from the Select menu to enter Find mode. A panel appears with the field names and blank spaces, much like what you see when you enter data for a record.
2. Make sure that your toolbar is showing. Click the toolbar button at the bottom of the screen if the bar is not in view.
3. Tab down to the field labeled City and type **Chicago**.
4. Click on the Find button in the toolbar or press the Return key on your keyboard.

You're done! No leafing, no looking. You should now be back in the Browse mode with only the people from Chicago showing. You can double-check to see that you are truly in the Browse mode by pulling down the Select menu and making sure that there is a check mark next to Browse.

Run through all the records in your database now. All you see are the two brothers from Chicago; the other records you typed in earlier are missing. Not to worry; they are not actually deleted, they are just hiding so that you can look at the specific data that you are interested in.

To bring all the records back, just choose Find All from the Select menu. Find All brings you back to where you were. All the records should now show in exactly the way you typed them into the address book.

Changing Your Layout

FileMaker Pro's *Layout* mode is where you do the actual design of your database file. To get into it, choose Layout from the Select menu. In Layout mode you can change every aspect of your database's appearance on screen and on paper. For example, you can change the type style of the field names to make them stand out, or you can change the arrangement of the fields to give certain information priority. In fact, you can even have several layouts that you switch between. In this section, we'll spruce up your address book a bit and create a new layout for it.

1. Select all of the field names. To do this, move the pointer to a position above and to the left of all the field names, then drag a selection rectangle down and to the right until it encloses all the field names completely. Release the mouse button and check that all of the names have *handles* (small boxes on the corners).

2. Now that they're all selected, pull down the Format menu to Font.

3. Choose Times from the Font submenu. (If Times isn't installed choose another of your favorite fonts.)

4. Choosing Times makes the type look a bit small, so pull down the Format menu again. This time go into the Size submenu and choose 14 or 18.

Great! Those field names look much better. It would be nice, however, if they were arranged a bit better. This is easy; just click and drag each field where you want it to go. Using this method, I moved the fields as in Figure 13.6. You can copy me or pick your own format. The style of your database file is entirely up to you, so be creative.

You can also change the size of your fields by dragging the handles. Make sure the tip of the pointer is on a handle, not on the whole field. To make a field larger or smaller just drag the handle until the field is the desired size, as shown in Figure 13.6.

Adding to the Database

Once you've set up the basic structure of your database, you're pretty much done. Oh, you'll add records, and delete them, and change them, but FileMaker Pro takes care of the real work—sorting records, finding them, keeping them safe.

There will be times, though, when you'll want to change your database's structure. Maybe your needs have changed, or maybe you have needs that you didn't anticipate when you planned your database. Then you'll want to add new fields. Let's add a Notes field and a Last Contact field to your address book, so you can keep track of your last contact with each person.

FIGURE 13.6
Reformatting the fields

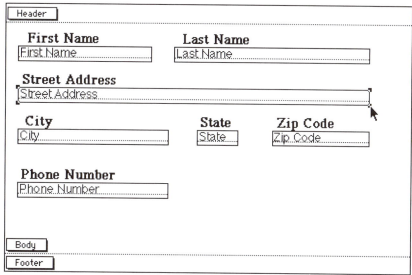

1. Pull down the Select menu and choose Layout. This takes you to Layout mode, where you can change the design of your database.
2. Choose Define Fields from the Select menu. You see the same dialog box that you began this chapter with.
3. Type **Notes** in the Name box and click on the Create button.
4. Type **Last Contact** in the Name box and click on the Create button.
5. Now you have two more fields to work with. Instead of clicking Done, this time click on the Options button to automate entry of the date in the last contact field.
6. Again you see a dialog box swarming with options. You don't need to learn them all now, but just think what you could do, given a little time and experience! For now, just click in the Creation Date check box under the heading "Auto-enter a value that is."
7. Place the pointer on the words Creation Date, pull down the menu and select Modification Date. By choosing this setting, you've told FileMaker Pro to automatically update this field to the current date every time something inside the record changes. Each time you talk to the person, you can make a note in the new Note field, and the date will change automatically, so you'll always know when you last talked to the person.
8. Click the OK button and then click the Done button to get back to your new layout.
9. Adjust the size and position of the fields to match the rest, as in Figure 13.7.

FIGURE 13.7

Formatting new fields to match a layout

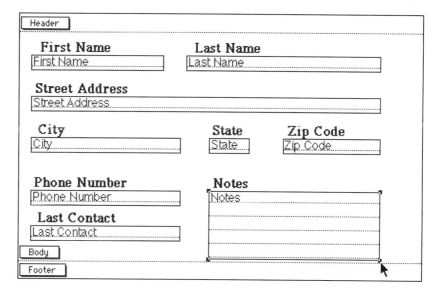

Creating a Mailing

For the grand finale, you can make your address book capable of producing envelopes. Creating mailings is one of the greatest features of databases. Once you set up FileMaker Pro to print out your envelopes, you can go have lunch. When you come back your printer will have produced a tremendous amount of work with only minimal effort on your part.

Before you envision a mass mailing to the world, create the new layout. Don't worry about the old layout; FileMaker Pro saves it and you can get back to it in the Layout menu at the top of your toolbar.

1. First, make sure you are still in the Layout mode. Choose Layout from the Select menu if you aren't.

2. To start a new layout, choose New Layout from the Edit menu. FileMaker Pro presents you with a dialog box to let you set the name and type of your new layout.

3. Type in **Envelope Layout** and click in the Envelope radio button.

4. Click the OK button. The dialog box that appears allows you to choose which fields you want to be printed on your envelope.

5. Click on each field you are interested in, then click the Move button. The field names for the envelope appear on the right side of the dialog box. The order is important, so be sure that your dialog looks like Figure 13.8 when you are all done. If you make a mistake, click the Clear button and start again.

6. When you're done, click the OK button to get back to designing the layout of the envelope. The fields you selected are stacked up at the bottom of the window.

7. Orient the fields so that each is on its correct line, as shown in Figure 13.9. This can be a little tricky when working with small fields. Here are a couple hints for moving fields around:

    - Use the magnification buttons (below the toolbar) to magnify what you're working with.

FIGURE 13.8

Setting up fields for an envelope

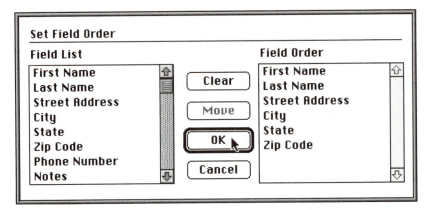

FIGURE 13.9
Adjusting the layout for envelope addresses

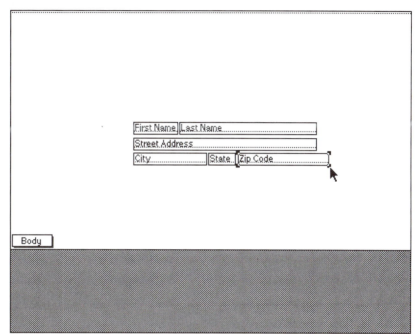

- A field can be moved by a single pixel by selecting the field and using the arrow keys. This is great for tiny adjustments.
- Drag a selection rectangle around all the fields if you want to move the whole batch to a better position on the envelope. To deselect the whole batch, click somewhere in blank space with the pointer.

When you get the layout looking something like Figure 13.9, pat yourself on the back. You have just created an envelope layout. You can switch back to the first layout by using the toolbar. Click on Envelope in the Layout box at the top of the bar and a pop-up menu will appear with all your layouts in it. Look at the first layout if you want, but then switch back to Envelope layout and try looking at some of the data in it by choosing Browse from the Select menu. You may want to go back to Layout mode to resize and move the fields a bit to line up the parts of the address.

Once the address looks good, everything would be dandy if you had envelopes preprinted with your return address. But preprinted envelopes are expensive, and you have a Mac to work with. So why not have FileMaker Pro print your name and address in the correct position of each envelope?

All you have to do is add a *header* that will be the same on every envelope. The header is separate from the *body* of the layout, where the record fields appear.

1. Go back to Layout mode by choosing Layout from the Select menu.
2. Make sure that you're back in the Envelope layout by using the pop-up menu for layouts at the top of the toolbar. Click on it and select Envelope Layout.
3. Click on the A tool in the toolbar. This allows you to create fields of text that don't relate to the data that you've entered in the records.
4. Move your cursor to the header section of the layout and type in your return address. Don't worry, the field expands as you type, and you can press Return to start a new line.
5. Click the pointer tool, then click in the return address to select it and drag it to the left side of the header area, as shown in Figure 13.10.

This example, although it looks great on the screen, is somewhat simplified. To actually make the envelopes print you have to set the computer up for your exact envelopes and your exact printer. The following example shows how to print envelopes on a LaserWriter NT.

FIGURE 13.10
The completed layout for an envelope

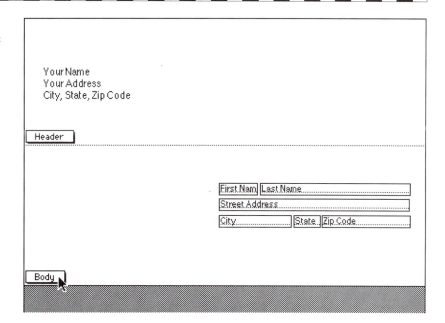

The steps may be different if you have a different printer, so see your printer's owner's guide for details.

1. Choose Page Setup from the File menu.
2. Choose Envelope - Edge Fed from the pop-up menu for the Tabloid option, and click OK.
3. In Layout mode, raise the address fields until they are in the center of the upper envelope, just under the header. Make sure your return address is still placed correctly in the header area.
4. Raise the body marker in the bottom left corner of the envelope until the slashed line below the address fields disappears, so your layout looks like Figure 13.10.
5. Choose Print from the File menu.

Chapter 13

6. In the Print dialog box, click the radio buttons for Manual Feed Paper Source and the Current record.
7. Open your LaserWriter NT multipurpose tray, as explained in "Manual Feed Printing" in the owner's guide. Place the envelopes face down in the feeder.
8. Click Print. Click OK in the two PrintMonitor dialog boxes.

Your envelopes print out!

Saving and Printing a FileMaker Pro Document

One of the best features of FileMaker Pro is that it saves your work automatically. You never have to choose Save while working with FileMaker Pro. In fact, it's not even an option. As soon as you enter data or change a layout it automatically saves everything for you in the FileMaker Pro folder. However, if you want, you can save a file to a different folder by choosing Save a Copy As from the File menu.

Printing in FileMaker Pro is not as cut-and-dry as saving, but there are quite a few added features to help you know when everything is going to print out well. To print the address book that was created in this chapter, simply choose Print from the File menu and then click the OK button in the Print dialog box.

For most cases this should be all you need to do to print out your file. However, there are a few exceptions. FileMaker Pro likes to print out everything, and if you have hundreds of people in your address book this could be pretty inefficient. In these situations it would be better to print only a portion of the file. Near the bottom of the Print dialog box there are a few options that allow you to print different portions of your file, such as just the current record. Choose the one that you need and go on printing as usual. For more information on printing, see Chapter 3.

Troubleshooting Problems with FileMaker Pro

The following subsections cover the problems you are most likely to have while working with FileMaker Pro.

Not enough memory.

This problem will only occur if you if you have just double-clicked on the FileMaker Pro icon. Since FileMaker Pro is an extremely complex program, it takes up a considerable amount of your Mac's RAM.

To solve this problem, you need to free up some memory to give to FileMaker Pro. Start by turning off any system extensions you don't need. These devices can be "turned off" by removing them from the System Folder or by holding down the Shift key when your Mac is starting up.

If this doesn't work, you might try increasing the amount of memory allocated to FileMaker Pro. See Chapter 7 for more information on memory allocation. If you can't give FileMaker Pro enough memory to start it, you'll have to add some RAM to your Mac. See a qualified technician for help.

When you press Tab, the cursor goes to the wrong fields.

Unfortunately, the computer is not quite intelligent enough to decipher in exactly what order you would like to cursor to go. It moves the cursor to the next field in the order that the fields were created. This is fine for most purposes, but when fields get moved around, then FileMaker Pro gets confused.

To fix this, choose Layout from the Select menu. Then choose Tab Order from the Arrange menu. A small window will appear on the screen to help with the different options for setting the tab order. In your database file, your fields should be displayed with an arrow next to them. If the Tab Order window covers your fields, you can move it by dragging it from its title bar. Each arrow now displays its current order. Click in the Create New Tab Order radio button to clear the incorrect order. To set their new order, click on each field in the correct order. When you're finished, click in the OK button and your troubles should be solved.

Missing records.

You may have accidentally deleted a record, so before trying anything else, see if you can undo the deletion by choosing Undo from the Edit menu. If this doesn't help, you may be in the wrong mode for viewing your records. For example, if you're in Find mode, only a small portion of your records are available for viewing. Just choose Find All from the Select menu, and you'll be back in Browse mode, and back in business.

CHAPTER 14

Managing Personal Finances

Do you need help with your financial affairs? You can't get cash advances from your Mac, but you can get help with the nitty-gritty chores of keeping your finances in order. Personal money managing applications make it simple to manage your checkbook and keep track of your financial situation. You can automate recurring transactions, print out checks, plan your budget, and check your net worth, all without having to scribble tiny ciphers in a giant double-entry ledger. And the Mac does all the calculating for you, so you can be sure your records are accurate when it comes time to prepare your tax returns.

The best personal finance applications make it easy to set up your check register and bookkeeping files. They automate repetitious tasks, but make it easy for you to enter the figures that vary month to month. You can keep simple records of where your money came from and how you spent it, or you can generate sophisticated reports to aid in financial planning.

 Which Money Managing Application for You?

There is a wide range of applications that can help you with your personal finances. The simplest ones are just computerized checkbooks with the ability to print out checks and keep a tabulated register. The most advanced financial management applications can do specialized tasks for different types of financial management. Some can take care of small business needs like accounts payable and receivable, inventory control, and payroll. Other money managing applications can track investments and project their future values, based on detailed analysis of data you enter.

Bargain Budgeting Tools

Of the personal finance tools that cater to the penny-pincher, Quicken is the most popular, and for good reason. The interface and documentation are easy; anyone who can keep a check register and balance their checkbook can master the Quicken system. Checkbook II covers most of the same ground, and although the interface is not so intuitive, the program provides tools to design your own checks, and it has a database for addresses. But the basic jobs of recording cash flow and preparing records for tax purposes are much easier to handle in Quicken. Quicken can memorize your regular monthly payments and print out the checks for you, and it makes budgeting a clear and simple process, because the categories of transactions are so intuitive. For more information, see "Using Quicken" later in this chapter.

There are also special-purpose applications, such as MacIntax, that do a great job of preparing federal and some state tax forms. TurboTax is another tax-preparation application, but it is much less intuitive and direct; you have to be a spreadsheet whiz to get all your data entered. Both of these tax tools can accept input from Quicken and from the more sophisticated financial management applications.

High-Cost Financial Management Applications

The higher-priced money managing applications aim at either the professionals who want investment portfolio management, or the small business people who want to take care of all their accounts, their payroll, and their inventory. Andrew Tobias's Managing Your Money

(MYM) is the leader in the investment managing arena and the most expensive choice. Mind Your Own Business (MYOB) is a good example of the small business package. MacMoney is cheaper than either MYM or MYOB, and is somewhere between the two in features; it can be used as a personal finance tool like Quicken, but it has more power to calculate things like loan payments and the ability to generate color graphs. If you have a simple business you may be able to get by with MacMoney. If you have a growing, varied business, MYOB would be a better choice. If you are developing an investment portfolio and are willing to do lots of data entry to make good projections and keep accurate records for taxes, get MYM and get busy.

 Using Quicken

Quicken takes the pain out of writing checks and keeping financial records. You set up one or more accounts, then enter transactions, categorizing each deposit, check, and withdrawal so you can track it later. If you order personalized checks for your type of printer, you can print checks instead of writing them out. This saves a lot of time and effort, and keeps your records up-to-date automatically.

When your bank statement arrives, you just enter the information and Quicken reconciles the account for you. You can create a wide variety of both personal and business reports that display transactions by time period, category, class, payee, or account. At the end of the year, at tax time, you have the information you need at your fingertips.

Creating a File for Your Quicken Accounts

When you first open Quicken, you have to start an account. You can keep bank accounts, cash accounts, and credit card accounts with Quicken, but to start with, you open a standard bank account for checking.

This section and the ones that follow use a simple account as a model. You can create this test model to become familiar with how Quicken works before you start entering your real-life checkbook figures. Take the following steps to create a first account called Home Checking:

1. Double-click the Quicken icon, as shown in Figure 14.1, to start the application. What you see depends of whether the application has been used before.

    - If the application has never been opened on your current disk, you see a message box asking if you're upgrading from an earlier version of Quicken. Click No. A dialog box for naming a new accounts file appears.
    - If the application has been opened before, you see the check register that was last open. For example, if you did the Quick Tour, you see one of the Sample Data accounts. Choose New from the File menu. In the small dialog box that opens, click New File. A dialog box for naming a new accounts file appears.

2. Enter a name for the file in the File for your accounts box. Click to put an X in the Home categories check box if there isn't one there already. Check the Business box too if you have both home and business accounts.

3. Click the New button. Quicken makes your file; a message box tells you how the category-copying is coming along. Then the Set Up New Account dialog box opens, as shown in Figure 14.2, but without the data filled in.

Chapter 14

FIGURE 14.1
The Quicken icon

FIGURE 14.2
The Set Up New Account dialog box

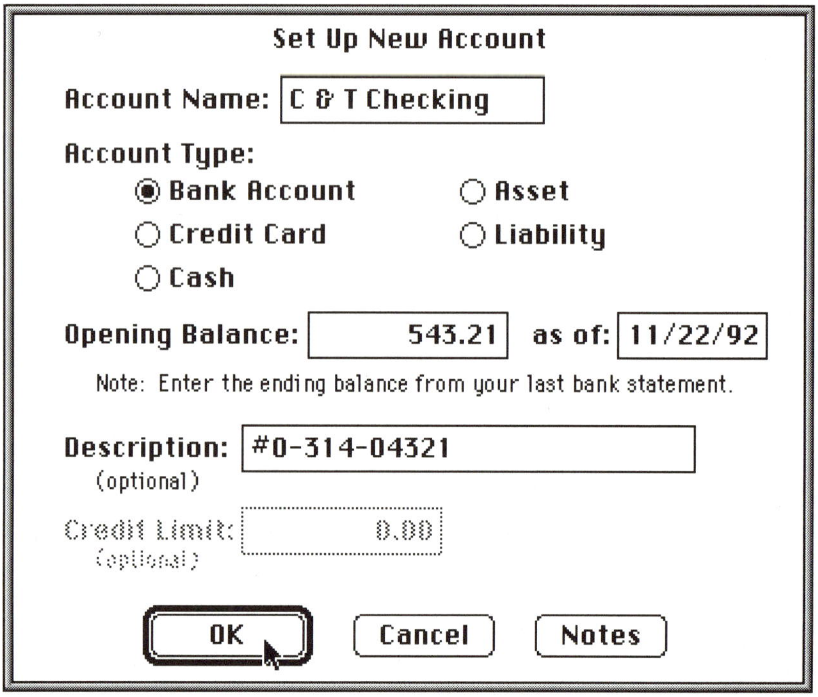

```
Set Up New Account

Account Name: C & T Checking
Account Type:
    ● Bank Account      ○ Asset
    ○ Credit Card       ○ Liability
    ○ Cash

Opening Balance:  543.21  as of: 11/22/92
Note: Enter the ending balance from your last bank statement.

Description: #0-314-04321
(optional)

Credit Limit:  0.00
(optional)

[ OK ]   [ Cancel ]   [ Notes ]
```

Opening a New Account

You are moving right along. You have created a file to keep all your accounts in, and now you are going right ahead and making your first account to put in that file.

1. Make sure you're looking at the Set Up New Account dialog box. Then enter an account name in the Account Name text box at the top. The name should tell what the account is for, or who uses it.
2. Leave the default Account Type selection at Bank Account. Press Tab to move to the next field.
3. Enter the opening balance of the account. This should be your ending balance from your last bank statement, and it should be reconciled.
4. Enter the date of the bank statement from which you took the ending balance.
5. Enter an account description, if you want; I put my account number here.
6. Click the Notes button at the bottom of the box if you want to add things like the bank's address and telephone number. Click OK in the Notes dialog box when you are finished.
7. Click OK in the Set Up New Account dialog box when you are satisfied with the entries. Quicken creates a new bank account and displays the account register as shown in Figure 14.3.

Using the Check Register

The register is a record of all the transactions that occur in an account. It looks like the paper check register you probably carry around attached to your checkbook, with entries for date and type of transaction, check number, description, amount, and account balance. There is also a column for a check mark to tell when a check or deposit has cleared.

Each account has a separate Quicken register. Although the registers for different account types display different column headings, all registers work the same way.

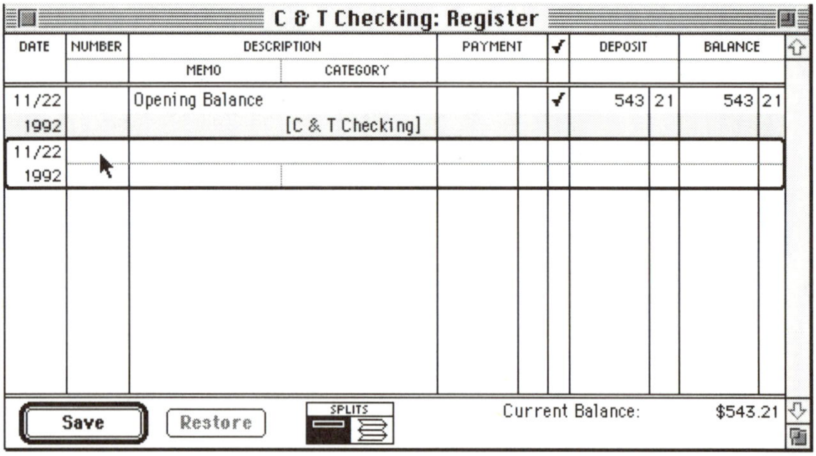

FIGURE 14.3
The Register window, showing a new checking account

DATE	NUMBER	DESCRIPTION		PAYMENT	✓	DEPOSIT	BALANCE
		MEMO	CATEGORY				
11/22 1992		Opening Balance	[C & T Checking]		✓	543 21	543 21
11/22 1992							

Current Balance: $543.21

The first empty transaction line in the register appears with a bold frame around it; this is the one you can fill in. You enter transactions in the register by typing information in the fields; the fields are just like the spaces you see in your paper check register. Press Tab to move from field to field. When you write a check using Quicken rather than by hand, Quicken enters the check information in the register automatically. See "Writing Checks" later in this chapter for details.

Once you have entered some transactions as described in the section that follows, you can use the scroll bar to move through the register window. A date box appears next to the scroll bar when you drag the scroll box. The displayed date shows you the date of the transaction that will be selected if you release the scroll box at that point.

You can search for, change, or delete transactions in the register at any time.

Recording a Check in the Register

To enter a transaction in the register, you just fill in the fields. If a blank transaction is selected, as in Figure 14.3, you can enter data. If it's not selected, choose New Transaction from the Edit menu (⌘-N). Once you have selected the blank transaction, you can enter the data for a handwritten check to the grocery store.

1. Enter a date. You can leave the current date, or type any date you want. Pressing the Plus (+) or Minus (-) key increases or decreases the displayed date by one day. After entering the date, press Tab.
2. Enter a check number as shown in Figure 14.4. Press Tab to move on.
3. Enter the description. When recording a check, enter the name of the payee. Otherwise, enter a word or phrase that describes the transaction. Press Tab to continue.
4. Enter the amount of the payment. That's the amount of the check in this case. Use this field for bank fees and withdrawals, too. Press the period key or spacebar to move from the Dollars field to the Cents field. Press Tab to go to the Memo field.
5. Enter a memo if you need to. This field is optional. You can use it to indicate an account or invoice number. Press Tab to go on.
6. Enter a category. You can type it in, or choose Category & Transfer List from the Shortcuts menu, then find the category that fits and double-click it. See "Using Categories" later in this chapter for details.
7. Click Save to complete the entry, as in Figure 14.4. Quicken does the arithmetic for you, and selects the next transaction line.

Skip the little field with the check at the head of the column (the one to the right of the Payment field). It is for checking off cleared checks as you reconcile your account when you get your monthly statement from the bank.

FIGURE 14.4
Recording a check in the register

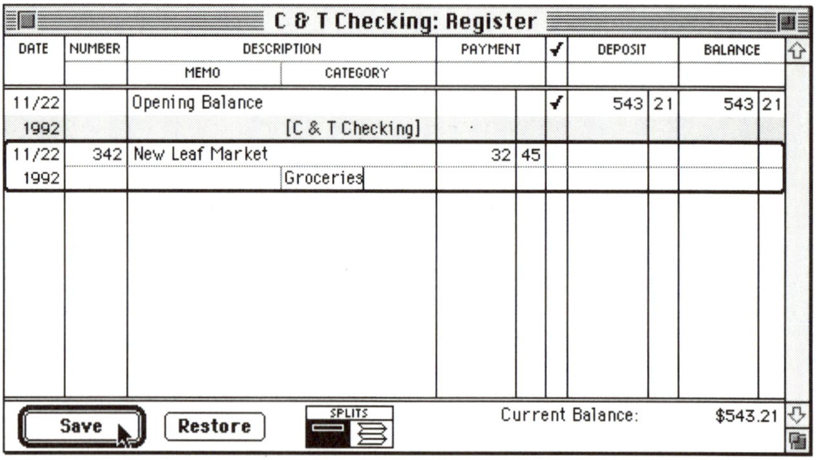

Entering Deposits in the Register

To get a little more practice, enter a couple of deposits in the register. Tab past the number field and enter a description instead of a payee. Tab past the payment field and enter the amount of the deposit. If you need to specify where the deposit came from, and it is a regular source of income, you can make a category for it, as described in "Setting Up a Category" later in this chapter. Click Save when you are done entering each deposit. Quicken does the math, and your balance goes up. A nice thing, even though it never lasts.

Correcting Mistakes in the Register

If you make a little mistake of just a couple characters in a field, press the Delete key to back up over them, then type in the correction. If you decide a whole field is wrong, choose Undo from the Edit menu, then start the field entry from scratch. If you decide a whole transaction is wrong and you haven't saved it yet, click the Restore button instead of Save. Quicken clears all the fields except the date, so you can start over.

If you decide a transaction is wrong after you have saved it, but before any money has changed hands, you can choose Delete Transaction from the Edit menu. Quicken puts up a little dialog box to make sure you want to do this risky thing. Click Delete if you do.

If you write a check and then void it after entering the transaction in the register, just select the transaction and choose Void Transaction from the Edit menu. Quicken undoes the change in your balance and puts the word *VOID* in front of the name of the payee.

Using Categories

The secret to controlling your finances is seeing the patterns that are hidden in all the detailed information in your accounts. The Category field is the tool that helps you see the patterns. Quicken uses the Category field to sort information into reports. You can create reports at any time to see how you are doing on the different categories of income and expenditure.

Categories let you track expenditures for specific items. For example, you might want to see how much money you have spent fixing up the old car you are driving. If you categorize these checks as car-repair transactions you can create a report showing all the money you have poured into that old heap. To limit yourself, you can create a budget and then compare budgeted items to actual amounts.

Your needs determine the categories you set up. Think carefully about the categories you want. If you want to compare what you budget with what you actually spend, you need a category for each comparison you want to make.

Quicken provides you with two lists of categories—one for home, and one for business. You can use these lists if you want, or you can create your own list of categories.

Choosing a Category or Transfer Account

When the cursor is in the Category field in the register, you can either type in the category if you know it, or you can choose it from a list. To get at the list, choose Category & Transfer List from the Shortcuts menu (⌘-L) or double-click on the Category field. Select a category from the list by double-clicking on the category name, as shown in Figure 14.5. Quicken copies the category name to the Category field.

If you can't find a category that the check fits into exactly, you can create your own category. See the section that follows for information on how to do this.

You can also specify transfers of money from one account to another by choosing the name of an account from the list. You must have several accounts set up to use this feature. See the chapter on transferring money between accounts in the Quicken *User Manual* for details.

Setting Up a Category

Use the following steps to define a new category and add it to the list so you can choose it for future checks or deposits.

FIGURE 14.5
Choosing a category from the Category & Transfer list

Category/Transfer	Type
Child Care	Expense
Clothing	Expense
Dining	Expense
Dividend Inc	Income
DYI videos	Income
Education	Expense
Entertainment	Expense
Gift Received	Income
Gifts	Expense
Groceries	Expense
Home Repair	Expense
Household	Expense

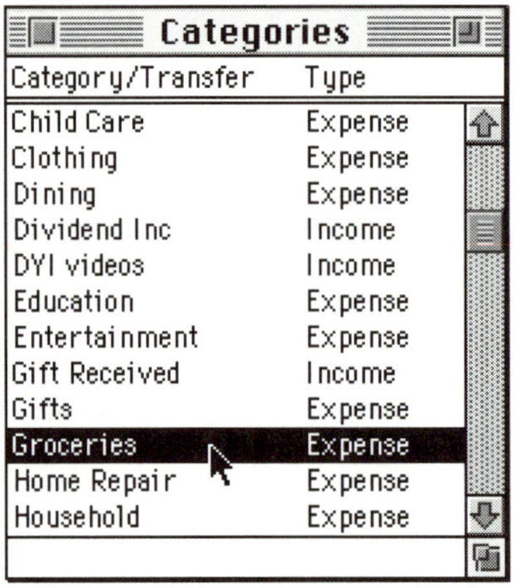

1. Choose Set Up Categories from the Shortcuts menu. The Set Up Categories dialog box appears.
2. Enter a category name and if you want, enter a description.
3. Specify whether the category is an expense or income item and if you want it stored as a tax-related item (anything you have to report for taxes is tax-related).
4. Click Save to add the new category to the list, as shown in Figure 14.6. Click Restore to discard it if you change your mind, then click the close box to exit the dialog.

If you type a nonexistent category name in the Category field on the register, Quicken tells you the category cannot be found, and offers you three options: select another category from the list, set up this category, or cancel.

Writing Checks

If you have ordered Quicken checks for your type of printer, you can make out a check on your Mac and Quicken will enter the information in

FIGURE 14.6
Setting up a new category

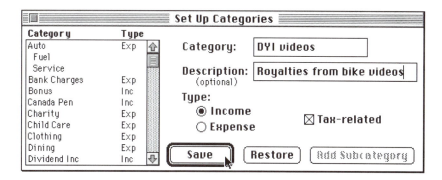

the check register and print the check for you. To do this, follow these steps:

1. Choose Write Checks from the Account menu (⌘-J). A blank check appears in a window.
2. Change the date if you need to. Press Tab to move to the next field.
3. Enter the payee name in the Pay to the Order of field and press Tab.
4. Enter the amount of the check in the $ field and press Tab. Quicken fills in the the next field for you. The cursor goes on to the Address box.
5. Fill in the payee name and address if you intend to mail the check in a Quicken window envelope. *Warning:* After typing the name, press *Tab* to move down to the next line of the address. If you press the Return key, the check is saved and a new blank appears. Press Tab to go on to the next field, also.
6. You can enter memo information if you want. You might want to give the payee additional information—memo information is printed on the check. Or, you might want the information for your own records. Press Tab to go on to the Category field.
7. Assign a category, in the same way you do for any other transaction.
8. Click Save when you are finished, as in Figure 14.7. If you click Restore, the transaction is deleted.
9. Click the close box when you are done. The register window returns.

Your check is recorded in the register. You can make corrections in the register and they will appear on the check, if you haven't printed it yet. If you saved a check with mistakes on it, you can select it in the

FIGURE 14.7
Writing a check

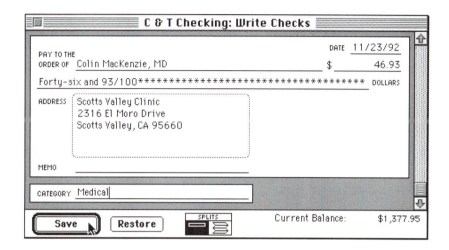

register and choose Delete Transaction from the Edit menu, then confirm the deletion in the dialog box.

Memorizing Transactions

If there are checks that you write every month, you can put them on a Memorized Transaction List. Then you don't have to reenter the information every month. If the amount of the check varies from month to month, you can leave the amount blank and fill that field in each time you make out a check.

To create a memorized transaction, use the following procedure:

1. Choose Write Checks from the Account menu.
2. In the Write Checks window, enter the check exactly as you want it to appear each month. For example, if the amount is likely to change every month, as it usually does with the telephone bill, leave the amount blank.
3. Choose Memorize Transaction from the Shortcuts menu (⌘-M). Quicken memorizes the transaction.

4. You can complete the check and save it as a specific transaction; for example, if you did not enter an amount, you can do so now.

Once you've created your memorized transactions, you can use them to write checks by following these steps:

1. Get ready to write a check. If you are already in the Write Checks window, you're set. If you're in the register, choose New Transaction from the Edit menu.
2. Choose Memorized Transaction List from the Shortcuts menu.
3. When the list displays, double-click on the item you want. Quicken creates the check for you.

If you decide the memorized transaction is not needed after all, you can select it in the register and choose Delete Transaction from the Edit menu, as long as you haven't printed out the check yet.

You can change information in a memorized transaction at any time by choosing Edit Transaction from the Edit menu (⌘-E). Just make your changes and click Replace in the dialog box.

To delete a memorized transaction, choose Memorized Transactions List from the Shortcuts menu. Then select the transaction you want to delete and choose Delete Memorized Transaction from the Edit menu (⌘-D). Click OK in the displayed dialog box to confirm.

Printing

You can use Quicken to print custom Quicken checks or checks made by other companies. You can also print reports that give an overall picture of your finances. How you do this depends on the kind of printer you have. The following sections tell you how to do some of the most common printing jobs in Quicken. Read your Quicken manual for more information on printer setup.

Printing Checks on a Page-Oriented Printer

Use the following procedure to prepare for printing and print checks by the page:

1. Load the checks in the paper tray. Make sure the checks are face up. The top of the checks should face into the printer. If you are printing to an Apple Personal LaserWriter or HP LaserJet IIP, load the checks face down. Since the printer pulls the top page off the pile, you have to reverse the order of the checks so the first sheet is on top when you're looking at the checks face down.
2. Choose Check Setup from the File menu. Make sure that the settings match the paper you have for checks and that the style suits you.
3. Choose Print Checks from the File menu and fill in the Print Checks dialog box.
4. Click OK, as shown in Figure 14.8.
5. Check the settings in the printer's Print dialog box and click OK to begin printing.
6. After your checks print, Quicken asks if they printed correctly. If they did, click Yes. If they didn't, click No and start the procedure over.

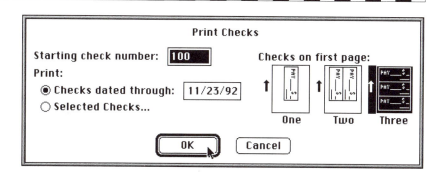

FIGURE 14.8
Printing checks to a page printer

Chapter 14

Printing Checks on a Continuous-Feed Printer

It's probably a good idea to do a test run before actually printing the checks on a continuous-feed printer, to make sure everything is lined up correctly. Then follow these steps to print your checks.

1. Load the checks in your ImageWriter.
2. Choose Print Checks from the File menu and fill in the Print Checks dialog box. If you are printing a sample check, click the Check Alignment Test button.
3. Click OK.
4. Position the top check. If you're printing to an ImageWriter I, align the fifth line of the check with the top of the type head. Snap the roller into place to hold the checks in place. If you're printing to an ImageWriter II, align the top of the check with the top of the plastic guard in front of the print head. If you're printing to an ImageWriter LQ, align the top of the check with the top of the print head.
5. Click OK.

If the checks do not come out with the text aligned correctly, start the paper again, adjusting the alignment to correct the problem.

Creating Reports

You can also use Quicken to create reports based on your transactions. Entering transactions in the register, whether by hand or by writing checks, creates a database of all your transactions that you can sort and summarize in a report.

For example, to create a summary of your tax-related information, first make sure you've designated your tax-related items. Then open the Reports menu and highlight Home. Move into the Home reports submenu and select Tax Summary. A dialog box appears. Specify the information you want the report to contain by filling out the dialog box. Quicken searches the account(s) you specified, collects the information you requested and displays it, as shown in Figure 14.9.

You can print out a report by choosing Print Report from the File menu when the report is in view. Select any options you need in the Print dialog box, and click the Page Preview button to see how the report will look. Click Print in the Preview window to begin printing.

Troubleshooting Problems with Quicken

The following subsections cover the types of problems you are most likely to encounter when using Quicken to keep your financial records.

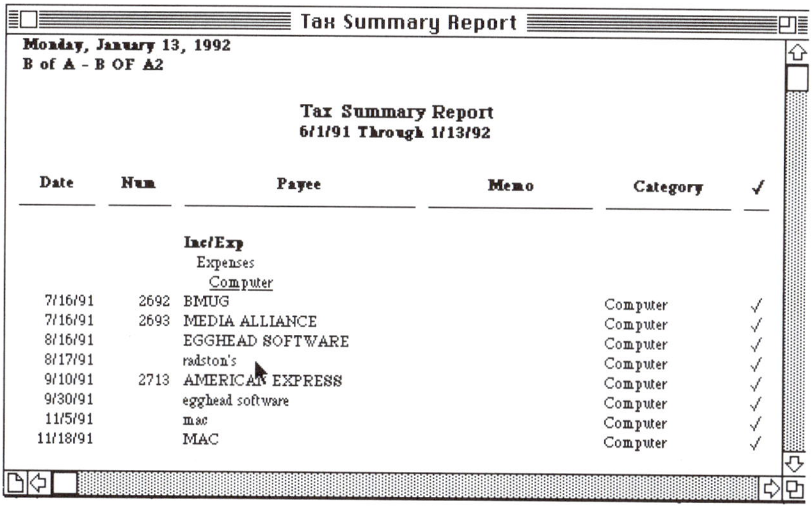

FIGURE 14.9
A tax summary report

Can't enter a transfer from one account to another without entering the data twice.

Quicken actually has a nifty way to transfer money and write both the withdrawal and the deposit for a transaction at the same time. You just write up the transaction for the withdrawal, then choose the name of the account you are depositing in the Category field of the transaction.

For example, to transfer money from your checking account to your savings account, first make sure you have created both accounts in the same file, then write out a check. When you get to the Category field, choose Category & Transfer List from the Shortcuts menu, then scroll all the way down to the bottom of the list and choose the name of your savings account. Bingo; two transactions appear in the registers: one for your check and one for the deposit.

Can't change a category or account name, or can't delete a category or account.

You can't make big changes to categories or accounts while you are looking at transactions in the register. You have to list the accounts or categories first. For example, to change the name of an account or to delete it, you first choose Account List from the Account menu. When the list of your accounts appears, select the name of the account you want to edit, then choose Edit Account from the Edit menu. The Account Info dialog box opens. You can edit the name, the type, and the description of the account, then click OK. If you want to delete an account after closing it, just select the account name in the Account List, then choose Delete Account from the Edit menu.

I keep saving my checks when all I want to do is move to the next field.

You have to press the Tab key to move from field to field when entering data in the check-writing fields. If you press the Return key,

Quicken thinks you are giving the keyboard shortcut for clicking the Save button. Most annoying. I really have a strong tendency to do it when I'm entering the address at the bottom of the check.

The answer is easy. Choose Other Settings from the Options menu, and when the dialog box opens, click in the check box next to the option that says "Pressing Return tabs to the next field." Click OK, and you can go ahead and enter data in checks without having to worry about those premature saves.

Can't figure out what to do with categories.

If you aren't an accountant, you may wonder what all those categories are about. Why fill in a category for a check, if you have already written in what the money went to in the description field? Or why have a category for income, if you know where the money is coming from?

The answer is that the description field is for telling *who* the money went to or came from. A category is a way of recording *what* you spend the money on, or what type of source it came from.

Categories are useful because you can tell Quicken what you are spending each check on, then make up a report at the end of a month and see how much you spent in each category. Usually, all you need to do is see how much money you have been spending on things, and then you'll learn to budget more wisely.

CHAPTER 15

Integrating Your Work

Once you have had some experience creating documents in two or three different applications, you will begin to see opportunities to include data from one type of document inside other types of documents. For example, you might want to include a graph from your spreadsheet application inside a financial report you are creating with a word processor. Or you might want to put titles you create in your word processor under graphics you create in your drawing application. The Mac makes it as easy to move things from one application to another as it is to move parts of the same document around. Practically any kind of data you can see in one document, you can move to another document, as long as the two documents have compatible formats.

    This chapter explains the different ways you can use your Mac to integrate the data you've created. The first section describes how to move and remove parts of documents by way of the Clipboard. The second section describes how to link documents that you've created within the same application and different applications. The third section explains the Publish and Subscribe features found in many Mac applications running under System 7. These features allow the exchange of information between documents belonging to different users and created by different applications.

Cutting, Copying, and Pasting

The simplest way to move and remove parts of your documents is to cut, copy, and paste data using the Clipboard. You can use the Clipboard to move material within a document, between documents, or between documents created by compatible applications.

Introducing the Clipboard

When you cut something out of a document, it is held in a special temporary storage place in your Mac called the *Clipboard*. You can undo the cut and bring the item back from the Clipboard, or you can paste the item that's in the Clipboard someplace else. You can also copy an item in a document, which leaves it where it is and places a duplicate in the Clipboard. This copy can be pasted into the same document or into other documents.

Working with the Clipboard is pretty easy, but there are a few things to keep in mind. First of all, you don't ever see the Clipboard. You can see what's in it in some applications (they have a Show Clipboard command in the Window or View menu, usually), but otherwise, the Clipboard does its work behind the scenes. If you are like me, and you are curious about where the heck the Clipboard actually is, just go to the Finder and open the System Folder. There it is. Double-click the icon, and you get a window showing what's in it.

You also need to remember that the Clipboard can only hold one item at a time. If you copy an item into the Clipboard so you can paste it somewhere else, but then cut something else before you get around to pasting, the copied item will be lost, and the cut item will be all that is left in the Clipboard. For a way to recover from this error, see "Undoing Clipboard Mistakes" later in this chapter.

On the other hand, pasting does not remove anything from the Clipboard, so you can paste an item as many times as you want. It will stay there until you either cut or copy something else, or shut down your Mac.

Cutting and Pasting to Move Parts of Documents

To move part of a document, you select it and cut it out of its original place, then move to the new place and paste it in. For example, if you are in Microsoft Word and you want to move a sentence that seems out of place, use this procedure:

1. Select the sentence that's out of place by dragging the I-beam over it, as shown in Figure 15.1. (In graphics applications, drag a selection rectangle or lasso around the image, or click on it if it is a selectable object.)
2. Choose Cut from the Edit menu, or press ⌘-X.
3. Place the insertion point where you want to paste the text, as in Figure 15.2. (If you are placing something in a graphics application, scroll the window until you can see the spot where you want to paste the item.)
4. Choose Paste from the Edit menu, or press ⌘-V. The new text appears, as in Figure 15.3.
5. In a bit-mapped graphics application, drag the pasted item to the place where you want it. In a text or object-oriented application,

FIGURE 15.1
Selecting text to move

Is there any better or equal hope in the world? Why should there not be a patient confidence in the ultimate justice of the people?

Abraham Lincoln, March 4, 1861

FIGURE 15.2
Placing the insertion point for a paste

|Why should there not be a patient confidence in the ultimate justice of the people?|

Abraham Lincoln, March 4, 1861

FIGURE 15.3
Text moved to the right place

Why should there not be a patient confidence in the ultimate justice of the people? Is there any better or equal hope in the world?|

Abraham Lincoln, March 4, 1861

adjust the pasted text style, or the surrounding text and images, so the old blends well with the new.

This procedure works for cutting items out of one document and pasting them into another one, too. If you have two or more documents open when using an application, make your cut in one window, then click in the second window, or choose the second window from the Windows or View menu. Find the place where you want to paste the item in the second window and paste it as described above.

One minor problem with cutting and pasting text from one document to another: the style of the cut and pasted text usually stays the same, so the newly pasted stuff (text, for example) may look different from the stuff all around it. To fix this, select the pasted text, then apply the style of the surrounding text to it.

Copying and Pasting

The procedure for copying and pasting items in a document or from one document to another in the same application is just the same as that for cutting and pasting. The only differences are that you choose Copy from the Edit menu instead of Cut (or press ⌘-C instead of ⌘-X) and that the original item stays in place.

Copying Parts of Documents between Applications

Moving items from a document created by one application to a document created by a different application requires a little more preparation and care than moving things around in the same application. It is better to do the moving process by copying items rather than cutting them, since a moved item may not come out exactly the same if you try to move it back to the application that created it. Follow these steps to move items between different applications:

1. Make sure the applications have compatible formats. If you are copying items from one bit-mapped graphics application to another, you will not have much trouble. But if you are trying to move an item from an object-oriented graphics application to a text processing application, you may need to take special preparatory steps. See Appendix A and read your applications' documentation for more information.

2. Open both applications. Then open the origin document, which has the item you want to move, and the destination document, where you want to paste the item. For example, I might open SuperPaint and Word, as in Figure 15.4.

3. Select the item in the origin document, as the graphic border pattern is selected in the SuperPaint window in Figure 15.4.

4. Choose Copy from the Edit menu, or press ⌘-C. Since SuperPaint is just working with a bit map, all I have to do is choose Copy from the File menu in the sample shown. But you may have to enter a special command to copy the format in a certain

FIGURE 15.4
Selecting a graphic to copy

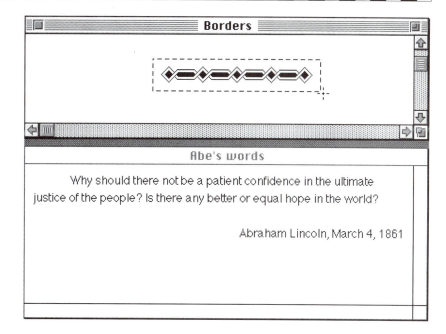

way. For instance, in order to copy something from some PostScript graphics applications to some word processing application, you must press the Option key when you choose Copy from the Edit menu.

5. Switch to the destination application and document. You can choose the destination application's icon from the Applications menu, or you can click in the window of the destination document. Window-clicking sometimes confuses the application, so I normally go via the Applications menu.

6. Place the insertion point or position the window where you want to place the item. In Figure 15.5, I placed the I-beam where I want the border to show up.

7. Choose Paste from the Edit menu or press ⌘-V. Your copied item appears, as shown in Figure 15.6.

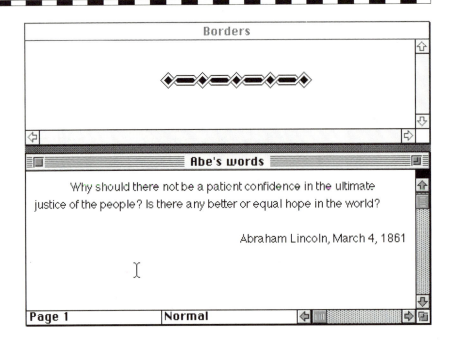

FIGURE 15.5
Placing the insertion point for a graphic

If the item isn't quite in the right place, you can often move it with tabs. In Microsoft Word, you can change the size and shape of placed graphics by selecting them and moving the corner handles in and out.

If the item does not appear, or if a blank space the size of the item appears in the destination document, see the "Troubleshooting" section at the end of this chapter.

Using the Scrapbook

The Scrapbook is a permanent storage place, unlike the temporary Clipboard. If there are things you want to have on hand to paste into documents over and over, put them in the Scrapbook. For example, if you wanted to end each of your Word documents with the border shown in Figure 15.6, you could put it in the Scrapbook.

FIGURE 15.6
A placed graphic

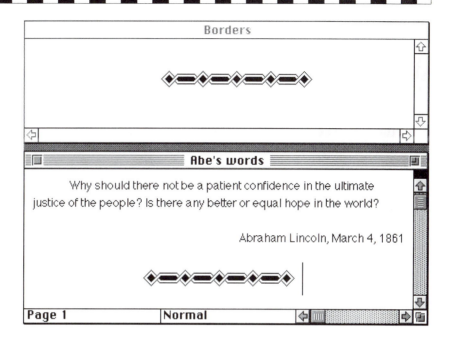

Use these steps to put an item into the Scrapbook:

1. Copy the item from a document into the Clipboard.
2. Choose Scrapbook from the Apple menu. The Scrapbook opens, with the item on the current page showing. You can scroll to a different page if you want. It's best to leave your most-copied item on the front page.
3. Paste the new item onto a page; it takes over that page and moves the other items in the Scrapbook back a page. You can cut and paste items from page to page in the Scrapbook if you want to rearrange their order.

If you have a Scrapbook item you think you'll be using frequently, you can leave the Scrapbook window open and switch to other applications, then choose Scrapbook from the Applications menu to get back to the Scrapbook when you need it.

To paste an item from the Scrapbook into a document, follow these steps:

1. Open the document you want to paste the item into, then open the Scrapbook.
2. Scroll through the Scrapbook to the item you want to paste.
3. Copy the item from the Scrapbook to the Clipboard; you do not need to select the item to do this.
4. Click in the document window or choose the document application from the Applications menu to make it active.
5. Paste the item into the document and adjust the surrounding text or images to blend well with the pasted item.

Figure 15.7 shows the path an item can take from an origin document to a destination document by way of the Clipboard and the Scrapbook.

If you do a lot of cutting and pasting, especially if you are designing page layouts, you may find the Scrapbook cumbersome. You can purchase other desk accessories, such as SmartScrap or ClickPaste, that serve the same purpose and provide sizing and hierarchical storage functions.

FIGURE 15.7

A way to cut and paste through the Clipboard and the Scrapbook

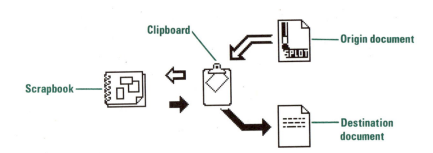

Undoing Clipboard Mistakes

If you ever cut an item from a document and realize it was a mistake, you can put the item back by choosing Undo Cut from the Edit menu or pressing ⌘-Z. If you do something else after the mistaken cut, you can still go back to the place where you made the mistake and paste the item off the Clipboard. As long as you haven't cut or copied anything else into the Clipboard, the item you cut by mistake will still be there.

You can even recover something you cut *after* copying or cutting another item into the Clipboard. Choose Undo from the Edit menu or press ⌘-Z to undo the last cut or copy: the Clipboard is restored to the previous item, the one you want to recover. Go back to the place where you mistakenly cut the item and paste it back into your document.

Dynamic Updating with Links

Some applications allow you to link one document to another, so that the data in the *dependent* document will update automatically when corresponding data in the *supporting* document is changed. Similar forms of linking are available in several different application groups, but in this section, I will describe linking as it works in Microsoft products such as Excel and Word.

Linking a Text Document to a Spreadsheet

You can copy and paste a chart from a spreadsheet into many word processing documents, but if you are using Microsoft Word and Excel, you can *link* the chart in your text document to the original spreadsheet document. Once you've linked the two documents, whenever there is any change in the spreadsheet, such as a bunch of sales figures changing when the company has a good month, the chart in the Word document is updated automatically. The following procedure tells how to create the link so the word processing document is dependent on the spreadsheet document.

1. Open Excel and open the supporting document, and open Word and the dependent document. Then display the chart you want to copy into Word. (If you created a sample chart in Chapter 12, you can use that one.)
2. Select the whole chart. First double-click in the middle of it to go into chart mode, then choose Select Chart from the Chart menu (is that redundant, or what?). Things should look something like Figure 15.8.
3. Choose Copy from the Edit menu.
4. Switch over into your Word document and place the I-beam where you want to place the chart. (Just type a simple sentence like the one in Figure 15.9 if you don't have a Word document you want to use.)
5. Choose Paste Special from the Edit menu. When the dialog box opens, click the Paste Link button. The chart appears in your Word document, as shown in Figure 15.9.
6. Now, if you want to see magic, go back to Excel, update a number somewhere deep in the spreadsheet, then check out the chart both in Excel and in your Word document. Wow.

Special Considerations for Linked Documents

As you might expect, there are a few little things you have to take care of with this automatic updating business. For one thing, the whole scenario works best if both the supporting document and the dependent document are in the same folder. So, if you are working on a project and

FIGURE 15.8
Selecting a chart in a supporting document

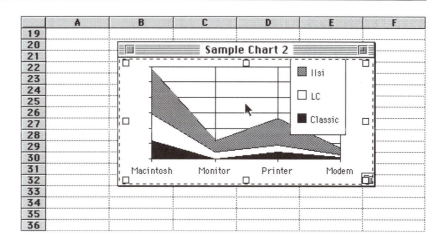

FIGURE 15.9
A linked chart in a dependent Word document

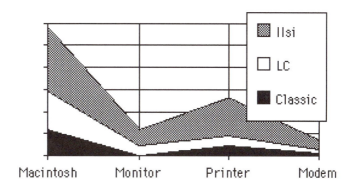

you have the supporting document (the Excel spreadsheet in my sample) in that project's folder, just put the dependent document (the Word one, in my sample) in that same folder. And if you ever update the supporting document when both it and the dependent document are open, save the supporting document first, then save the dependent document. If you save the dependent document first, the references can get mixed up.

Publishing and Subscribing to Parts of Documents

Some applications allow you to create items that automatically update after being copied to other documents. It is as if these applications can cut and paste new information into your documents all by themselves. Applications with this automatic updating feature will have commands such as Create Publisher and Subscribe to in the Edit menu.

When you make a change in a document with a *publisher* item, the change will also occur in any *subscriber* items that have been placed in other documents. This automatic updating is especially useful if there are several users on a network relying on the same information in different documents. Each user can work on a part of a project and publish the parts of their documents that need to be put into the final document for the whole group. Other users can see the updated version of the final document as work by each member progresses. They can also subscribe to specific parts of each other's work in order to keep abreast of day-to-day developments without having to exchange barrages of memos or phone calls.

For example, if a construction team is working on a bid for a big job, one of the people would make a spreadsheet of estimates, in Resolve perhaps, and another might write up a proposal in MacWrite. Both of these people could publish and subscribe to each other's work. The manager might subscribe to both the spreadsheet and the text proposal, to see how things are going without having to pester the team workers.

To create a publisher item and an *edition* file that contains the updatable information, follow these steps:

1. Select the item you want to make into a publisher. For example, you might have a table of time and cost estimates for making a construction bid.
2. Choose Create Publisher from the Edit menu. The Publisher dialog box opens.
3. Enter a name for the edition file that will contain the Publisher item. For the example described above, the edition file could be called Estimates.
4. Click the Publish button.

The edition file appears on the desktop, with a gray textured border, as shown in Figure 15.10.

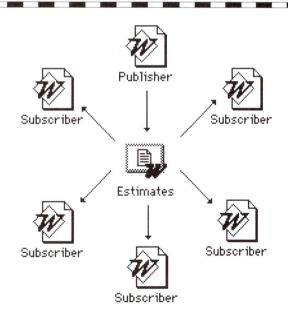

FIGURE 15.10
An Estimates edition file, with its publisher and subscribers

To tap into the updatable information in the edition file, follow these steps:

1. Open the document in which you want the information from the edition to appear, and place the insertion point.
2. Choose Subscribe to from the Edit menu. A dialog box opens, with a list of files; the edition files have a gray rectangle icon.
3. Find the edition file you want and select it.
4. Click the Subscribe button. The item in the edition file appears in your document. If you select this item, it displays a linked pattern border. The linked pattern border does not show if the item already has a border, so if you subscribe to a table like the estimates one, you will not see the telltale border.

Use the Publisher options and Subscriber options commands in the Edit menu to update editions automatically or manually, to see when the edition was updated last, to cancel updating, or to locate and open the publisher document. For more information on using published information, see the *Macintosh Networking Reference*.

Troubleshooting Problems with Data Integration

The following sections cover the problems you can have when cutting and pasting, using linked documents, or using publisher and subscriber documents.

Pasted graphic doesn't appear in text document.

You paste a graphic into a document created by a word processing application, and the graphic doesn't appear, or just an empty frame appears. Try displaying the item by choosing Show Clipboard in the origin application (if the application has that menu option) or choosing Show Clipboard from the Edit menu in the Finder. When you have seen the graphic in the Clipboard, paste it into the the destination document. If that does not work, try pasting the item via the Scrapbook, as described in "Using the Scrapbook" earlier in this chapter.

Can't find an item quickly in the Scrapbook.

You want to copy something out of the Scrapbook often, but you get sick and tired of scrolling through all the other stuff in there to get at your item. The answer is simple. Scroll to the item, cut it to the Clipboard (choose Cut from the Edit menu), then scroll to the first item in the Scrapbook and paste the often-used item over it (choose Paste from the Edit menu). Now that item you want will be right up front every time you open the Scrapbook.

Can't save a dependent linked document.

You created a link to a brand new document by placing an item that was copied out of it, but when you try to save your dependent document, you get an error message about saving to an untitled file. The problem is that you haven't saved the supporting document yet. Switch over to that supporting document, save it and give it a name, then switch back to the dependent document. Now you can save it just fine.

By the way, if you ever rename a supporting document that is not in the same folder as its dependent document, or if you ever move supporting and dependent documents to different folders, you may have to redirect the links so the dependent documents can find their supporters. For more information on this, see your application's user's guide.

Can't subscribe to an edition you can see in the file list.

If you are working on a network and you can see an edition file listed on your network, but it does not have the correct border or you cannot see it at all, then the file may have limited viewing permissions, or you may not have access rights on that server. See your network administrator, or see Chapter 6, "Linking Programs Over the Network," in the *Macintosh Networking Reference*.

Only part of an Excel edition appears when you subscribe to it.

If an Excel edition has both data and a graph in it, you can only subscribe to the data. To see the graph and the data, you have to subscribe to it all as a picture; just hold down the Shift key when you click the Subscribe button in the Subscribe To dialog box. The data and the graph both appear.

Can't tell if an edition you subscribed to is updated or not.

To make sure you are looking at an updated version of the edition you have subscribed to, select the subscriber item, then choose Subscriber Options from the Edit menu. When the dialog box opens, check the date in the lower left corner to see when the edition was last updated by the publisher. If you think that this date was after you got your last update, click the Get Edition Now button and your subscriber item will be updated immediately.

Can't tell what items in a document are subscribers.

If you are wondering what parts of your document are subscribers, you may be able to find out by one of a couple ways. Some applications, such as Excel, have a Links command in the File menu. If you choose that command, you can choose Subscribers in the Link Type box and see a list of all the subscribers in your document. In other applications, the subscribers have patterned borders or double brackets around them. For example, in Microsoft Word you can choose Show ¶ from the View menu, and gray double brackets appear at the beginning and end of each subscriber.

P A R T
four

Utilities and Communications for the Mac

The next few chapters of this book describe some small programs, called utilities, that you can use to make your work on the Mac go smoothly. The Mac has a few weaknesses that can lead to problems unless you take care of them, but there are many wonderful little utilities that can work hand in hand with your system software to help you keep ahead of trouble and save time in the process. You can use utilities to find files quickly, to automate repetitious tasks, or to organize things on the Mac so it works better. You can also find utilities that will protect your files from viruses or accidents.

The final chapters explain how you can use your Mac to communicate with other Macs over networks and telephone lines. You can share ideas and information with other users in several ways; there are sections that help you decide the best means of communication for your needs, and sections that show how to use the media effectively.

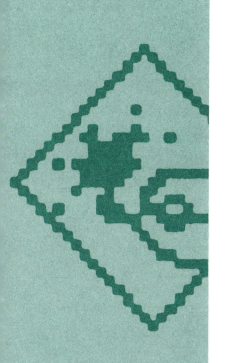

CHAPTER 16

Time-Saving Utilities

Time-saving utilities are little applications you can use to make your work on the Mac go faster and easier. When you're working on a computer, the last thing you want to do is repeat some tiresome task over and over. The Mac is supposed to do that repetitive stuff, not you. But oddly enough, some things about the Mac's system software and some things about many applications are like hurdles that make it so you *have* to do repetitive tasks to get your work done. Sometimes these hurdles were made with the best intentions; the software engineers wanted to keep the flow of decisions as clear and simple as possible. But they made it so you have to do simple stuff too many times, or in slow, tedious ways. In response to this problem, clever programmers have figured out ways to get around most of the hurdles in the Mac system software and in the commonly used applications.

One word of caution. Any add-on utility that tries to sneak by the limitations built into system and applications software is walking on thin ice. If *two* add-on utilities try to walk on the same ice, they tend to fall through. So buy and use only one utility for any given time-saving task, and if you can get by using the standard system or applications software (they often have ways to get around their own hurdles), do so. See your local user group for tips and tricks that can help you make the most of what you have. Then find out if there is *one* utility that will do what you need, and install and use that utility. Don't just load up your Mac with every time-saving gimmick that comes along, or you'll waste a lot of time recovering from system bombs and applications that quit unexpectedly.

Which Time-Saving Utilities for You?

You can spend a lot of time checking out time-saving utilities. First, ask yourself how you waste time doing your work now. When you know what you want, check out the utilities described in this chapter, talk to experienced users, then pick the one that will work best for your specific needs.

Be cautious when you shop for your utility. Keep in mind that utilities are always changing. They are quick and easy to write, compared to major applications, so developers are churning them out all the time. They tend to be buggier than major applications, especially if you don't use them as intended. Shareware and freeware can be just as good as commercial software, but the odds are much higher that the free stuff will be untested and therefore buggy. Before you install any utility, make sure that it's guaranteed to work with your version of the system software, and that it is not known to conflict with any other utility you have installed. User groups and utilities like INITInfo can give you help with compatibility issues.

Utilities that Get at Things Quickly

Most of the time you waste at the Mac is either waiting for it to do something, or having it wait for you to remember how to get at something that you have forgotten. There isn't a utility that makes the Mac think faster, but there are several that can help you find and get at things that *you* can't think of.

Fast Find is my favorite. It is included with the Norton Utilities, a group of small, powerful programs sold as a package. There are other packages of "tools" like the Norton Utilities, but none, in my experience, are so consistently reliable and easy to use. Fast Find is about the best of the Norton Utilities. It is so fast and so simple to use that I recommend it to anyone with a slow or poor memory. See "Using Norton Fast Find" later in this chapter for more information.

If you put aliases for all the applications and documents you use frequently on the Apple menu, so that it gets ridiculously long and messy, you need HAM. Once you've installed HAM, you can organize all your Apple menu items into hierarchies. Only the top item of each hierarchy appears in the Apple menu; the lower-level items are in submenus that branch out to the right side of the Apple menu. For more information on this great tool, see "Using HAM" later in this chapter.

If you use lots of different fonts, and can never remember which keystroke produces which special character (how *do* you make an O with an umlaut in Palatino?), you should use KeyFinder, another great little utility that comes in the Norton package. See "Using Norton Key-Finder" for details.

Utilities that Do Your Repetitive Work for You

There are a few utilities that can do tiresome repetitive jobs by making *macros*, commands that incorporate two or more other commands. The easiest way to make macros is with a utility that has a *recorder* built into it. You just turn on the recorder, enter your keyboard commands, then turn off the recording and assign a keystroke combination to it. Whenever you press those magic keys, the recording of the commands runs, executing them one after another, automatically.

There are some tricks to using macros, and each of the utilities for making them has some compatibility problems with major applications and other utilities, but if you do lots of repeated tasks and aren't afraid of doing a little setup work, you should try either the HotKeys Macro-Maker or QuickKeys. See "Using HotKeys MacroMaker" for some hints on the subject.

Using Norton Fast Find

Fast Find is one of the Norton Utilities, that excellent collection of Mac utilities that you can buy for less than some individual mini-applications. When you install the Norton Utilities, you'll see a new DA (desk accessory; another name for a utility) in your Apple menu called Fast Find. You can use it to find and display files before you open or move them. It works much faster than the Find command in the Finder, and it shows you much more, both when it's looking and when it finds things.

For example, let's say you have several files called Ch4—one's about headsets, one's about System 7, and one is full of short inserts. You can't remember where they all are, much less which one is the one about headsets. Here's how you use Fast Find to find out.

1. Choose Fast Find from the Apple menu. The Fast Find window opens.
2. Choose where you want to look. If there is more than one disk icon showing at the top of dialog box, choose the disk you want to search through. The hard disk is chosen in Figure 16.1.
3. Enter the name of the file you want to look for, or as much of the name as you can remember, in the Search For box.
4. Click on the runner guy, or press Return. The bar above the file name fills as the search progresses. Fast Find lists the files that match or come close to the name you entered, and gives you a beep when it has finished searching. The number of found files appears to the left of the progress bar. You can stop the search by clicking on the hand icon or pressing the Esc key.
5. Select a file to see information about it and where it is in your folder hierarchy. For example, if I select the Ch4 Headset file, I see the information in the lower left panel, and the location in the lower right panel, as shown in Figure 16.1.

FIGURE 16.1
Fast Find showing information and location of a found file

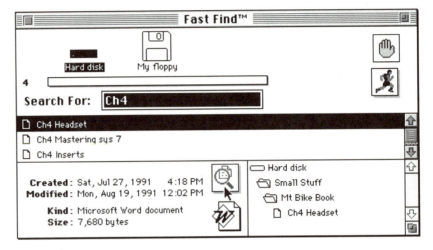

6. Do what you want to do with the file. To open it, double-click it. To get just a peek at the data in it, without opening the application that made it, click on the magnifying glass icon, as shown in Figure 16.1. To move the file directly to the desktop so you can put it somewhere else without having to open and close a bunch of windows, choose Move to Desktop from the Fast Find menu.

7. When you're done with Fast Find, choose Quit from the File menu. You go directly back to the Finder or whatever application you were working in.

It's a fine thing, this Fast Find. For more information on how to use it, see the Norton Utilities documentation.

 Using HAM

Simplicity is a lovely thing. HAM makes life with the Apple menu amazingly simple. All you have to do is install this little utility, and you can bring the same sort of hierarchical order you see on the desktop to your Apple menu.

HAM works by letting you put many of the things that are now in your Apple menu into submenus that branch off it. You get to see a good example of HAM in action just as soon as you have installed it. Just pull down the Apple Menu until you highlight the Control Panels command, then slide the mouse to the right when the submenu pops open. All the control panels are listed in the submenu, as shown in Figure 16.2. You'll never have to see your Control Panels window again.

FIGURE 16.2
HAM view of Apple menu contents

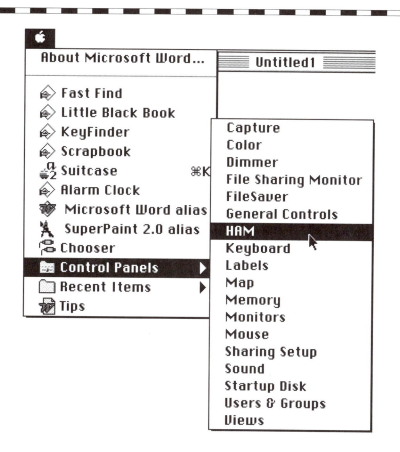

Choose the HAM control panel from the submenu. It opens immediately. While you're in the HAM control panel, check the Use "Resume HAMlet" at Startup check box at the bottom of the panel. This turns on HAM's ability to remember what application and document you are using when you shut down, so it can open them up automatically the next time you start your Mac. To take advantage of this feature, don't close your current document and quit its application before shutting down. Just save your work, switch to the Finder, and choose Shut Down from the Special menu. It seemed weird to me the first time I did this; I'm so used to the ritual of closing documents, quitting applications, *then* shutting down. But I got used to the HAM way; it's too easy to pass up.

To get immediate access to your most-used documents and folders, all you have to do is make an alias of the folder that contains the folders and documents, then drag the alias to the Apple Menu Items folder in your System Folder. The alias for the often-used folder appears in the Apple menu. When you highlight it, the folders and documents inside it appear in a submenu. Each folder in the submenu opens a second level submenu when you highlight it, and so on. Whee, what fun; cascading menus!

After you have used HAM for a few sessions, you can take yet another shortcut to your last-used documents and applications. Just highlight the Recent Items choice in the Apple menu, then go into the submenu and choose either Applications or Documents, then choose the item you were recently working on. Oh, it's so nice to have the Mac remember these things, so you don't have to remember and go hunting for them.

It takes a little practice to zip down through the submenu hierarchy, but it is so much faster than opening windows or clicking little list view arrows that you soon get hooked on it. Once you have set up the folder choices in your Apple menu, you can take all those individual

DAs and stuff out of the Apple Menu Items folder. The Apple menu gets nice and short, so you can choose things in it quickly.

To make it even easier to choose the things you use most often in the Apple Menu, you can rearrange the items in it. Just open the HAM control panel and use the grabber hand to push things higher or lower in the menu list on the right side of the panel.

The only problem with HAM is that the items in the Apple menu use up RAM. Don't put huge folder hierarchies with thousands of documents in there. Just put in the folders with the applications, utilities, and documents you use most. And if you find that you use one item constantly, and it is buried deep in a submenu hierarchy, just make an alias for it and put it directly in the Apple Menu Items folder.

Using Norton KeyFinder

Use Norton KeyFinder to find out how to make special characters appear in each of the different fonts you use. The utility is placed in your Apple Menu Items folder when you install the Norton Utilities. It's a breeze to use. In the following example, you'll find out how you make an O with an umlaut in Palatino font.

1. Choose KeyFinder from the Apple menu. The KeyFinder window opens, with the first font displayed. Usually this font is Chicago, unless you have installed some custom fonts.

2. Choose the font you want to see from the font list in the lower right corner of the window. When I choose Palatino, the characters appear. I like them.

3. Click the character you want to enter. The keystrokes for it appear in the box in the upper right corner of the window, as shown in Figure 16.3.

FIGURE 16.3
The KeyFinder window, with an umlaut O selected

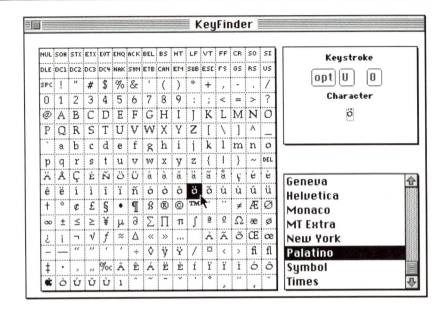

4. Close the KeyFinder window and enter the letter in your document. In my sample, I would memorize the sequence of Option-U and then the letter O (notice that there is a gap between the U and the O, which means you release the Option and U keys before pressing O).

If you are a real font fiend, you may want to leave the KeyFinder window open all the time, and slide it down to the bottom of your screen. Then you can raise the bottom of your document windows a bit, and just click your way to KeyFinder and back.

Using HotKeys MacroMaker

Macros are tools for making your own series of commands and executing them all at once with a single keyboard command. You can use macros to automate almost any repetitive process, from adding four dots to the end of a word to reformatting a whole paragraph.

HotKeys MacroMaker is just one of several utilities you can use to create macros. It is a pretty powerful tool, but you must remember that you are messing with the Mac's brain when you use it, so you can get into trouble pretty easily. The same is true of any of the other macro-creating utilities. They work fine in many situations, but they can give you trouble if they aren't compatible with the applications you use, or if they aren't compatible with the newest version of the system software. To be honest, I have to say that I had trouble using MacroMaker with Microsoft Word 5 under System 7, and I'm not sure it will be compatible with your software, either. So beware.

No matter which utility you use to create your macros, the process is pretty much the same. First, you decide what sequence of commands you want to make into a macro, then take a practice run through them to make sure they do what you want. Next, you use the utility to record the macro. Then you name the macro and assign it a keystroke combination that will make it run. Finally, you play back the macro, to make sure it works right.

The following exercise is a simple example of how to use MacroMaker to automate the tiresome process of changing a bunch of folder titles with numbers. MacroMaker must first be installed in your System Folder.

1. Select the first folder title you want to change.
2. Take a practice run. Enter the new title, without the number of the chapter, then back the insertion point up to the spot where the number will be entered. For example, to make meaningful titles for the folders with the short titles shown in Figure 16.4. I could enter **Chapter Art** (with two spaces between the words) and then use the left arrow to back up to the middle of the double space, so everything is set for entering the chapter

FIGURE 16.4
Folder names to be changed with a macro

▷   ▇ 1 ar   — folder
▷   ☐ 2 ar   — folder
▷   ☐ 3 ar   — folder
▷   ☐ 4 ar   — folder
▷   ☐ 5 ar   — folder
▷   ☐ 6 ar   — folder
▷   ☐ 7 ar   — folder
▷   ☐ 8 ar   — folder
▷   ☐ 9 ar   — folder

number. After doing the practice run, change the title back to its original form, and select the title.

3. Choose Start Recording from the MacroMaker menu (the menu under the little cassette icon in the menu bar to record the macro). The icon starts blinking.

4. Repeat the actions you practiced. In my example, I would type **Chapter Art** and press the left arrow key until the insertion point went back to the middle of the space between the two words.

5. Choose Stop Recording from the MacroMaker menu. The Macromaker window appears, with the title bar for your new macro selected, as shown in Figure 16.5.

6. Enter a name, description, and ⌘-key sequence for your macro. If you have a long list of macro names, it's good to choose a new one that begins with an *A* so you don't have to go hunting for it later.

7. When you finish entering the ⌘-key sequence, click the Store button, as shown in Figure 16.5. The storing process takes quite a while sometimes. Be patient. If you start clicking and mousing

FIGURE 16.5
Storing a macro

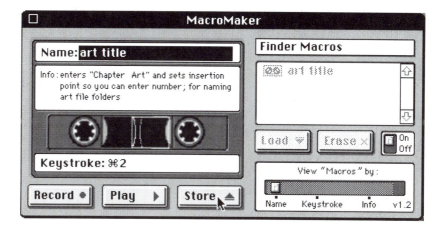

around, you can really confuse MacroMaker. Eventually, the new macro appears in the macro list at the left side of the Macro-Maker window.

8. Close the MacroMaker window. This sometimes takes a while too. Remember, you've been messing with your Mac's gray matter. Let it get back to normal.

Now that we've recorded the macro, let's try it out.

1. Select a folder title that needs to be changed. The title must be framed, not just highlighted.
2. Press the ⌘-key sequence for your macro. If you forget the key sequence, just pull down the MacroMaker menu and choose the macro by name (it'll be near the top of the list if it begins with A). The actions you recorded play out on the screen.
3. Finish the folder title. In my example, all I have to do is enter a number, then go on to the next folder title.

If I wanted to take the time, or if I had a hundred folder titles to change, I could even automate the numbering. You can do all sorts of tasks with macros, but until you have experience, work with the simple ones; they are the ones that are the most bothersome, anyway.

Troubleshooting Problems with Time-Saving Utilities

The following subsections cover the problems you are most likely to have while working with the time-saving utilities described in this chapter.

Out of memory messages or bombs after adding a new control panel or extension.

Well, well. You added the latest utility gimmick (INIT, CDEV, special customizing file, "little program," or whatever you want to call those things that show their icons during the startup sequence), and now the Mac just isn't running like it used to.

You probably have a conflict between your new utility and one of the old ones, or some incompatibility with either your applications or the system software itself.

First, try removing the last control panel or extension you added. See if the Mac runs OK again. If it does, check with the dealer who sold you the utility, and see if you need a later version. Sometimes there may be incompatibilities that you can't do anything about; you'll have to give up the new utility or the thing it was conflicting with. If it conflicted with the system software, you have no choice; the utility must go.

Sometimes you have to get rid of all the control panels and extensions. To test the Mac without them, restart it with the Shift key depressed. That bypasses all of them; if the Mac works fine, you have to take strong measures.

Start the Mac with an emergency or other startup floppy. Move your non-Apple control panels and extensions to a new folder, then move them back to the System Folder one at a time. Run your favorite applications on the Mac after moving each one in. When the Mac starts acting up, take out the last control panel or extension you added.

Then read the warnings about too many utilities at the beginning of this chapter.

Fast Find can't find files you know are there.

Usually, the problem is that you have not entered the name correctly. Make sure there are no extra spaces, and that the spelling is correct. If you are not sure how you spelled the name of the file, just enter the letters you are most sure of. Fast Find is very forgiving. It may turn up a bunch of files that aren't the one you want, but if you give it a free rein, it will usually come up with what you're after, too.

Some keys don't work as KeyFinder says they should.

Do you have a standard ADB keyboard? Some keyboards don't deliver the right codes for your Mac, so it won't do some of the special keys indicated in the KeyFinder window. Replace your keyboard with one that's made specifically for an ADB connection.

MacroMaker macros not working.

Your carefully made macros in the MacroMaker file are not working at all. Check the Caps Lock key. If it is locked on, none of the ⌘-key sequences will work. You may also be having a conflict with another utility or special customizing file installed on your Mac. Try removing the last control panel or extension you installed. If you don't have any luck, call Hot Keys support.

CHAPTER 17

Organizer Utilities

Organizer utilities are small applications you can use to keep things in order on your Mac. One of the best things about the Mac is that it lets you put things wherever you want, and keeps track of things wherever you put them. But it's easy to let things get disorganized. A file here, a font there, a funny beep sound somewhere else—pretty soon you can't remember where you put anything, and your System Folder is bulging with fonts and sounds you'll never use. Your Mac is a disorganized mess.

There is also a hidden type of disorganization that happens as you add things to your Mac, erase other things, and add new things in their place. It's called fragmentation. It happens because your hard disk separates your applications and documents into pieces to store them on your hard disk, and when you take things off the Mac and put new things on, the Mac starts breaking everything into smaller and smaller pieces and putting them in more and more places on the hard disk. Pretty soon it's like a patchwork quilt of all the pieces, and every time you try to do anything, the Finder has a heck of a time finding the pieces and putting them together so you can work with them. If you let the process go on too long, the hard disk can get so fragmented the Mac grinds to a halt.

You can do a lot to help keep your documents and applications in order if you put them in a clear hierarchy as described in Chapter 5, "Using Folders to Organize Your Files." But that doesn't take care of all those little utilities and funny sounds and exotic fonts you can't resist adding to your System Folder. And it doesn't keep your hard disk from being fragmented.

Fortunately, there are clever Mac programmers who have made utilities that manage your font and sound resources, and other utilities that can defragment your poor patchwork hard disk.

 ## Which Organizer Utilities for You?

There are a number of utilities that can help you organize things on the Mac, but there are a few that stand out head and shoulders above the rest. Since you use organizer utilities regularly and build up your organization over time, you should find the ones that do just what you want, then stick with them. Organizer utilities are less likely than time-savers to cause problems with your system software; in fact, the best ones are a big help to the system software because they give it an orderly world to operate in.

Utilities that Organize Your Resources

Fonts, sounds, and utilities that you keep in your Apple menu (formerly called desk accessories or DAs) are all resources. These are the things that can clog your System Folder, or get lost if you take them out of the System Folder and store them somewhere else. Fonts and sounds are kept in the System file suitcase. If you have hundreds in there, it's hard to find the ones you want, and it slows the system software down whenever it has to use the System file.

Suitcase and MasterJuggler are two utilities that can manage resources effectively. I use Suitcase because it was the first to be compatible with System 7, but there are many who favor MasterJuggler; it handles sounds better. If you use lots of fonts, you can get the Adobe Type Manager utility and use it with either Suitcase or MasterJuggler. This will allow you to reduce the number of screen fonts you have and organize all your fonts neatly in one place, outside the System file. For details on how to organize and use your fonts, see "Using Suitcase" and "Using Adobe Type Manager" later in this chapter.

Utilities that Organize and Defragment Your Hard Drive

There are several utilities that can defragment or optimize your hard disk so all the pieces of your documents and applications are put back together. Of these, I've found Speed Disk to be the clear leader. It is part of that great team of tools, the Norton Utilities. It is faster than the other utilities I know about, and it has the most incredible interface of any utility I've ever used. I mean, you can just *watch* the thing reorganize everything on your hard drive, and the results are so dramatic it will make an instant believer out of you.

I always avoided defragmenting my hard drive before I got Speed Disk, I confess. I used to just copy all the files over to a friend's bigger hard disk, then reformat mine, then copy everything back. And I only did that about once a year. Now I do a Speed Disk optimization on my hard disk about once a month or so.

Among the other utilities packages, MacTools Deluxe and SUM II both have defragmenting utilities that work OK, and DiskExpress has an optimizing utility that works in the background, but it is pretty intrusive (it gets so busy in the background, you can't do anything in the foreground!) until it has the disk thoroughly defragmented and reorganized. For more details on how to defragment your hard disk with my favorite organizer, see "Using Norton Speed Disk" later in this chapter.

Other Organizer Utilities and Screen Savers

There are whole groups of organizer utilities that are less important to the big picture, but that might still be useful to you. There are utilities that let you reorganize the look and feel of your desktop and its menus, such as On Cue and Layout Plus. There is HAM (see Chapter 16) that lets you organize your Apple menu into hierarchical menus.

While we're talking about look and feel, you can change how the blank desktop and how the idle screen looks if you want. If you want your desktop pattern to look different, there is Wallpaper. And if you want to see anything when you leave your Mac idle—from fireworks to famous quotations—you can get screen savers like After Dark and Pyro. I get sick and tired of screen savers. They make me feel like I should have turned the Mac off and conserved the energy. I use a cheap little thing called Dimmer; it just turns down the brightness if I leave the Mac idle for a while. And it doesn't conflict with screen capture utilities like Capture or ScreenShot the way the screen savers do.

There are also some utilities for organizing your life, as well as your Mac. There are little programs you can put in your Apple menu to help you plan your day and remember phone numbers and addresses. I just use the Alarm Clock DA to tell me what day it is, and I write my appointments on a wall calendar. I keep my phone and address list in a tiny DA called Little Black Book. Simple, but cheap and quite adequate. If you want to put a little money into getting organized, try DayMaker, QuickDEX, or Address Book Plus.

Using Suitcase

Suitcase is a utility for organizing fonts and desk accessories. Since you can keep your desk accessories organized easily within the normal folder hierarchy, I'm just going to cover using Suitcase to keep your fonts in order.

When dealing with fonts, I have to put my cards on the table. I'm not a font fondler. I mean, I like a handsome font as well as the next person, but I don't have this overwhelming urge to put every nice font I see into my System file. I get along fine with Times and Helvetica, thank you. I do have to work with different fonts now and then, and I understand why many of you desktop publishers need to use a number of different fonts. But I still think you should be sparing in your use of fonts and organize them in a clear, simple manner. Suitcase provides a great way to do the organizing.

Now, most people keep their fonts all over the place, without much organization at all: a bunch of PostScript outline fonts in their Extensions folder, and another bunch of bit-mapped fonts and TrueType fonts in the System file, and still more fonts stored in folders here and there. Things get pretty scattered.

To organize things better for using PostScript outline fonts, here's what you should do: Get rid of your TrueType fonts if you have them, then use Suitcase to organize your PostScript printer fonts and your screen fonts in sets of suitcases. Each suitcase will contain one font, and you will keep them all in one folder, so there is no confusion. If you follow the procedures below, you can wind up with a few sets of fonts you use regularly, and a tidy storage place for all the other fonts you rarely use.

Before we start, though, let's make sure we're all talking the same language. When I say font, I mean the whole collection of styles and sizes in one design, such as Helvetica. People in the printing trade call this a typeface. Most of us Mac users call it a font. OK?

If you use lots of different fonts, chances are you use PostScript *outline fonts* whenever you can. They look so good and you can do all those wonderful stretching and resizing things to them. But you need to have bit-mapped *screen fonts* too; they are the versions you see on the Mac screen, and you have to have one for each size you use. So you wind up with a lot of fonts. The TrueType fonts that came with your system software just add to the jumble; if you look in your System file and your Extensions Folder, you may see fonts with all of the different icons shown in Figure 17.1.

You need Suitcase to get your fonts in order. With it you can put all the different sizes of each screen font in a single suitcase. You should also get Adobe Type Manager (ATM) to reduce the number of screen

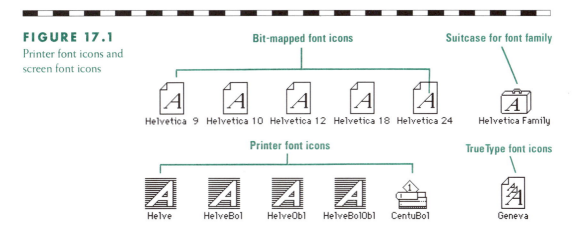

FIGURE 17.1
Printer font icons and screen font icons

fonts you need, and to ensure that your fonts look as good as possible on screen and in low-resolution printouts. The following procedures for setting up a font system with Suitcase will work best if you already have ATM working for you. For details, see "Using Adobe Type Manager" later in this chapter.

Creating a Fonts Folder

To start the process of organizing your fonts into sets and suitcases, you have to make a folder to keep the whole collection in. Then you can use Suitcase to finish the job. This procedure is a short version of one that the Suitcase documentation describes.

1. Install Suitcase according to the *User Manual* instructions. If you have not installed ATM, do that now, too.
2. Close any applications you have open and open your startup hard disk window.
3. Choose New Folder from the File menu, and name the new folder "Fonts." Shrink the hard disk window so it shows the Font folder and not much else, then move it to one side of your screen.

4. Open your System Folder, and when it opens, open the System file. Move the System file window to the other side of your screen, so you can see it and the shrunken hard disk window at the same time, as shown in Figure 17.2.

Take a deep breath and get focused before you go on to the next step. You are about to deal with the basic resources your Mac uses to display and print text. Mistakes can make life hard on the Mac, and can make things look wrong on the screen and in print. So proceed with care.

5. If you are planning on using PostScript fonts (and you shouldn't be doing all this unless you are), you must select and remove the TrueType fonts, other than three very important exceptions: Chicago, Geneva, and Monaco. The Mac uses these fonts in the Finder and in its code. If you are looking at a list view of the System file, as in Figure 17.2, the TrueType font resource files are

FIGURE 17.2
Preparing to move TrueType fonts out of the System file

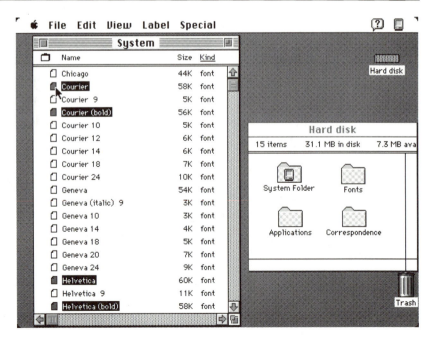

the ones that do *not* have size numbers after the names. So Shift-click the TrueType fonts like the Courier and Helvetica ones shown, but *don't* select the TrueType Chicago, Geneva, and Monaco resources. Leave them for the Finder to use.

6. Drag all the TrueType fonts to a folder outside the System Folder, or to a floppy disk, or to the Trash. This is a heavy thing to do, I know; TrueType is great for low-end Macs with low-end printers. But if you are into PostScript fonts, and especially if you use applications and printers that depend on PostScript fonts, then you have to get TrueType out of the picture.

7. Next, select all of the bit-mapped font resource files other than the Chicago, Geneva, and Monaco ones. Leave these three for the Finder to use. The bit-mapped resource files have numbers after the names. When they are all selected, as the Courier and Helvetica ones are in Figure 17.3, drag them into the Fonts folder in your little hard disk window. This should leave only the Chicago, Geneva, and Monaco fonts in the System file, along with some sounds.

8. Close your slimmed-down, fit-for-fast-work System file.

9. Now you can put all your PostScript fonts in the Fonts folder. Open the Extensions folder in your System Folder. Select and drag all the PostScript printer font *resource* files from the Extensions folder to your Fonts folder. The icons look like the ones on the bottom row in Figure 17.1. If you have PostScript fonts on floppies or stored in other folders, drag them all into your Fonts folder. If you have dozens of fonts, it may seem like you are making more of a mess rather than less. Fear not. You will straighten it all out in a few moments.

10. Open the Fonts folder and choose by Name from the View menu. The font resource files form a long alphabetical list. Notice that there are groups of bit-mapped font resource files,

Chapter 17

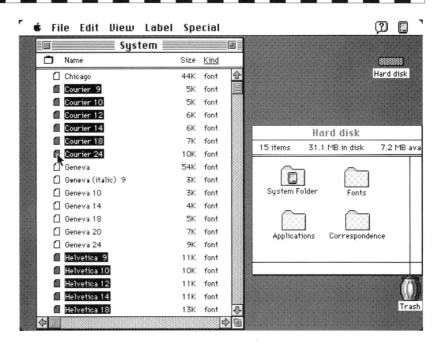

FIGURE 17.3
Bit-mapped font resource files selected

each with a size number after it, and groups of PostScript font resource files, which have no numbers after them.

11. Weed out duplicates and any TrueType font resource files you missed before. If you see two files that have nearly the same name, and neither has any style attribute letters at the end, such as Helve and Helvetica, select each of the files and choose Get Info from the File menu. If they are identical font resource files (the icons, names, and sizes are the same), throw one in the Trash. If one is a TrueType font you missed (as Helvetica is in Figure 17.4), move it to a storage folder or to a floppy or the Trash. Your font icons may have A's in them, depending on what size you set them at in the Views control panel. If you don't have hundreds of fonts, you can choose by Small Icon from the

View menu and look for the TrueType font resource files with three A's on the icons.

If you have hundreds of PostScript and bit-mapped fonts and the Fonts folder is really hard to hunt through even after you have weeded out the chaff, you can create a Fonts II folder, and put the fonts in it that you are least likely to use. You can use it just like the original Fonts folder; whenever you use one font in it, it becomes a viable source of font resource files. When you have cleaned out all your extra fonts and you have one or two tidy Fonts folders, you are ready to organize the resources into suitcases and sets.

Building Font Family Suitcases

Now you are getting to the nitty-gritty of organizing your fonts. You are going to make a bunch of suitcases, each of which holds all of the bit-mapped resource files for a particular font. Then, in the next section, you will organize the suitcases into sets.

1. Make sure you have saved your work and quit any application you were using.

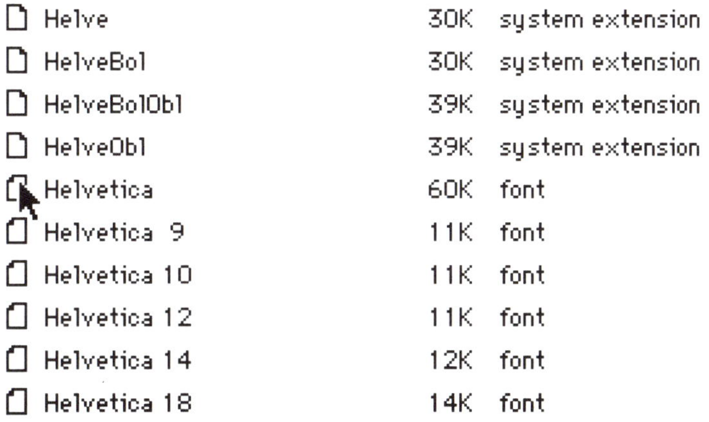

FIGURE 17.4
A TrueType font resource file among PostScript font resource files

Helve	30K	system extension
HelveBol	30K	system extension
HelveBolObl	39K	system extension
HelveObl	39K	system extension
Helvetica	60K	font
Helvetica 9	11K	font
Helvetica 10	11K	font
Helvetica 12	11K	font
Helvetica 14	12K	font
Helvetica 18	14K	font

Chapter 17

2. Choose Suitcase from the Apple menu. The Sets and Suitcases window opens. Ignore it for now.

3. Choose Create Empty Suitcase from the Suitcase menu. An odd variation on the Save As dialog box appears, as in Figure 17.5.

4. Use the pop-down menu under the title for the file list, just as you would in a Save As dialog box, and change to your hard disk listing. Then double-click the Fonts folder, so you have a listing similar to the one shown in Figure 17.5.

5. Enter the name of a suitcase for a group or *family* of bit-mapped fonts. For example, I have a bunch of Helvetica bit-mapped font resource files, so I need a suitcase called Helvetica Family.

6. Make sure the Fonts radio button at the bottom of the dialog box is selected.

7. Click the Save button.

8. Repeat this procedure for each group of bit-mapped font resource files you have; you want to make a suitcase for each

FIGURE 17.5
Creating a suitcase for the Helvetica family

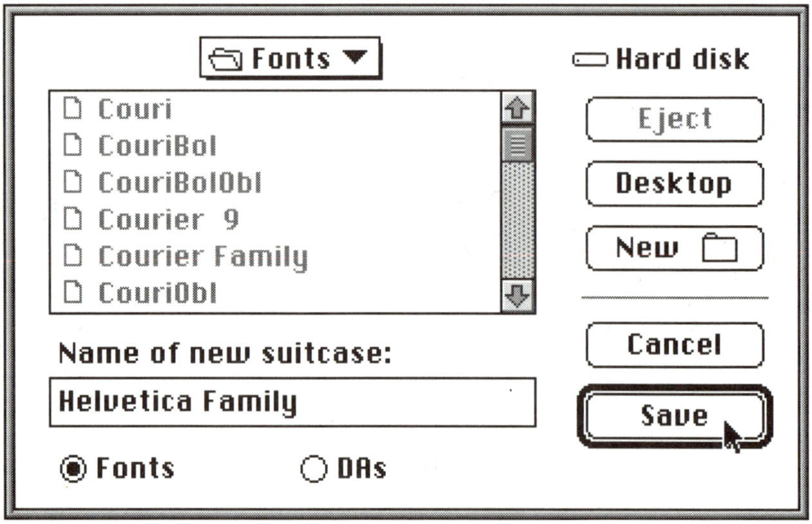

family of bit maps. It's OK to have just one resource file in a family, as long as you are using ATM.

9. When you have made all the suitcases you need, switch to the Finder by way of the Applications menu and go to the Fonts folder window. Select all of the bit-mapped font resource files for a given font and drag them into the appropriate family suitcase. For example, I would select all the Helvetica font resource files with numbers after them, as in Figure 17.6, and drag them into the Helvetica Family suitcase. Make sure you don't drag any PostScript font resource files in there, too; that can confuse some applications. Leave the PostScript font resource files where they are, at the top level of the Fonts folder.

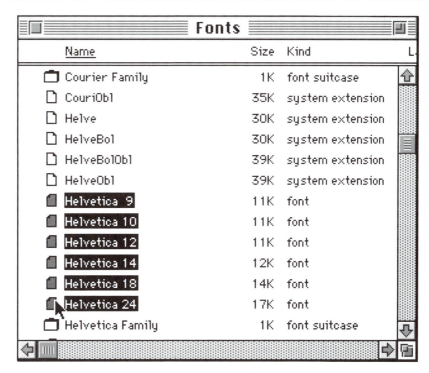

FIGURE 17.6
Selecting bit-mapped font resource files to put into a suitcase

Delete any bit-mapped font resources you don't need. You may need all the resources in each family, or you may need only a couple, or you may need only one, depending on your situation:

- If you have a relatively slow Mac, like a Plus or early Classic, and you plan to print to an ImageWriter or StyleWriter, leave all of the bit-mapped font resource files in each family suitcase. Your Mac and printer need all the bit-mapped resources they can get in order to work at a reasonable pace and print out bit-mapped fonts.
- If your Mac is relatively fast and you print mostly to laser printers, leave only a couple of bit-mapped font resources in each family suitcase. Leave the ones you use most commonly on the screen, such as 9- or 10-point and 12-point. Adobe Type Manager can recreate the other sizes, and if you have a fast Mac, it won't bog down on the font-making job.
- If your Mac is a screamer, like a IIci or faster, and you use only laser printers or even higher resolution printers, you need only one bit-mapped font resource file for each family suitcase. You're going to be printing PostScript fonts, and ATM can make the screen fonts by using the single bit map for each family.

When you are all done whittling down your bit maps and putting them in suitcases, check your work. Make sure there are no bit-mapped font resource files left outside suitcases in the Fonts folder, and make sure no PostScript font resource files have snuck into the family suitcases.

Organizing Suitcases into Sets

OK, you have the bit-mapped font resource files organized into suitcases. Now you can put suitcases together in useful sets. To start with, you need to make a set that becomes available every time you turn the Mac on, your Permanent set. Then you can make other sets for special situations. This means you will never have a Font menu that is fifty names long, and you will never have to hunt around your folder hierarchy for a missing font, either. Oh, how sweet that is.

1. Switch back to Suitcase by way of the Applications menu, and look at the Sets and Suitcases window as shown in Figure 17.7. Whew. This organization business is pretty rigorous, isn't it? But you're almost done. The top part of the window lists the sets that exist; the most important one is called Permanent (Open at Startup). You can ignore the others for now. The bottom part of the window is a list box for the suitcases that are in the set that's

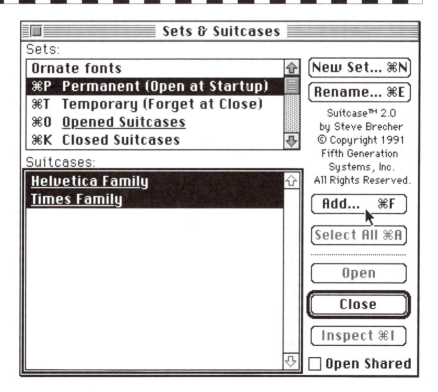

FIGURE 17.7
Preparing to add suitcases to the Permanent set

selected. Since you haven't added anything to the Permanent set, your list box should be empty. In Figure 17.7 there are a couple of families listed, just to show you what they look like.

2. With Permanent selected, click the Add button. A dialog box opens, and it is like an Open or Save As dialog box again, with a list box and some buttons. Make sure the Open Added Files check box at the bottom of the window is checked, and that the Show All Types option is *unchecked*. Leave the Shared box unchecked too, unless you are sharing fonts on a network. Use these settings for *all* set building you do.

3. Use the pop-down menu over the list box to go to your hard disk, then open the Fonts folder. A list of font families appears.

4. Select a font family you want to add to your Permanent set and click the Add button, as shown in Figure 17.8. The screen blinks and the font family disappears from the Add list.

5. Add the other font families you want in your Permanent set. When you are done adding families, click the Done button. The Sets and Suitcases window comes back with a list of the familes you added. They should all be underlined, indicating they are open, available for use in all applications. To remove a family you decide you don't want in a set after all, select it in the suitcases list, click Close if it is open, then choose Cut from the Edit menu. Make sure no applications are open when you do this. Also make sure the Suitcases panel is active, not the Sets one, or you will cut out the whole set and have to put it back together again.

6. To create a new set, like the Ornate fonts one shown in Figure 17.7, just click the New Set button in the Sets and Suitcases window, name the set, and add suitcases to it as you did for the Permanent set. You can use a suitcase in two sets without causing any problem.

FIGURE 17.8
Adding the Courier Family suitcase

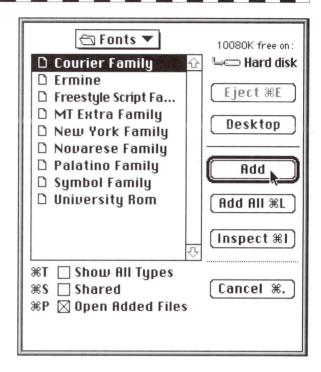

7. When you have all the sets you want, choose Quit from the File menu. Open your favorite application and check the Font menu. If you hold down the Option key as you open the menu, the font names appear in their own fonts, in most applications.

Suitcase has a lot of other options that I can't cover in this book; you can make a DAs folder like your Fonts folder and put DAs in sets with your fonts. You can organize sounds and F-keys in the same way. But frankly, unless you have lots of sounds or DAs, I don't think it's worth the trouble.

Making Font Sets Available

Once you have set up your suitcases and sets, you can use one or more sets of fonts at any time. Your Permanent set is available every time you turn the Mac on. To make another set available, like the Ornate fonts set in Figure 17.7, follow this simple procedure.

1. Choose Suitcase from the Apple menu. The sets and suitcases window lists your sets.
2. Select the name of the set you want to make available in the sets list.
3. Click the Open button. All of the font family names become underlined.
4. Choose Quit from the File menu.

The next time you open an application, the new set of font names will appear in the Font menu. To take the extra fonts out of the menu, quit the application, go into the Suitcase Sets and Suitcase window and close all the fonts in that set, then quit Suitcase.

If you want to use a font or two during just one session, such as when you have somebody else's document with weird fonts in it, you can add those fonts to the Temporary set. When you finish the session and shut down the Mac, the fonts will become unavailable all by themselves.

Using Adobe Type Manager

Adobe Type Manager, or ATM, is one of those Mac utilities that you hardly have to know about. It does its work in the background, for the most part, and you don't have to fiddle with it.

ATM will make nice screen versions of PostScript fonts at any size (you just need to have one bit-mapped font resource installed for each font) and it will make your PostScript fonts print out OK on low-resolution printers and dot-matrix printers like the ImageWriter.

The one drawback to using ATM on a low-end Mac is that it makes things slow. If you get more memory for your Mac you can increase the Font Cache, and this will speed up things like scrolling and displaying large fonts.

Once you have installed Adobe Type Manager, all you need to do is choose Control Panels from the Apple menu, double-click the ATM icon, and make sure ATM is turned on. If you have a lot of RAM and expect to use lots of big fonts, you can increase the Font Cache from the default of 96K to 192K or 256K, as in Figure 17.9; but if you have 2Mb of RAM or less, you should leave it at 96K. Leave the Preserve Line

FIGURE 17.9
The ATM control panel

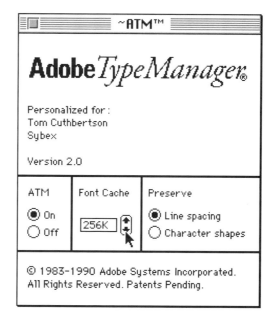

spacing button selected, unless you are using special fonts with big descenders and you *must* see those descenders on the screen.

Using Norton Speed Disk

Speed Disk is one of my favorite Norton Utilities. It defragments your disks, quickly and safely. This may not seem like such a big deal to you if you have never had a hard disk crash that destroyed a lot of valuable data. But even if you just talk to someone who has had a hard disk crash, you'll become a believer. And Speed Disk makes defragmenting, or *optimizing*, as they call it, a short and painless job. The following procedure takes you through checking and optimization. If you have a 40Mb hard drive, the whole thing usually takes less than fifteen minutes. Very cheap insurance, it seems to me.

1. Back up your data and applications. Speed Disk is a very reliable defragmenting program, but there still is a slight risk of losing data as files are shuffled, and there's always the threat of a power surge during the optimization process. See the next chapter for details on backing up.

2. Start the Norton Utilities. Just double-click on the icon to bring up the main menu window, which lists the utilities, as shown in Figure 17.10.

3. Click on the Speed Disk icon in the main menu window. The Speed Disk window opens. It shows a picture of the data on your current disk, with the filled sections in black and the empty parts in white as shown in Figure 17.11.

4. To get a better idea of how much fragmentation you have on your hard disk, click the Check Drive button near the bottom of the window. If you want to check another hard disk or a floppy

Organizer Utilities

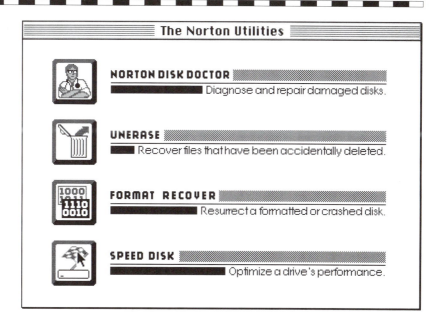

FIGURE 17.10
The Norton Utilities window

FIGURE 17.11
The Speed Disk window

disk that is mounted (any disk with its icon showing on the desktop), click the arrows under the icon for your current disk. When you see the disk you want, click the Check Drive button. As soon as you click, Speed Disk takes a quick look at your current disk, and when it is done, you see a picture of the disk, with different shades for things like applications and documents, and blank space for empty sectors on the disk. This picture of the disk, as seen in Figure 17.12, is much more detailed than the first look you saw, as shown in Figure 17.11. If the shades are all mixed in patches, and if there are lots of little blank spaces and no big blank space in the picture, you can bet you have fragmentation. In the text box at the right side of the window, you see a report of how much fragmentation there is. If you have anything more than moderate fragmentation, optimize. You should optimize for sure if your hard disk is more than 9/10 full and even moderately fragmented. The sample shown in Figure 17.12 doesn't really require optimization, but I might do it anyway if I hadn't done so for several months.

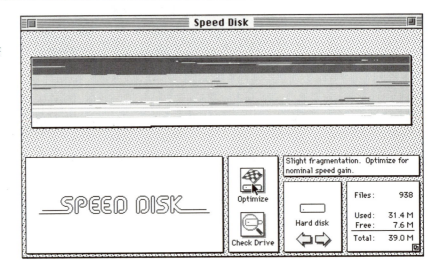

FIGURE 17.12
The Speed Disk window with results of a disk check

5. If you need to defragment a disk, you do one of two things, depending on whether the disk is your current startup disk (the one with the system software you are running) or not. You can't defragment the disk that is running your Mac, for sure. That would be like dismantling a car and reassembling it while zooming down the freeway.

   - If the disk is your current startup disk, restart your Mac and insert the Norton Utilities Applications disk. When it starts up, it puts you right into the Speed Disk window. Click the arrow under the Norton Utilities disk until you see your startup hard disk. Click the Optimize button, as shown in Figure 17.12.
   - If the disk you want to defragment is not the current startup disk, just click the Optimize button, as shown in Figure 17.12.

   Speed Disk chugs through the optimization process, and you can watch as it verifies the media, then optimizes the directories, system files, applications, documents, and finally the desktop, in that order. You can go away and get a snack or something, and if you come back to check, you can tell how far along it is by what it is optimizing. When it is done it plays a pretty chord, and the message box on the right side of the window tells you that now there is no need to optimize. The picture of the disk has a wonderfully organized, straightened-out look to it.

6. If you want to get a closer look at the different layers of stuff on the disk, choose Go To Expert from the Options menu, then move the pointer (it becomes a magnifying glass) up and down the picture of your disk. The chart to the right of the big magnifying glass thing tells you what you are looking at. It's really grand. By the way, Expert mode gives you all kinds of powers over the optimization process, but it can slow things down; I

just do the Easy mode approach, and let Speed Disk do the job as it sees fit. I trust it. To get out of Expert mode, choose Go To Easy from the Options menu.

7. Choose Quit from the File menu. If you were optimizing your startup disk and running Speed Disk from the Norton Applications disk, just click the Restart button in the dialog box, and you'll go back to running on your nicely defragmented hard disk.

That's all there is to it. It's so easy, you may be tempted to optimize frequently, but I wouldn't do that. Why dismantle your car and reassemble it if it's running OK? I check my hard disk once every week or two, but I don't optimize unless there is at least moderate fragmentation and/or the disk is 9/10 full. If the disk is that close to full, I clean out old unused files and applications *before* I defragment; that makes for a disk that is tidy and roomy too. One last hint: After defragmenting, it's a good idea to rebuild your desktop. Just hold down the ⌘ and Option keys, then restart your Mac. Then *everything* is cleaned up and put in order. If you look real close the first time you start your Mac after doing all these things, you might notice that the happy Mac smile is pixel or two broader. I wouldn't swear to it, but it seems that way.

Troubleshooting Problems with Organizer Utilities

The following subsections cover the most common problems you can have working with utilities that keep your Mac organized. The problems and solutions discussed apply to the specific utilities described in this chapter, but you can use the concepts as guidelines for solving problems with other similar utilities.

A font that's in a suitcase in the Fonts folder doesn't appear in an application's Font menu.

The problem may be that the suitcase is not in a set that you have made available, or the Family suitcase may not be open. Choose Suitcase from the Apple menu, then select the set with the font you want. The font families appear in the Sets and Suitcases window, all selected. Click the Open button. Then quit Suitcase, go back to your application, quit it, and start it up again. The font should be there.

If that doesn't take care of the problem, make sure the actual font resource files are in the Family suitcase. If they aren't, go to the Finder, open your Fonts folder, and drag the bit-mapped font resource files (the ones with numbers after the names) of that font into the Family folder. If there aren't any bit-mapped font resource files for that font in the Fonts folder, install them from a floppy or drag them in from wherever you store your font resource files.

No outlined size number appears for a font size that is in an open suitcase.

You *know* you have a bit-mapped font resource file for a particular font and size, but the Font Size menu in your application refuses to show an outlined number for that size. The problem is probably that you have mistakenly left font resource files for some sizes of that font (but not the one you want) in your System file. The Mac looks there first, and if it finds any resources, it ignores other suitcases. Take the font resource files for that font out of your System file.

There is one exception to this rule. If you are dealing with Chicago, Geneva, or Monaco fonts, you gotta leave them in the System file. If you want more sizes for those fonts to appear, you have to install the bit-mapped font resource files for the sizes in the System file. Drag the resource files to the System file from your Fonts folder suitcase for that font family, or drag them in from a floppy or your storage folder.

Some font sizes contained in open suitcases are not available after installing new system software.

Apple can be a little pushy about fonts. The Apple Installer program puts *their* fonts in your System file when it installs a new version of the system software. So you update your system software to the latest version, and you get Apple's fonts, and the system software uses them and ignores yours. If the Apple-installed fonts have fewer sizes than you do in your Family suitcase, you get fewer sizes. If you are using ATM, you don't have to worry about printing noninstalled sizes; ATM will make them for you, even if you print to a low-resolution printer like an ImageWriter. It may take a long time to print the stuff, but it will look good when it finally comes out.

An application cannot open due to insufficient memory after you open a set of suitcases.

You have too many suitcases open, you font fondler. Get a clue. Open suitcases use up system memory, you know. Your applications need system memory, and the system software needs system memory. All Mac's children need memory. So choose Suitcase in the Apple menu, and close the suitcases you don't really need, then try opening the application again. Sheesh. Can't you leave those new fonts *alone?*

Two fonts have the same name or ID number.

You try to open a new suitcase, and you get a dialog box telling you a selected font has the same name or ID number as another one. The problem is that two fonts can have the same name; they should have different ID numbers, but the assignments get messed up in some cases. There is no easy solution. It is best to just close one of the two suitcases to get around the conflict. If you can't do that, and it is an ID number conflict, use the number that Suitcase suggests. If you have to change the font name, be aware that you might run into trouble when working on documents or in applications that expect the original name to be attached to that font. For more information on this touchy issue, read the "Troubleshooting" section in the Suitcase *User Manual.*

Jagged characters still appear while using ATM.

You still see jaggies on the screen or you still get jagged characters in your printout, even though you are using ATM to give you nice fonts. Make sure that ATM is turned on, that the font you are looking at or printing is in an open suitcase, and that there is only *one* bit-mapped font resource file for the font is in the suitcase. If you have a bit-mapped font resource file for the jaggy font in that family's suitcase, ATM uses it instead of making a nicer outline font. Take out all but one bit map to force ATM into making its nice version. If the jaggies are appearing in the printout only, and you are using a low-resolution printer (such as an ImageWriter), make sure you have chosen Best Quality in the Print dialog box. If you are using Chicago, Geneva, New York, or Monaco fonts, you are stuck with the quality the resources in the System file can produce; switch to other fonts.

Line spacing and page breaks are different on the screen from what comes out of the printer.

If you are using ATM, click the Preserve Line spacing button in the ATM control panel. This may mean that some of the characters loose the bottoms of their descenders (like the bottom of the *y* and *g*), but the lines and pages will match. You may want to switch fonts to prevent the clipping of the descenders.

If you have any TrueType font resource files and you are printing on a hot-shot laser printer or other high-resolution printer, TrueType may be the cause of the problem. Take all TrueType font resource files out of your Fonts folder and System file, unless you want to use TrueType instead of the PostScript fonts.

Printing is very slow when using ATM.

You are printing out a document with nifty fonts to an ImageWriter and it takes forever. ATM is having to make up the fonts as printing goes along. To speed things up, stop the printing job, open the ATM control panel and increase the Font Cache as much as possible for your Mac. ATM likes to have 50K for each font you use often. You may have to experiment with the size, especially if you only have 2Mb or 4Mb of RAM.

When printing documents to an ImageWriter, some characters overlap.

Choose Page Setup from the Find menu of your application and see if there is a Fractional Widths option. If you have the Fractional Widths option and it's checked, uncheck it. If that doesn't help, you are using a font that ATM can't redraw for the ImageWriter. You have to change fonts.

Character spacing looks uneven on the screen.

Your application is doing fractional-width spacing. You can turn off that option in the Page Setup dialog box (as explained in the preceding problem), but you should reselect it before printing out to a PostScript printer. You can also minimize uneven spacing by installing more bit-mapped font resource files for each font Family.

When optimizing with Speed Disk, you get a message that the disk has weak or defective sectors.

This means that Speed Disk has found some real problems on the disk that defragmenting can't fix. You can try to optimize anyway, but it may be risky. First choose Go To Expert from the Options menu. Then pull the Options menu down again and choose Verify Data if it has a check in front of it. With Verify Data turned off, you may be able to optimize. If the problem recurs, it is time to copy all your data and applications off the hard disk. Do so, then reformat your hard disk and check it again with Speed Disk or Disk Doctor. If the bad sectors persist, take the drive to a qualified technician for repair. Don't risk crashes by continuing to use it.

While optimizing a disk with Speed Disk, you get a message about the disk being completely full.

Whoa, there. You are really running that hard disk too full! Either that or it is a floppy and it is filled to the brim. Take 20K or 30K worth of data off a floppy disk, or at least a megabyte off a hard disk, and try again.

You see a message about Speed Disk not being able to optimize your startup drive.

You are trying to defragment the drive that your Mac is running off. You need to restart the Mac, inserting the Norton Applications disk at the beep. The Speed Disk window appears when the startup sequence ends. Click the Optimize button, and Speed Disk will go to work on your startup drive. When it finishes, Choose Quit from the File menu, then click the Restart button in the dialog box that appears. Your nicely defragmented hard disk will start up again.

CHAPTER 18

Data Protection and Recovery Utilities

This chapter covers utilities designed to protect your Mac, your files, and your disks. Your Mac is a pretty reliable thing, but it was designed and made by humans like you and me, and we are fallible. Some of us are more than fallible, in fact; we are devious, or at least negligent. It's our careless neglect that leads to things like crashes that wipe out data. It is the deviousness of a few of us that leads to virus infections.

Ah, viruses. A *virus* is any program that gets into your computer without your consent. It may just duplicate itself in your system software and cause little harm, or it may go after data files and really do major damage. Fortunately, there have been very few Mac viruses so far that cause major file loss or damage on the computers they invade, and Apple has fixed the system software so it eradicates some of the most bothersome existing viruses. You still need to prepare for new viruses though; they are, I'm afraid, as inevitable as the common cold. Cold viruses are a part of nature, and so are humans who like to create computer viruses. Their deviousness is part of human nature. So we all need protection from viral invasion.

But data damage due to virus infection is really quite rare. More commonly, data damage is caused by power or hardware failure, or operator error. Whether it's a power surge, a bad power supply, or your own lack of brain-power that leads to a crash of your hard drive, you have the same reaction; you *really* wish you had backed up your work. You'll learn how to back up your work in this chapter, and how to do it with a minimum of time and disks wasted. And for those cases where hardware or media failure leads to loss of data, there is a section on recovering data with disk repair utilities.

Which Data Protection Utilities for You?

The following subsections cover the utilities that can do the most to protect your Mac and all the stuff you keep on it. Pick a good antiviral utility to keep your system clear of viruses, then get a good back-up utility to make sure you have all your data backed up in case of a crash. Finally, get a good disk repair utility to recover data and fix your disk if you ever do have a crash.

Antiviral Utilities

There is a wide spectrum of utilities designed to protect your Mac and its files, from humble freeware to complex applications that cost a pretty penny. I can only cover a few of the outstanding examples and hope that you will use the concepts you learn for the samples to find a protection utility that suits your specific needs. The two recognized leaders in the antiviral field are Virex and SAM (Symantec AntiVirus for Macintosh). They are both good at detecting and eradicating the common viruses, they cost about the same amount (quite a bit, as utilities go), and each has ways of looking for new viruses and giving you upgrades when they appear. SAM has a hotline for the latest virus news, and it makes special efforts to keep up system software changes. SAM also has a one-step method to update whole networks with new protection when new viruses appear. For more information, see "Using SAM" later in this chapter.

There are several other good but less thorough antiviral utilities, such as Rival, VirusDetective, and Antitoxin. Any of them will protect your Mac from the common viruses, and some are cheaper than SAM and Virex. They may have less support and updating capability, however, so there is always the risk of a new virus getting past them. If you tend to be paranoid, you'll probably want something more powerful and up-to-date.

One other alternative is Disinfectant. It is free. It comes from John Norstad, one of the unsung heroes of the Mac community. He and his cohorts wrote Disinfectant for the Mac networks at Northwestern University. They wrote great online docs for it too. They keep it up-to-date and circulate Disinfectant to user's groups and the general public by means of information services such as America Online and CompuServe. Thanks from all of us, John. Disinfectant can check your disks and eradicate any virus known to the Mac community. Just keep in touch with your user's group or information service to make sure you always have the latest version of Disinfectant, and you will be relatively safe from virus attacks. The program is anything but slick, and it does not watch your system for hints of virus activity the way others do. But if you use Disinfectant properly and don't trade disks with lots of runny-nosed users, or do a lot of downloading off sneezing information services, or run lots of floppies through germ-spattered copy-service rental Macs, then you probably won't have to worry about virus infection. For more information, see "Using Disinfectant" later in this chapter.

Backup Utilities

There are three basic categories of backup tools: global utilities that just back up everything on a disk, incremental utilities that back up changed files and make new archives at each backup, and incremental utilities that replace old backup files with your new ones. The global approach is very thorough, but wasteful. The two incremental types of utility are better; you do one global backup, then just add little daily increments of your changed files to the big backup. The archival approach is more thorough; you can go back and get an old version of a file if you don't like the newer version. The nonarchival approach takes a lot less time and uses fewer disks, but you can't go back to old backup files if you don't like the latest ones.

A good example of a utility that does archival backups in increments is Fastback Plus. You do one global backup with it, then each day you do an archival backup of the files you have changed. Fastback Plus gives you the choice of overwriting or not overwriting previous backup files with the same names, so in a way it is only archival if you want it to be. It compresses all the files into one big dense one, so you don't have to use dozens of disks. The only problem with this is that you must have the utility in order to restore your files. Other backup tools such as Backmatic keep all your files separate, so you can restore a file by just dragging it off the backup disk onto your hard disk. This takes more disk space, however. If you have time and disks to spare, try Backmatic; it has a nice feature of reminding you to do a backup at each shutdown. If you're short of time, disks, and patience, and can keep track of your utility master disk, try Fastback Plus. For more information on it, see "Using Fastback Plus" later in this chapter.

Examples of backup utilities that do incremental backups and replace the old files with the new changed ones are Redux and DiskFit. Redux is easy to use and quick, so it is a good choice unless you make lots of big files every day. For more information on backing up in this simple incremental way, see "Using Redux" later in this chapter.

File Recovery Utilities

There are tools that can recover files you lose when a disk has a problem, and there are tools that recover files you have thrown in the Trash by mistake.

You get a primitive recovery tool with your system software. It's called Disk First Aid, and it can find and fix some minor problems, but it isn't nearly as good as some of the other tools available. My favorite is Disk Doctor, in the Norton Utilities. It works with Filesaver, a little program that records all the file moves and changes you make on your disks. If you have a disk problem, the Disk Doctor can check the disk, then check the Filesaver records and fix any file info problems it finds. It can also fix lots of directory and allocation problems. Disk Clinic in the SUM (Symantec Utilities for Macintosh) collection is also good, and MacTools has a similar utility. I just prefer Disk Doctor because it works so reliably and is so easy to use. For more information, see "Using the Norton Disk Doctor" later in this chapter.

As for recovering files you have trashed by mistake, you can use Complete Undelete in the Microcom 911 Utilities, or UnErase in the Norton Utilities, or Guardian in SUM. They all just drag the file remainders out of your Trash and list them for you. For an example, see "Using Norton UnErase" later in this chapter.

 Using SAM

You can use SAM at many levels, depending on how rigorous you want to be about watching for viruses, and depending on how much RAM and disk space you have. The following procedure tells how to do your first scan with the SAM Virus Clinic, and how to install SAM Intercept Jr., a small, fast version of the SAM program that checks everything you put into your Mac for viruses. Note the unusual order of events. You scan *first,* then install. You do this to make sure you get rid of any viruses on your hard disk *before* you put the SAM clinic on there where it might get infected. Then you can scan all your other disks.

To get your system free of viruses, follow these steps:

1. Lock your SAM Program Disk #1, then insert it in your Mac and start it up. Enter your name and company when a dialog box asks for them. The SAM window opens on the desktop.

2. Double-click the SAM Virus Clinic icon. The Virus Clinic window opens. Make sure your hard disk icon is showing at the top

of the window. It's already selected, so don't click it; if you do by mistake, just click it again to make that X go away.

3. Click the Scan button. The scan proceeds. It may take a few minutes.
4. If alert boxes appear, saying virus infections have been found, click OK in each one. When the scan is complete, the Clinic window shows the results, as in Figure 18.1.
5. What you do next depends on if infections were found:

- If no infections were found, click Quit and go on to the next step.
- If infections were found, double-click the name of each one in the box, then click the Copy/Repair button in the Repair dialog box. After repairs, scan the disk again. Click Quit when you get a clean scan.

FIGURE 18.1
Scan report with no viruses found

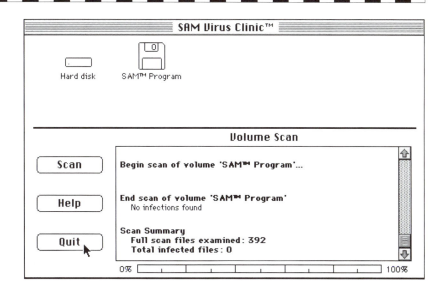

6. Restart your Mac; let it kick out the SAM startup disk, so it runs on the hard disk's System file.
7. Insert the SAM Program Disk #2. The SAM window opens.
8. Drag the SAM Intercept Jr. icon and the SAM Virus Definitions to the System Folder icon in your hard disk window. When the message box asks if you want to put SAM Intercept Jr. in your Extensions folder, click OK. You can install SAM Intercept instead of Intercept Jr. The full Intercept has more custom options; Intercept Jr. just gives you Basic Protection, but that is adequate for all known viruses.
9. Click in your hard disk window, then choose New Folder from the File menu and name the folder SAM.
10. Drag the SAM Virus Clinic icon from the SAM Program Disk #2 window to the SAM folder in your hard disk window.
11. Restart your Mac. The Intercept Jr. icon appears along with your other extensions and control panels during startup.
12. Double-click the SAM Virus Clinic icon on your hard disk. When the window opens, insert one of your floppies.
13. Click Scan. Scan *all* of your floppies and Copy/Repair any infected ones.
14. Check for a magnifying glass pointer each time you insert a floppy. It tells you that Intercept Jr. is scanning the floppy to see if there are any viruses or suspicious file irregularities on it.

That's all there is to it. You should scan your hard disk with the Virus Clinic tool every once in a while, and check now and then with your user group or Symantec to see if you need a new version of SAM for a new virus, but basically, your virus worries are over. Of course, if you ever insert a floppy disk and an alert box pops up to tell you a virus has been detected, run the Virus Clinic and give it the cure.

Using Disinfectant

You can use Disinfectant in much the same way you use SAM, except you have to make the program-startup disk yourself. Some people even use both SAM *and* Disinfectant. If you have a SuperDrive, it's easy; just copy Disinfectant and a System 6.0.7 System Folder onto a blank 1.4Mb disk, then drag the Disinfectant Preferences file to the System Folder. Make your Disinfectant startup disk on a system that has been using Disinfectant and is known to be virus-free. Then lock the disk to protect it from virus infection. If you have to use 800K floppies on your Mac, you need to pare down a 6.0.7 System Folder so both it and Disinfectant can fit on the disk. Or you can use your Disk Tools disk as a startup disk and run Disinfectant from a second floppy; this involves a lot of disk swapping if you don't have two disk drives.

When you have a Disinfectant startup disk, start your Mac with it in the drive. Open Disinfectant, and when you see your hard disk icon at the top of the window, click the Scan button to scan your hard disk. You see a scan report at the end, as shown in Figure 18.2.

Scan all of your floppies. If Disinfectant finds viruses, click the Disinfect button to take care of them. Then, before closing Disinfectant, choose Install Protection INIT from the Protect menu to install the Disinfectant INIT in your system folder. Then restart your Mac and check to make sure the Disinfectant INIT icon appears during startup.

The Disinfectant INIT doesn't do a thorough scan of every floppy you insert, like the SAM Intercept or Intercept Jr., but it does detect viruses when they appear. Your Mac will beep ten times and an alert box will come up, telling you what kind of virus you have. Run Disinfectant and eradicate the virus. If the infected file is an application, you may want to reinstall the application from an uninfected master disk, just to make sure you aren't using a damaged version of the application.

FIGURE 18.2
Disinfectant scan report

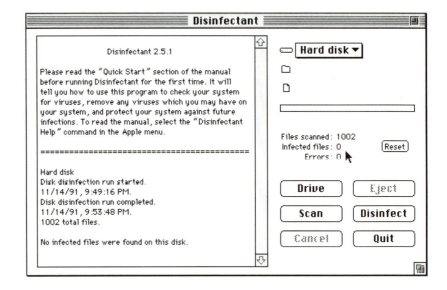

 Using Fastback Plus

Use Fastback Plus to compress your files and save them onto a floppy or alternate hard disk. When you restore files from your backups, use Fastback Plus to decompress the files and put them back on the hard disk.

Doing Your First Big Backup

Use the following procedure to back up the files on your hard disk by making an archive on floppy disks:

1. Collect enough floppy disks of one type (800K or 1.4Mb) for the backup. Figure on about one 800K floppy for each megabyte you need to backup, or one 1.4Mb floppy for each 2Mb to be backed up. Format them and put blank labels on. Have a pen handy to write on the labels.

Data Protection and Recovery Utilities   449

2. Start Fastback Plus. The Fastback Plus Express window appears.
3. Check the settings. The boxes should say Fastback Plus will back up all files from your hard drive to floppies in the internal drive, as shown in Figure 18.3.
4. Click on any box that is wrong and change the setting. For example, if your floppy disks are 800K and the To box says "Media: 1.4M high-density floppy," click the To box. When the dialog box opens, use the pop-up media menu to select 800K floppy, then click OK. To back up a different hard drive, choose it from the pop-up menu in the From box.

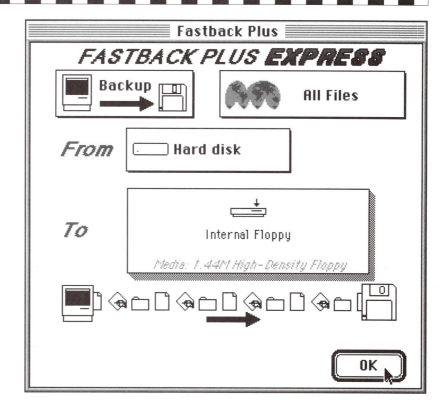

FIGURE 18.3
The Fastback Plus Express window

5. Click OK when everything is right. The Backup Progress window appears, with everything blank.

6. Click Start Backup. A highlighted bar appears at the bottom of the screen telling you to insert volume 911115A #001 (or a similar long number) in the internal floppy drive. Pretty rude message, I'd say.

7. Ignore the tone of the message and write the number it says (yours will be different from the example above) on the floppy disk label, then insert it. The circle in the Progress window shows the floppy disk filling up.

8. Label and insert more floppy disks as Fastback Plus asks for them. Make sure they are all of the same type, 800K or 1.4Mb. When the backup is complete, the window looks like Figure 18.4.

9. Choose Quit from the File menu.

FIGURE 18.4
The Backup Progress window at the end of a backup

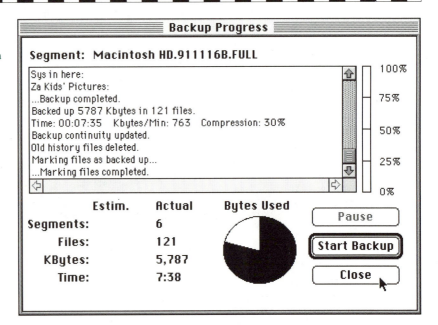

Keep your backup floppies in a safe place. Many people say you should have two copies of every backup, but I don't. I back up daily to an old hard drive, and then at the end of a big project, I make floppies of all the data for the project. I have never heard of anyone losing both their originals and their backup copies. But if you have lost stuff, you'll want to make two backups.

Daily and Partial Backups

To make a daily backup of just the things you have changed, follow the procedure above, but when you are in the Express window, open the pop-up menu under All Files and choose All Changed Files Except Applications. The backup will be short and sweet, for sure. I'm always surprised, though, at all the little housekeeping files that have changed. Makes you appreciate how much work the Mac does to keep itself in order for you.

To make a backup of just a particular folder and all its contents, follow the procedure above, but when you get to the Express window, choose Files I Choose from the pop-up menu under All Files. Fastback Plus takes an inventory of your disk, then lists all the folders in the Choose Backup Files window. Scroll through the folder list and find the folder you want to copy. If you select a folder, the files in it appear in the panel on the right side of the window. Hold down the Option key and double-click a folder to select it and all that is in it. Click OK in the Choose Backup Files window, as shown in Figure 18.5.

Click OK in the Express window, then click Start Backup in the Backup Progress window and be ready to label and insert a floppy disk. When the backup is complete, choose Quit from the File menu.

Restoring a File to Your Hard Disk

If you lose a file or you can't read it because the hard disk goes sour, you tend to go into a panic and want to drag the backup right off the

Chapter 18

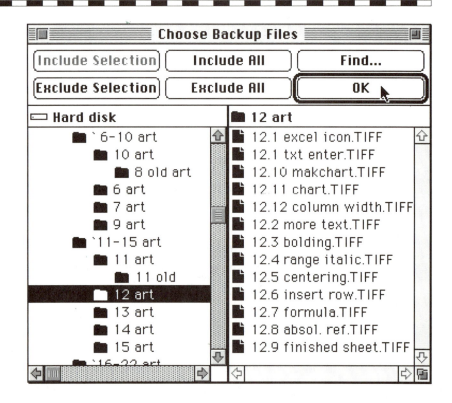

FIGURE 18.5
Selecting files to back up

backup floppy, RIGHT NOW. You can't do this with compressed archive backups like Fastback Plus makes. So take a deep breath, calm down, maybe get up and stretch a bit. Have faith in Fastback Plus. It is a very reliable keeper of data.

To restore a file from your backup archive, you have to open Fastback Plus, look through the archive listing, then insert the floppy Fastback Plus asks for, so it can decompress the file and put it back on your hard disk. Get out your backup floppies and use the following steps to get the job done, so you can start breathing normally again. Do things carefully. Fastback Plus is a bit picky about how you set up restores.

1. Open Fastback Plus. The Express window appears.
2. Use the pop-up menu under Backup to change it to Restore. The train of stuff at the bottom of the screen switches direction.
3. DO NOT change the All Files pop-up yet. First check the From and To box settings.
4. To change the From setting, click on the From box and use the Media pop-up menu to choose the type of floppy you have the archive on. Don't change anything else in that box unless you are restoring from a hard drive. Click OK.
5. To change the To setting (if you have more than one hard drive), use the To pop-up menu to select the hard disk you want to restore to.
6. Got your From and To right? Good. Now choose Files I Choose from the All Files menu. Fastback Plus does a quick check of backed up files and the Choose Restore Files window opens.
7. Find the files you need to restore (isn't it great to see them in the list?) and double-click each one, so it is highlighted AND the icon is in reverse video (white on black). It's not enough to select the file. You have to double-click it, or select it and then click the Include button. Picky, picky Fastback Plus. If you need to restore a folder and all its files, double-click the folder. Option–double-click to restore a folder and all folders and files inside it.
8. When the files you want to restore are all selected and reverse video, click OK. The Express window appears.
9. Click OK. You may see a dialog box asking what you want to overwrite; just click OK so you don't wipe out any new files. The Restore Progress window appears.

Chapter 18

10. Click Start Restore. Insert the backup disk with the number Fastback Plus asks you for at the bottom of the Restore window, as in Figure 18.6.

11. When the restore is complete, choose Quit from the File menu. Then go look in the folder where your lost files used to be. Oh yeah. There they are again.

Fastback Plus may have a prickly interface, but it sure is nice when it works. There are many, many other things you can do with it, from automatic backups that happen in the middle of the night, to customized backups you make with Fastback Plus's built-in language of macro keywords. Oh, boy. I'm sorry, but I'm just not turned on by that stuff. If you are, go for it. Good luck with the *User Manual*.

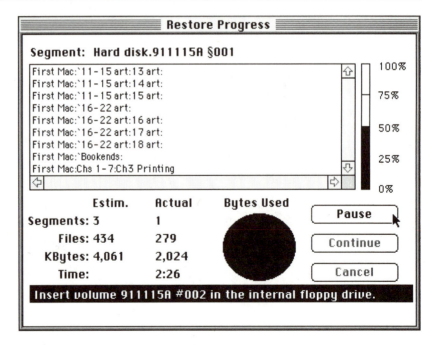

FIGURE 18.6
Restoring files from a floppy disk

Using Redux

It may not be as fast, powerful, and penurious with disks, but Redux is a lot easier to use than Fastback Plus. To do a total backup, just follow these steps:

1. Get a bunch of disks; you always seem to need a couple more than you'd expect from the amount of stuff you have to back up. Get a pen to write on labels, too.
2. If the disks have data on them, erase it; Redux does full, slow reformats if it finds files on a disk and you tell it to erase the files to make room for your backup.
3. Open Redux. You see the Redux window, with source drives listed.
4. Select a source drive, the one you're going to back up.
5. Click the Backup button. The target disk list appears; the target disk is the one you put the backup on.
6. Write 1, dot, and your hard drive name on a floppy label and insert the floppy. For example, I would write **1.Macintosh HD**. The target disk shows up in the list; it may not have the right name yet, but don't worry, Redux will soon rename it.
7. Click Proceed. A dialog box appears, asking if you want to erase the first disk to start the backup. You can change the BackupSet name if you want, but I don't.
8. Click Erase. This seems a bit spooky the first time you do it; it's just the way Redux clears each backup disk so it can make full use of it.
9. Label the backup disks and feed them in as Redux asks for them. Click Proceed and Erase for each disk. When the backup is complete, Redux asks for the first disk again.

10. Insert the first disk (1.Macintosh HD in my case) and click Proceed one last time. Redux updates the backup directory and tells you you're done, as shown in Figure 18.7.

Oh, it's so nice and easy. And it doesn't really take much longer than doing a compressed backup, and it doesn't take many more disks.

Doing future backups is even easier. All you have to do is get all the disks ready, plus an extra or two, then open Redux. Select your hard disk as the source if it isn't selected, and click Backup. Then insert your first backup disk (1.Macintosh HD in my case) and click Proceed. In the dialog box that appears, you can see how much is going to be backed up; click Backup, then insert any disks that Redux asks for. At the end, insert the first backup disk again so Redux can update the directory.

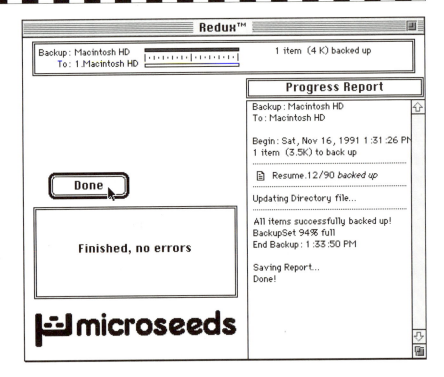

FIGURE 18.7
Finished backup

To restore a file, you have to do a bit more, but it's still very simple:

1. Get your backup disks out, then open Redux.
2. Select your hard disk as the Source (this seems backwards, but you are restoring files back to their source, right?) and click Restore.
3. Insert the first disk of your BackupSet and click Proceed. A file list appears on the right side of the window.
4. Choose Uncheck All Files from the File List menu.
5. Find the files you want to restore and click in the box next to each one to check it, as shown in Figure 18.8. The file list works somewhat like a list view in the Finder; you can open folders to check files inside them.
6. Click Begin when you have checked all the files you want to restore. Redux goes to work; it asks you if you want to replace files that still exist on your hard disk and tells you what the last modification dates were.
7. When the restore is done, choose Quit from the File menu.

That's all there is to it. There are two things you have to keep in mind about Redux, though. If you do daily backups, it replaces old files with new ones; so if you back up a file that is a mess, you can't go back to yesterday's backup. This saves a lot of space, but it can lead to grief. Also, if you drag a file on your hard disk to the Trash and then do a daily backup, Redux deletes the backup of the file, too. So if you drag a file to the Trash by mistake, restore it *before* you do your daily backup. If you forget, see "Using Norton UnErase" later in this chapter.

Redux can do some other nifty stuff, too, like copying files instead of making backup archives, so you can use them straight off your floppy, and setting up scripts to automate backups. See the clear, concise *User's Guide* for details.

FIGURE 18.8
Selecting a file to restore

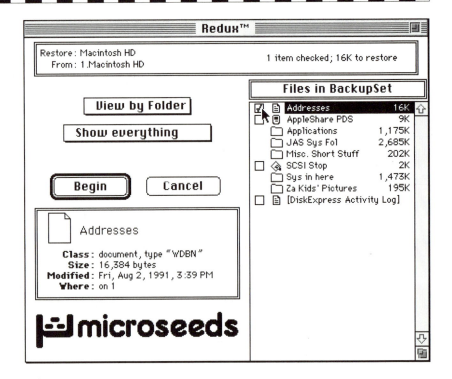

Using the Norton Disk Doctor

Disk Doctor is a very easy utility to use, and that's a good thing, because when you need it, you're not in the mood to fiddle around with multiple dialog boxes. All you have to do is start the Norton Utilities and click the Disk Doctor icon. When the dialog box appears, insert the disk you want to fix, or click the Drive button to show it if it is already in the drive. Then click Open, as in Figure 18.9. The Disk Doctor window appears; click Start and you can watch as the doc checks everything out. When he finds an problem, a box appears, describing it. Click

Data Protection and Recovery Utilities

FIGURE 18.9
Starting the Disk Doctor checkup

Yes to correct the problem. In very rare cases, you have to click No to avoid file damage; the doc will tell you.

When the doctor is done, you see a little clipboard dialog box, telling you that everything is fixed or no problems were found. If you want to see details, click the More Info button. Otherwise click Done, then choose Quit from the File menu.

That's all. But don't think the doctor is a wimp, just because his interface is bedside-friendly. I've had some real scares with unreadable disks and missing files that the Disk Doctor saved me from. And he's the cheapest specialist ever.

 ## Using Norton UnErase

Like its Norton partner, Disk Doctor, UnErase is easy to use, and when you need it, you'll be glad it is so easy. Just remember one key thing about using UnErase to get things back out of the emptied Trash: the sooner you fish the file out of the dumped Trash, the less decayed it will be. The Mac writes over stuff that you dump out of the Trash. If you retrieve quickly, there's a good chance the file will be intact. If you wait a day or two, or do a defragment after emptying the Trash, your chances are very poor that the dumped file will be usable.

To go after a dumped file, start the Norton Utilities and click the UnErase button. A dialog box comes up; click the Drive button if you don't see your current startup disk icon at the top. Leave Quick UnErase selected and click OK. A file list appears, showing all the files that can still be unerased out of the Trash. Just hunt through the files, and if the one you want is in either Excellent, Very Good, or Good condition, select it and click the UnErase button up at the top of the window, as shown in Figure 18.10. The file is restored and placed in your hard disk window. When UnErase is done, choose Quit from the File menu. You can open the file with the application that created it, then save it. With luck, it will work fine.

FIGURE 18.10
Recovering a file from the Trash with UnErase

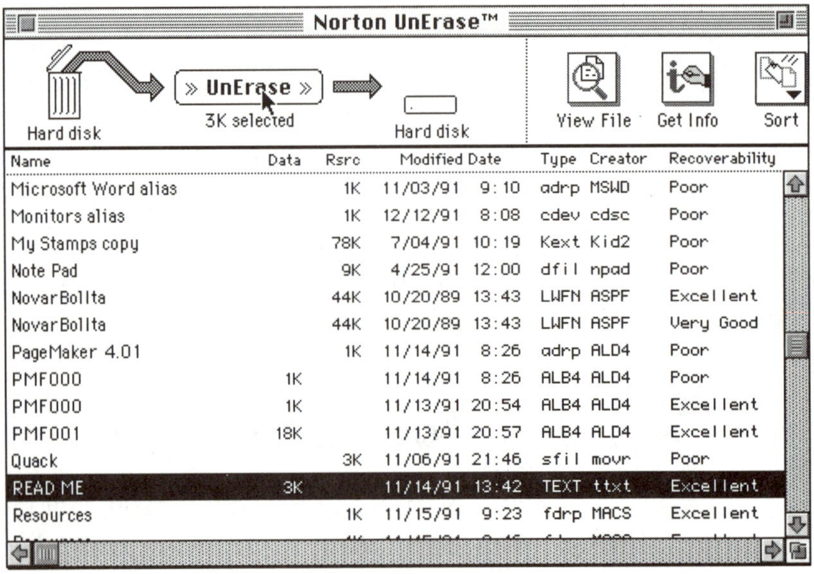
Norton UnErase™
» UnErase »
3K selected
Hard disk
Hard disk
View File
Get Info
Sort
Name Data Rsrc Modified Date Type Creator Recoverability
Microsoft Word alias 1K 11/03/91 9:10 adrp MSWD Poor
Monitors alias 1K 12/12/91 8:08 cdev cdsc Poor
My Stamps copy 78K 7/04/91 10:19 Kext Kid2 Poor
Note Pad 9K 4/25/91 12:00 dfil npad Poor
NovarBollta 44K 10/20/89 13:43 LWFN ASPF Excellent
NovarBollta 44K 10/20/89 13:43 LWFN ASPF Very Good
PageMaker 4.01 1K 11/14/91 8:26 adrp ALD4 Poor
PMF000 1K 11/14/91 8:26 ALB4 ALD4 Poor
PMF000 1K 11/13/91 20:54 ALB4 ALD4 Excellent
PMF001 18K 11/13/91 20:57 ALB4 ALD4 Excellent
Quack 3K 11/06/91 21:46 sfil movr Poor
READ ME 3K 11/14/91 13:42 TEXT ttxt Excellent
Resources 1K 11/15/91 9:23 fdrp MACS Excellent

Troubleshooting Problems with Data Protection Utilities

The following subsections cover the problems you are most likely to have while working with data protection and recovery utilities.

SAM keeps telling you that your files have irregularities.

SAM is trying to sell you a laxative. No, it just keeps seeing the same problem over and over. Start SAM Virus Clinic and choose Scan Options from the Options menu. If that command isn't in the Options menu, choose Advanced Menus from the Options menu. In the dialog box that appears, choose Complete Check, then choose Use filters. Rescan the problem disk. If the file is a commercial product and you still get bad reports on it from SAM, check with the manufacturer or Symantec support.

Can't move or change SAM Intercept.

If you locked the SAM Intercept extension, you cannot modify it in any way; this is so nobody can disarm Intercept and sneak things into your system. For information on how to assign a password to SAM Intercept so you can lock and unlock the extension at will, see the SAM User Manual.

Fastback Plus won't accept your backup disk.

As you are doing a backup with Fastback Plus, you stick a backup floppy in the drive when it asks for one, and you get a message box that tells you the volume is locked or incompatible with the media selection. First check the floppy to see if it is locked (close the little tab over the square hole in the corner). Then check to see if it is the same size floppy as the others you are using; if you are backing up to 800K floppies, for instance, Fastback Plus won't accept a 1.4Mb floppy.

System crashes during a Redux backup.

It isn't the end of the world, as you might expect. All you have to do is find the file called Directory, stored in the same folder with Redux, and drag it to your first backup disk. Then start Redux and start the backup over; Redux will pick it up just where it left off!

First backup disk of Redux backup is lost.

To rebuild the file directory that Redux keeps on your first backup disk, open Redux and choose Rebuild Directory from the Disk menu. Redux asks you for the first target disk. If you still have it, insert it. If not, choose Missing Backup Disk from the Disk menu. Redux asks for the second target disk; insert that one. Redux will ask for all the backup disks so it can rebuild the directory. When it asks you for another one after you have inserted your last one, click Done. Redux then asks for the first disk again. If you have it, insert it, if not, insert a blank disk. Redux puts the directory on this disk; use it as your first disk from now on.

CHAPTER 19

HyperCard

HyperCard is a new kind of application. It is a tool you can use to look at a wide variety of files that contain user-friendly information, and, at the same time, it is a programming tool that you can use to make full-fledged Macintosh programs of your own, complete with a nice graphic interface and the power to do all sorts of tasks. And the most surprising thing about this application is that you receive it with your system software, free.

If the Macintosh is the computer for the rest of us, HyperCard is the programming tool for the rest of us. The programmers at Apple developed HyperCard to give ordinary Mac users a chance to make up programs that work on their own machines. You don't have to study programming for ten years to get started with programming in HyperTalk, the HyperCard programming language. You can use some of the basic functions in making simple home-spun applications like an interactive address book or a calendar.

The key to understanding HyperCard lies in understanding the metaphor it's built upon. Information is placed on *cards*, each of which focuses on a specific item, and the cards are arranged in *stacks*. The cards and stacks work like interactive flash cards: you click on a button or icon, and HyperCard gives you more information or moves you somewhere else in the stack.

The best way to get started with HyperCard is to experiment with a premade stack. You can buy HyperCard stacks with illustrations and sound covering every subject from comic strips to languages to the anatomy of birds. There are also a few simple stacks that come with your system software, including the stack you'll experiment with in this chapter. You can use these stacks as reference material or as a quick way to learn just what you want on a subject, with visual and often audio reinforcement.

If experimenting with premade stacks just whets your appetite, you can advance to creating your own stacks. First, read the *HyperCard Basics* booklet that you received with your Mac for more information on programming with HyperCard. If you're still interested, you can obtain the full HyperCard development kit from Claris.

Using HyperCard Stacks

HyperCard can be used to access the information in any of the HyperCard stacks that have been created and distributed for users by Apple Computer, Claris Corporation, and thousands of other Macintosh programmers. In the rest of the sections of this chapter, you will learn how to open, move around in, add to, and print a HyperCard stack.

Starting HyperCard and Opening a Stack

To start HyperCard and open a stack that lets you make an address book, use the following procedure:

1. Lock your HyperCard master disk and make a copy of it. Always use the working copy. Using HyperCard changes it, and if you use your master copy's Home stack, any changes you make to it will be permanent .

2. If HyperCard is not installed on your hard disk, drag it there from your working disk.

3. Drag the Home stack, the Addresses with Audio stack, and the Audio Help stack from the HyperCard disks to your hard disk and put them all in a HyperCard folder.

Chapter 19

4. Open the HyperCard folder and double-click the HyperCard icon. You see the first card in your Home stack, as shown in Figure 19.1.

5. Click with the browse tool (a pointing finger) on the More button if you want to read more than the first page of the introduction to HyperCard.

6. Use the browse tool to click the Addresses with Audio button on your Home stack. The first card of the Addresses with Audio stack appears. Address cards look like the one shown in Figure 19.2. You may see notes about the card, too; click the Hide Notes button to see the rest of the address card.

Click the browse tool in the right and left arrows to move from card to card, as shown in Figure 19.2. Notice that the cards are in an endless loop. When you go past the last card in a stack, you come back to the first one; it's as if the cards were on a rolodex.

FIGURE 19.1
The first card in the Home stack

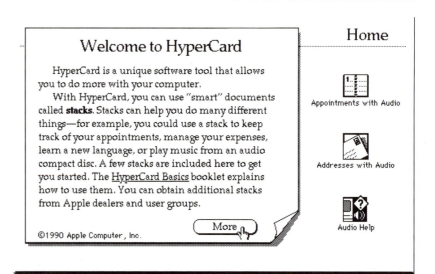

FIGURE 19.2
A card from the Addresses with Audio stack

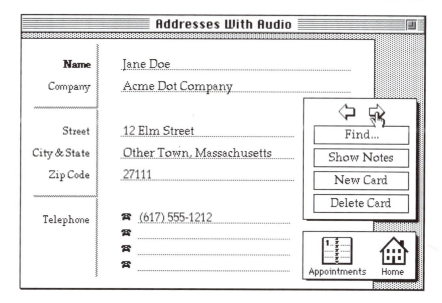

Adding and Sorting Address Cards

To make the rolodex address card stack more useful to you, add a bunch of cards for people you need to contact often. Use the following procedure to add new cards:

1. Click the New Card button. A blank card appears, with the cursor at the beginning of the Name line.
2. Type in the name of the first person you want to make a card for. Put the first name first, as on the example cards.
3. Press the Tab key to move the insertion point to the next line, or *field*. If the person does not work for a company, press Tab to move on to the Street field.
4. Fill all the address fields, and one or more of the telephone fields, depending on how many phone numbers the person has.

5. Click New Card to add another person's address and phone number. Add all the cards you want.

If you want to add a note about a person, such as a reminder about an impending address change, click the Show Notes button, then click in the empty note box and type in a note. Click the Hide Notes button when you are done, as shown in Figure 19.3.

The stack updates as you work on it; you do not have to save the changes as when you are working with other applications. But you must keep this fact in mind when you make permanent changes to the stack. For example, if you sort the stack into alphabetical order, it stays sorted. You can't go back to your unsorted stack. If you want to have access to the unsorted version of the stack, choose Save a Copy from the File menu *before* you sort.

To sort the cards alphabetically by last name, follow these steps:

1. Choose Sort Preferences from the Utilities menu.

FIGURE 19.3
Adding a note to an address card

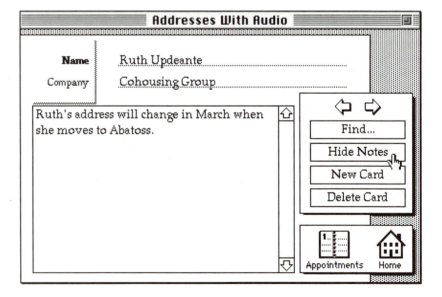

2. Click the radio button for First name first.
3. Click the button for Sort by last name, as shown in Figure 19.4.
4. Click Return to Addresses.
5. Choose Sort by Name from the Utilities menu. HyperCard sorts the address list.
6. Check the order of the cards by clicking the right arrow.

All of the cards should be in alphabetical order now. If one is out of place, it may have an extra suffix on the end, such as Jr. or III. Otherwise, the stack sorts very reliably.

Finding Cards in the Stack

Once you have added a large number of address cards to your stack, it becomes hard to get to a card by clicking the arrows over and over. To move quickly to a card, just click the Find button. A small dialog box appears. Enter the name of the person whose card you want

FIGURE 19.4
Setting sort preferences

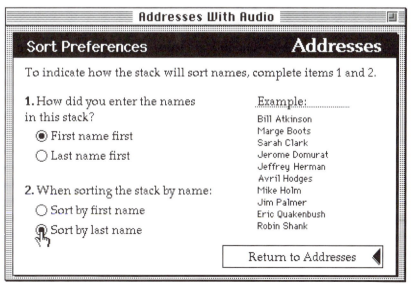

to see and click OK. HyperCard takes you directly to the card of the specified person and puts a box around the name.

If you forget a person's name, you can enter the town they come from or another piece of information about them, such as part of their name, in the Find dialog box. For example, if I know a fellow in my Cohousing group comes from Manteca, but I can't recall his name for the life of me, I can put Manteca in the Find dialog box, as in Figure 19.5. HyperCard takes me right to his card, as shown.

FIGURE 19.5
The Find dialog box and the card it found

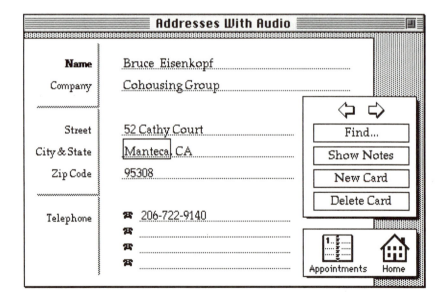

If there is more than one card with the text you typed in the Find box, press the Return key to see the other cards. If the Mac beeps and doesn't find any cards with the text you entered, check your spelling.

Fixing Mistakes

If you make a mistake while entering text in a field, just backspace over it with the Delete key or select the mistaken words and enter the correct ones. If you make a mistake in the name and this puts the card out of alphabetical order, first edit the name, then choose Sort by Name from the Utilities menu to straighten things out.

If you want to remove a card completely, just bring it into view, then click the Delete Card button and click OK in the dialog box. For example, if you want to dump the two sample cards for Jane Doe and A. Royce Walthrup, just go to each one and click Delete Card. Click OK in the dialog box that asks if you want to delete this card.

Printing

You can print all or parts of a HyperCard stack. To print all of the addresses listed on the cards, follow these steps:

1. If you plan to print out mailing labels, put the label paper in your printer's paper carrier.
2. Choose Print Addresses from the Utilities Menu. A dialog box appears, asking if you want to print the addresses as mailing labels or as an address book.
3. Choose the type of printout you want and click the appropriate button:

    - If you want mailing labels, check the Labels button; the phone numbers do not appear on this printout.

- If you want to see a list of all the addresses and phone numbers, click the Book button.

HyperCard puts up a message box that tells you how the printing preparations are going. When they are done, the job goes to the printer.

To print out the current card, just the way it looks on the screen, choose Print Card from the File menu.

To print out a nicely formatted address list made out of the information on the cards, you make it into a report, then print the report. Take these steps:

1. Choose Print Report from the File menu. The Print Report window appears, showing the current report layout. Reports are ways of formatting information from the cards.
2. Choose Name and Address List from the Reports menu. The format for the list appears on the left side of the window.
3. Enter a title for your report in the Header text box at the bottom of the window.
4. Click Print in the Print Report window, as shown in Figure 19.6.
5. In the dialog box that appears, click Yes. Then click Print in the Print dialog box.

The address list prints out, with the names of the people in bold typeface, the phone numbers under the names, and the addresses on the right.

Quitting HyperCard

To stop creating cards or reading from them, choose Quit HyperCard from the File menu or press ⌘-Q. You are not prompted to save your work because it is saved as you do it. It gives you an eerie feeling the first time you quit without saving, but you soon find that the stack shows the results of your work when you come back to it, so you soon

FIGURE 19.6
Printing an address list

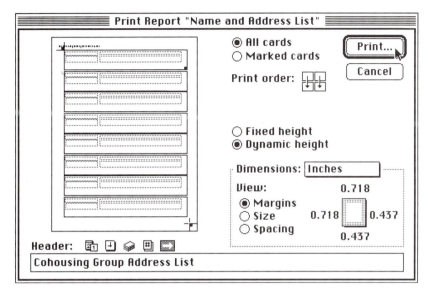

trust HyperCard to save all your modifications. The concept is perfectly logical; whatever you do to a card becomes a part of it. Just keep this in mind when you are looking at your Home stack; you don't want to change that unless you are ready to live with your changes or reinstall the Home stack from your floppy.

Troubleshooting Problems with HyperCard

The following subsections cover the problems you are most likely to have working with HyperCard.

Chapter 19

HyperCard does not start.

You probably do not have the latest system software. New versions of HyperCard will not run on older versions of the Mac system software. Install the latest.

When you start HyperCard, you get a message about a font missing.

The HyperCard Home stack calls for some fonts that aren't in the standard bunch you find in every System file. Palatino is the one people usually don't have and the Home stack uses it for its text and titles. You can run the stack without it; the text and titles appear in Geneva instead. If you want to see the Home stack in all its finery, though, either drag the Palatino fonts into your System file, or, if you are using Suitcase, select the Palatino font family in the Sets and Suitcases window and click Open. Even though I'm not a font nut and normally would not be bugged by a problem like this, I have to admit that I'm quite fond of Palatino. It's a graceful font.

You can't see the menu bar when you are using a stack.

When you open a stack, the menu bar goes away. Some stacks want things that way; they are intended to guide the user through a single track, with no options to get out. If you want to get out anyway, just press ⌘-spacebar. There's your menu. You are free to choose commands again. If you press ⌘-spacebar again, the menus disappear.

CHAPTER 20

Networking

A network is a collection of computers, printers, and other devices that can communicate directly with each other. Since the introduction of System 7 in 1991, all Macs have had built-in networking capabilities that let you share printers and other peripherals and link up programs and data in ways that were unimaginable just a few years ago.

Most Mac networks are Local Area Networks (LANs), which means that they are connected by special cables or adapted phone wires, and they are all in a relatively small area. A typical small Apple-Talk network (that's the term used for the kind of network using the software you get with the Mac) might have three or four Macs, a printer, and a modem, all hooked together with special connectors and phone wiring. Any user on the network could print on the printer, and a user at home could dial up the network via the modem connection. Users could also share files, and if an electronic mail system was installed, they could write messages back and forth.

Some LANs are much more complex. They can have a hundred Macs and dozens of printers and modems, special computers reserved for file storage, and all kinds of peripheral attachments from scanners to mainframe connections. But once you are hooked up to a big network properly, you use it just as you would a small one. And the powers of a Mac network can be truly amazing; many applications let you share and link up the data in separate files, on separate Macs, so changes in one document are reflected in another.

For example, a spreadsheet on one Macintosh can be a source of data for a report that another user is writing with a word processor on a different Mac in a separate office. Yet when the original information in the spreadsheet is changed to reflect new circumstances, the updating of the report on the second Mac happens automatically. This new feature is called Publish and Subscribe. All you have to do to use it is hook your Mac to an AppleTalk network; you just plug the cable into the printer port on the back of your Mac and you're ready to go.

 ## AppleTalk and Ethernet Networks

Any Mac that is connected to a PostScript LaserWriter constitutes a network, although typically people think of a network as a bunch of Macs connected together. There are a variety of different Mac networks available today, but the most popular are LocalTalk (often referred to as AppleTalk), Ethernet, and Token-Ring. These networks can mix and match Macintoshes and PCs, powerful workstations, minicomputers, and mainframe computers.

Although the setup of each of these types of networks is different, they are all designed to send information to unique *nodes*, or addresses, that are assigned to each and every device on the network. The *protocols* (standardized procedures) that define how they do this are given names such as AppleTalk, EtherTalk, Novell Netware, DECNet, TCP-IP, and TokenTalk, to mention but a few. In the Macintosh world, you will principally be concerned with AppleTalk, which is the protocol used on LocalTalk networks; EtherTalk, which is the protocol used on Ethernet networks; and TokenTalk, which is the protocol used for Token-Ring networks.

Each type of network has its advantages and disadvantages. AppleTalk is the cheapest and least complex to set up, but it is slow and it can handle only a limited number of computers and devices. Phase II implementation of AppleTalk, for example, can only transmit 230 kilobits per second (that's about 5000 words of text). AppleTalk networks have a maximum cable length of 1000 feet (this can be extended to 3000 feet with a different kind of cable called PhoneNet, which resembles telephone wire). Only 32 devices, including Macs and printers, can be on a single AppleTalk network, unless you add expensive routers, bridges, and repeaters to extend the network's range and power. AppleTalk's great advantage, though, is that it is built into every Mac and requires no extra cost to install, other than the cable and connector boxes to connect the network together. It is a plug-in-and-play setup.

An Ethernet network, with the EtherTalk protocol, offers much greater speed and capacity. You can transmit data at up to 10 megabits per second over an Ethernet network: that's about 40 times faster than AppleTalk. And you can hook up as many users or devices as you want, within reason. The drawbacks of Ethernet are, of course, that it is not built into each Mac; you have to buy an expensive Ethernet transceiver card and install it in the expansion slot of every Mac on the network. Also, laser printers and any other devices on the network need to have special Ethernet connectors or be connected through a print server, since they are LocalTalk devices designed to work with AppleTalk.

Although this all adds up to a big original cost for an Ethernet network, it is well worth the money if you have ten or more users or who demand a lot of the printers and other shared devices such as file servers. In this day of increasingly complex electronic mail, voice-annotated documents, and full-color graphics, more and more data needs to be transmitted over network lines. Ethernet is so much faster that it is the only way to go, unless you are willing to put up with agonizing delays.

Networking

Setting Up an AppleTalk Network

An AppleTalk network is slow to transmit data, but it can be quick and easy to set up. If you will only be connected to an AppleTalk laser printer, for example, all you need to do is plug a LocalTalk cable into your printer port, then plug the other end into a single LocalTalk connector and plug that into your laser printer. On the other hand, if you are going to connect up more than one printer, or connect other Macs, then you will need to purchase a LocalTalk Connector Box for each Mac and printer. You connect the two incoming cables from the other Macs or printers into the box, and plug the single outgoing cable from the box into your Mac's printer port, as shown in Figure 20.1.

AppleTalk networks with LocalTalk cabling use a "daisy chain" topology. What this means is that each device on the network, be it a printer or computer, has two cables coming out of its connector box, so it occupies a spot in a linear chain that connects one machine to another.

Think of the configuration as a group of people all holding onto a single rope in a long line. If one person lets go, the others are still connected. However, if the rope is broken, the people split into two separate groups. Similarly, if you disconnect a Mac from an AppleTalk network, it can still work, but if the cabling between the connectors is

FIGURE 20.1
LocalTalk connector box showing single cable to printer port and two incoming LocalTalk cables

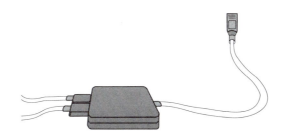

Chapter 20

disconnected, the network is split into two distinct entities that can function independently, but no longer transmit data to each other. Notice also that an AppleTalk network must have a beginning and an end; it cannot be connected in a circle. Circular networks are called "ring" topology networks. Figure 20.2 illustrates an AppleTalk network.

To make a daisy chain work, your LocalTalk Connector Box must always have cables that connect up to some other AppleTalk device. If a cable is plugged in that is not properly terminated in a printer or other computer, your AppleTalk network will crash and no one will be able to print or share information. So make sure your LocalTalk cables are always firmly connected to your connector box. If your Mac is at the end of the daisy chain, make sure there is one socket in your connector box with no cable plugged in, as shown in Figure 20.2, and make sure your Mac is always firmly connected to the cable at the printer port.

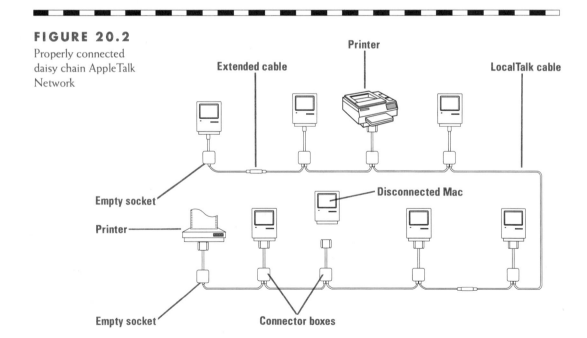

FIGURE 20.2
Properly connected daisy chain AppleTalk Network

Setting Up an EtherTalk Network

Setting up the hardware of an EtherTalk network is beyond the scope of this book, since it requires the installation of specialized cabling and tranceiver cards. For these tasks, see the documentation of the hardware, and work with the hardware dealer to ensure that your network is properly installed.

There are, however, a number of concepts you can learn in order to better understand how your network functions. First off, it will help to recognize the cabling for your network, so you never disconnect it by mistake. Depending on what kind of network you have, your cable will resemble the coaxial cables that connect VCRs to TVs, or it may be run on what is known as "twisted-pair wiring," which looks like telephone wire. Coaxial cable comes in two varieties, one known as "thick" and the other as "thin." Ethernet technology is also turning to fiber optical cables to enable speeds of up to 100 megabits per second and greater. Compare this to AppleTalk's measly 230 kilobits per second, and you can quickly see why many companies are abandoning LocalTalk networks in favor of Ethernet.

In addition to cabling, your Mac must have an Ethernet interface card to enable you to connect up to the network. Special cards are sold from various manufacturers to enable you to connect up any Mac SE, Notebook, LC, or II series to the particular kind of cable you have.

There are several different ways that Ethernet networks can be connected together. In contrast to AppleTalk's daisy chain topology, many Ethernet setups use what is known as a star topology. All the computers on the network are arranged in a star, with each person having a line dedicated to their computer. All the branches of the star merge in a central hub or nexus where there is typically a *file server*. A file server is a computer that stores applications and documents for all the users on the network. A file server can also be a central distribution point for electronic mail and a center for accessing commonly used databases and files. The advantage to the star configuration, besides greater speed, is that if one Mac on the network crashes, it does not impair or disrupt the rest of the network. By contrast, in AppleTalk, if one Mac crashes and interrupts the network chain, the entire network can come crashing down.

Installing EtherTalk Drivers

After you install the interface card in your Mac and hook it up to the network, you need to install the special System 7 *driver* for EtherTalk. The driver is the software that enables your Mac to talk to the network. It is included on your System 7 installation disk. The EtherTalk driver isn't ordinarily loaded unless you have previously installed an Ethernet card in your Mac. If you need to install these drivers, just follow these steps:

1. Insert your Install 1 disk into your floppy drive. The disk's window opens.
2. Double-click the Installer icon. A welcome dialog box opens.
3. Click OK in the welcome dialog box. The Easy Install dialog box appears.
4. Click the Customize button. A dialog box appears, with a list of software options.
5. Scroll down the list of software options, and highlight the EtherTalk Software option. Below you will see information about the option you have selected.
6. Click the Install Button, as shown in Figure 20.3, to begin the custom installation.
7. When prompted, insert the appropriate installation disks. A dialog box appears when installation is complete.

FIGURE 20.3
Installing an EtherTalk driver

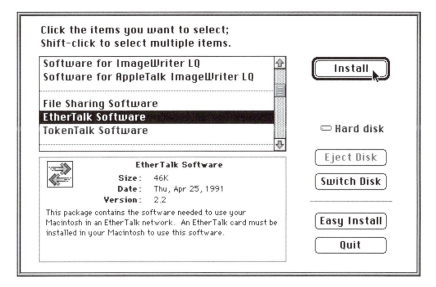

8. Click the Restart button in the dialog box to restart your computer and activate the new network drivers installed into your operating system.

Selecting Your Network Connection

To get started with your EtherTalk network connection, you need to select the icon of the EtherTalk connection in your Network control panel. Follow these steps to make the connection:

1. Choose Control Panels from the Apple menu. The Control Panels window opens.
2. Double-click the Network control panel. The Network window opens.
3. Click on the EtherTalk icon.

If you are connected to an AppleTalk network, you see a dialog box warning you that you may lose any network services that you may have been using. Don't worry, just click OK and close the Network control panel. You are now connected to the Ethernet network, but you still have to open the Chooser and choose your printer and the file servers you use.

Connecting to a Shared Printer on the Network

Before you can print documents from your Mac, no matter which kind of network you have, you must pick a printer on your network by using the Chooser. Once you have chosen a printer, you can change to another one at any time by opening the Chooser from the Apple menu and clicking on a printer. In the left panel of the Chooser window, there is a list of icons depicting various types of printers, as shown in Figure 20.4. These icons represent the *device drivers*, the software that your Mac uses to communicate with printers. You must pick one to let the operating system know what printer you plan on using. Ninety-nine percent of the time, if you are using PostScript laser printers, you will select the LaserWriter icon with the large ampersand character symbol, as shown. Once you select an icon, a list of printers appears in the right panel of the window. Click the name of the one you want to use.

If you are choosing a LaserWriter, you will want to click on the Background Printing radio button in the lower right side of the window. This allows you to continue working while your document gets processed as a "background" activity that won't interrupt you. Background printing is often referred to as *print spooling*, since it stores your print jobs in a queue and then spools the documents out one by one, first-come, first-served, as the printer becomes available for new documents. Note that the Background Printing feature is only available for

FIGURE 20.4
Selecting a Laser-Writer in the Chooser

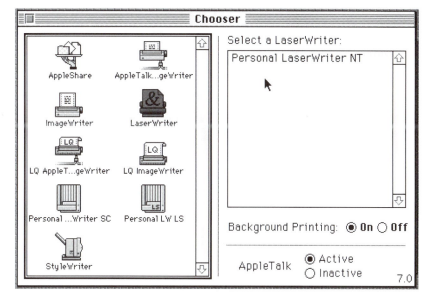

LaserWriter and compatible printers on a network. For other printers you must purchase separate spooling software to take care of this important job.

Once you have turned on Background Printing in the Chooser, you can use the PrintMonitor, a desktop accessory, to monitor the progress of your print jobs. The PrintMonitor allows you to see what document is being printed on a printer as well as a chronological list of the documents to be printed next. For more information on the Print-Monitor, see "Using the PrintMonitor" in Chapter 3.

Using a Print Server

The main problem with shared network printers is that often two or more people on the network want to print at the same time. This means that everybody is vying for the printer's attention, and somebody who has a long or complex document can hog the printer's time, to the detriment of others. Unfortunately, when this happens, your computer is forced to wait and wait until it hears that the printer is free. But you never have to wait if your network has a computer known as a *print server* to handle all requests for the printer. When a job comes in addressed to a particular printer, the print server immediately stores it on a hard disk and puts it into a queue, or waiting list. It sends the job out to the printer when it is ready for the next job. The order in which the documents are printed is first-come, first-served, so nobody is forced to wait for an unreasonable length of time. For more information on purchasing and installing a dedicated print server, see your computer dealer.

Using an ImageWriter on the Network

Most models of the ImageWriter printer cannot be networked. Although you hook the printer up to your printer port, the ImageWriter can only be used by the Mac it is hooked up to. That's because Image-Writers are *serial devices*, meaning that they communicate by sending bits of data one by one, in sequential order. They are relatively slow, to say the least.

However, some of the later ImageWriter models *can* be hooked up to your AppleTalk network and shared. You need to select the AppleTalk ImageWriter icon device driver in your Chooser before you can print to this type of printer over a network. See your printer owner's guide to determine whether your ImageWriter can be networked or not.

 ## Sharing Files on a Network

System 7 includes built-in networking features. What exactly does this mean? Well, if you are in an office hooked up to an AppleTalk network, you can share files and folders between any Macs on the network, complete with security and password protection. You can operate or run any application or program on any other Mac, while sitting in the comfort of your own easy chair. You can see what's on somebody else's hard drive, in another office, or you can use their CD-ROM drive. However, you can also limit the access other users have to your computer, and you can give some people more access than others, through password restrictions. If you give yourself access rights, you can log into your computer from anybody else's computer on the network and access any file you wish, all by using your own personal owner password. With System 7's Publish and Subscribe feature, you can create data in a document that is electronically linked across the network to other people's documents. You make a change in your data, and presto, the change is instantaneously recorded in all of your colleague's documents. Oh, it's so slick.

Distributed and Dedicated File Servers

Along with the sophisticated networking power it gives to the average user, System 7 has incorporated a feature known as *distributed file sharing*. This means that file sharing is not limited to one or two machines, but is distributed among many machines on a network. Any one user can publish the contents of his or her hard drive and make it available as a resource for anyone else on the network. At the same time, this person can keep on using the computer while others remotely access his or her machine.

Many older computer networks operate on a principle known as *dedicated file sharing*, where only a few machines, which are solely devoted to sharing files and nothing else, can act as file servers. Under this setup, network users cannot send files directly to one another; they must send and receive files through the focal point of a central file server, which serves as a storing place for documents and applications that network users can access. Novell Netware is one such example of a dedicated file server type of network.

If you want to set up your computer so that others can get access to the files on it, you must use the Network Setup control panel, as explained in the next sections of this chapter. If you are only interested in getting files from somebody else's Mac, all you need to do is log on to their computer through the Chooser. This is explained in "Getting Access to Other Users' Files" later in this chapter.

Preparing to Share Files

Before you can share files on your computer, you must establish your network identity by entering your name, password, and a name for your Mac. The reason for this is important: you want to identify your Mac on the network as belonging to you, so others can determine whether to give you access to their files. You also need to create a unique password that will protect your computer from unauthorized intrusions over the network. Only you will be able to set your computer's access privileges through this "owner" password. Data security is important if you have sensitive information that you want to restrict others from viewing.

Use the following steps to establish your network identity and start up file sharing:

1. Make sure all networking software is installed on your Macintosh. This includes the File Sharing and Network extensions, and the AppleShare, Sharing Setup, Users & Groups, and File-Sharing Monitor control panels. Use the Installer on the Install 1 disk of your system software to put all those things in the right places in your System Folder.

2. Close all applications and choose Control Panels from the Apple menu.

3. When the window opens up, double-click the Sharing Setup control panel.

4. Type your name in the Owner Name text box.

5. Press the Tab key to jump to the Owner Password text box.

6. Type in a password of up to eight characters. Choose a memorable, unique password that others can't guess. *Root*, *Fido*, and *mom* are bad passwords; *wyLE&1* and *lockMuP* were good until I blabbed them. Memorize your password carefully, including which letters are capitalized.
7. Press the Tab key to jump to the Mac Name text box. Your password turns into a row of asterisks as in Figure 20.5; you did memorize it, I hope.
8. Type in a name for your Mac. Use a distinctive name that other users will remember. For example, if your name were Nick Dargahi, you could just call your computer Nick's Macintosh.
9. Click the Start button to turn the file sharing feature on.

FIGURE 20.5
Giving yourself a network identity

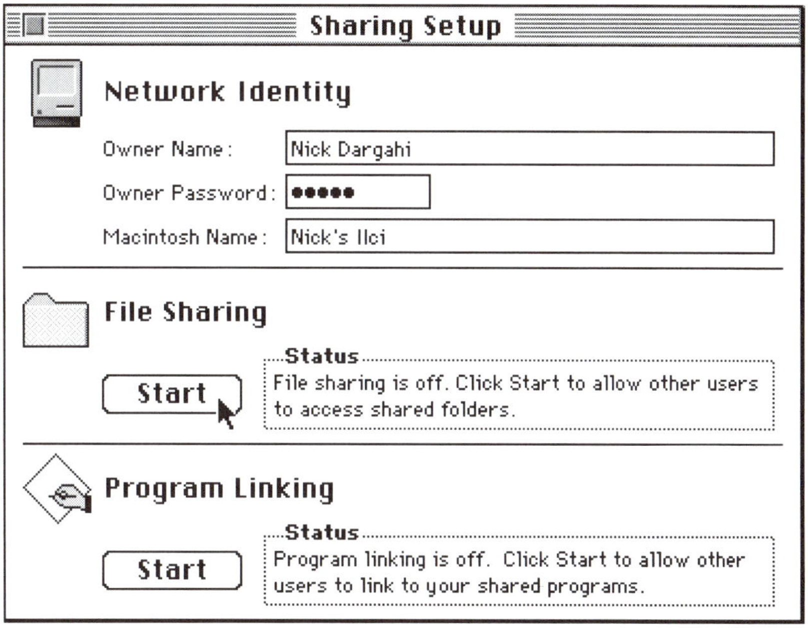

Later, if you want to disable file sharing, come back to this control panel and click the Stop button.

Setting Up Your Macintosh as a File Server

After identifying yourself and turning on File Sharing, decide which folders and/or hard disks on your computer you want to share. If you don't care about security, then you can share the entire contents of your hard disk with everyone; but if you are concerned about prying eyes, then you can selectively allow only certain folders to be shared. If you like, you can allow only one person sharing privileges, or if you prefer, you can give them to a specific group of people of your choosing. And, for even finer control, you can specify whether people can change or see any files or folders you have in your shared portions of your folders and disks. Note that you cannot share an individual file or application by itself; you can share it only if the folder or disk that contains the file or application is shared.

Sharing a Folder with Everybody

Any folder, hard disk, or CD-ROM drive that is attached to your computer can be shared over a network. If you have turned on file sharing as explained above, you can follow the procedure below to share a folder so all other network users have completely open access to it. The same procedure could be used to share a hard disk or CD-ROM drive. This is a nice, simple procedure, but you should only use it on a network where there is mutual trust among the users and no concern about outsiders gaining access to confidential files.

1. Select the folder you wish to share. For example, if I were on a product development team, I might want to share a Team projects folder on my hard disk, so other people on my product team could use the plans I had developed.

2. Select Sharing from the File menu. The sharing window appears. If the Sharing command is dimmed, it means you haven't selected a shareable item.
3. Click the box labeled "Share this item and its contents" to put an X in it, as shown in Figure 20.6. This enables file sharing.
4. Close the sharing window by clicking on the close box. A dialog box appears. It asks if you want to save your changes to access privileges for the folder.
5. Click on the Save button to confirm your choice.
6. To check and see if your folder is now available over the network, look at the folder to see if it has network cables below it, as in Figure 20.7.

FIGURE 20.6
The Sharing window

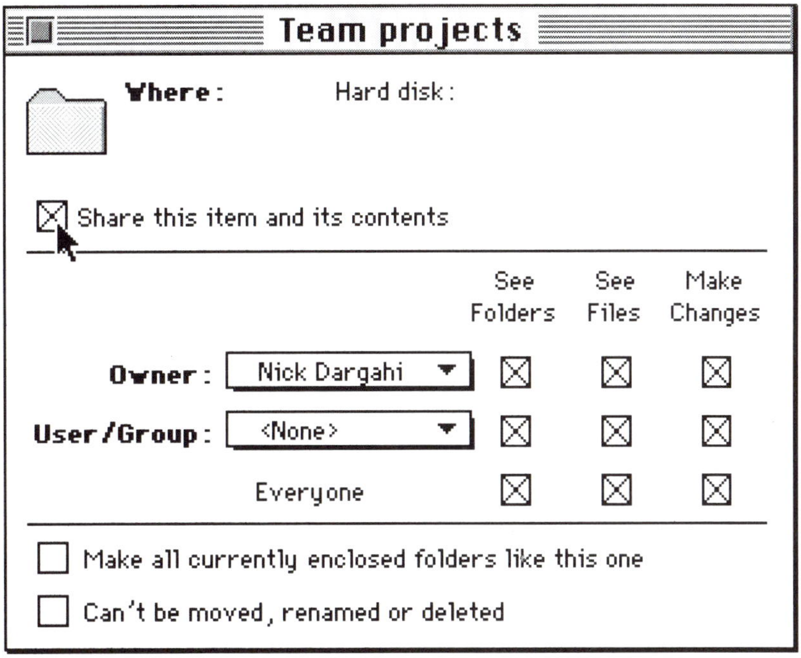

Chapter 20

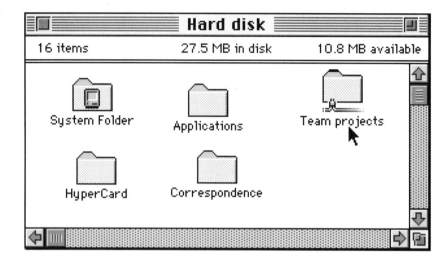

FIGURE 20.7
A shared folder

That's all there is to sharing a folder. The files within the shared folder are now freely available to everyone on the network.

If you share a disk or a CD-ROM, the disk or CD-ROM icon on your Mac does not show the cables; only your shared folders do. However, disk icons representing other computers that you are accessing over the network will show the cables to indicate that they are being networked.

If you want to name specific people to share the information in a folder, or limit what they can do with the data, you need to restrict the access rights, as explained in the next section.

Limiting Access Privileges

The System 7 networking software gives you the power to select who can use your computer remotely. You just have to name each user, give them a password, and specify what access privileges they will have to your files. There are three classes of users: guests, registered guests, and registered groups. Guests are anyone who connects to a computer without having to give a name or password. Registered guests (or registered users—the terms are interchangeable) are those whose names and passwords are recorded by your computer and who must correctly enter their name and password each time they log onto your computer. Registered groups are groups of registered guests who collectively share the same resources that other members of the group have access to. An example of this third category would be a group of designers, engineers, and writers who are working on a development project. Each member of this group would need to work with the same project information, so it makes sense to group them for common access rights.

To limit access to a shared folder, you first deny access to guests in general, then you give access rights to specified users. Start by using the following steps to deny access to unregistered guests.

1. Choose Control Panels from the Apple menu.
2. Double-click the Users & Groups control panel. Its window opens, with icons for you and an unregistered guest user, as shown in Figure 20.8.

FIGURE 20.8
Users & Groups window

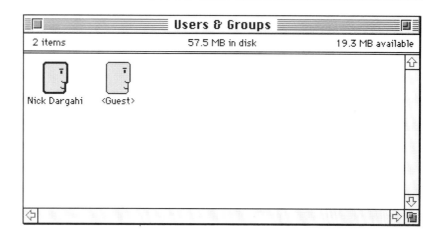

Chapter 20

3. Double-click the <Guest> icon. The Guest window opens, as in Figure 20.9.
4. Uncheck the box for allowing guests to connect to your shared folder.
5. Close the Guest window and click Save in the dialog box that asks if you want to save your changes.

Now that you have denied access to unregistered guests, take the following steps to specify the users and groups you want to give access rights to.

1. Select New User from the File menu while the Users & Groups control panel is still open. A new user icon appears in the Users & Groups window.
2. Type in the name of a user that you want to share files with. This person will become a registered guest.
3. Double-click the icon to open the user's window.
4. Type in the registered user's password and specify whether they can connect to shared files or change their own password, as shown in Figure 20.10.

FIGURE 20.9
Guest window

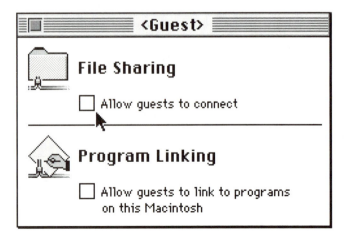

FIGURE 20.10
New registered user's control panel

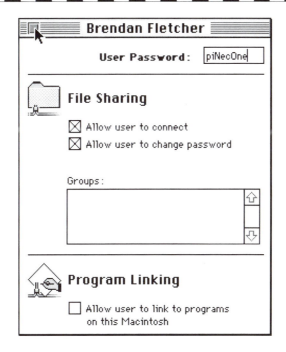

5. Close the window and click Save in the Changes dialog box. Repeat steps 1 through 5 for each registered guest you want to give access rights to.

6. When you are done with the registered guests, double-click your own icon to open the owner window, as shown in Figure 20.11. In this window you set what aspects of your computer you yourself can access from someone else's computer.

7. To give yourself the various access rights, take one of the following actions:

- Leave an X in the Allow user to connect check box to give yourself access to your computer from another machine.

FIGURE 20.11
Owner's control panel

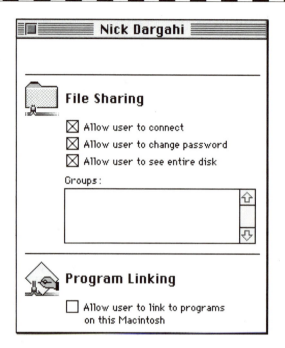

- Leave the Allow user to change password box checked if you want to be able to change your password externally from another Mac.
- Leave the Allow user to see entire disk box checked if you want complete, unrestricted access to everything on your disks, shared and unshared folders alike.

8. Close the window and click Save in the Changes dialog box.
9. To name a group of users, select New Group from the File menu while the Users & Groups control panel is still open. A new group icon appears.
10. Type in a descriptive name for the group.

11. Drag the registered users' icons to the Group icon. Each icon disappears into the Group icon momentarily; a dialog box says they are being added to the group, then the icon reappears in the Users & Groups window. All registered users inside the icon are now attached to this group name.
12. To see which users are in the group, double-click the Group icon. A window opens, showing you the group members' icons in frames. Close the window.
13. Close the Users & Groups control panel.

You are now finished naming all your guests, registered guests, and groups. Your next step is to assign privileges to the various users you have named. To define what folders or disks your users have access to, use the following procedure:

1. Select the folder, hard disk, or CD-ROM icon that you want to define access rights for.
2. Choose Sharing from the File menu. A window for the selected item appears.
3. Click in the check box for "Share this item and its contents" to put an X in the box.
4. Place the pointer on the little arrow in the User/Group text box and open the pop-up menu, as in Figure 20.12.
5. Choose the user, registered guest, or group in the menu that you want to assign sharing rights to.
6. Remove all the checks from the row of check boxes marked "Everyone" if you want *only* the group or registered guest to have access to this shared item.

Your folder is now available to the people you have specified. If new people join the group, just give them icons in the Users & Groups window, then drag their icons to the group icon.

FIGURE 20.12
Assigning access privileges

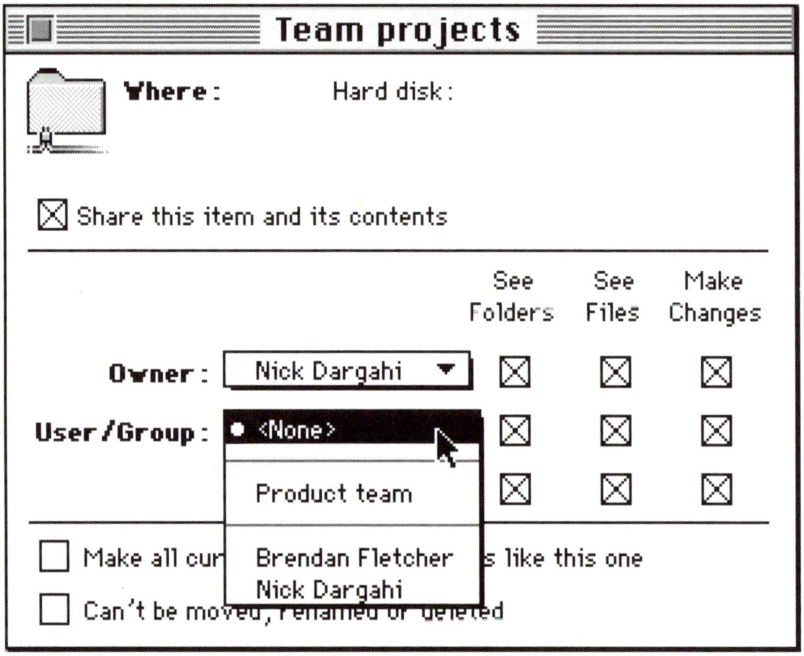

Shutting Off File Sharing on Your Computer

All you have to do to stop file sharing is click on the Stop button in the File Sharing panel of the Sharing Setup control panel. This action will prevent everyone, including yourself, from accessing your computer from another computer on the network. Your computer will be completely isolated from other users, although you will still be able to log in to other computers on the network. In other words, you will be able to see them, but they won't see you.

Getting Access to Other Users' Files

You don't need to start up sharing on your computer in order to get files from other computers on the network. All you have to do is choose the Chooser in the Apple menu, select the AppleShare icon, then choose the name of the file server and the AppleTalk zone you wish to access.

If your network has no zones (none are listed in the lower left corner of the Chooser window), you can skip this next paragraph. If you have zones, here's what they're all about. An AppleTalk zone is a group of devices that are organized by a network administrator to make the network more manageable. For example, all the Macs on the fifth floor of a company could be organized into Zone V (any name will do), while all the Macs on the sixth floor could be included in the Zone Spock. If you want to print to a LaserWriter on your floor, you select your *local* zone, the one your Macintosh is located in. The zone feature of the network helps prevent you from accidentally selecting a device that is not nearby. If you need a file server or printer in another zone, you must select the proper zone before you can see its list of computers and printers in the Chooser. If you are running an EtherTalk or Token-Talk network, you also have to select the appropriate network driver in the Network control panel.

Logging In to a File Server and Getting a File

To log in to another Mac on the network, follow these steps:

1. Select the Chooser from the Apple menu.
2. Select the AppleShare icon.
3. If you have zones and are looking for a Mac in another zone, select the appropriate zone from the list .
4. Pick the name of the Mac you wish to access in the right panel of the window, as shown in Figure 20.13.
5. Click the OK button. A dialog box appears with your name in it.
6. Enter your password, exactly as the host owner specified. If you want to change your password, click the Set Password button.

FIGURE 20.13
Using the Chooser to log on to another Macintosh file server on the network.

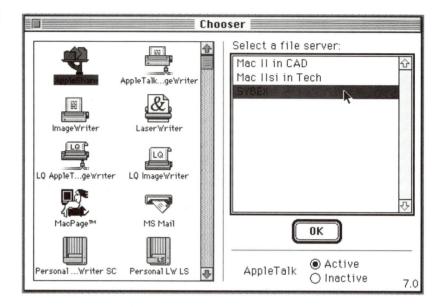

This only works if the owner has given you permission to do it. You can register as a guest if the owner permits it; otherwise the Guest option is dimmed.

7. After entering your password, click OK. A selection dialog box appears, as shown in Figure 20.14.

8. Highlight the volumes or disks that you want to use. Shift-click to select more than one disk to access at the same time.

9. Check the check box to the right of an item if you want it to open up automatically the next time you start your computer, without you having to go through the whole logging-in rigmarole. Of course, the host computer must be turned on with sharing activated before you can log on.

If you have registered as a registered user, two other radio buttons appear that allow you to control the automatic login procedure:

- Click the first button, Save My Name Only, if you want to enter your password each time your machine is started up.
- Click on the second button, Save My Name and Password, if you want to log in to the host computer without any password interruption.

The latter approach has risks; anybody who turns on your machine will be able to log in to networked file servers in your name without your permission.

11. Click OK when you are finished with all your selections.
12. Close the Chooser. In a few moments the shared disk icon appears below the icon for your hard drive. Double-click this drive icon to open up the shared disk so that you can access its files.

FIGURE 20.14
Selecting Shared Items dialog box

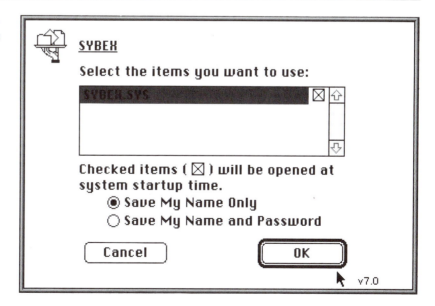

Login Shortcut: Creating Aliases

There is a neat way to automate logging in to a colleague's networked Mac: You use an alias.

What you do is simple. The first time you log on to someone's computer, follow the procedure outlined in the previous section. When you open up the shared disk icon, however, go to the file or application that you need to use and highlight it. Next, choose Make Alias from the File menu. The alias appears. Drag it to your own hard disk. The next time you want to open up the shared disk to obtain the file you just aliased, simply double-click on the alias and you will instantly be logged on to the networked drive, and the file or application will open.

Disconnecting from Someone Else's Computer

To disconnect a shared disk that you have logged on to from your computer, simply drag the icon of the disk on the right side of your desktop to the Trash. Don't worry when you do this; you are in no danger of erasing or trashing any files on the remote computer. The disk icon just vanishes from your desktop. When you no longer see the icon of the hard disk or CD-ROM, you will know that you are now disconnected from the other computer.

Linking Programs

Another new feature of System 7 is the ability to link up programs (applications) over the network to exchange information. This is called Program Linking, and in order to use this feature, you must properly configure your computer for it. Only programs that are purposely designed to take advantage of this unique new ability of System 7 can benefit. To link programs, use the following procedure:

1. Set up your Mac for network sharing, as described in the "Sharing Files on a Network" section earlier in this chapter.
2. Quit the application that created the document you want to link, if it is open. Then start up Program Linking by opening the Sharing control panel and clicking the Start button in the Program Linking portion of the window.
3. Select the program that you wish to link and choose Sharing from the File menu. The Sharing window for the program opens.
4. Check the check box labeled "Allow remote program linking."
5. Close the program's Sharing window.
6. Choose Control Panels from the Apple menu and open the Users & Groups control panel.
7. For each guest or registered user that you want to allow program linking with, double-click the guest icon to open up the icon's window and check the check box named "Allow guests to link to programs on this Macintosh." For registered users, the check box is called "Allow user to link to programs on this Macintosh."
8. Close each guest or user's window, then start up the program you wish to link.

Program linking is now enabled.

Troubleshooting Problems with Networks

The following subsections cover the problems you are most likely to have while working with your Mac on a network. If you are just connecting your Mac to a new network, especially an Ethernet one, you can expect to have a few problems with the printers and file servers. It may take some time for the network manager to adjust the network's tuning and check all of the connections. Just be patient during the first days on a new network, and you will soon be thankful for the convenience it offers once it is working smoothly.

You can't find or can't open the Sharing Setup control panel.

The networking software has not been installed correctly. Make sure the File Sharing extension and the Network extension are in the Extensions folder in your System Folder. Also make sure the Sharing Setup control panel is in the Control Panels folder in your System Folder. If one or more of these files is not where it should be, install them, then restart your Mac. You should be able to open the Sharing Setup control panel now.

The Sharing command is not available.

When you pull down the File menu to choose Sharing so you can share a folder or something, the command is dimmed. This is probably because you have not selected the folder. Select it first, then choose Sharing from the File menu.

EtherTalk icon doesn't appear in Network control panel.

The EtherTalk icon will only appear if you have an EtherTalk expansion card installed in your Mac and the EtherTalk software installed in your System Folder. Make sure your expansion card is properly installed; see the dealer for assistance if you need it. To install the EtherTalk software, use the Installer on the Install 1 disk of your system software disk set. Choose the Customize option in the Installer. For details on installing with the Customize option, see Chapter 2 of the *Macintosh Reference*.

The name or password you enter when trying to get access to shared files is not accepted.

You aren't entering the name or password the way the owner of the shared item specified. See the owner of the folder for the correct spelling. If you have permission to change your password, you can enter a new one, but make an effort to memorize it so you don't have to keep making up new ones.

You can't locate a file or folder inside a shared folder or disk.

The file may not be there anymore, or you may not have access rights to see it. Check the small icons in the upper left corner of the window to see if there is a document icon with a line through it; this little icon means that you do not have the right to see or open any of the files in the folder.

Your owner icon does not appear in the Users & Groups control panel.

You probably have not identified yourself on the network. You have to open the Sharing Setup control panel and put your name in the Name box, then enter a password and a name for your Mac as well. See "Preparing to Share Files" earlier in this chapter for details on identifying yourself to the network.

Intermittent and unpredictable network failure.

The network stops working for no apparent reason. First, see if any of the Macs on the network have crashed in the middle of a network operation. Next, check the network cable connections; the connection at the printer port on the back of each Mac is not as important as the connections of the inter-Mac cables to the connector boxes. The Macs or printers at the ends of the network must be firmly connected, however. Check to see that you have not exceeded the maximum length of cables or number of nodes on your network. See a qualified technician for recommendations.

Check to make sure all Macs on the system are using the same version of the system software, and that everyone has the same versions of the printer drivers in use.

The network is working, but you can't print or get access to anything over it.

You probably don't have something set up right on your Mac. Make sure AppleTalk is active in the Chooser if you are on an AppleTalk network. Make sure the correct network driver is installed on your Mac; the AppleShare icon or the EtherTalk or TokenTalk icon should be selected in the Chooser.

CHAPTER 21

E-Mail

Electronic mail is the easiest way to communicate with other users over a network. Once you set up an E-mail system on your network, you can exchange important messages, crucial files, and the latest gossip with anybody on the network. If your network has telephone connections and either a gateway or access to an information service such as CompuServe or MCI Mail, you can exchange E-mail with millions of users all over the world.

Electronic mail systems let you send and receive messages, but the better ones let you do a lot of other things, such as sort and store your incoming messages and keep track of your outgoing ones. The best E-mail systems do all these things quickly. If you are on an AppleTalk network, you can't expect blazing speed if you are trying to mail huge enclosures, but you can at least expect the mail server (the big Mac that runs the E-mail system) to do the work instead of your personal Mac.

Which E-Mail System for You?

There are two basic categories of electronic mail system: ones that will work on small networks, and ones that are made for large networks. On a low-end mail system, you can send one message to one other person at a time. Needless to say, this kind of mail system only makes sense on a very small network, and only if you are willing to keep track of all the messages you send and receive. This is a very limited type of mail, but if you get a file-transfer utility like Flash, which includes message sending, you can get by on a shoestring and do big file transfers without a file server, too.

For any network with more than five users, you need a better E-mail system than the one-to-one type. The high-end E-mail systems all have one powerful Mac as a *mail server*. The mail server is like the post office; it keeps track of the messages between the time you send them and somebody else reads them, so anyone can send and receive messages whenever they want.

There are a number of different ways of dividing up the work of sending, receiving, and storing E-mail messages, and you probably don't want to know all the details of the client-server relationship and whether your mail server is saving messages as separate files or in a database. Suffice it to say that some E-mail systems, such as InBox Plus, have a good interface and are easy to use, but they can be slow and cumbersome, especially if people send messages to many recipients.

Other E-mail systems, such as cc:Mail, QuickMail, and WordPerfect Office, are medium-fast performers; they are fine for most networks, but may bog down in certain heavy-use situations. As long as you don't have more than 20 users on each mail server, and as long as people aren't over-using the E-mail instead of doing their work, any medium-fast performer will work OK.

The best E-mail system I've seen is Microsoft Mail. It lets your network's big Mac mail server do all the heavy mail work, so your personal Mac never has to slow down, and it handles messages in a very elegant, efficient way, so that even if you and ten other users are addressing long letters to everybody on the net, the server keeps up with the traffic. Microsoft Mail isn't cheap, but then, it can save a lot of time and money by keeping the network working smoothly. For more details, see "Using Microsoft Mail" below.

Using Microsoft Mail

Before you can use Microsoft Mail, you have to make sure your network manager (or administrator, as they say on most networks) has set up an E-mail account for you on the network. The network manager is the person in charge of running the mail server. This person will tell you how your name is entered for your account and how to set up your password. Memorize these two things; they are your keys to the E-mail kingdom. And don't share them with others, any more than you would share your keys to your castle. Also, ask your network manager if you need to choose a zone or a particular server for your mail use. These are all things you need to know to get started on the E-mail system.

If you have not installed the Microsoft Mail software on your Mac, do so according to the instructions in the Microsoft Mail *User's Guide*. Your network manager can give you help with this installation if you need it.

Keep in mind as you do the sample exercises in this section that your network manager may set some of the preferences differently than I did, so you may see some different dialog boxes and you may have to take a step more or a step less here and there. If a step is unclear, see your Microsoft Mail *User's Guide* for details, or ask your network manager how to use the particular setup you have for E-mail.

Selecting a Mail Server

You have to tell your Mac which mail server you are going to use, even if there is only one on your network. After you choose the server once, the Mac will remember the choice so you never have to do it again. Use the following steps to pick your server:

1. Choose the Chooser from the Apple menu. Its window opens, with some icons in the left panel.

2. Click on the MS Mail icon, as shown in Figure 21.1. The names of the servers on your network appear in the list box on the right side of the Chooser window. If your network has zones, a list of zones appears below the icon panel.

3. If there is a list of zones, select the zone that has the mail server you should use; the network manager can tell you which one to use if you don't know.

4. Select your mail server in the Select a Mail Server panel.

5. Click the Set Up button. The Mail Sign-In Preferences dialog box appears, as in Figure 21.2.

6. Click the check box for the Sign in to Mail automatically setting so an X appears in it, and type in your name. Leave the radio button for the Password must be typed option selected. The other

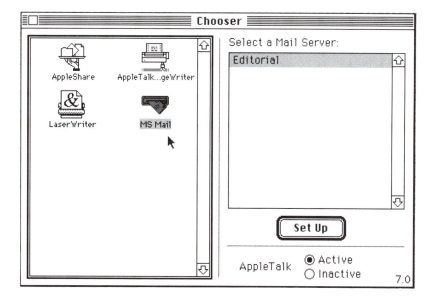

FIGURE 21.1
Selecting a mail server in the Chooser

Chapter 21

FIGURE 21.2
Setting mail sign-in preferences

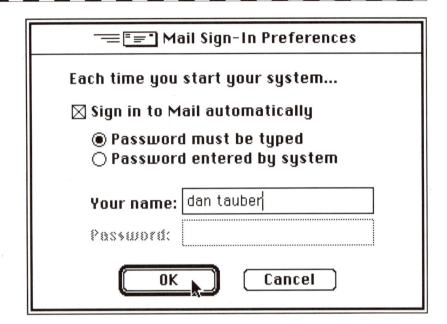

option is risky; if you select it, anybody using your Mac can get into your mail automatically.

7. Click OK to close the dialog box.

You have done all the setup you need for using Microsoft Mail. Now you can start sending those hot gossip messages to your friends. Be careful what you say on E-mail, though; it is much, much easier to copy an embarrassing E-mail message to a bunch of the wrong people than it is to have a copy of a paper letter get into the wrong hands. For more information, see the "E-Mail Etiquette" section later in this chapter.

Starting E-Mail

You can get into your mail at any time, via the Apple menu. Just follow these steps:

1. Choose Microsoft Mail from the Apple menu. The sign-in dialog box appears, as in Figure 21.3. If you are on your own Mac, your name is there already.
2. Enter your password and click OK. Your Mailbox window appears, with all the messages you have recieved listed in it, as in Figure 21.4.
3. Select a message you want to see and click the Read button at the bottom of the window, or just double-click the message. The message appears.
4. When you are done with the message, click the up or down arrows at the bottom of the message window to see other messages, or close the message window to go back to your Mailbox window.

Sending a Message

To send a mail message, you have to pick a type of message first. There are five buttons along the left side of the Mailbox window that

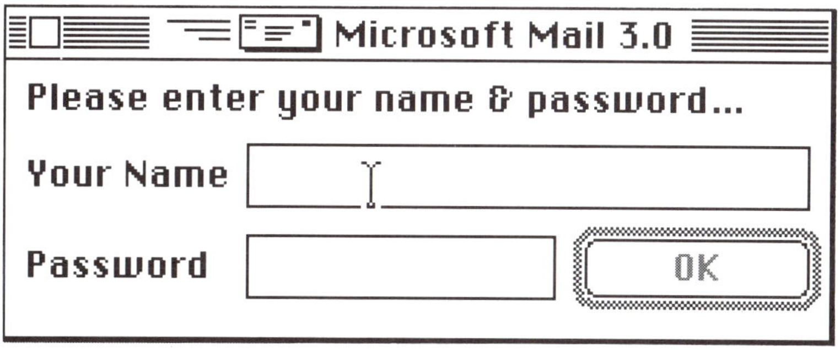

FIGURE 21.3
Signing in to Microsoft Mail

FIGURE 21.4
The Mailbox window with three messages

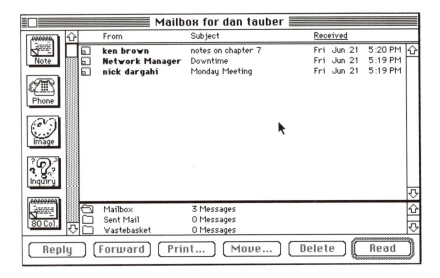

allow you to send different forms of messages. The Note form is the one you will use most. The 80-column form is good for sending E-mail via a gateway to a user on some other mail system (UNIX and DOS mail systems often use 80-column format).

To send a short message, just follow these steps:

1. Click the Note icon on the left side of the Mailbox window. The Address Mail dialog box appears, as in Figure 21.5.
2. Click the name of a user you want to send the message to.
3. Click Add to add the user to the list of recipients.
4. If you want people to receive copies of the letter, even if it isn't addressed directly to them, you have two options:

   - Click Cc in the Add as box if you want them to get a carbon copy.
   - Click Bcc if you want them to get a "blind" copy without anyone else knowing they got it.

FIGURE 21.5
Choosing recipients for a message

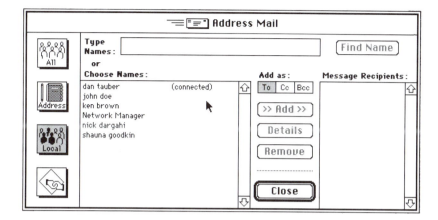

5. If you want to see address lists other than the one with all users on the network, click the Address button (for your personal list), the Local button (for users on your server), or any special button you have (for external users).
6. Click Close to finalize your addressing. The Send Note window appears.
7. Enter a subject for your note; keep it short and to the point.
8. Enter your message. You don't have to use salutation and sign-off lines to begin and end your message, as shown in Figure 21.6, but it helps identify both the recipient and you if they forward your message later.
9. Click the Options button to see the options shown in Figure 21.7:

- Urgent displays the message immediately, if the proper feature is enabled on the recipient's Mac.
- Return receipt informs you when your message has been read.

FIGURE 21.6
Writing a note

FIGURE 21.7
Options for sending mail

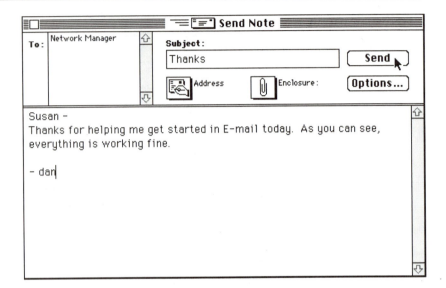

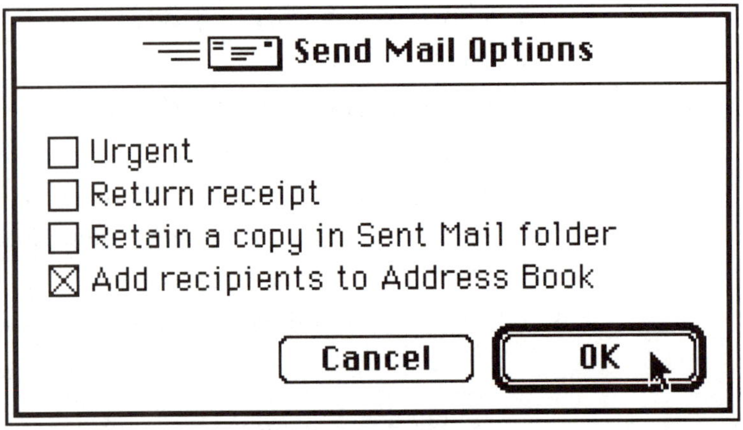

- Retain a copy in Sent Mail folder keeps a copy so you know what you sent.
- Add recipients to Address Book adds the users' names to your private address list.

Click OK when you've chosen your option.

10. You can attach any document file created in any Mac application to your note. Just click the paper clip icon. An Open-type dialog box appears. Find and select the file you want to enclose in the file list box, and click the Add button to put it on the Enclosures list. Then click Done. Send attached files only to other Microsoft Mail users; they can't be read by other mail systems.
11. Click Send to mail the message.

When you send a message, it goes to the mail server, and the server sends a reminder to the recipient. If the system is set up so the recipents see these reminders, a reminder box appears, like the one in Figure 21.8. The recipient can read the note immediately or later.

If you decide you don't want to send a message, you can close the Send Note window before you click the Send button. The Mail program

FIGURE 21.8
A mail reminder dialog box

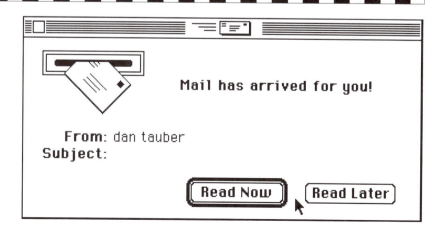

warns you that you'll lose the stuff in the window if you close it. Just click OK and it all goes away.

Replying to a Message

To begin a reply to a message in your mailbox, just click the Reply button, whether you are looking at the Mailbox window or reading the message itself.

A reply window appears, with the text of the message and a header telling who the letter was from, the subject of the letter, and the other users it was addressed to. The Subject box for the reply contains the subject of the original letter, with the letters *RE* in front of it. The cursor appears in a blank space above the header, as shown in Figure 21.9. Enter your reply, then click Send.

You can either append the original message or leave it out of your reply. You can also address the reply to all original recipients. To set these options, choose Preferences from the Mail menu, click the Other

FIGURE 21.9
Replying to a message

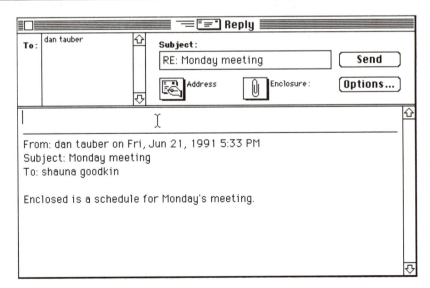

icon, and check or uncheck the check boxes for the appending and addressing replies.

Using E-Mail inside Other Applications

A number of Macintosh applications, such as PageMaker, Excel, and Microsoft Word, have built-in support for Microsoft Mail. This means you can send and receive documents as enclosures without having to do any file transfer procedure.

For example, if you have connected your Mac to a mail server and chosen it in the Chooser, any copy of Microsoft Word you run will have the Open Mail and Send Mail options available in the File menu. If you want to mail a document to a coworker, just take these steps:

1. Open the document you want to send as you would open any Word document.
2. Choose Send Mail from the File menu. The Address Mail dialog box appears.
3. Select the user or users you want to mail the document to, and click Add.
4. Click Close when you have the recipients listed. A Send Document window opens. Your current document is listed as an enclosure already.
5. Click in the message box if you want to add a note to the recipients of the document.
6. Click Send. Mail tells you that it is taking the document to the server.

That's all you have to do. The recipients can open the message in Mail and save the document to any folder, or they can open it directly from Microsoft Word. Oh, it's a great bit of office communication. Never again will you have to use the old sneaker-net, which required that you make a floppy of a document, put on your sneakers, and run over to your coworker's desk to deliver it.

Quitting Mail and Signing Off

There are two ways to get out of Mail, and you should pick one or the other, depending on whether you are going to be the next one that goes into E-mail from your computer.

If you are going to continue working on the computer, and no one else is going to have access to it if you leave for lunch or something, you can just choose Quit from the File menu in Mail. But this is a little risky. Anybody can come up to your Mac if you step out, and choose Microsoft Mail from the Apple menu. Then they can read all your gossip.

If other users have access to your Mac, you should sign off of the mail server. Choose Close & Sign Out from the Mail menu. The next time you or anybody else opens Mail, the name and password dialog box appears, so the user must sign in properly.

Mail Etiquette

As more and more people have begun to use E-mail, certain customs and unwritten rules have developed to make communicating easier and more pleasant. The most important things for you to keep in mind as you write and read mail are these:

- Don't be rude. You are sending messages to a person, not a computer.
- Write in an informal manner. E-mail should be clear and easy to read, so it helps communication rather than hindering it.
- Keep your messages short and to the point. Brief messages encourage quick replies.
- Don't over-quote messages when you reply. Although most E-mail systems make it easy for you to include the original

message in your reply, your correspondent doesn't want to reread the whole message. Just quote the parts of it that you are commenting on, and delete the rest.

- Don't under-quote messages. It is just as rude to pull tiny bits of a message out of context and misuse them in a heated response.
- Respond to important inquiries, even if simply to acknowledge receipt. If you don't have time to make a full response, just state that you got the inquiry and will look into it.

Finally, don't get upset and send an angry reply if you get a message with a little collection of funny symbols at the end of it. Symbols such as :-) are just clever homemade icons thought up by folks who are stuck on systems that don't have graphic interfaces like the Mac. If you look at each symbol sideways you can figure out what kind of face it is supposed to be. The one above is a smiley face; it indicates that the writer of the message wants you to take the message lightly, or as a joke. The sad face :-(indicates the writer is unhappy about something. Other symbols have more esoteric meanings, but you get the idea.

 ## Using Information Services

Even if your Mac isn't connected to a network, you can still send E-mail to millions of people all over the world. All you need is a modem, some terminal software such as Microphone, Zterm, or Smartcom, and an account on an information service, and you can send your E-Mail over the phone lines. Just remember that the slower your modem is, and the longer your E-mail messages are, the more you're going to pay to the service and your phone company.

CompuServe

CompuServe is one of the largest information services available. It serves all kinds of computer users and allows you to send and receive E-mail, take information off huge databases, get into bulletin-board discussions, and download public domain software and shareware.

Once you connect to CompuServe, all you have to do to get into E-mail is type **go mail**. A menu for the CompuServe mail system appears. You can also purchase a program from CompuServe that makes the interface more Mac-like, with standard pull-down menus and dialog boxes.

CompuServe's E-mail system has lots of nifty little features, like Congressgrams, which lets you send a telegram to your Representative or Senator, right from your Mac. The only problem with CompuServe is that it has so many tantalizing features you can easily waste hours wandering around inside it.

There is another information service that is comparable to CompuServe but not quite so vast. It is called America Online, and the interface is so Mac oriented, it can almost be tiresome. There are shortcuts you can learn to get around all the friendly sights and sounds, however, and many Mac fanatics prefer it.

MCI Mail

MCI Mail is designed for one thing: E-mail. Once you have an MCI Mail account, you can send E-mail not only to MCI Mail users, but CompuServe users and people on Internet—the network used by most universities and research facilities around the world.

Internet connections require a different form of addressing than you use in normal E-mail, and if you plan to do a lot of communication over this wonderful tool of the research community, you should learn how to address mail properly. For details, read the book with an odd, but very apt title: *!%@:: A Directory of Mail Addressing and Networks*, by Donnalyn Frey and Rick Adams, published by O'Reilly and Associates.

From MCI Mail you can also send E-mail direct to any telex machine or fax machine in the world. This is a very powerful communication tool.

You can also purchase a Microsoft Mail gateway, such as CommGATE, that lets you send and receive E-mail from all over the world and read it in your Mail program just like E-mail from your coworkers.

Public Access Systems

Many grass-roots, decentralized computer network systems have sprung up all over America, such as San Francisco's Wetware Diversions. In addition to offering public messages like most bulletin boards run by local user groups and information services, these large systems usually offer E-mail connections to other systems and to Internet. Public access systems don't guarantee quick or infallible delivery of E-mail, but they are much less expensive than the large commercial services.

Troubleshooting E-Mail Problems

The following subsections cover the problems you are most likely to encounter when using electronic mail. Many of the problems only occur if you are sending and receiving mail from remote systems that are running on different platforms, such as VAX, DOS, and UNIX.

Mail is returned to sender, or bounced.

This usually happens when you send mail to a nonexistent recipient. In Microsoft Mail you see a dialog box with "Return to

Sender" stamped across the top. Other E-mail systems send you a message from the mail daemon (the program that manages mail) or the gateway with a subject that says "returned mail." If you are sending mail to someone on your network, you probably just entered their name wrong. When you send E-mail to someone on a remote system, it is common for many computers to transfer the message along the way. Any one of these computers will bounce the message back if it doesn't know where to send the message next. The top few lines of the bounced message should contain the name of the computer that returned the mail. The easiest solution to the problem is to telephone the recipient and ask them for a different routing, or ask your network manager about different gateways you might use.

E-mail enclosure files arrive corrupted.

Someone sent you an enclosure, and when you open it, part or all of it has turned into gibberish. Unfortunately, the general rule is that you cannot send binary files, like Excel spreadsheets or Quicktime movies, through gateways. You can always try it and see what happens, but the chances are not good for a perfect file transfer. A lot of E-mail systems still use 7-bit data links to transfer messages. While 7-bit links are fine for text, they destroy any binary data sent over them.

International or special Macintosh characters disappear from a message.

This problem is probably caused by sending a message over a data link that does not support binary data. Unfortunately, there is not a lot you can do to fix the problem, other than avoid using the characters. If you have a different gateway available to you, you can try sending the message over it.

Mail arrives with lines truncated.

Many E-mail systems cannot deal with lines longer than 80 characters. They just remove all the text beyond the 80th character in each line. Microsoft Mail includes a special 80-column form for sending E-mail to such systems.

End of E-mail message is missing.

This is due to the fact that many E-mail systems have a maximum message size. If your message is too long, the remote system may cut off the ending. In Microsoft Mail, the network manager can set the maximum size for messages. The default size is one megabyte, more than enough for the longest memo or the entire text of this book. Many other systems use 64K as the maximum message size. If you don't know what the maximum size is for a remote system, assume that it is 64K.

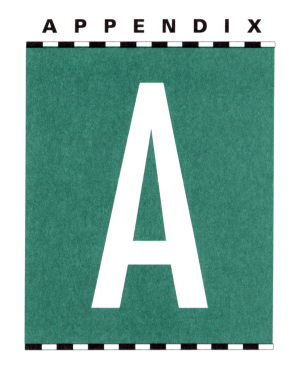

APPENDIX A

Graphics
File Formats

Table A.1 below summarizes the compatibility of the most common graphics file formats with the major graphics applications described in this book. The formats, starting with the lowest resolution and working up, are defined as follows:

- MacP (MacPaint): The original Macintosh paint format; 72-dpi resolution, black and white images. Widely supported, even by DOS graphics and publishing applications. Prints on many printers, but jagged.
- PICT (Picture): Format for many object-oriented draw-type graphics. PICT 2 can be high resolution and color, but the format does not do well in publishing applications or on non-PostScript printers.
- EPS (Encapsulated PostScript): Format for high-end drawing and illustrating applications. Each image has a low-resolution screen version and a high-resolution PostScript code. Widely supported by desktop publishing for PostScript printers; not good for scanned images or color bit maps, and non-PostScript printers can only print the low-resolution screen version.
- TIFF (Tagged Image File Format): Bit-mapped format that can be any size and resolution. The higher the resolution and the more color/grayscale involved, the more gigantic the files. Widely used, in compressed forms, by publishing applications in both Mac and DOS worlds. Most high-resolution printers do well with TIFF.

TABLE A.1: Compatibility of Major Graphics File Formats

APPLICATION	IMPORT/ OPEN	EDIT/CREATE	EXPORT
Adobe Illustrator	EPS, MacP, PICT	EPS	EPS, PICT
Aldus Freehand	MacP, PICT, TIFF	EPS, PICT	EPS, PICT
Aldus PageMaker	Place: MacP, EPS, PICT, TIFF	Resize: MacP, some PICT, EPS, TIFF	PICT via Clipboard
Aldus SuperPaint	MacP, EPS, PICT, TIFF	EPS, TIFF. Resize only: EPS	EPS, PICT, TIFF
Claris MacDraw Pro	PICT	MacP, PICT. Resize only: EPS	EPS, PICT

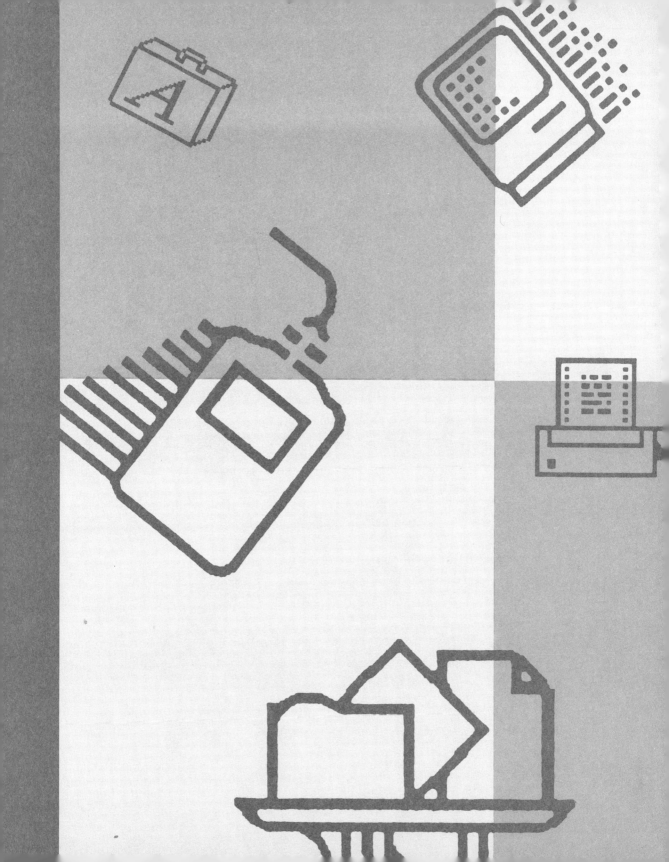

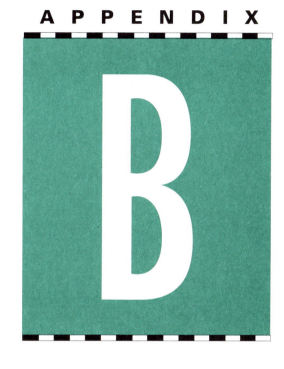

APPENDIX B

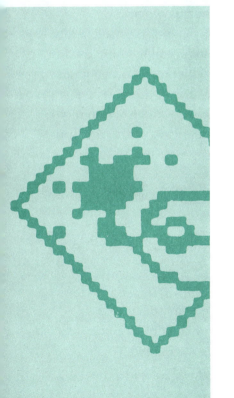

Intalling the
System Software on
a Customized Mac

If you have done a lot of work to customize your System Folder, adding special fonts and sounds, adding special customizing files and control panels, and setting up your Apple menu and lots of application preferences, you don't want to lose all these specifications and customizing files when you install System 7. If you just run the Installer program that comes with the new system software, you can be sure it is going to clobber most of your customizing work.

To avoid this catastrophe, do not install System 7 as instructed by Apple in their installation procedure, and do not install by using the Installer. Instead, use the following procedure, which saves all your custom files and preferences, and puts them back into the new System Folder after you have installed Apple's system software. Keep in mind as you do this procedure, though, that the goal is to put as much of Apple's new software in the System Folder as possible, and to merely add your customizing stuff on top of that base.

To install new system software and preserve your customizing, follow these steps:

1. Start up your Mac using a floppy startup disk, such as the Disk Tools disk that you get with the system software set.

2. Open the System Folder on your hard disk. If you have lots of special fonts (or only a few fonts because you use Suitcase) in the System file, drag that file out of the system folder into a folder that you name something like "Sys file in Here."

3. Drag the Finder from your hard disk's System Folder to the Trash.

4. Change the name of your System Folder to something like "Old system folder."
5. Get out all your system software disks and restart your Mac, inserting Install 1 at the startup beep or chime.
6. Click OK in the Installer's welcome screen. When the Easy Install dialog box appears, you can do a full, easy install, or a custom install, depending on your situation:

    - If you have enough disk space or aren't sure which drivers you're going to need for printers and/or networking, click Install in the Easy Install dialog box.
    - If you want to save space on your hard disk and you know what printer and/or network drivers you need, click Customize, Shift-click the things you need to install, then click Install button.

7. Feed the Mac the disks it asks for, until you see the message box telling you that installation was successful.
8. Click the Quit button and restart your Mac on the new system software.
9. Open the new System Folder and your old System Folder; place and size the windows so you can see both at once.
10. Choose by Name from the Views menu when each window is active, so you can compare the contents.
11. Drag your custom files from the old System Folder to the new one, but do so carefully. Close the new System Folder each time you want to add a new file, and drag the file to the System Folder icon, so the file gets put in the right place inside the System Folder. Add your special custom extensions and control panels, and all the preference files for your applications and utilities, but do NOT copy over any files that Apple has just installed. For example, don't copy old extensions like your printer

drivers and the PrintMonitor over the new ones. Leave the new Apple control panels and Apple Menu items in place, too.

12. Close the old System Folder and open the old System file and the new System file, so you can see what's in both windows.

13. Close the new System file and System Folder and drag your special custom fonts and sounds (if you have any in the old System file) to the new System Folder. Do not copy over any of the Chicago, Geneva, and Monaco font resource files that have size numbers after the titles. Leave the Indigo sound, too. If you are using Suitcase and PostScript fonts, you don't have to do this step: just drag all the TrueType fonts in the new System file to the Trash.

14. Restart your Mac.

You now have all new versions of the Apple system software, including fonts, extensions, control panels, and Apple menu items. To this base you have added your fonts, your custom files, and the preferences for your applications and utilities.

If you have problems with some of your custom files not working, try reinstalling fresh copies of the latest versions to make sure your old version wasn't corrupted. Also, make sure you have the version that is the most likely to work with the new system software.

Index

!%@:: *A Directory of Mail Addressing and Networks* (Frey and Adams), 523
****, in spreadsheet cells, 319
####, in spreadsheet cells, 319
⌘ key (Command key), 37

A

About This Macintosh command (Apple menu), 39
About This Macintosh window (Finder), 154, 159
absolute cell referencing
    in Excel, 301–302
    in Resolve, 314–315
accented characters, printing, 79
access privileges
    assigning to users, 497
    limiting on networks, 492–497
    to your own computer, 495–496
active window, 40–41
ADB socket, 16
Address Book, for Microsoft Mail, 517
Address Book Plus, 413
Adobe Illustrator, 216–217, 232–252. *See also* Illustrator
Adobe Type Manager (ATM), 75–76, 81, 411, 414–415, 426–428
    and jagged characters, 435
    troubleshooting problems with, 83
After Dark, 413
Alarm Clock, 166, 413
Aldus Personal Press, 257
alert boxes, 43–45
    bomb, 50, 132
    emptying Trash and, 42
alert sound. *See* beep
aliases, 166
    in Apple Menu Items folder, 100–101
    for application, 94
    for automating login procedure, 502
    finding originals for, 156
    of folders, 400
    in Startup Items folder, 167
America Online, 168, 522
American Cartridge Recycling Association, 65
Antitoxin, 441
antiviral utilities, 441–442
Apple Desktop Bus (ADB) icon, 15
Apple HD SC Setup program, 130
Apple menu
    About This Macintosh command, 39
    vs. Applications menu, 100–101
    Chooser, 499. *See also* Chooser (Apple menu)
    Control Panels, 24, 157, 168–169. *See also* Control Panels (Apple menu)
    creating hierarchy in, 398–401
    Key Caps, 78–79, 82
    opening applications from, 100–101
    Scrapbook, 379
    Suitcase, 411, 420, 426
Apple Menu Items folder, 165–166
Apple Personal LaserWriter, printing checks on, 365
AppleShare icon, 59
AppleTalk network, 476, 477
    features of, 477–478
    printer for, 57
    for printer connection, 59–61
    server for, 11–12
    setting up, 479–480
AppleTalk zone, 499
application disks, 137
application icons, dragging document icon over, 95
"Application is busy or missing" message, 134, 145–146
applications, 90–91
    backup copies of, 133, 137–139
    copying between, 376–378
    cutting, copying, and pasting between, 373–381
    E-mail support in, 519–520
    hiding windows of, 102–103
    installing, 92–93

managing, 100–103
memory for, 39, 154–157, 434
opening, 94
opening document from, 95
opening from Apple menu, 100–101
opening multiple documents in, 104
placement on Apple menu, 101
quitting, 51, 109–110
restarting to free memory, 160
specifying for startup, 166–167
switching between, 101–103
troubleshooting problems with, 108–110
unavailable, 109
unexpected quitting of, 161
Applications menu
   vs. Apple menu, 100–101
   Finder. *See* Finder (Applications menu)
   Hide Others, 101, 103, 121
   Scrapbook, 166, 378–380, 387
ATM. *See* Adobe Type Manager (ATM)
audio output plugs, 16

B

background printing, 60–61, 69, 232, 484–485
Background Printing (Chooser), 69
Backmatic, 443
backup copies, 97, 100, 132–133
   of application and system disks, 137–139
   of files, 22
backup process
   daily and partial, 451
   major, 448–451
   utilities for, 442–443. *See also* Fastback Plus; Redux

battery, for portable Macintosh, 13
BeagleWorks, 292
beep (alert sound), 47, 176
   dialog box and, 44
   setting, 177
Before You Install System 7 disk, 20
bit-mapped fonts, 75, 77
bit-mapped graphics
   jagged text in, 252
   moving part of, 223
   painting programs for, 215
bit-mapped resource files, 417
black and white, setting display for, 172
blend tool (Illustrator), 246
blends, creating and hiding, 245–247
Blesser, 27
block of text. *See* selected text
bomb alert box, 50, 132
bombs, 161–162, 406–407
brightness control, 24, 172
Browse mode (FileMaker Pro), 332
bytes, 126

C

cables
   for AppleTalk network, 478
   connections of, 505
   for hard disk, 143
   for network, 481
cache. *See* disk cache
calculation of formulas, manual or automatic, 320
canceling print job, 69
"Cannot resolve circular reference" message, 320
Canvas, 215
Capture, 413
cards (HyperCard), 464

Caution icon, 45
cc:Mail, 509
CDEVs, 20, 161, 164
CD-ROM drives, sharing, 490, 492
cells, in spreadsheets, 293, 307
centered text
   in MacWrite II, 206
   in Microsoft Word, 197
Central Processing Unit (CPU), 5
characters
   printing accented, 79
   uneven spacing of, 436
charts
   in Excel, 303–305, 320–321
   in Resolve, 317
check register. *See* register (Quicken)
Checkbook II, 351
checks from Quicken
   printing, 364–366
   voiding, 359
   writing, 361–363
   writing with memorized transactions, 364
Chicago font, 416–417, 433
Chooser (Apple menu), 499
   Background Printing, 69
   closing, 60
   for Microsoft Mail, 510–511
   printers in, 58–62, 80, 484
circular networks, 480
ClarisWorks, 292
Clean Up Window, 52
cleaning hard disk vents, 131
cleaning mouse, 48–49
Cleaning Page document, 66
clicking, 35
   troubleshooting problems with, 46–47
ClickPaste, 380
clip art, 215, 256

Clipboard, 373–374
    copying graphic to, 73
    for customizing icons, 180
    file for, 166
    losing information on, 195
    size of data in, 160
    undoing mistakes on, 381
clock, 12- or 24-hour, 171
closed paths, 216, 236
    filling with gray shades, 244–245
    matching, 240–244
    paint can for, 229–230
    splitting into two shapes, 237–239
closing Chooser, 60
closing control panels, 179
closing window, 41
coaxial cables, 481
color
    control panel settings for, 172–174
    custom, 174
column guides, in PageMaker, 284
columns
    creating in PageMaker, 266
    hiding with Views control panel, 107
    inserting in Resolve spreadsheet, 311
    missing from list view window, 181
    problems in PageMaker, 285
Command key (⌘ key), 37
commands, selecting from menus, 36–37
CommGATE, 523
compact Macintosh, 8
Compatibility Checker, 21, 168
Complete Undelete (Microcom 911 Utilities), 444
CompuServe, 508
    E-mail on, 522

extensions and control panels from, 168
confidential files, on networks, 490
Contents card, Compatibility Checker, 21
Control Panels (Apple menu), 24, 157, 168–169
    ATM, 427
    Keyboard, 175–176
    Memory, 179
    Mouse, 176
    Network, 483
    Network Setup, 487–488
    Sound, 176–177
    Users & Groups, 493
    Views, 177–179
control panels, 20, 164, 168–179
    for brightness, 172
    for color, 172–174
    closing, 179
    default settings for, 84
    General Controls, 170–171
    problems from, 161–162, 181–182, 406–407
Control Panels folders, 166–167
Copy (Edit menu), 73
copying
    document parts between applications, 376–378
    entire floppy disk, 139–140
    text, for moving, 192
    to and from floppy disks, 135
Courier font, 73
cover page, printing, 69
CPU (Central Processing Unit), 5
Create Publisher (Edit menu), 385
cursor, 5, 35
customer support, information for, 52
customization, 164–182
    of icons, 179–180
    and System 7 installation, 532–534

troubleshooting problems with, 180–182
customizing files, 20, 164, 167–169
    and bombs, 161
    memory for, 160
cutting and pasting, 373–381

D

daisy chain network, 479–480
damaged disks, 146
DAs. *See* desk accessories
data, 5
data disks, 137
data entry. *See also* editing
    in Excel, 294–296
    in FileMaker Pro, 332–333
    in HyperCard, 467–469
    in MacWrite II, 202–203
    in Microsoft Word, 191
    in Resolve, 308–310
data integration, 372–389
    cutting, copying, and pasting, 373–381
    links for dynamic updating, 381–384
    publishing and subscribing, 384–386
    troubleshooting problems with, 386–389
data protection utilities, 440–462
data security, 488. *See also* passwords
data sharing, 476–477. *See also* networks
database applications, 324–348. *See also* FileMaker Pro
    choosing, 325–329
    troubleshooting problems with, 347–348

databases
    design of, 329–330, 340
    header in layout of, 344
    moving through, 334–335
dates, 171
Date view of documents and
    folders, 106
DayMaker, 413
dedicated file servers, 487
defragmentation of disks, 412, 428
    for hard disks, 133–134
    rebuilding desktop after, 432
    for startup disk, 437
deleting files, 42–43
    recovery from, 43, 451–454
deleting text, 38
    in MacWrite II, 204
    in Microsoft Word, 192
dependent documents, 381, 387
desk accessories, 20, 411, 413
desktop, 32–34, 165
    color of, 174
    in file hierarchy, 112–113
    folders on, 114
    help for, 39
    icons on, 52, 143, 149
    insertion point on, 37
    pattern for, 171, 413
    rebuilding, 131–132, 143, 145
    rebuilding after defragmenta-
        tion, 432
    settings for, 170
    troubleshooting problems
        with, 46–53
    view of documents and folders
        on, 105–106
desktop publishing, 256. *See also*
    Pagemaker
DeskWriter, 57, 63–64
device drivers for printers, 484
dialog boxes, 43–45
    exiting, 44

for installing applications, 92
dimmed commands, 36–37
Dimmer, 413
directories, rebuilding with Redux,
    462
disconnecting from remote com-
    puter, 502
Disinfectant, 168, 442, 447
disk cache
    adjusting, 157–159
    memory for, 133
    reducing size of, 160
    setting, 179
Disk Clinic, 444
disk crash, 144–145
Disk Doctor (Norton Utilities),
    146–148, 443–444,
    458–459
Disk First Aid, 146–148, 443
disk icon
    question mark on, 26–27
    with X, 25–26
disk information header, turning
    off and on, 178
Disk Tools, 26, 130, 145
disk windows, hierarchies inside,
    114
DiskExpress II, 134, 412
DiskFit, 443
disks, 6, 124–150. *See also* defrag-
    mentation of disks; floppy
    disks; hard disks
    checking capacity of, 142
    damaged, 146–147
    defective, 436–437
    full, 144
    name of, 135
    selecting, 127–128
display screen. *See* monitor
distributed file servers, 487
document icons, dragging over ap-
    plication icon, 95

documents, 90–91. *See also* open-
    ing documents
    attaching to E-mail, 517
    Cleaning Page, 66
    cutting and pasting to move
        parts of, 374–375
    finding, 103–104
    management of, 103–108
    naming, 97, 224
    saving, 97–100
    selecting in multiple folders,
        107–108
    specifying for startup, 166–167
    switching between, 104
    troubleshooting problems
        with, 108–110
    viewing on Desktop, 105–106
domestic keyboard, 172
Domestic U.S. Keyboard file,
    keystrokes for accented
    characters, 79
DOS mail systems, 514
dot-matrix printers, 58
double-clicking, 36
    to open applications, 94
    settings for, 176
    troubleshooting problems
        with, 47
drag-and-drop method, for
    moving text, 192
dragging icons, 36
draw layer, in SuperPaint, 230–231
driver software, 128, 484
dynamic updating. *See* links

E

Easy Install screen, 22
Edit menu
    Copy, 73
    Create Publisher, 384–385

Paste, 180
Paste Special, 382
Subscribe to, 384, 386
Undo, 210, 381
Edit menu (Excel)
  Fill Right, 301
  Insert, 297
Edit menu (FileMaker Pro), New Layout, 342
Edit menu (Illustrator)
  Bring To Front, 250
  Preferences, 236
  Undo, 248
Edit menu (Kid Pix), Undo, 219
Edit menu (Microsoft Word), 194–195
  Clear, 195
  Undo, 193
Edit menu (PageMaker), Edit story, 285
Edit menu (Quicken)
  Delete Transaction, 359, 362
  Edit transaction, 364
  New Transaction, 357
  Void Transaction, 359
Edit menu (SuperPaint), Undo, 229
editing
  in MacWrite II, 203–204
  in Microsoft Word, 192–193
  saving documents during, 98
editions
  creating, 385
  determining updating of, 388
  problems subscribing to, 388
Eject Disk (Special menu), 140
ejection of floppy disks, 19, 126, 135
electronic bulletin boards, extensions and control panels from, 168
electronic mail. *See* E-mail
E-mail. *See also* Microsoft Mail

attaching document files to, 517
enclosure files in, 524
etiquette for, 520–521
maximum message size for, 525
selecting system for, 508–509
starting in Microsoft Mail, 513
troubleshooting problems with, 523–525
Empty Trash (Special menu), 42
Encapsulated PostScript (EPS) format, 216, 528
enclosure files, in E-mail, 524
enlargements in printing, 71
entry bar, in spreadsheets, 294–295, 308
entry of text. *See* data entry
envelopes, printing, 344–345
EPS (Encapsulated PostScript) format, 216, 528
Erase (Special menu), 142
eraser options, in Kid Pix, 219
erasing floppy disks, 142
ERR 46, in Resolve, 321
Ethernet network, 10, 476
  features of, 478
  interface card for, 481
  server for, 11, 12
EtherTalk icon, in Network control panel, 504
EtherTalk network, 499
  installing drivers for, 482–483
  selecting connection for, 483–484
  setting up, 481–484
EtherTalk protocol, 478
Excel, 291–306
  absolute cell referencing in, 301–302
  charts in, 303–305
  data entry in, 294–296
  E-mail support in, 519–520
  fill function in, 301

formatting numbers in, 298–299
formulas in, 299–301
inserting rows in, 297–298
manual or automatic formula calculation in, 320
opening spreadsheets in, 293
range selection in, 298–299
removing gridlines in, 319
saving and printing in, 305–306
and subscribing problems, 388
totals in, 302–303
type style and format in, 296–297
expansion cards, 504
  installing, 16
  NuBus, problems with, 28
expansion slot, 9–11, 16
extensions, 20, 164, 168
  changing name of, 182
  disabling during startup, 169
  problems from, 169, 181–182, 406–407
Extensions folder, 167
Extensions Manager, 182
external hard disks, 128, 130

F

fanfold paper, 67
fans, 7, 23
Fast Find (Norton Utilities), 395–398
  problems with, 407
Fastback Plus, 443, 448–454
  problems with, 461–462
fiber optical cables, 481
fields, in FileMaker Pro, 329–330
file compression, 448
File Force (Acius), 328
File menu
  Find, 110, 120

Find Again, 120
Get Info, 122, 155–156, 180, 418
Links, 388
Make Alias, 94
New, 97
New Folder, 37, 138, 415
New Group, 496–497
New User, 494
Open, 45, 95
Open Mail, 519
Print, 68
Print Window, 72
Put Away, 43, 135, 149
Save, 98, 231
Save As, 45, 99, 210
Send Mail, 519
Sharing, 491, 497, 503–504
File menu (Excel), Print Preview, 306
File menu (FileMaker Pro)
　Page Setup, 345
　Save Copy As, 346
File menu (HyperCard), Save a Copy, 468
File menu (Illustrator), Save, 251
File menu (MacWrite II)
　Print, 208
　Save, 208
　Undo, 204
File menu (Microsoft Word)
　Print, 200
　Save, 200
File menu (PageMaker), Place, 268
File menu (Quicken), Print Checks, 366
file recovery utilities, 443–444
file servers, 481–482
　distributed and dedicated, 487
　logging on to, 499–501
　setting up Macintosh as, 490
file sharing, 486–503
　shutting off, 498

File Sharing (Sharing Setup control panel), 160, 498
File Sharing extension, 504
FileMaker Pro (Claris), 328–348
　creating fields in, 331–332
　creating mailing with, 341–346
　finding records in, 337–338
　layout mode in, 338–339
　opening documents in, 330–331
　record entry in, 332–333, 339–340
　saving and printing in, 346
　sorting records in, 335–337
　Toolbar in, 334–335
　troubleshooting problems with, 347–348
files, 91. *See also* documents; sharing files on networks
　finding, 110, 150, 505
　lost, 120–121
　moving between folders, 118
　order of listing in folder, 118–119
　organizing, 112–122
　recovering from Trash, 460
　restoring to hard disk, 451–454
　selecting from list, 108
　sharing on networks, 486–503
　slow speed of loading, 145–146
　troubleshooting problems with, 119–122, 146
Filesaver, 443
fill function
　in Excel, 301
　in Resolve, 314
fill patterns, 229–230
　leaks with, 252
　in SuperPaint, 225
Find (File menu), 110, 120
Find Again (File menu), 120
Find Original button (Alias Info window), 156

Finder (Applications menu), 34, 101, 103, 113, 131, 165
　About This Macintosh, 154
　customizing, 20
　fragmented files and, 133–134
　vs. Norton Fast Find, 397
　printing window in, 72
　request for disk, 148–149
　switching to, 132
finding cards, in HyperCard stacks, 469–471
finding files, 103–104
　on floppy disks, 150
　after moving, 110
fixed-size fonts, Mac use of, 77
Flash, 508–509
flat-file databases, 325, 328
floppy disks, 6, 125–126
　800K vs. 1.4 Mb, 126–127
　care of, 135–136
　copying, 135, 139–140
　ejecting, 19, 27, 92, 126, 135
　erasing, 142
　finding files on, 150
　inserting in drive, 15, 135
　locked and unlocked, 122, 140–141
　preparing for use, 136
　recommended use of, 127
　stuck in drive, 149
　System Folder on, 51
　troubleshooting problems with, 143–150
　uses of, 136–137
floppy drives, for PowerBook Macs, 13
folder hierarchy menu, 95, 100
folders, 91, 112
　aliases of, 400
　for applications, 92
　backups of, 451
　creating, 113–114
　creating for fonts, 415–419

Index **541**

determining current, 109
displaying contents of, 107
hiding contents of, 107
hierarchy of, 112
list views to work with, 117–119
locating inside shared folder, 505
lost, 120–121
moving files between, 118
moving selected icon to, 107
naming, 114
nesting, 91, 114–117
parent, 119
printing list of, 72
problems changing name of, 122
putting file into, 114
selecting from list, 108
shared, 490–492
troubleshooting problems with, 119–122
users' access to, 497
viewing on Desktop, 105–106
Font Cache, 427
font resource files, 417–418, 421, 433
font sets, availability of, 426
Font Smoothing (Page Setup dialog box), 81
Font Substitution (Page Setup dialog box), 81
fonts. *See also* screen fonts
building suitcases for, 419–422
creating folder for, 415–419
in graphics, 231
in Illustrator, 249
Key Caps to view changes in, 78–79
KeyFinder and, 401–402
memory for applications and, 434

organizing, 411, 413–426
in PageMaker, 276–278, 284
serifs, 74
size of, and jagged text, 82–83
style and format in Excel, 296–297
style and format in Resolve, 310–311
in System file, 165
temporary set of, 426
troubleshooting problems with, 433
TrueType, 73–77, 414
vs. typeface, 414
for views, 178
fonts for printers, 73–79
installing, 76–77
removing, 77
and screen fonts, 79
types of, 73–76
Form Feed button (ImageWriter), 86
formatting floppy disks, 136
formatting of text, mixed in paragraphs, 211
formulas
in Excel, 299–301
problems with, 320
in Resolve, 312–314
4th Dimension (Acius), 326–327
Foxbase Pro, 326
fractional-width spacing option (Page Setup dialog box), 81, 436
fragmentation of disks, 145–146, 410
fragmented memory, 160
FrameMaker, 257, 259
FreeHand (Aldus), 216
compatible graphics file formats for, 529
freehand drawing, in Illustrator, 247–249

freehand tool (Illustrator), 238, 248
freeware, 395
full disk, Speed Disk and, 437
Full Impact, 291

G

gateways, 524
General Controls panel, 170–171, 174
Geneva font, 82, 416–417, 433
Get Info (File menu), 122, 155–156, 180, 418
ghost icon, 36, 140
gigabytes, 126
glare on screen, correcting, 25
Goodies menu (Kid Pix), Small Kids Mode, 218–219
graphic files
compatibility of formats for, 528–529
for screen dump, 72
storage size of, 126
graphics
adding freehand drawing to, 247–249
adding text to, 249–250
placing in PageMaker, 270
problems integrating, 386–387
wrapping text around, 279–281
graphics applications, 215–253. *See also* Illustrator; Kid Pix; SuperPaint
choosing, 215–217
troubleshooting problems with, 252–253
gray shades
filling Illustrator closed path with, 244–245
for Kid Pix graphics, 222

selecting number for display, 172
gray waves, on screen, 25
grayed commands, 36–37
grayscale graphics, printing, 253
grid, for icons, 178
gridlines in spreadsheets, turning off, 319
group, adding icon to selected, 41
grouped objects, 236
groups of users
　adding members to, 497
　giving access rights to, 494–497
　naming 496–497
Guardian (SUM), 444
guests on network, 492–493, 500

H

HAM, 396, 398–401
Happy Mac icon, 17, 25–27
hard copies, 56. *See also* printing
hard disk icon, 28–29
hard disks, 6, 124–125
　advantages of, 127–128
　capacity of, 131
　care of, 129–134
　checking with Speed Disk, 430
　connecting and initializing, 19–22, 129–130
　defragmenting, 133–134, 412
　driver software, 128
　fragmentation of, 145–146
　installing applications on, 92
　major backup of, 448–451
　moving, 15
　and RAM amounts, 153
　restoring files to, 451–454
　system software on, 19
　troubleshooting problems with, 143–150

hardware, 6
　failure of, 440
　troubleshooting problems with, 23–29
head crash, 131
head parking, 128, 130
header, in database layout, 344
headings, in PageMaker, 276–278
help balloons, 39
Help menu
　Hide Balloons, 39
　Show Balloons, 39, 154
Helvetica font, 74
Hewlett-Packard LaserJet, 64
hidden files, 142
Hide Balloons (Help menu), 39
Hide Others (Applications menu), 101, 103, 121
hiding application windows, 102–103
hierarchy of folders, 112, 117–118
　creating, 114–117
　file placement in, 119
　menu of, 109
highlight colors, selecting, 173
highlighting icons, 35
Home stack, 20
horizontal printing, 71
Hot or Cool (Label menu), 178
hot spot of pointer, 35, 46
HotKeys MacroMaker, 396, 402–405
HP LaserJet IIP, printing checks on, 365
hung up, 50
HyperCard, 464–474
　installing version 1.2.2, 20
　quitting, 472–473
　saving in, 468
　sorting and data entry in, 467–469
　starting, 465–466

troubleshooting problems with, 473–474
HyperCard folder, 115
HyperCard stacks, 465–473
　correcting mistakes in, 471
　finding cards in, 469–471
　opening, 465–466
　printing, 471–472
HyperTalk, 464

I

I-beam, 37, 190, 192
icon views, 105, 178
icons, 34, 91
　adding to group, 41
　on alert boxes, 45–46
　Apple Desktop Bus (ADB), 15
　customizing, 179–180
　disk with X, 25–26
　for floppy disks, 125
　Happy Mac, 17
　hard disk, 28–29, 124
　labels for, 38
　lost on desktop, 52
　moving, 36
　moving selected to folder, 107
　opening, 36
　question mark, 17, 19
　question mark disk, 143
　Sad Mac, 27
　selecting, 35
　selecting dispersed, 107
　selecting multiple, 41, 108
　size on list views, 178
　suitcase, 77
　telephone, 16
ID number
　for fonts, 434
　for system error, 51
Illustrator, 216–217, 232–252

Index

adding freehand drawing to graphic in, 247–249
adding text to graphic in, 249–250
blends in, 245–247
closed paths in, 236
compatible graphics file formats for, 529
filling closed path with gray shades, 244–245
general steps for using, 233–234
layers for depth effects in, 250
matching closed paths in, 240–244
opening documents in, 232–235
saving and printing in, 250–252
sketching as beginning, 235–236
splitting closed paths in, 237–239
ImageWriter
　care of, 67
　connecting, 59
　fonts for, 422
　magnetic fields from, 136
　on networks, 486
　overlapped characters on, 81, 436
　printing checks on, 366
　troubleshooting problems with page breaks on, 86
InBox Plus, 509
indents
　consistent sizing of, 210
　in Microsoft Word, 195–197
Info boxes, rebuilding desktop and, 131
information bar, in disk window, 142

information services, 521–523
initialization
　customizing files for, 167
　of floppy disks, 136
　of hard disk, 129–130
INITPicker, 182
INITs, 20, 160, 164, 167
ink cartridge
　changing on DeskWriter, 63–64
　changing on StyleWriter, 63
ink ribbon, changing on ImageWriter, 67
inkjet printers, 57
input, 5
inserting spreadsheet rows or columns
　in Excel, 297–298
　in Resolve, 311
insertion of floppy disks, 15, 135
insertion point, 37, 171, 190, 202
Inside Macintosh, 6
installation
　of applications, 92–93
　of EtherTalk drivers, 482–483
　of expansion card, 16
　of fonts for printers, 76–77
　of System 7 on customized Mac, 532–534
　of System 7 on hard disk, 19–22
　troubleshooting problems with, 23–29
installer, 22
interface, 6, 32
internal hard disks, 128
international characters, in E-mail, 524
international keyboard, 172
Internet, 523

J

jagged text
　Adobe Type Manager and, 435
　correcting in printing, 81
　font size and, 82–83

K

K (kilobytes), 126
Key Caps (Apple menu), 78–79, 82
key repeats, setting, 172
keyboard, 5, 15, 37–39
　control settings for, 175–176
　for PowerBook Macs, 13–14
　shortcuts for, 37
　troubleshooting problems with, 49–50
KeyFinder (Norton Utilities), 396, 401–402
Kid Pix, 215, 217–222
　correcting mistakes in, 219
　drawing lines in, 219
　opening documents in, 217–219
　saving and printing in, 222
　stamps in, 220
kilobytes (K), 126

L

Label menu, Hot or Cool, 178
Label view of documents and folders, 105
LANs (Local Area Networks), 476
laser printers, 57–58
LaserWriter
　care of, 64–67

connecting, 59
ink smudges from, 85
Page Setup dialog box for, 71
selecting on network, 484
LaserWriter Font Utility, 66
LaserWriter IInx, 58
LaserWriter NT, 58
layers in Illustrator, 234–235
for depth effects, 250
objects disappearing behind, 253
Layout Plus, 413
line breaks, fonts and, 76
line spacing
on MacWrite II ruler, 206
in Microsoft Word, 195, 197
screen vs. printer, 435
lines
drawing in Kid Pix, 219
forcing straight from pencil tool, 228
spaces between, and color leaks, 228
linking programs, over network, 502–503
links, 381–384
Links (File menu), 388
Linotronic commercial printers, 75, 216
list of folders, printing, 72
list views, 106–108
appearance of, 177–178
column missing from, 181
determining kind of, 109
icon size on, 178
to work with folders, 117–119
Little Black Book, 413
loaded icons, 268, 285
loading files, problems of slow speed when, 145–146
Local Area Networks (LANs), 476
LocalTalk, 477. See also AppleTalk network

LocalTalk Connector Box, 479
locked files
and changing name, 122
and emptying trash, 48
locked floppy disks, 122, 140
login procedure
alias for automating, 502
automatic, 501
to file servers, 499–501
lost files, 120–121
lost folders, 120–121
lost windows, 53

M

MacCalc, 291
MacDraw Pro (Claris), compatible graphics file formats for, 529
MacIntax, 351
Macintosh Basics disk, 15, 32
Macintosh characters, in E-mail, 524
Macintosh Classic/Classic II, 7–8
Macintosh computers
communication with printer, 80
extra connections to, 16
parts of, 4–6
selecting, 7–14
setting up, 14–18
shutting down, 18–19
total memory in, 154
Macintosh II, 10-11
automatic shut off of, 18
problems with, 28
Macintosh LC, 9–10
Macintosh Plus, 7–8
Macintosh Quadra, 12
Macintosh Reference manual, 170
Macintosh SE/30, 9
MacMoney, 352
MacP (MacPaint) format, 253, 528

MacroMaker (Hotkeys), 402–405
macros, 396, 402
playing, 405
storing, 404–405
MacTools, 444
MacTools Deluxe, 412
MacWrite II, 188, 201–208
editing text in, 203–204
opening documents in, 201–202
saving and printing in, 208–209
text entry in, 202–203
text style in, 207–208
Mail menu
Close & Sign Out, 520
Preferences, 518
mail server, 509
selecting in Microsoft Mail, 510–512
mailings, creating with FileMaker Pro, 341–346
Make Alias (File menu), 94
Managing Your Money (Andrew Tobias), 351–352
Manual Feed button (Print dialog box), 66, 69
margins
correcting ragged right, 81
on MacWrite II ruler, 205, 206
in Microsoft Word, 197
and off-center printing, 84
in PageMaker, 262–263, 265
marquee, 242. See also selection rectangle
master pages, creating in PageMaker, 265–268
MasterJuggler, 411
Mb (megabytes), 7, 126
MCI Mail, 508, 522–523
megabytes (Mb), 7, 126
memory, 5–6, 152–162
amounts needed, 152–153
for applications, 39, 155–157

control settings for, 179
and desktop, 34
for disk cache, 133
for FileMaker Pro, 347
for fonts and applications, 434
fragmented, 160
and graphics applications selection, 215
in Mac Plus or Classics, 8
monitoring use of, 154–155
and multiple applications, 101
for outline fonts, 82
overload of, 161
for spreadsheets, 318–319
for System 7, 34
troubleshooting problems with, 28, 159–162
for word processors, 209
memory (PRAM), problems with, 27
Memory icon (Control Panels window), 158
menu bar, 33
menus
to adjust brightness, 24
selecting commands from, 36–37
messages
"Application is busy or missing," 134, 145–146
"Cannot resolve circular reference," 320
"Not enough memory," 159, 406–407
"Out of Space," 132
"This disk is unreadable," 147–148
Microcom 911 Utilities, 444
microphone, 16, 177
Microphone, 521
Microsoft Mail, 509, 510–521
Address Book for, 517

mail server selection in, 510–512
quitting, 520
replying to message, 518–519
"Return to Sender" message, 523–524
sending message in, 513–517
starting E-mail in, 513
Microsoft Word, 187, 189–201
Clipboard to move and replace text in, 194–195
cutting and pasting in, 374–375
document window in, 190
E-mail support in, 519–520
editing in, 192–193
opening documents in, 189–190
ribbon in, 199–200
ruler to format text in, 195–199
saving and printing in, 200–201
text entry in, 191
text style in, 199–200
Microsoft Word User's Guide, 189, 200
Microsoft Works, 292
Mind Your Own Business (MYOB), 352
modal dialog box, 44
modeless dialog box, 44–45
modem port, 16
for printer, 59
Monaco font, 416–417, 433
money management applications, 350–369. *See also* Quicken
monitor
for Macintosh IIsi, IIci or IIfx, 10
for Macintosh LC, 9
setup steps for, 15–16
Monitors control panel, 172
mouse, 5, 15, 32, 34–35
cleaning, 48–49
control settings for, 176

troubleshooting problems with, 46–53
mouse pad, 35, 49
moving
files, 110, 118
icons, 36
items from System Folder, 21
text in Microsoft Word, 192
windows, 41

N

Name view of documents and folders, 105
names
for disks, 135
of extensions, 182
of file, problems changing, 122
naming documents, 97
nesting folders, 114–117, 91
Network control panel, 483, 504
Network extension, 504
network manager, for Microsoft Mail, 510
network server, Macintosh Quadras for, 12
Network Setup control panel, 487–488
networks, 476–506. *See also* E-mail
access to files from other computers on, 498–499
advantages and disadvantages of, 477–478
confidential files on, 490
limiting access privileges on, 492–497
linking programs over, 502–503
preparing to share files on, 488–490
print server on, 485–486

printer connection on, 60–62, 80, 484–486
sharing files on, 486–503
troubleshooting problems with, 503–506
unpredictable failure of, 505–506
zones for, 61
New (File menu), 97
new accounts, in Quicken, 354–355
New Folder (File menu), 37, 138
New Group (File menu), 496–497
New User (File menu), 494
nodes, 476
Norton Utilities, 395
   Disk Doctor, 146–148, 443–444, 458–459
   Fast Find, 395–398, 407
   KeyFinder, 396, 401–402, 407
   Speed Disk, 134, 147, 412, 428–432, 436–437
   UnErase, 444, 459–460
"Not enough memory" message, 159, 406–407
Note icon, 45
notebook-size computers, 13
Novell Netware, 487
NuBus expansion cards, problems with, 28
Number 2 Kit, 19
number formatting
   in Excel, 298–299
   in Resolve, 312

O

object-oriented drawing programs, 215–216
objects, grouped, 236

off-center printing, 84
On Cue, 413
on/off switch, 18
online information services, extensions and control panels from, 168
Open (File menu), 95
   dialog box from, 45
   keyboard shortcut for, 37
Open Mail (File menu), 519
opening applications, 94
   from Apple menu, 100–101
opening balance, for Quicken account, 355
opening documents, 94–97
   in Excel, 293
   in FileMaker Pro, 330–331
   in Illustrator, 232–235
   in Kid Pix, 217–219
   in MacWrite II, 201–202
   in Microsoft Word, 189–190
   in PageMaker, 261
   in Resolve, 307
   in SuperPaint, 223–225
opening HyperCard stacks, 465–466
opening icons, 36
optimization. *See* defragmentation of disks
organizer utilities, 410–437
orientation of printing, 71
"Out of memory" message, utilities and, 406–407
"Out of Space" message, 132
outline fonts, 75, 414
   installing, 77
   memory for, 82
output, 5
owner icon, for shared files, 505
owner password, 488
owner window, 495

P

page breaks
   fonts and, 76
   ImageWriter problems with, 86
   screen vs. printer, 435
page icons, in PageMaker, 265
page layout applications, 256–287. *See also* PageMaker
page numbers, in PageMaker, 266
page orientation, setting in PageMaker, 262–263
Page Setup (File menu), for special printing, 70–72
Page Setup dialog box
   Font Smoothing, 81
   Font Substitution, 81
   fractional-width spacing option, 81, 436
Page setup dialog box (PageMaker), 262
PageMaker (Aldus), 257, 259–287
   adjusting document layout in, 273–276
   adjusting text blocks in, 272–273
   compatible graphics file formats for, 529
   creating columns in, 266
   document window in, 264–265
   E-mail support in, 519–520
   font size and style in, 276–278
   graphic placement in, 270
   master page creation in, 265–268
   opening documents in, 261
   page numbers in, 266
   page view in, 270–272
   preliminary page settings in, 262–263
   vs. QuarkXPress, 258–259

rough sketch for, 260–261
saving and printing in, 281–282
text placement in, 268–269
troubleshooting problems in, 282–287
Tutorial folder in, 261
wrapping text around graphic in, 279–281
pages
locating center in PageMaker, 283
printing range of, 68
paint can (Kid Pix), 221–222
paint can (SuperPaint), 229
paint layer, in SuperPaint, 224, 227–228
Palatino font, 474
Panorama (ProVUE), 328
paper, 56
fanfold, 67
inserting in LaserWriter, 64
source for printing, 69
paper copies, 56
paper jams, 83–84
paper size
for LaserWriter, 71
and off-center printing, 84
paragraphs, mixed formatting in, 211
parent folder, 119
partial backups, 451
partitions, 134
passwords, 305, 499
changing, 496
for E-mail, 510
for network access, 487–489, 493, 505
for SAM Intercept, 461
Paste (Edit menu), 180
pasteboard, 265, 283
path of graphic line, 216, 236
patterns, in SuperPaint, 225

peripheral devices, problems from, 51
Personal Press, 257
personalizing program copy, 92
PhoneNet, 478
phono-plug adapter, 16
PICT (Picture) format, 72, 253, 528
pivot points, 248
platters, in hard disks, 124
playing macros, 405
pointer, 34–35
port, for printer, 59
portable Macintosh, 12–14
hard disk for, 128
shutting down, 18–19
turning on, 16
PostScript font resource files, 421
PostScript format file, 69
PostScript laser printers, 58, 484
PostScript outline fonts, 75
creating screen versions of, 427
organizing, 414
power
troubleshooting problems with, 23
turning on, 17
power failures, 97, 440
power surge, 144
power switch, 15
PowerBook Macintosh, 12–14
hard disk for, 128
turning on, 16
PRAM (memory)
control panel settings in, 179
problems with, 27
Print (File menu), 68
Print dialog box
Best Quality, 81
Manual Feed button, 66, 69
print server, 485–486
print spooling, 484

Print Window (File menu), 72
printed graphics, poor quality of, 253
printer driver, 80
printer icon, on Chooser, 80
printers. *See also* fonts for printers
blinking status lights on, 84
care of, 62–67
connecting, 16, 59–60
connecting to one on network, 484–486
direct connection to, 59–60
paper jams in, 83–84
selecting, 56–58
setting up on networks, 60–62
printing, 56–86
accented characters, 79
canceling, 69
checks in Quicken, 364–366
Chooser to set up, 58–62
cover page, 69
default settings for, 68
in Excel, 305–306
in FileMaker Pro, 346
HyperCard stacks, 471–472
in Illustrator, 250–253
in Kid Pix, 222
list of folders, 72
in MacWrite II, 208–209
in Microsoft Word, 200–201
multiple copies, 68
page ranges, 68
in PageMaker, 281–282, 286–287
paper source for, 69
screen snapshot, 72–73
speed of, ATM and, 436
in SuperPaint, 231–232
troubleshooting problems with, 80–86
window in Finder, 72

PrintMonitor (System Folder), 69–70, 83, 200, 232, 485
    Documents folder, 166
    icon, 70
program disk, 92
programming, with HyperCard, 464
protocols, 476
public access systems, 523
Publish and Subscribe, 384–386, 477, 487
Publish It Easy, 258
publisher item, creating, 385
Put Away (File menu), 43, 135, 149
Pyro, 413

Q

QuarkXPress, 257–259
question mark disk icon, 17, 19, 26–27, 143
QuickDEX, 413
Quicken, 351–369.
    check register in, 355–356
    check writing in, 361–363
    creating accounts in, 354–355
    creating file in, 352–353
    dates in, 357
    memorizing transactions in, 363–364
    reports from, 359, 366–367
    troubleshooting problems with, 367–369
    voiding checks in, 359
QuickKeys, 396
QuickMail, 509
quitting applications, 51
    HyperCard, 472–473
    Microsoft Mail, 520
    problems with, 109–110
Quote Init, 168

R

RAM (random access memory), 5–6, 124, 152. *See also* memory
RAM cache. *See* disk cache
range selection
    in Excel, 298–299
    in Resolve, 312
Read Only Memory (ROM), 5
reading files, problems with, 146
records, in FileMaker Pro, 324–340
recovering files, from Trash, 460
recycling cartridges, 65
reductions in print, 71
Redux, 443, 455–457, 462
registered guests on network, 492–493
    automatic login procedure for, 501
    giving access rights to, 494
    including in group, 497
relational databases, 325–328
remote computers, disconnecting from, 502
replacing text
    in MacWrite II, 204
    in Microsoft Word, 192
reports
    from Quicken, 359, 366–367
    word processors for, 188
Resolve, 291, 306–318
    absolute cell referencing in, 314–315
    charts in, 317
    data entry in, 308–310
    fill function in, 314
    formatting numbers in, 312
    formulas in, 312–314
    inserting columns or rows in, 311
    manual or automatic formula calculation in, 320
    range selection in, 312–314
    removing gridlines in, 319
    starting new document in, 307
    totals in, 316
    type style and format in, 310–311
Restart (Special menu), 19, 51, 84
restoring files
    to hard disk, 451–454
    with Redux, 457
"Return to Sender" message (Microsoft Mail), 523–524
ribbon, in Microsoft Word, 199–200
right-justified paragraphs, correcting problems with, 81
ring topology networks, 480
Rival, 441
ROM (Read Only Memory), 5
row insertion
    in Excel, 297–298
    in Resolve, 311
ruler
    in Illustrator, measurement units on, 236
    in MacWrite II, 204–206
    in Microsoft Word, 195–199
    in PageMaker, 265, 284
ruler guides, 237–238

S

Sad Mac icon, 27
SAM (Symantec AntiVirus for Macintosh), 441, 444–446
sans serif font, 74
Save (File menu), 98
Save As (File menu), 45, 99, 210
saving, 19, 97–100
    in Excel, 305–306
    in FileMaker Pro, 333, 346
    frequency of, 132
    in HyperCard, 468

Index

in Illustrator, 250–252
in Kid Pix, 222
in MacWrite II, 208–209
in Microsoft Word, 200–201
for multiple versions of document, 99
in PageMaker, 281–282
for PageMaker master pages, 267
in SuperPaint, 231–232
switching documents and, 104
scalable fonts, 77
Scrapbook, 166, 378–380, 387
screen
correcting glare on, 25
dark, 181
expanding window to fill, 107
frozen, 50–52
gray waves on, 25
printing snapshot of, 72–73
text appearance vs. printed copy, 81
troubleshooting problems with, 23–24
screen capture programs, 162
screen dump, 72
screen fonts, 414
created by ATM, 427
and fonts for printers, 79
screen savers, 24, 162, 181, 412–413
ScreenShot, 413
scroll bars, 41–42, 265
SCSI (Small Computer System Interface) hard drives
cable for, 129
driver software for, 128
external, 28
socket for, 127
SCSI ID number, problems with, 143
SCSI ports, 12

selected text
changing size of, 192, 204
in MacWrite II, 203, 206
for Microsoft Word editing, 192
multiple formats in, 198
selection
of commands from menus, 36–37
of files for restoring, 453
of icons, 35, 41
selection handles, and text wrap, 279
selection rectangle, 41, 114, 242
Send Mail (File menu), 519
sending mail messages, 513–517
sentence spacing
by MacWrite II, 203
by Microsoft Word, 191
serif font, 74
server, for network, 11
setting up Mac, 14–18
setup disk, 92
7-bit data links, 524
shared folders, 490–497
Shareware, 395
Sharing (File menu), 491, 497, 503–504
sharing files on networks, 486–503
Sharing Setup control panel
File Sharing, 160, 498
locating, 504
Shift-clicking, 41
Show Balloons (Help menu), 39, 154
Shut Down (Special menu), 18, 400
shutting down Macs, 18–19
SIMMs (Single In-line Memory Modules), 153
Size view of documents and folders, 105

Sleep (Special menu), 19
Small Icon view of documents and folders, 105
Small Kids Mode (Kid Pix, Goodies menu), 218–219
Smartcom, 521
SmartScrap, 380
sorting
of FileMaker Pro records, 335–337
in HyperCard, 467–469
sounds
control settings for, 176–177
as input, 16
organizing, 411
in System file, 165
speaker volume, setting, 176
special characters
KeyFinder and, 401
keystrokes for, 82
special effects in printing, 71
Special menu
Eject Disk, 140
Empty Trash, 42
Erase, 142
Restart, 19, 51, 84
Shut Down, 18, 400
Sleep, 19
Speed Disk (Norton Utilities), 134, 147, 412, 428–432
defective disk reported by, 436–437
and full disk, 437
splitting closed path, 237–239
spreadsheets, 290–321. *See also* Excel; Resolve
links to text document, 381–384
selecting, 290–292
troubleshooting problems in, 318–321

stacks, 464. *See also* HyperCard stacks
stamps, in Kid Pix, 220
star topology, 481
start pages, preventing, 66–67
starting Mac
    disabling extensions during, 169
    setting up hard disk for, 19–22
    strange sound at, 28
    troubleshooting problems with, 23
startup applications, specifying, 166–167
startup disk, 137
    defragmenting, 431, 437
    for Disinfectant, 447
    floppy disk as, 51
startup documents, specifying, 166–167
Startup Items folder, 166–167
static electricity, and floppy disks, 136
Stop icon, 45
storage. *See* disks; floppy disks; hard disks
storing macros, 404–405
style of text
    in MacWrite II, 207–208
    troubleshooting problems with, 209–210
styles, in Microsoft Word, 198
StyleWriter, 57
    care of, 62–63
    connecting, 59
    fonts for, 422
    paper feeder on, 83–84
stylus pointers, 16
Subscribe to (Edit menu), 386
subscribers, 388–389
Suitcase, 411, 413–426
suitcase icon, 77
suitcases

building for font families, 419–422
organizing into sets, 422–425
problems with fonts in, 433
SUM II (Symantec Utilities for Macintosh), 412, 444
SuperDrives, 127
SuperPaint (Aldus), 215, 222–232
    compatible graphics file formats for, 529
    creating shapes in, 225–226
    freehand outlines with, 227
    opening documents in, 223–225
    paint can in, 229–230
    saving and printing in, 231–232
    text in draw layer of, 230–231
supporting documents, 381
switching between applications, 101–103
switching between documents, 104
Symantec AntiVirus for Macintosh (SAM), 441, 444–446
Symantec Utilities for Macintosh (SUM), 412, 444
Symbol font, 74
system disks, 137–139
System Extensions folder, outline fonts in, 77
System file, 112, 160, 165, 433
System Folder, 22, 115, 164–166
    Clipboard, 373
    Extensions folder in, 504
    on floppy disks, 25–26
    on hard disk, 131
    installing software on, 20
    moving items from, 21
    PrintMonitor, 69–70
    problem of multiple, 180–181
    resources in, 411
    on startup disk, 137
    updating without losing customization, 532

system heap, 161
System 7
    installing for first time, 19–22
    installing on customized Mac, 532–534
    linking programs in, 503
    memory for, 34
    networking capabilities of, 476
    TrueType fonts and, 273
system software, 6
    and fonts, 434
    on hard disk, 19, 131
system software extensions, 168
System Startup disk, 19
System Switcher, 27

T

Tab key, in Quicken, 368–369
tab settings
    on MacWrite II ruler, 206
    in Microsoft Word, 195, 197
tables, margins and column widths in Microsoft Word, 197
Tagged Image File Format (TIFF), 528
target folder, for dropping files, 110
tax-preparation applications, 351
TeachText, 72, 115, 188
temporary storage. *See* Clipboard
terminator, for SCSI drives, 129–130
text. *See also* data entry; editing
    adding to graphic, 249–250
    deleting, 38
    disappearance of, in word processors, 210
    formatting with ruler in Microsoft Word, 195–199
    graphics manipulation of, 216
    links to spreadsheets, 381–384

placement in PageMaker, 268–269
style in Microsoft Word, 199–200
threading in PageMaker, 284
"This disk is unreadable" message, 147–148
Tidbits disk, 66
TIFF (Tagged Image File Format), 286, 528
time-saving utilities, 395–407
Times font, 73–74
title bar
    of active window, 40
    generic titles in, 98
    in MacWrite II, 201
    in Microsoft Word, 190
toggling, 39
Token-Ring network, 476
Token-Talk network, 499
toner cartridge, 65, 85
Total memory amount (About This Macintosh window), 154
Touch Base (After Hours), 329
trackballs, 14, 16, 49
transactions, memorizing in Quicken, 363–364
transfers, between Quicken accounts, 360, 368
Trash, 21, 36
    dragging disks to, 126, 135, 149
    dragging hard disk to, 125
    dragging things to, 42–43
    for floppy disk ejection, 92
    recovering files from, 460
    troubleshooting problems with, 47–48
troubleshooting problems
    with applications and documents, 108–110
    with customization, 180–182
    with data integration, 386–389
    with data protection utilities, 461–462
    with E-mail, 523–525
    with FileMaker Pro, 347–348
    with files and folders, 119–122
    with graphics applications, 252–253
    with hard and floppy disks, 143–150
    with hardware and installation, 23–29
    with HyperCard, 473–474
    with memory, 159–162
    with mouse and desktop, 46–53
    with networks, 503–506
    with organizer utilities, 432–437
    with PageMaker, 282–287
    with printing, 80–86
    with Quicken, 367–369
    with spreadsheets, 318–321
    with time-saving utilities, 406–407
    with word processors, 209–211
TrueType font resource files, 435
TrueType fonts, 73, 77, 414, 416–417
TurboTax, 351
turning on Mac, 15–17
type tool (Illustrator), 249
typeface, 414

U

Undo (Edit menu), 210, 381
Undo (Illustrator, Edit menu), 248
Undo (Kid Pix, Edit menu), 219
Undo (MacWrite II, File menu), 204
Undo (Microsoft Word, Edit menu), 193
Undo (SuperPaint, Edit menu), for fill pattern removal, 229
Undo memory, clearing, 160
UnErase (Norton Utilities), 444, 459–460
UNIX mail systems, 514
unlocking floppy disks, 140
unregistered guests, denying access to folder, 493–494
updates, automatic. *See* data integration
urgent mail messages, 515
Users & Groups control panel (Apple menu, Control Panels), 493, 505
users of network
    classes of, 492–493
    giving access rights to, 494–497
utilities. *See* data protection utilities; organizer utilities; time-saving utilities

V

variables in spreadsheet formulas, 299–300, 313
video card, 11
View menu, 105–106
    by Label option, 178
    Show ¶, 210
View menu (Illustrator)
    Actual Size, 238, 242
    Artwork Only, 247, 249
    Preview Illustration, 247, 249
    Show Rulers, 236
View menu (MacWrite II), Show Invisibles, 206
View menu (Microsoft Word)
    Ruler, 196
    Show ¶, 199

View menu (PageMaker), Fit in window, 283
view of page, in PageMaker, 270–272
Views control panel, 177–179
    to display missing columns, 181
    hiding columns with, 107
    Show label box, 178
Virex, 441
VirusDetective, 441
viruses, 440
    freeing system of, 444–446
    protection against, 168
voiding checks, 359
voltage, 23
volume, speaker, 167

W

wacky brush (Kid Pix), 221
Wallpaper, 413
welcome screen, 21
window boxes, 45
windows, 36, 40–42
    closing, 41
    expanding to full screen, 107
    finding buried, 121
    hiding application's, 102–103
    lost, 53
    moving, 41
    scroll bars for, 41–42
    size changes for, 41
windowshade handles, 272–273, 285
Wingz, 291
word processors, 186–211. *See also* MacWrite II; Microsoft Word
    features of, 186
    choosing, 187–189
    troubleshooting problems with, 209–211
word wrap
    in MacWrite II, 203
    in Microsoft Word, 191
    phrases split by, 211
WordPerfect, 187
WordPerfect Office, 509
worksheet, 306
wrapping text around graphic, 279–281
WriteNow, 188
writing files, problems with, 146

Z

zones for network, 61, 499, 511
zoom box, 41
Zterm, 521

Selections from The SYBEX Library

APPLE/MACINTOSH

Desktop Publishing with Microsoft Word on the Macintosh (Second Edition)
Tim Erickson
William Finzer
525pp. Ref. 601-4

The authors have woven a murder mystery through the text, using the sample publications as clues. Explanations of page layout, headings, fonts and styles, columnar text, and graphics are interwoven within the mystery theme of this exciting teaching method. For Version 4.0.

Encyclopedia Macintosh
Craig Danuloff
Deke McClelland
650pp. Ref. 628-6

Just what every Mac user needs—a complete reference to Macintosh concepts and tips on system software, hardware, applications, and troubleshooting. Instead of chapters, each section is presented in A-Z format with user-friendly icons leading the way.

Encyclopedia Macintosh Software Instant Reference
Craig Danuloff
Deke McClelland
243pp. Ref.753-3

Help yourself to complete keyboard shortcut charts, menu maps, and tip lists for all popular Macintosh applications. This handy reference guide is divided into functional software categories, including painting, drawing, page layout, spreadsheets, word processors, and more.

Introduction to Macintosh System 7
Marvin Bryan
250pp; Ref. 868-8

An engaging, plain-language introduction to the exciting new Macintosh system, for first-time users and upgraders. Step-by-step tutorials feature dozens of screen illustrations and helpful examples drawn from both business and personal computing. Covers the Desktop, working with programs, printing, customization, special accessories, and sharing information.

Mastering Adobe Illustrator
David A. Holzgang
330pp. Ref. 463-1

This text provides a complete introduction to Adobe Illustrator, bringing new sophistication to artists using computer-aided graphics and page design technology. Includes a look at PostScript, the page composition language used by Illustrator.

Mastering Microsoft Word on the Macintosh
Michael J. Young
447pp. Ref. 541-7

This comprehensive, step-by-step guide shows the reader through WORD's extensive capabilities, from basic editing to custom formats and desktop publishing. Keyboard and mouse instructions and practice exercises are included. For Release 4.0.

Mastering PageMaker 4 on the Macintosh
Greg Harvey
Shane Gearing
421pp. Ref.433-X

A complete introduction to desktop publishing—from planning to printing—with emphasis on business projects. Explore the tools, concepts and techniques of page design, while learning to use PageMaker. Practical examples include newsletters, forms, books, manuals, logos, and more.

Mastering Ready, Set, Go!
David A. Kater
482pp. Ref. 536-0

This hands-on introduction to the popular desktop publishing package for the Macintosh allows readers to produce professional-looking reports, brochures, and flyers. Written for Version 4, this title has been endorsed by Letraset, the Ready, Set, Go! software publisher.

PageMaker 4.0 Macintosh Version Instant Reference
Louis Columbus
120pp. Ref. 788-6

Here's a concise, plain-language reference, offering fast access to details on all PageMaker 4.0 features and commands. Entries are organized by function—perfect for on-the-job use—and provide exact keystrokes, options, and cross-references, and instructions for all essential desktop publishing operations.

Up & Running with the Mac Classic
Tom Cuthbertson
160pp; Ref. 881-5

A fast, breezy introduction to computing with the Mac Classic. In just 20 steps, you get the fundamental information you need—without the details you don't. Each step takes only 15 minutes to an hour to complete, making this book a real timesaver.

Up & Running with Macintosh System 7
Craig Danuloff
140pp; Ref. 1000-2

Learn the new Mac System 7 in record time. This 20-step tutorial is perfect for computer-literate users who are new to System 7. Each concise step takes no more than 15 minutes to an hour to complete, and provides needed skills without unnecessary detail.

Up & Running with PageMaker on the Macintosh
Craig Danuloff
134pp. Ref. 695-2

Ideal for computer-literate users who need to learn PageMaker fast. In just twenty steps, readers learn to import text, format characters and paragraphs, create graphics, use style sheets, work with color, and more.

Up & Running with Norton Utilities on the Macintosh
Peter Dyson
146pp. Ref. 823-8

In just 20 lessons, you can be up and running with Norton Utilities for the Macintosh. You'll soon learn to retrieve accidentally erased files, reconstruct damaged files, find "lost files," unformat accidentally formatted disks, and make your system work faster.

Using the Macintosh Toolbox with C (Second Edition)
Fred A. Huxham
David Burnard
Jim Takatsuka
525pp. Ref. 572-7

Learn to program with the latest versions of Macintosh Toolbox using this clear and succinct introduction. This popular title has been revised and expanded to include dozens of new programming examples for windows, menus, controls, alert boxes, and disk I/O. Includes hierarchical file system, Lightspeed C, Resource files, and R Maker.

FREE BROCHURE!

Complete this form today, and we'll send you a full-color brochure of Sybex bestsellers.

Please supply the name of the Sybex book purchased.

_____

How would you rate it?

_____ Excellent _____ Very Good _____ Average _____ Poor

Why did you select this particular book?

_____ Recommended to me by a friend
_____ Recommended to me by store personnel
_____ Saw an advertisement in _____
_____ Author's reputation
_____ Saw in Sybex catalog
_____ Required textbook
_____ Sybex reputation
_____ Read book review in _____
_____ In-store display
_____ Other _____

Where did you buy it?

_____ Bookstore
_____ Computer Store or Software Store
_____ Catalog (name: _____)
_____ Direct from Sybex
_____ Other: _____

Did you buy this book with your personal funds?

_____ Yes _____ No

About how many computer books do you buy each year?

_____ 1-3 _____ 3-5 _____ 5-7 _____ 7-9 _____ 10+

About how many Sybex books do you own?

_____ 1-3 _____ 3-5 _____ 5-7 _____ 7-9 _____ 10+

Please indicate your level of experience with the software covered in this book:

_____ Beginner _____ Intermediate _____ Advanced

Which types of software packages do you use regularly?

_____ Accounting	_____ Databases	_____ Networks
_____ Amiga	_____ Desktop Publishing	_____ Operating Systems
_____ Apple/Mac	_____ File Utilities	_____ Spreadsheets
_____ CAD	_____ Money Management	_____ Word Processing
_____ Communications	_____ Languages	_____ Other _____
		(please specify)

Which of the following best describes your job title?

____ Administrative/Secretarial   ____ President/CEO

____ Director   ____ Manager/Supervisor

____ Engineer/Technician   ____ Other _____
                                              (please specify)

Comments on the weaknesses/strengths of this book: _____

_____
_____
_____
_____

Name _____
Street _____
City/State/Zip _____
Phone _____

PLEASE FOLD, SEAL, AND MAIL TO SYBEX

SYBEX, INC.
Department M
2021 CHALLENGER DR.
ALAMEDA, CALIFORNIA USA
94501

SEAL

Keyboard Shortcuts on the Mac

Finder Shortcuts

Copy (not move) icon to another window	Option + drag icon
Select icon by name	Begin typing name (without pauses between characters)
Select multiple icons	Shift-click, or drag selection rectangle
Select name of selected icon for editing	Return or Enter
Eject a floppy disk	⌘-Y (leaves no ghost icon)
Temporarily eject floppy disk	⌘-E (leaves a ghost icon)
Take a picture of the current screen	⌘-Shift-3
Stop a switch-disk nightmare	⌘-. (period)
Rebuild the desktop file	⌘-Option + start up Mac
Disable all extensions at startup	Shift + start up Mac

Window Shortcuts

Open window of application or Finder and close current window	Option + choose application or Finder from Applications menu
Zoom a window to largest size possible	Option + click zoom box
Move a window without making it active	⌘ + drag the window
Close all Finder windows	Option + click a close box
Escape from application window to Finder	⌘-Option-Esc